D1490077

GETTING THERE BY DESIGN

An Architect's Guide to Design and Project Management

Kenneth Allinson

Architectural Press

Architectural Press
An imprint of Butterworth-Heinemann
Linacre House, Jordan Hill, Oxford OX2 8DP
A division of Reed Educational and Professional Publishing Ltd

ℛ A member of the Reed Elsevier plc group

OXFORD BOSTON JOHANNESBURG
MELBOURNE NEW DELHI SINGAPORE

First published 1997

© Ken Allinson 1997

All rights reserved. No part of this publication
may be reproduced in any material form (including photocopy-
ing or storing in any medium by electronic means and whether
or not transiently or incidentally to some other use of this publication) without the written permission of the copyright holder
except in accordance with the provisions of the Copyright,
Designs and Patents Act 1988 or under the terms of a licence
issued by the Copyright Licensing Agency Ltd, 90 Tottenham
Court Road, London, England W1P 9HE. Applications for the
copyright holder's written permission to reproduce any part of
this publication should be addressed to the publishers.

British Library Cataloguing in Publication Data
A catalogue record for this book is available from the British
Library

ISBN 0 7506 2623 2

Library of Congress Cataloguing in Publication Data
A catalogue record for this book is available from the Library of
Congress

Graphic design, cover, diagrams and illustrations are by Ken
Allinson

Printed and bound in Great Britain

● Contents

Contents

PART FIVE: CONCLUDING SECTION

Preface

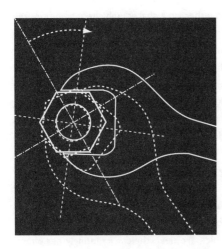

Born from the shifting currents of constant socio-economic change, project management is overwhelmingly dominated by the concern to plan and control the project process in its voyage toward the realisation of its goals. It has an entirely instrumental intent, even when this includes value-laden and qualitative criteria of success. Its roots are in forms of technical rationality, in systems theory and analytical technique. Its paradigm is the sophisticated mechanical control device and its most deep-rooted maxim is: know what it is you want to do, then do it in a controlled fashion. Its twin gods are economy and effectiveness. However, when faced by design, project management theory confronts a difficulty and the need to acknowledge its sister discipline: design management. Design is concerned with economy and effectiveness, too, but it has an irreducible core concerned with issues outside the boundaries of instrumentality. Conversely, design cannot restrict itself to a cultural and aesthetic agenda and must accommodate itself to the realities of purposive thinking: i.e. what project management is all about. This book is about the pragmatics of that accommodation, but its underlying value system is architectural. It discusses project and design management from the architect's viewpoint. And it sees no contradiction between these two enthusiasms. Unashamedly, it aims to persuade architects that management is an interesting subject.

Design is invariably considered to be a *wild card* in the project management pack because its values are poorly understood and its methods are difficult to explain, even by designers (see Allinson, 1993). In the first place, the concept is hard to define. Perhaps the nearest one can get to it is the notion that *design is the deliberate placing of intent into events*, somewhat in the sense that Isaac Newton would talk about the design of things as something fundamental to their nature. Whilst such a definition might touch upon the challenge to act both appropriately and authentically with regard to key, underlying issues - the major, implicit ambition of all forms of design worthy of the name - it fails to suggest the manner in which all kinds of design (including architecture) *mediate* between the instrumental mind-set of most project initiators and what has been described the cultural and symbolically-loaded 'life-worlds' of end-users (see Habermas, 1987, for a lengthy explication of this concept). It is this mediation which both motivates designers and engenders headaches for some project managers.

Defining design as a wild card might be a sensible way of ostensibly obviating risk, but it courts another danger: of seriously delimiting project potential.

The instrumental mind-set of managers - more often than not motivated toward goals expressed in terms of those two great media of contemporary economies, money and power - bears an impassive face toward elusive argumentation which draws design into a cultural realm of ambiguity and subjectivity. On the other hand, architects can be equally intransigent in refusing to acknowledge and accommodate managerial values - for example, the *a priori* contextural imperatives lending projects their bald, purposive meanings sometimes exasperates them, appearing to nullify architectural potential and emasculate the architect's agenda. With such a potential for misunderstanding on each side, mutual respect can be a good starting point: the client who accepts an architectur-

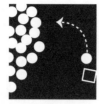

Project management's role is to shepherd the project through a critical period of exposure to risk, to get the project to the safe haven of successful completion. This can sometimes entail the sacrifice of some project potential - an issue which is usually (and quite properly) of deep concern to designers.

The RIBA Strategic Study (Phase two, 1993), included a section on the client's perspective of architectural services. Its conclusions were to the point:

'While a number of clients felt that architects would never regain what they felt had been a privileged position in the past, some 30% were willing to reconsider their opinion on the basis that the profession meet the following stringent criteria:

• An improved awareness of the context of the project in hand in terms of the client's business or personal needs and situation
• A more responsible attitude toward the control of costs on projects
• The introduction of thorough management procedures to ensure the smooth running of projects
• A willingness to seek an optimum balance between what are often seen as conflicting parameters by architects: quality, cost and time.'

These simple criteria are hardly different from calls for managerial competence made in the RIBA's study, *The Architect in His Office,* published thirty years earlier. The key is an emphasis upon instrumental intent. It is also upon reasonableness, consideration and common sense. RIBA sponsored research published in the Architect's Journal, 7.3.96, confirmed the Strategic Study. Key findings included the comment that, 'There is a critical difference of perception between clients and architects', and 'Clients see architects as having a hidden agenda of seeking peer approval'.

al agenda but insists upon a fastidious regard for their functional criteria; the architect who vigorously pursues an architectural agenda but is wary of imposing architectural meanings on others and is mindful of the need to serve and of the risks any project courts.

Managers and architects are brought together on a shared vehicle of ambition: the project itself. However, because projects are undertakings concerned with realising change, risk is endemic to them. Project managers exist in order to shepherd a project through a period of exposure and risk to the safe shores of project completion. Their services, especially once the architect has formulated a design content, are insurance of the client's expectancy of reasonable certainty and predictability. Their mode of thinking leans toward a technical, rule-governed rationality. The language of their assurances speaks of performances, budgets, and schedules. Their agenda is concerned with planning, monitoring and analysis, and control. The concepts they employ (such as fitness for purpose, quality assurance, cost targeting and the like) are all framed instrumentally.

Such a mind-set can provide good service to the project, but it has two principal difficulties: it confronts both the motivational and interpersonal issues informing design team performances and design's mediation between purposive thinking and the sphere of cultural meanings, as important factors which are nevertheless irritatingly peripheral to the project manager's main agenda. However, such difficulties can be obviated. A sensitivity to team issues can be cultivated once the project's reliance on important and complicated nature of human relations is appreciated. And project space can be given to design by acknowledging that thorough scheme preparation is when it best fulfils its role - after which (when the project content is agreed) project management can assist design toward the realisation of its ambitions. This last phase - what some construction experts like to describe as the engineering phase of project development - is especially risky. All too often, project management's view is that, since what needs to be done is now known and agreed, there is nothing left but instrumental execution. This argument is at the root, for example, of design and build modes of procurement. It's a notion originating in neo-militaristic attitudes separating strategy from tactics and Taylorist attitudes separating policy from execution (one which architects themselves foist onto builders), but it does design a disservice, failing to accept that even door handles, to offer a mundane example, can have conceptual and strategic significance. Nothing is more depressing to many architects than this misunderstanding - that the architecture is only strategic and then superficially cosmetic, that detail is simply about proper workmanship. This is where the designer's opposition to value engineering comes from - not as a resistance to the principal of sound economy itself. On the other hand, it is architects who have the responsibility of arguing their case. And this has to be done in terms which give project management values their due place. All too often this does not happen: architects fail to validate their case, are prejudiced against managerial issues, and characterise project managers as philistine power freaks. To the extent this occurs, it is usually an unfair prejudice.

The sub-text of this book is an attempt to bridge between these perspectives, to suggest that there is much common ground between the disciplines who seek to get there 'by design'. Take, for example, the following writer's comment on the nature of business strategy - one of the most important topics in management theory. His 'essential insights' would hardly be news to any designer :

> *Strategy develops around a few key concepts and thrusts that provide cohesion, balance, and focus. Strategy deals with the unknowable as well as the unpredictable. Its essence is therefore, necessarily, to build a posture strong*

enough and flexible enough to allow the business organisation to realise its
goals despite the unforeseeable interventions of external events (1)

This could also be a description of design strategy. And there are other common denominators. If, for example, it can be argued that architecture clothes itself in imprecise cultural pretensions which are sometimes difficult to validate, project management clothes itself in precise techniques which are, in reality, founded - like much design - upon intuition, judgment and experience, the crucial skills once observed by Henry Mintzberg as the very ones business schools fail to teach (2). In fact, the more the much-vaunted techniques of project management are examined, the more they become revealed as tools which, no matter how useful, are founded on the employment of judgement. Techniques are about the ideas and concepts which underly them. Designers hoping to use them as some form of life-belt will be sorely disillusioned. And yet, ironically, if they would only ask about what is beneath the surface they might find much of interest. Only in this way can managerial techniques be appropriated and usefully employed.

In any case, architects have no choice but to accept purposive-rationality and a success-oriented agenda seeking forms of technical competence to further its ambitions. (Policies and values derive from mind-sets and the instrumental mind-set is not about to evaporate overnight.) But they simultaneously need to persuade management that concerns with broadly defined cultural and aesthetic considerations (especially the latter) amount to more than a cosmetic palliative of style grafted onto technique (as merely other functional attributes of the architectural equation). Management is often willing to accept the argument, but only if its goals are not compromised, its project is not to be subject to unnecessary risk, and it can be seen to be properly managed. The difficulties are shared.

The premise of this book is that a mutual accommodation of viewpoints and value systems is not a contradiction. Upon that basis it offers to expose the foundations of project management and to suggest how the successful management of architectural design can be considered. Two broad strands run through the content: techniques of planning, monitoring, analysis and control (including consideration of the project life-cycle and cost estimating); and issues of team management.

The book begins with a discussion of the nature and features of project and design management, underscoring their contemporary importance and the issues involved. Part One ends with a parable of misfortune - an illustration of how projects can go wrong.

Part Two (Decisions and Techniques) raises a broad range of project management issues, at the heart of which are planning difficulties and the importance of heuristic. It addresses issues raised during design development and is especially concerned with 'mapping' the project's future path forward.

Part Three (Managing Costs and Fees) moves on to the issues of managing costs and fees, demonstrating how a fee calculus can be constructed for specific firms.

Part Four (Cultures as Action Systems) looks at the cultures of architectural practice, arguing that it is practice culture - as ways of action unselfconsciously infused with appropriate values - that is the bottom line to the discussion about project and design management. It addresses fundamental issues of teamwork, motivation and leadership.

Part Five (Concluding Remarks) is accompanied by a short project and design management dictionary, and a guide to further reading. The latter is intended to take those who are interested to more specialised texts and their sources.

Acknowledgments

In a profession where few architects will admit to an interest in managerial issues, acknowledgments are due to a number of people who have supported this book: Fiona Duggan, Paul Hyett, Niall McLaughlin, Bill Ungless, and Justin de Syllas - each of whom has commented upon parts or the whole of the manuscript and provided both criticism and encouragement; Neil Warnock-Smith and Sarah Leatherbarrow, both at Butterworth Heinemann; colleagues at Oxford Brookes University School of Architecture and Planning, who provided the opportunities to present the ideas in seminars and lectures; students at a number of other schools who have heard some of the ideas in professional practice seminars; and Victoria Thornton, who proved that not all acts of authorship are grounds for divorce.

Part One:

The Project Context

*Yesterday's a memory; tomorrow's only a vision;
but today's a real bitch.*
Project maxim

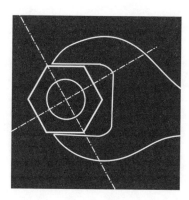

The contemporary concept of the project has developed from Cold War roots within US aerospace industries after World War II via a suitable intellectual and economic climate, and large engineering and building construction sites, to become an increasingly common feature of current business practice.

Similarly, design management - a product of the development of design disciplines during the middle and later parts of the 20th century - has become headlined as a key to corporate innovation and business success in a post-modern era. Toward the end of that century neither of these current enthusiasms is, from an architectural viewpoint, particularly new. On the contrary, they have always been fundamental to architectural practice. But it is for this very reason that architects are all too often blind to the fact that theirs is a design discipline rooted in the use of a managed project method. Universally, architects learn contract and practice administration on their architectural courses, not project and design management. It is their clients who have focused upon the discipline of project management as an instrumentally useful tool and imposed it upon their architectural designers. And now these same clients talk of design management.

Part One places project and design management into the context of architectural design, setting the basis for later sections. The emphasis is upon the project method, the importance of time management, and of realising the potential of 'good' design in order to 'add value' within the context of the project process.

The subject: purposive action

1 There are two, principal aspects to most project management theory: considerations almost entirely deriving from *planning* issues and usually quantifiable or measurable ('hard' considerations), and factors almost entirely focused upon *people* issues ('soft' issues). Together, a planning content and the consideration of human relations form the essence of project management practise. The success of this practise is framed in terms of the skill and judgement with which planning techniques are employed, leadership and, of course, the degree to which project outcomes meet the project sponsor's objectives and criteria.

Techniques and the schedules derived from them, however, are best employed when *what* has to be done is fully known and residual uncertainty only concerns *when* and, to some extent, *how* the project is to achieve its ends. Such information is not always available or consistent, complete or reliable. It is less likely to be certain and complete than provisional and plausible (but no less valued for all that). To the extent that planning exercises are, necessarily, a conjectural imagining and structuring of what lies ahead (this is the essence of 'projecting'), much depends upon the art of apposite, forward mapping. This mapping must be founded upon a concept of the undertaking and of how this can be usefully imagined as a planning exercise. In this sense it becomes implicitly *heuristic* i.e. a way of proceeding which employs rules of thumb derived from experience. In addition, research (as well as common sense) suggests that beneath the planning considerations determining project success lies a host of subtle, people-centred issues such as staff motivation and the adequacy of interpersonal communications. In other words, 'hard' planning techniques are invariably a lot 'softer' than planners care to admit. This is especially true when project success is strongly dependent upon design inputs.

Two considerations dominate most project management theory: planning and human relations. Whilst these concerns are hardly unique, they have to be seen within the specific content of projects - their uniqueness, goal-orientation, concern with change, mix of agencies and temporary nature.

2 **Means and Ends.** The significance of planning techniques and the formal reliance place upon them derives from the purposive ambitions informing project management. These ambitions characterise and legitimate the discipline - these, and a self-consciousness regarding the medium (or context) of action: *the concept of the project as a tool for realising business and organisational change.*

Such a tool constructively or reconstructively takes the client from A to B, instituting a new state of affairs. The discipline of project management exists in order to ensure this change is competently achieved. However, in a design context, there is more to the competent management of projects than planning and control. When change is reliant upon design content, then project management is, simultaneously, *design management* - aimed at realising the potential design can unlock.

Architectural designers have always worked on projects as the natural medium of practice. They take it for granted. However, managerial and design agenda can be different - their concepts of value to be realised by the project frequently lie poles apart. Furthermore, their working methods are also different. For example, architects typically enjoy a tolerance for *ambiguity* that is the antipathy of project planning and its anxious pursuit of certainties and fixed outcomes. The meeting ground between these mind-sets is design-project management, where different notions of 'deliberately and appropriately placing intent into events' have to be reconciled.

As a form of risk management, as well as a means of enhancing project instrumentality, clients have explored varieties of procurement route for getting from A to B and have increasingly resorted to using *project managers* - a body of people better characterised by an attitude of mind than any particular disciplinary training or particular empathy with designers - as a key component of achieving their goals. And this draws our attention to a third dimension of project management: the dialectic between the

Projects:

• *Are unique goal-oriented events, set up in order to get a client from A to B, from a less preferred set of conditions to a more preferred set of conditions. They are mediums for realising change and vehicles for realising ambitions. They have specific goals and criteria of success.*

• *Are unrehearsed events happening in real-time. They have start and end points, without which they loose definition and cannot be meaningfully managed except as on-going programmes.*

• *Have specific budget allocations without which, again, they cannot be meaningfully and economically managed or feature as components of larger programmes.*

means of getting there and the *end* objective itself. Clients are interested in both - in the end as a more preferred place to be, and in the means as a way of getting to their desired objective. However, the project ends are frequently instrumental vehicles serving other, higher level goals e.g. value added to the business enterprise or process, social benefit realised for the community, and so on. On the other hand, architects project forward to the designed end as valid in its own right: at least a coherent, advantageous reconciliation of project content; at best, the poetic formulation of this content. How the outcome of a project feels is as important as what it does.

A definition of ends is adopted as the architect's ambition and responsibility. The means - as a project effort - are of secondary importance - a point which requires no apology, but one which can lead many a designer astray. A holistic concern with the whole outcome is followed by a concern with constructional issues, *then* with issues of process.

From the viewpoint of the construction professional - a third player in the game - both the client's long-term, instrumental concern with the outcome a new building realises, and the architect's concern with the building as an end in itself, are alien to constructive interests and the profit to be derived from the building process. Like the construction contractor, project managers are also oriented toward means rather than ends. To some extent they, too, must concern themselves with the accommodative and programmatic content of the project deliverable (as it is called), but they do so in terms of control and the pursuit of an economy of means. Their concern is getting there rather than being there.

Clearly, one person's means are another person's ends. The point is that all viewpoints are (self-evidently) valid and have their place - a clear argument for the teamwork from Day One which is only just beginning to establish itself within many sectors of the building industry.

Form and Content One

'We are seeking outstanding technical architects who can translate business and systems strategies into an integrated set of architectures then deliver an infrastructure to support our clients' national and international business processes. You should have a proven track record in corporate systems architecture design and implementation, and be able to rise above the detail to think and act strategically.'

Advert in newspaper, 1997, underscoring the precise and colloquial understanding of 'an architecture' which, paradoxically, eludes some architects. The media have many references, especially to politicians and business people who create schemes.

Means and Ends - Different Priorities

Managers talk about 'means - ends' thinking. This conventionally implies a purposive way of thinking concerned with means only to the extent they serve some apriori or macro end. However one person's means (say, a client) can be another person's end (for example, the architect).

Both the manager (as client) and the architect share a concern to 'get there' (to the project goal), but their values are prioritised in different ways. The client will enjoy the building in its own right, but it will have been justified as a means to some larger end which it serves. Typically, this will be the ubiquitous commercial media of money and power, but it could well be the restaurant that is enjoyable to run or the house extension coping with a growing family. The architect will acknowledge this mind-set but will be motivated by the building as an architectural end in itself.

On the other hand, there are ways of prioritising the process of getting there. Builders and project managers exemplify professional types who are naturally process oriented. The building contractor is concerned with the building simply as a construction and the PM as the satisfactory completion of the project.

The extent to which these perspectives and values overlap or pass each other by makes up much of the content of projects.

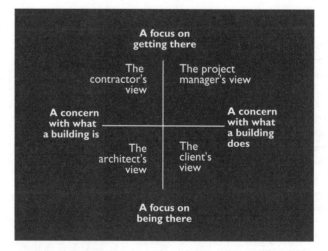

A focus on
getting there

The contractor's view | The project manager's view

A concern with what a building is

A concern with what a building does

The architect's view | The client's view

A focus on
being there

These disparate perspectives and emphases tend to confront one another during a crucial part of the project process: after scheme design approval and during the critical stage of design development and the preparation for work on site. At this point project management asks, "Now we've agreed what it is we're doing, let's do it - what's the *plan of action?*" The project has now entered what managers like to term its 'engineering' phase. In other words, the nature of the game has shifted its bias toward technocratic factors and implementational criteria. The architectural designer - still (quite rightly) concerned to pursue informing design concepts through to the detail of the building design - is now enmeshed in a complex interactive equation demanding cooperation, coordination and, above all, strategic effectiveness. The context of actions will be a planning framework and the schedules it fosters. These, in turn, will facilitate monitoring and the control of performances. Unavoidably, the architect faces a requirement for the exercise of project management expertise, especially if he or she wants to be perceived as a credible team participant, able to act instrumentally as well as artfully.

It is at this point in the project process that the architect's vulnerability is most exposed. The competence that alchemically produced an exciting scheme now has to turn itself inside out. The tolerance for ambiguity that fostered a comfort with being in control without knowing the outcome (a disturbing condition for many people) is reversed. The ability that produced a design from a blank sheet of paper has to be translated into a predictable, carefully choreographed and staged process, orchestrated as a performance between quite disparate disciplines. On what basis can drawing and specification production be predicted? What of content, effectiveness, productivity and, especially, available resources and fees? How is the architect to plan his or her own actions as well as the building being worked upon? How does intuitive, reconstructive problem-solving become externalised as planned, instrumental action? How does the design manager embrace project management? At its worst, the imaginative practises of *projet* become entangled with pragmatics and expediency. At best, imagination becomes limited only by what is possible.

3 Art and Commerce. It is arguable that a polarisation between the instrumentality of purposive, means-ends thinking and the curious alchemy at the heart of the design enterprise is most acute within the architect's own firm: how are fee-bids to be estimated and, later, the expenditure of fees to be properly utilised and controlled when the motivation of most architects is of a different kind?

Such issues have been sublimated beneath the teaching of 'practice management' - for example, as taught to students sitting a Part Three qualifying examination - as an aspect of *administrative*, ethical, legal and contractual topic rather than one concerning the fundamentals of design and project *management*. For too long, the differences have been concealed within the vocational posture of an architectural professional whose dedication is still redolent with 18th c. gentlemanly and amateurish undertones, whose cultured focus upon artistic ends and a dependency upon imaginative vision tends to hover above a concern with mere means, and whose commitments are coloured by the 19th c. notion that the practice of architectural design is essentially an artistic endeavour aimed, as Tom Wolfe would say, at shocking the bourgeoisie (or, at least, at freeing itself from bourgeois values). The latter concept, in particular, remains a bastion of resort within many schools of architecture, but nothing could be further from the truth and inimicable to successful architectural practise than this pernicious confusion of design and art.

The fact is that most practising architects are either in business - providing a useful service within the broad context of current socio-economic praxis - or out of practice. The successful contemporary architect is both celebrated by colleagues and end-users, *and* a commercial figure able to play an instrumentally-minded client at their own game. The successful contemporary architect is not only an artful cultural intermediary, but must also be a skilled project and design manager. In fact, project and design management must stand at the core of any architectural firm's endeavours. Necessarily, architectural values will be affected by a concern with process - but they are being transformed anyway, especially by the radical transformations wrought by digital technologies and their cultural by-products, as well as by a prevailing hegemony of instrumental values seeming to continually extend their penetration into the cultural heart of

Form and Content Two

There are two aspects to project management: what is on the surface and underlying structural features of the subject which lie buried from normal view. H.G. Wells's Invisible Man is a useful metaphor. Whilst his bandaged and clothed form facilitates meaningful interaction with other people, his inner, invisible substance is the significant power and energy within. Without that inner, structuring content, the bandages and clothing are merely a bundle of useless and meaningless cloth; however, without these wraps the inner form's interaction with the world is frustrated. What you see on the surface of project management are the techniques of planning, monitoring and control. What lies beneath are aspects of 'deep structure' which determine and inform the techniques i.e. distinctive ways of framing problems, particular value systems, and a purposive-rationale and instrumental way of thinking upon which the disciple depends. An appreciation of project management depends upon an understanding of both these dimensions of the subject.

Unfreeze / Freeze

A project is initiated in order to realise some form of change. Inception, by its nature, produces all kinds of 'unfreezing' and commitments which it is intended to bring to a condition of closure (a refreezing), ending the 'inbetween-ness', the exposure and risks which the project engenders. Project Management exists in order to manage the project, in order to ensure its potentiality is envisioned, harnessed and realised, and in order - once a scheme has been agreed - to ensure a reasonable degree of predictability and certainty of outcome.

There is an anomaly called 'the on-going project' which expects only a partial goal achievement, which expects to continually roll-over in a series of incremental adjustments, each of which becomes a mini-project in its own right. 'Refreezing' becomes a satisfactory and viable holding stage prior to a subsequent readjustment. However, most projects reach a more complete stage of closure. The extendable, changeable building (such as Richard Rogers' Lloyds building) merely holds within it the potential to form the schematic basis of future projects. It is a part of an on-going project only in the sense that Lloyds itself subscribes to such a background project concerning its facility needs. Similarly, Rogers' Pompidou Centre reached its own completion, although it facilitates a range of other projects within its framework. Except in the case of 'the folly', a project's architectural content is normally incidental to another project purpose (such as providing facilities for insurance trading or cultural events).

society. Already, architecture is frequently valued as a feature of the average consumer's aestheticised landscape of imagery and entertainment. New ideological frameworks must be borne out of this circumstance. If they are not, then architecture is doomed to become a moribund discipline.

4 Seeking a Middle Ground. It is against the background of such issues that this book has been written. Its principal aim is to be useful to architects and help them be effective in the contemporary project management climate. Its method is to describe and discuss topics in such a way that both the surface and deeper undercurrents can be recognised in relation to one another. Changing techniques can then be appreciated in reference to underlying issues and these, in turn, can become a source of better practice management.

A fundamental premise of the book is that architects can be expert managers. However, this does not mean they should rush toward classical management ideology and its flawed dependence upon purposive-thinking and the employment of technique. The notion that project and design management are about technique is as misguided as many architect's ideological orientation toward the art paradigm.

There is a middle ground - one that eschews certainties and accepts ambiguities, that leans upon heuristic rather than analytical technique and accepts architecture as a design discipline whose 'sister arts' are not painting and sculpture, but the likes of contemporary graphic and product design. This is a territory where designers and managers can find they have much in common. This is where the creative, expert and inventive wit of the designer is not a million miles away from the manager who must 'satisfice' and rely upon judgement and intuition (3). This is a domain mapped out long ago by people like Charles Lindblom, an administrative scientist who facetiously argued for a real-world science of 'muddling through' as a counter-vision to a post-war managerial ideology obsessed with quantitative values, strategic thinking and the rational-deductive ideal in problem-solving (4). It's a realm which fascinates commentators such as professor Donald Schon, a sociologist and management writer who sat in on MIT architecture classes, achieved a better understanding of design that most architects ever do, and became an advocate of design teaching methods in other professions (5). It is an area of actions and decisions where creativity (a word that was not in the Oxford dictionary before 1972) has been acknowledged as both profoundly important to rational, scientific endeavour, yet deeply mysterious and incapable of being explained.

Whilst this book does not dwell on such ideas, it is coloured by them. Its focus is upon architectural design practice as a set of actions and commitments. Its aim is to be pragmatic, bridging between architectural design and managerial practises in the same way that it seeks to inform everyday, mundane issues by illuminating the structural premises to project management theory. It discusses techniques, but hopes the reader will understand their limitations as well as their utility.

The reader will find there are recurring interests permeating the text: the usefulness of heuristic as a method of orientating practice; the imperative that architects make effective use of their key resource: available time; the need for a focus upon comparatively crucial success factors rather than attempts at synoptic coverage of every project consideration; and the fact that theory and commentary tend to wilt in the face of the need to act. In the end, that is what this book is about: purposive action.

Thinking about managing projects

The concept of Project Management is straight-forward - the conflation of two terms: project and management. It follows that an understanding of the subject will come from appreciating the relative meaning of each word.

Projects are a ubiquitous form of socio-economic activity. They always have been. The building of pyramids and the construction of medieval cathedrals were enormous projects, as was the building of canal and railway systems during the Industrial Revolution or, more recently, sending Apollo modules to the moon, setting up North Sea drilling platforms and constructing the Channel Tunnel. Of a different tenor, the masques of Inigo Jones for King Charles 1st and Millennium celebration programmes are also projects among the many examples that can be chosen.

Architects tend to think of projects principally in the construction realm, but projects have now become a common feature of business and government activity and all kinds of business change are now considered as projects, as well as the provision of new buildings. Researching biomedical and pharmaceutical innovation is frequently undertaken on a project basis, as is software development, moving office or the implementation of new equipment systems. At the opposite extreme, mundane activities having little or nothing to do with large enterprises or construction can also be thought of as projects. For example, a vacation or a birthday party can legitimately be considered as projects, as can setting up a small exhibition or a summer fete.

Projects concern themselves with initiating *change,* moving from a less to a more preferred state of affairs, either as a one-off, short term phenomenon (e.g. a birthday party) or as a new condition of indeterminate longevity (e.g. a new building). Their underlying presumption is the acceptance of continual change as a cultural norm i.e. no sooner do we move from a fixed condition, through a process of change to another fixed condition, than we can expect to move on once again. If this weren't the case, projects would become bogged down in the relative values associated with the change from one condition or another.

All projects share common features: they are one-off, unique, finite, purposive, goal-oriented enterprises undertaken in real-time. They all involve the act of projecting forward (for example, in terms of time, place, and situation), but rehearsals are rarely possible. They require vision, ambition, some form of inception, planning, monitoring, control, the coordination and synchronisation of proposals, the allocation of responsibilities and roles, and some final closure that brings the project to an end. If they are to be successful and reasonably economic, hassle-free undertakings, they must be managed as purposive, instrumental vehicles.

Another way of thinking of projects is to differentiate them from long-term *operations* in the sense of undertakings that are on-going, but without a predetermined conclusion (although there might be operational criteria which will prompt termination). For example, setting up a car manufacturing plant will almost certainly be a set of projects; the actual manufacturing, maintained so long as there is a market, will be a set of operations functioning so long as certain criteria are satisfied (Ford's famous Model T was just such an operation - followed through beyond the point at which it should have been superseded by superior products, as Chrysler developed). Most departmental functions within universities are operations in this sense, even though the content of the curricula might be largely made up of projects. Similarly, the architectural firm is an organisational entity that seeks to be operational over an indefinite long-term period and is quite distinct from the discrete projects it undertakes and which give it viability.

Projects and More Projects

Automation and empowerment take away the need to have managers oversee the day-to-day work. Everything has become projects. This is the way Fannie Mae does business today.
Spokesman for the Federal National Mortgage Association, 1995.

Project management is going to be huge in the next decade. The project manager is the linch-pin in the horizontal / vertical organisations we're creating.
Partner at Price Waterhouse, 1995

Project management is moving from a speciality to the mainstream.
Forsberg et al. (1996)

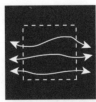

Operations are ongoing, systemic activities framed by a larger, organisational context. Projects are temporary, unique, definable organisational entities in themselves, subscribed to by contributing departments and / or agencies . They exist only until project goals have been realised, then they are concluded.

A Tool for Change

Projects have become increasingly important to contemporary business enterprise. Today's reality of a free-trade, competitive, global economy, characterised by accelerating technological innovation and enjoying trans-national commercial activities and operations has engendered so much change and flux that the idea of the project has become an important business tool. Recent symptoms of change have included managerial enthusiasms for down-sizing, flat hierarchies, re-engineering, out-sourcing, just-in-time techniques, incrementalism, customer-oriented strategies, team-working, emphases on quality, cross-border production and marketing, the need for focus and, especially, timeliness.

Within this climate of constant change and regular adaptation, the project - as a vehicle of unique, one-off change - has become an important tool for managing and effecting business strategy and realising its ambitions. Projects - once a mundane characteristic and taken-for-granted feature of architectural practice - have become high-profile business tools.

Typically, project-implemented change has three dimensions:

1. Meeting organisational objectives, which includes structural changes to support new technologies, ways of managing the business, etc.

2. Meeting human objectives e.g. so that the right people with the right skills are available to operate new technologies.

3. Meeting technical objectives which provide management with new technologies and systems e.g. a new building.

These three dimensions of change often coincide - something which is at once an enhanced challenge to architects and a delimitation to their arrogance.

Where do Projects Begin?

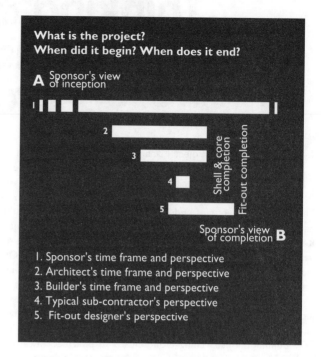

What is the project?
When did it begin? When does it end?

A Sponsor's view of inception

Sponsor's view of completion B

1. Sponsor's time frame and perspective
2. Architect's time frame and perspective
3. Builder's time frame and perspective
4. Typical sub-contractor's perspective
5. Fit-out designer's perspective

Projects are bound to contexts. For example, the clients who come to an architect and commission the fit-out of a retailing shell as a restaurant might be fulfiling a dream they have had for years. The project is borne of that context and, when the architect's design role is finished, the product of that project (its 'deliverable') sinks back into that context - now a one concerned with acting out the dream.

All buildings have this aspect to them. It engenders the tension between client and architect - the former concerned with the architecture as part of a larger set of concerns; the latter concerned with the architecture as an end in itself (or a part of another context pertinent to the architect). The tension can be creative or destructive.

The contemporary language for an underscoring of why projects exist often expresses itself in terms of 'user needs' and 'conformance to requirement'. This is a very instrumental approach. The opposite - when the architectural agenda entirely takes over - has traditionally been called 'a folly', something either literally foolish and ill-conceived, or indulgently fulfiling a pleasure principle and nothing else.

Many contemporary projects marry these two polarisations together. Examples would those pitched at selling stylistic posturing and ambience as the crucial ingredient offered to customers. Arguably, these are increasingly common - separating aesthetic content (whatever its rationale) from the forms of instrumentality also present. Conventional project management theory is ill-adapted to these forms of project (an area for further consideration).

Organisational, staffing and other considerations might be quite different within the parent organisation that fosters projects and within the project enterprises themselves. This has generated a whole body of organisational theory concerned with the managerial relations between line staff (as they are called) and project staff. These are usually variations on 'matrix' organisations seeking to establish workable ways in which line staff can also be a part of project teams and deal with two supervisors (line and project). In many organisations line roles predominate, giving the project manager serious problems of authority and delimiting his or her leadership role. In architectural practices it is the project staff who predominate, leaving line roles to be differentiated into non-professional support staff and those professionals who are a part of a core (operational) team, usually made up of partners, directors and associates. The implication is that other staff are a part of the organisation on a less secure, project-by-project basis.

2 Contexts. It is important to acknowledge that projects belong within *a context*: a specific background of financial, technical, moral, cultural and other considerations out of which they arise - a fluid, dynamic milieu of factors from which they are born and back into which they sink. They are rarely born in some neatly formatted configuration. More often, they will slowly come into definition, their goals and criteria sometimes reflecting a messy inceptural evolution characterised by analysis, debate, and conflicting calls upon limited resources that might be allocated to the undertaking. This background context is implicitly dominated by the strategic interests of the project sponsor, for whom the project exists as an *instrumental* means of getting from A to B. This is true even when goals are described according to subjective and aesthetic criteria.

Imagine a company dealing with the many issues of production, R & D, the employment of capital, marketing and sales, personnel issues, new products and services, and the similar factors common to a competitive business enterprise - or, if you prefer, the policy-making of a local authority considering capital expenditures for a variety of social projects, or an individual client considering, for example, a restaurant conversion or a new home extension. The need for building work crystallises out of such contexts and is usually justified as a crucial feature of the way forward to a more preferred state of affairs long before any designing architect comes on the scene. The architect will then become involved as specialised design expert long after the inception of an unfolding set of conditions that result in his or her involvement.

The implication is that the involvement of professional expertise has to be *goal-oriented*. What that goal is and which criteria apply depends largely upon the initiating client, although professionals might be asked to clarify and develop them (as in a feasibility study), statutory authorities might impose constraints, and a wide spectrum of social representatives might have a legitimate voice that has to be heard before 'a brief' can be finalised. Professionals are principally employed as experts capable of realising the project ambition within its frame of reference and in terms of stated criteria - which might explicitly invite aesthetic considerations or merely presume them as a natural consequence of the architect's involvement.

The down-side of this reality is that briefing statements implicitly carry typologically rooted notions of the solution to initiating project prompts. Sometimes they can be wrong. This can happen in competitions, where the brief denies the legitimacy of efforts to think laterally or to engage in a dialogue with the client that might enrich consideration of the issues. (Norman Foster's approach to the Hongkong and Shanghai bank competition was an example.) The point can be exaggerated, but it underscores two aspects of contemporary commissioning: the possible need for specialist briefing consultancy at the front-end of a project, and the client's intention of instrumentality which conventionally informs the process.

3 Interests and Enthusiasms. Professionals ostensibly engage with projects as *disinterested* experts - disinterested in the sense of bias in the administration of contracts, of placing their interests before those of the project sponsor, or of securing personal gain (especially in a financial sense). This is a convenient socio-economic pretence founded upon the notion that professionals are neutral appliers of technical expertise (in the tradition of *noblesse oblige* service, from which it originated and informed the 19th c. development of the profession). In fact, professionals play a project

Gestation

Boeing's 777 project was born from a long period of looking at what was happening in the market before they were brought to the decision that they should be considering a new aircraft which filled a gap in their family of products. Millions of dollars were spent on designer and engineering time to make provisional drawings, calculations and models, and many hours were spent with potential customers giving orientation to a potential project and investigating feasibility before commitments were made. Even then, there was no firm project committed to development and production before a first-batch buyer was found.

In essence this is no different from the way in which architectural projects are given birth, whether they be a Boeing office building or a small house extension. Architects also enter a stream that is already flowing, leaving it when their service has been rendered and their role is complete.

The Manager's Role

'When introducing change, the manager's role becomes crucial. On the one hand, he must determine what changes are necessary for the effective survival of the organisation, and on the other, he must secure and maintain the effective co-operation of individuals and groups to insure their acceptance.'
T. Miller

Two fundamental questions have to be addressed:

What are we doing?
How are we going to do it?

Strategic behaviours and debate engenders idenetified business needs. From these comes:

* benefits derived from current operations.
* benefits sought from current projects.
* benefits sought from proposed projects.

Each is subject to review and prioritisation. As a collectivity, the operations and projects form a portfolio of business activities from which benefits are realised - and their content feeds back into strategic considerations.

Projet

The word 'project' comes from the Latin pro, a prefix signifying fore, before, in favour of, and jet - that which spouts, issues, juts or shoots forward, having its roots in the French jeter, to throw, from the Latin iacere. A thesaurus offers a host of associations emphasising links with planning and risk taking: scheme, contrivance, rationalisation; programme, proposal, intention; master plan, blueprint, draft, prototype; undertaking: contract, engagement, promise; task, programme, plan; enterprise, quest; venture, gamble; occupation, matter in hand, etc. Imaginative (even visionary) and calculated projecting forward are fundamental to design thinking.

To engage in a project is not only to imaginatively anticipate the future, but also to plan, organise, orchestrate and control that future so that the result is a desired outcome. With the realisation of that outcome, the act of projecting is at an end. As vehicles of change, projects are to be differentiated from on-going operations (in the sense of purposive, organised practises with an indefinite life). But there is the concept of an 'on-going project' - meaning one whose end is indefinitely postponed because a condition of completion or closure is never achieved. They are comparatively rare.

Since the founding of the French Royal Academy of Architecture in 1671 the term projet has been employed in the sense of the draft of a proposed measure by students to characterise their proscribed learning vehicle - a teaching method for inculcating architectural values and a visionary medium by means of which imaginative creative ability was expressed and honed - the more flamboyantly the better. This was to such an extent that, in the 19th century (just as management and, especially, engineering were developing into their modern guise) the term acquired overtones of divorce from mundane realities. Coming from a haughty cultural tradition that held bourgeois preoccupations with material production to be unworthy of cultured gentlemen, French architects visiting the 1877 American Centennial, held in a self-evidently practical-minded country, disdainfully noted that, "Neither do we find anything of what with us is so appropriately termed projet. This last deficiency arises from a very simple cause. Taste is not yet sufficiently developed to permit the purely utilitarian side of questions to be forgotten, nor disinterested enough to lead one to make drawings for a scheme which he is not almost sure in advance of carrying out". (6)

By the turn of the century it had become commonplace for American practices - even midst enthusiasms for Beaux-Arts fashions - to accept the importance of business acumen as a basis for architectural practice. And along with this went an implicitly instrumental ingredient to mix with artful ambitions, one that was not seen to be inimical to art-architecture. However, the 19th c. French architects' attitude still haunts European practice, despite the fact that contemporary usage massively favours the American interpretation of 'projet'.

role for both material and vocational reward. Architects have a propensity to engage in project work because the client is the potential vehicle for a vocational agenda i.e. architects are unavoidably predatory (but no more than the heart surgeon thrilled at new operational possibilities, or the lawyer excited by the challenge of a new case). This fact ensures vocational commitment and underpins the architect's enthusiastic service which aims to insinuate an aesthetic and cultural agenda into the facts of utilitarian need and strategic intent. This is why their contribution is valued. But it is also why the client is fearful: the primacy of fundamental instrumental goals and criteria might be compromised by the designer's vocational ambitions. The building might be too late, cost too much, or be produced in such a manner that the client's pockets are emptied by contractor's claims. Most importantly, predictability of outcome might be lost.

As a partial answer to such criticisms, as a displacement attempt drawing attention away from risk, and as a claim to validation, the architect's professionalised design service has always been founded upon the maxim that, 'Good design need not cost more'. This is the true 'added value' the more able designer lends to a project. However, this ignores the reality that, on its own, an architectural agenda rarely provides project justification (the 'folly' and the monument to political vanities are notable exceptions) and it can only be realised if all other project criteria are respected, particularly a law of reasonable economy of means (why spend more, take longer, suffer inadequacies or hassle?). Whilst such an agenda is usually embraced wholeheartedly and incorporated into project ambitions, design is, nevertheless, often seen as a project wild card threatening the instrumentality and predictability of outcome any sponsor expects with regard to budgetary, temporal, and performative criteria. 'Good design' is rarely defined as embracing these kinds of process criteria and is almost invariably restricted as a reference to ends rather than means. However, if a practice cannot be trusted to respect these project criteria, some other agent can take its place as 'the client's friend': enter the manager of projects.

4 Roots. As a contemporary discipline, project management has its roots in American post-war efforts to deal with the Cold War and rationally manage a military-industrial complex characterised by large-budget projects. It's theoretical roots are in war efforts to manage the economy in the context of a prevailing concept of scientific management, of operations research, systems theory and the theory of cybernetic controls, and in efforts to manage government policies and budgets - such as the Program Planning Budgeting System, with its emphases upon strategic planning and a concern with goal-oriented budgeting (see Allinson, 1993). Climatically, it was born in an era obsessed with quantitative thinking and the notion of rational, strategic management. The aerospace industries were at the forefront of developing the discipline, but it soon spread to all kinds of government contractors engaged on large contracts and hence to private enterprise engaged on civil projects. First and foremost, the discipline is a managerial device concerned with the instrumental, goal-oriented focusing of project efforts. This ambition is all important. *Change is neither initiated for the sake of it or to give the architect an opportunity to design - it exists to address specific prompts for change acknowledged by the sponsor.* From this comes a focus upon planning, monitoring and control.

Project management is usually considered in terms of a single function or person (the executive project director) but, in fact, it operates at many levels and locations within the project as an attitude of mind and value orientation among disparate project agencies. This has to be achieved despite the fact that each project agency has a different viewpoint, dependent upon discipline, role and responsibility. Each will 'frame' a contribution in terms of its own own agenda - both in vocational and business terms. The architect, for example, aims to insinuate an agenda amounting to more than a cosmetic palliative - i.e. style grafted onto the technique of expertise. Society and many a client also expect this, but the right has to be earned, and the content has to be appropriate and validated. The architect's alchemical marriage between a contemporary client's systemic orientation and society's cultural values must be rooted in an ideology of legitimation which some architects lack. Faced with a hegemony of managerial values their constrained egos bleat in protest when they should be attempting to understand both what they confront and who they are. There is more at issue than disparate values. Mind sets and, in particular, ways of working can be at odds. The architectural designer has to understand both sides of the argument if he or she is to comprehend the project management phenomenon and realise the potential of design.

Project Justification Over-view

• Economic Justification *(all simple, bottom-line analyses): break-even analysis; incremental rate of return; net present value; return on investment (ROI); payback period, etc.*
• Analytic Justification: *more complex, sometimes dealing with uncertainty, economic and non-economic benefits and risks. Typical: value analysis; portfolio analysis; (non-numeric and numeric scoring techniques, and goal programming models); risk analysis; sensitivity analysis, etc.*
• Strategic justification: *less technical, directly linked to the goals of the firm e.g. technical importance; business importance; competitive advantage; research and development.*

• **Non-numeric models:**
• *The Sacred Cow (the boss wants it!)*
• *The Operating Necessity (we need to do it)*
• *The Competitive Necessity (competitiveness requires it)*
• *The Product Line Extension (new products or services require it)*
• *Comparative Benefit Model (comparing and contrasting alternatives, as in Q-sort)*

• **Numeric models:** *formal, numeric procedures for the evaluation and selection of projects. The emphasis is usually upon profit. Computer scoring and simulation modelling (considering multiple criteria) are becoming more common.*
Profitability models:
• *Payback Period (investment : cash flow generated)*
• *Average Rate of Return (average rate of return : initial or average investment required)*
• *Discounted Cash Flow (as above, but using present value method)*
• *Internal Rate of Return (discount rate relating sets of expected cash inflows and outflows)*
• *Profitability Index (cost benefit ratio - net present value of all future expected cash flows : initial cash investments)*
• *Other models which introduce risk, the effects on other projects and activities, etc.*

• **Criteria scoring models:**
• *Unweighted 0-1 Factor Model (yes / no against criteria)*
• *Unweighted Factor scoring (scoring against criteria on a 5-point scale)*
• *Weighted factor Scoring (as above, but criteria weighted)*
• *Sensitivity Analysis (what happens if we change this or that feature . . ?)*
• *Constrained Weighted Factor Scoring (some criteria fixed for all options e.g. it must . . . or, it must not . . .)*
• *Other numeric models introduce uncertainty and risk e.g. Risk Analysis - describing the variables and outcomes statistically, taking into account probabilities; General Simulation Analysis (machine simulation of all the variables), etc.*

A Good Business Approach

• *Intended projects are fitted to the business strategy.*
• *Disparate projects are tackled in terms of generic frameworks of planned project stages.*
• *Project content is reviewed before progression from one stage to another.*

Two Aspects of Project Context

• *The client's motivation, business case and intentions.*
• *The cultural context within which projects are tackled i.e. the culture of the architectural practice and of the other agencies participating in the project team. Practice cultures are different.*

Today's Best Firms

Truly dynamic companies concern themselves with constant, fluid change - projects become a way of life. Project roles - not job descriptions - are married with accountability. The opposite form of organisation (like the RIBA) is something like the professional institution organised on a committee basis.

Membership of the Project Management Institute (USA)

1984   1995

Value added

Goods are Consumed and Services are Experienced.

A differentiation has to be made between quality of work and quality of service. Clients expect the former and will usually make a choice between what are presumed to be equal technical competences. However, as non-experts they are unlikely to be able to judge the difference between merely competent and excellent work, especially when contingent and subjective factors are involved (the less-than-competent is a more obvious failure). The excellent standard - embodied in the service maxim that 'good design need not cost more' - might also be irrelevant or insignificant to the client. Good work might be done but neither recognised or wanted. Unforeseen contingencies grappled with and accommodated might be seen by the client as things that should not have happened in the first place.

David Maister (7) expresses the situation very well in a simple formula: Satisfaction equals Perception minus Expectation

(See section on Motivation, p136)

If service is perceived to be less than expected, the client will be dissatisfied. Expectations relative to actual delivery is a vital dimension of service management. Maister's extensive experience in providing consultancy to professionals leads him to believe that most firms are very poor at providing this kind of quality service, often dismissing it as client massaging.

It follows that an experiential, perceived quality of service is important. This can mean many things, from the enjoyment of working with certain people to the various ways in which a client can feel considered, consulted and looked after. Clients want their professional agents to care as well as to be competent. In other words, apart from the measurable, instrumental and technical dimensions of a project lies a domain of subjectivity which is immensely important but hardly debated.

The concept of *value added* - the difference between the comprehensively accounted inputs and outputs of a process - has become fundamental to business enterprise and is its central purpose. An example: the harvested coffee bean has a market value when sold; middle men bulk together farm products and sell them at a higher wholesale price - value is added by the service. The beans might be purchased and shipped by foreign distributors who sell at a higher price; other distributors will market in a local economy and a restaurant will purchase quantities of beans - value being added at each stage. Finally the beans are ground and made into an expensive cappuccino offered in a fine setting. The cost of that cup of coffee will be a high multiple of the value obtained by the farmer; measurable value will have been progressively added and realised at each stage. (Alternatively, a company might purchase the beans, process them into freeze-dried granules which consumers like for their convenience, package them into an appropriate format and market them to supermarket chains, who distribute them to consumer outlets - value is added at each stage.) Any business manager concerned with criteria such as organisational effectiveness, process engineering, productivity, customer satisfaction and so on, will inevitably, at some point, talk about adding value.

Architectural services are argued to be caught up in added value equations in a similar way. *Value added by design* (or created and accounted for by design) has two aspects:

1. That realisable by the architects themselves in the form of a fee income generated by the employment of professionalised human capital, and

2. Those forms of added value provided to the client by a completed building project or the services involved in creating one.

The principals of an architectural firm will seek to add (and realise) value by placing the design capability of themselves and their staff in contact with clients; they will also seek to formulate that capability as a service match to market need. Each becomes a form of 'added value' as defined above. Firms also seek effective internal process management in order to maximise net benefit to themselves (most significantly, by enhancing service value delivered to clients, but also by becoming more efficient and profitable). Externally, the architectural profession as a whole seeks ways of enhancing value by controlling what sociologists call 'jurisdiction'. They compete and jostle for market position - between professional disciplines as well as between themselves - in order to control a market sector. (This is sometimes the basis of what has been called the 'social contract' between a profession and the State in return for market privileges, such as protection of the title 'architect'.) Project management services exemplify a relatively new discipline carving out a niche at the expense of the established professions (to some extent, at least - they have also created a new service). When practised by, say, quantity surveyors, project management is a service enhancing the creation of value within quantity surveying firms and that profession. Adding value is about professional politics as well as service.

2 **Issues of Value.** From the client viewpoint, the architect's project role is to add value by re-forming available capital resources into a useful and attractive building. Traditionally, this form of value has three principal dimensions (i.e. forms of benefit to be derived from the project):

1. *Commodity (or exchange) value*: the value that can be realised and banked e.g. the market value of a speculative office building. It is a common form of value added by product design, packaging design, etc., where the excellence and appeal of the design are two aspects of value acknowledged in higher market

share and/or market returns.

2. *Operational value*: value enhancement relative to business operations and the criteria which make define their viability e.g. designs making the life and work of users easier and/or more productive, removing risk, hassle and sources of dis-satisfaction, housing new enterprises or processes, reducing operating and life-cycle costs, helping to grasp business opportunity, etc.

3. *Aesthetic value*: an appreciative value e.g. the perception of poetic qualities or a cultural and heritage content, or the perceived resolution and harmonisation of what is experienced - even including what value engineers sometimes call 'esteem value'. Like operational value, aesthetic value can be transformed into commodity value or its enhancement, but it can also become perceived to be a negative when it constrains other values (e.g. the added costs of dealing with the listed historical building or archaelogical find).

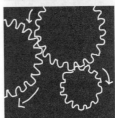

There are three aspects of architectural value to be envisioned, harnessed and realised: commodity, operational, and aesthetic. 'Good design' indissolubly links them intio a whole. It also binds them to a specific context and set of prompts which define the viability and validity of a design.

Architects can expect to deal with variations of these kinds of value as project deliverables which are the outcome of reforming the project inputs of time, resources, site, opportunity, etc. However, it is worth noting that architectural design is likely to be only *one* issue in the client's overall perspective and it is usually *the project as a whole* that adds or creates value for the project sponsor. Take a restaurant, for example: the kitchen staff, the menu selection, the quality of produce used and dishes served, the taste of that cup of cappuccino, the attitude and skill of the waiters, promotion, reviews and reputation, economic issues and many similar factors are all as important as the interior design of the restaurant in producing the right kind of ambience. Good design in this context has to imbue the entire endeavour and has diffuse boundaries.

It might be gratifying to consider the initiation of projects simply in order to cre-ate purely architectural kinds of value, but it is for good reason that such gestures are sceptically viewed as 'follies' - an uncommon basis for the employment of an architect. Building projects usually include more mundane prompts. The stated goals and criteria are also likely to be the chosen outcome of the consideration of a range of possible options to which resources might be beneficially applied. In other words, even the ambition of having the best restaurant in town has, in some terms and at some point, to be translated into a purposive, *strategic* format in order that project actions can be undertaken and change effected. Without some form of strategic content (the 'business case', for example, or a social programme), a design project loses its grounding in the world of praxis.

Against such a background the content of the architect's claim that *good design*

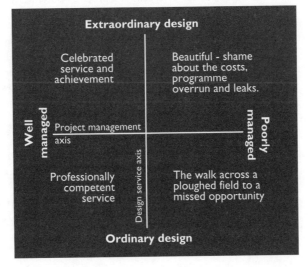

Service and Value

By setting an axis of 'design services' against one of 'project management', we generate four sectors defining kinds of service and value creation.

Briefs

'But a brief is more than a statement of the problem. That's only the first of its three roles. Its second is that of a tool, an ally, the partner in the journey to the solution which the designer embraces in creative conflict . . . The brief's third role is as a checklist . . of the mimimum criteria to be satisfied. because, as Alan Fletcher has said, 'solving the problem is not the problem. The problem is adding value'.
David Berstein

Seeking Potential

Projects have different kinds of potential. The so-called 'bad client' limits that potential. Circumstances can limit the potential. A designer's job is to optimistically seek out, pursue and realise whatever potential there might possibly be. And there is a sense in which they must do this both self-referentially and with regard to the client's instrumental intent. To deny the validity of either kind of motivation would be to miss the point.

need not cost more is somewhat ambiguous. Sponsors might ask for project goals to be achieved which satisfy performative, temporal and financial criteria in specific, quantitatively described terms, but they can only ask for 'good design' in the vaguest language - especially if their mind-set is instrumentally oriented. What is 'good' design? How do you appraise it? What is its opposite, 'bad' design? Is it the design that fails to achieve even a bench-mark of what can be reasonably expected (or even produce a subtraction from expected value)? What is the underlying bench-mark against which performance and achievement are to be measured? What is 'good design' in the context of a differentiation between quality of service and quality of work? The adage of good design not costing more may be correct (in the sense that poor design doesn't necessarily cost less), but it fails to help the client understand what it truly means and even underscores that ambiguity.

Similarly, questions of 'value added by design' are also fraught with ambiguity. What is the nature of the good value in question? Value for whom: client, designer, users or the general public? Value added to *what*? What if *your* value is not *my* value? How does one decide between added value options? How are conflicts to be resolved? Self-evidently, value might be added to the building site, the client's operations or their enjoyment, but the concept requires, at least, some form of bench-mark. How is this to be validated if projects are always unique, as architects emphasise?

Given such difficulties, it is understandable that many clients generalise projects and resort to performative terms such as 'fit for purpose', 'defect free' and similar implicitly negative quality concepts denoting *an avoidance of possible causes of dissatisfaction* and *an emphasis upon instrumentality*. This underlining of purposive rationality does not imply the denial of aesthetic value in general or the architect's agenda in particular - it simply doesn't know how to articulate or accommodate these forms of value nor avoid incompetence or charlatanism in the guise of artistry.

3 **Realising Potential.** From both the client and designer's viewpoint, a discussion about value added by design begins to make more sense when that value is considered as the challenge of a *potentiality to be realised*. This does not resolve the above issues, but it orientates project participants away from abstractions and toward a sphere of action.

Every project has some form of potentiality (some more than others) - a basic premise to the notion of design alchemy, especially when this is understood as more than the rule-governed application of technical expertise. In terms of this potentiality, there are four important dimensions to the project challenge: the need to *envision, to harness, to realise, and to experience*.

1. First, potential value has to be *envisioned* and formulated as a valid and attractive proposition, i.e. as the product of creative problem-finding, problem-framing and conceptualising, as in a scheme design which describes a specific set of proposed forms of benefit. If a project's potentiality is not realised in the initial scheme design, as a projected vision, then it is lost.

2. Second, potential value has to be *harnessed* in building specifications during design development. This is a stage of problem-solving when there is a shift toward the dominance of technical competence in order to realise the promise of the design proposition. What appeared feasible now has to become viable.

3. Third, the potential formulated as a set of specifications has to be *realised* in a substantial form i.e. as a construction. This challenge includes issues of 'buildability' incorporated into the design, as well as the responsibilities of the builder.

4. In addition, there is another stage: when the potential is occupied and *experienced* as a user benefit. (There have been excellent designs which reached the point of delivery, but failed to be occupied or were used in ways not intended e.g. the Richard Rogers Billinsgate building in the City of London.)

For example, the architect can be expected to create value as a design or consultancy service near the front-end of a project i.e. when available project leverage might lend the opportunity to provide an especially advantageous 'architecture' or structural configuration of attributes to the scheme formulation. Master planning, feasibility studies, space-planning and facilities management consultancy are typical front-end services of this kind. Contractors and specialist consultants can also make significant contributions during the early project stage by anticipating buildability issues and, sometimes, by expertly revealing potential resulting from the interplay of construction and building use. The potential value inherent in a scheme design has then to be harnessed and realised during design development and construction. This is the stage when it is easy for things to go wrong and for potential to be compromised and even aborted: for example, by inadequate or late information resulting in unexpected and unnecessary costs, delay, lost revenue, etc. If this happens, the potential value added can translate into a negative figure! Inappropriate or undesirable change - sourced from either the designer, the client, the users or the project environment - can severely undermine work in this stage, emasculating the potential and turning the project into a proverbial walk across a ploughed field. Team chemistries and inter-agency co-ordination are also significant factors in fulfilling potential success.

The inherent success potentiality of specifications (ideally incorporating a full anticipation of buildability issues) will be important to the final stage when attempts are made to realise the design, but so will the skill and contractual attitude of the building team. All too often, builders adopt a predatory and claims-conscious approach aiming to maximise their own benefit from arising project difficulties and construction problems - i.e they perceive a different form of potential. (See the section on classical and relational contracts.)

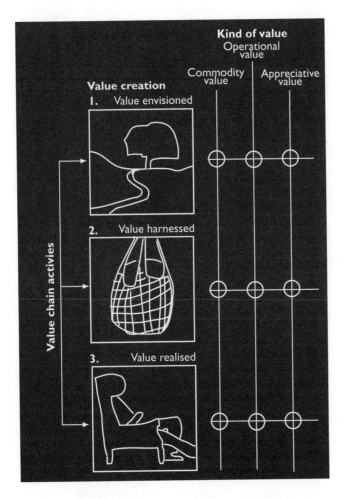

Kinds of Value to be 'Added' by a Project

In analysing what Michael Porter has called 'value chains' like that On the left (from envisioning, through harnessing to realisation), it is helpful to differentiate between two generic categories of activity: primary and support.

The primary activities are directly fee-earning and deal with (a) any marketing and sales promotion; (b) gathering and formulating base knowledge and material; (c) the operations which transform material into design propositions and services; (d) delivery logistics to others in the team; and (e) any post-delivery services offered.

Typical support activities cut across the entire range and all stages and deal with (a) general procurement (purchasing and the like); (b) technologies which enable processing, etc.; (c) human resource management; (d) and the firm's infrastructure (admin, legal, quality management, etc.).

It also helps to identify three kinds of activity types: (1) those activities directly concerned with creating value; (2) those activities which enable direct processing to be performed (all cultural factors and studio disciplines which contribute to quality assurance); and (3) those activities concerned with quality assurance (i.e. inspecting, testing, reviewing, etc., not quality management activities).

4 **Frames of Reference.** Because of such possible difficulties, especially during the harnessing stage, architects commonly find it necessary to frame service claims in terms that are implicitly defensive - claims seeking to obviate the perception that design is a project wild card. The claim that 'We *deliver on time and to budget, as well as being architects acclaimed for our design quality*' is another way of saying, 'We *will not go over schedule, we will not go over budget, and we can be expected not to deliver an unattractive building*'. From this perspective, the designer's claims are a contribution to risk management. This also applies to the offer of quality assurance, particularly when embodied in audited, procedurally articulated, quality assurance certification which seeks to reassure the client that a strongly framed technical rationality will be applied to the project content.

The more tightly a project sponsor frames and states instrumental project criteria, the more necessary are these assurances that the architect's service will be worry-free. The appointment of a project agent representing instrumental ambitions (i.e. the project manager) stands out among kinds of risk-limitation strategies employed by the client. As an insurance policy, the project manager is there to imbue the project with a goal-oriented, managerial rationale and to deal with project issues that can compromise success. The service is not there to *add* value; however, it can be instrumental in obviating potential risk and consequent damage to added value interests. In this sense it should further a realisation of a minimum value to be reasonably expected or, better still, the optimisation of the potential value inherent in the project. Design and project management has that goal.

Taking projects for Granted

During their long 'training', many architects are implicitly taught to take the project-situation for granted, to use it as a vehicle of creative enterprise offered as an end in itself, rooted in the paradigm of artistic endeavour. The products they concern themselves with are as much gestural, expressive statements as design resolutions of situational problematics. The student's experience of projects has beginning and end, but goals, methods and success-criteria are often (and necessarily) vague and encouraged to be open-ended. Whatever is incomplete can be later revisited and improved for portfolio presentations. Project content almost always addresses cultural programmes and rarely anything to do with work or commerce. In a discussion about means and ends, this content, ironically, emphasises aspects of process, but as worthy ends in themselves, often as solutions looking for problems, concepts referring only to themselves, and the by-products of creative endeavour celebrated as significant outcome.

The aim is to foster structural thinking and creativity, design inventiveness and wit. And it often works. However, it follows that the typical architectural

graduate's conception of the project is that of a creative situation to wallow around in. Success is not considered in specific instrumental terms, but with reference to generalised design criteria celebrating novelty, expressive concerns, intellectual content, and inevitably, skill in drafting. Maxims such as 'head in the clouds and feet on the ground' might encourage imagination coloured by pragmatism, but they sometimes pay little or no heed of process criteria such as a need for effectiveness in terms of performative and temporal criteria.

In practice - after the trauma of transition and adjustment - the architectural graduate must, unavoidably, learn to insinuate the design agenda into instrumentally-conceived projects. Even clients expect this, but the implicit disparity of position, perception, prioritisation of criteria and values can lead to a mutual lack of understanding. The student will have been ill-equipped to cope and ostensibly preparatory courses in 'practice management' will have done little apart from convey information about administrative, legal and ethical issues.. Managerial ones - and debate about the true meaning of professionalism in contemporary society - will have been hardly touched upon. True edu-

cation begins on the job, where the architect meets managers who employ the project as a useful, instrumental tool and deal with the project situation as a purposeful, goal-oriented undertaking from which they expect a high degree of predictability and certainty of project outcome.

There are two implications: on the one hand, clients learn that architects are a wild card and that architectural projects carry risks and uncertainties that have to be carefully managed; on the other hand, architects confront the need for a contemporary design ideology which can persuade clients and users in favour of their compelling commitments and the importance of their creative insinuations into other project criteria.

Debate on these issues within educational circles inevitably polarises into an argument about creativity within a liberal humanist tradition, versus training needs and fitting students for practice, as if it were a matter of either / or. However, the real issue at stake concerns the inculcation of inappropriate project values which can have a profoundly adverse effect upon the success and image of some members of the profession.

Four Strategic Points

It has been pointed out that many successful sports teams appear to deal with each game and season in a similar way to how projects are approached. Those who have achieved success over a long period have something in their favour which is more than the individual team members - somehow, the club maintains success as individual players and managers come and go. Architectural practices confront similar difficulties in managing themselves: in being 'game-specific' in the short term, and maintaining a distinctive capability over the long term. From this perspective project management is more than a discipline concerned with forms of technical rationality and the manipulation of process.

What everyone on a project team wants is very simple and can be generalised in the following way:

1. They want to get there - to the project goal.
No one wants the enterprise to be curtailed or to drag on indefinitely. They aren't in the project situation to wallow around. The whole point is to realise change, to get there - to the more preferred configuration.

2. They want to get to there successfully.
That is, they want to realise the quality / performance ambition which is the project goal and the situation's potential. Success is an implicit goal of all project undertakings - simply getting there is not sufficient. What is the point of a project if you get there, but consider the end result is compromised or unsuccessful?

3. They want to get there economically.
That is, in terms of the expenditures of available time, resources, effort and capital. Why spend more than you have to or take longer than necessary in instituting the desired change? A universal law of natural economy must prevail. Parkinson's rule that 'work expands to fill the time available' must be countered by effective management of the project enterprise.

4. They want to get there with minimum hassle (*the avoidance of process dissatisfactions*) *and as enjoyably as possible* (*the promotion of process satisfactions*)*. The latter includes the personal satisfactions that come with empowerment, knowing a job is being done effectively and well, and feelings of personal growth. What is the point of it all if there is no feeling of personal satisfaction? The alternative is , at best indifference and, at worst, alienation.*

Most architects and clients will share these goals and often subscribe to the same project criteria, but the above four points can mean different things to different people. For example, sharing criteria and ambitions has not been the architect's traditional attitude to client service. In 1925 Erich Mendelsohn idiosyncratically commented, "The client is in all cases a petty grocer, who only respects intelligence when it delivers the goods to him. He is only too glad to declare his respect for art but only in order to get a thousand pound pig for the price of a piglet." This prejudice continues. According to a recent RIBA survey, current attitudes still leave something to be desired. Architects complain that:

> Even clients who want 'dreams' are increasingly dominated by time and budgetary constraints. And, as managers reporting to bosses and/or shareholders, the professionalised clients of the 1990's are likely to be looking for ways of yet further reducing rick and uncertainty.

Perhaps as a consequence it was noted that:

> Virtually all the practices expressed their aspirations and motivation in terms of providing good/high quality design. Only a few mentioned client satisfaction!

Both comments form the RIBA Strategic Study, 1993

Design artistry

Architectural design is often discussed as a form of personal expression, almost in the sense that art is similarly valued. One recent book on the management of building design even drew a parallel with portrait painting (8). This misreads the motivations and vocational commitments that inform the architect's work, and misunderstands the nature of design. A more cogent description of how designers work, the nature of their form of rationality and its relation to other forms (for example, that characterising project management), comes from Donald Schon, who has written two books centred around the concept of what he calls the 'reflective practitioner' (Schon, 1983, 1987).

Schon is refering to people like architects. His message is that their education fosters a kind of creative 'artistry' which he considers to be desirable in the training of other professions. At the root of Schon's thesis is the difficult predicament of the contemporary professional in an age when everyone is professional, true professionals are sometimes held in comparatively low esteem and the term is becoming so ubiquitous that it is losing meaning. Schon places much of the blame at the door of educational institutions who encourage the notion that professionalism is a form of systematic, technical rationality founded upon the value of scientific knowledge and applying generic solutions to problems. Teaching is first of all in relevant basic science, then in applied science, and finally involves a 'practicum' in which students are meant to apply research-based knowledge in everyday practice. The idea that a rule-governed technical means should be applied toward achieving the goal of stated ends is the premise at the heart of much of this educational concept and the professional method it endorses.

There is certainly a skill called for in applying technical rationality. For example, the subject has been explored at length, from another viewpoint, in *Zen and the Art of Motorcycle Maintenance* (Pirsig, 1974), but this is only one form of action-competence. Furthermore, as Schon argues, the traditional notion of professionalism exercised by the problem-solver as an embodiment of instrumentally applied technical expertise tends to ignore what he calls the issue of 'artistry' - especially the artistry of *problem-finders* attuned to kinds of unique and indeterminate situations where intuition, judgement and experience have to be exercised, as well as a technocratic form of professional knowledge. This 'artistry' is now a kind of *knowing-in-action* because that is how it manifests itself. The knowing is in the action - informed by a kind of 'unselfconscious virtuosity' which, characteristically, we cannot make verbally explicit. A tennis player, for example, knows how to hit the ball right; a doctor might immediately intuit what is wrong. When such a knowing-in-action is exercised, rules and procedures are of secondary importance or even put aside. Barristers, for example, popularly exemplify one form of artistry, one that is reliant upon forms of creative *problem-framing*. However, Schon acknowledges yet another kind of artistry, one concerned with *reflection-in-action* as well as knowing in action. This is a form of creative problem solving with a critical content. It has to *reconstruct* the nature of the problem as well as reframing it and is crucially different from knowing-in-action. Designers are called upon to exercise this form of artistry all the time.

2 **Four Competences.** The different forms of professional competence Schon describes (which includes my own invention of a fourth kind, and which are not at all mutually exclusive) have been schematically arranged in the diagram overleaf. Each of these competences can be considered as a kind of *artistry* in the sense of 'a knowing more than we can say':

1. An *implementational* art reliant upon technical training and exemplified by the technician's ability to problem-solve.

2. An *improvisational* art such as that exemplified by the barrister's ability to problem-frame.

On Being Chewed Over

The manager's instrumental agenda

PRACTICE

The architect's design agenda

Architectural practice is increasingly sandwiched between its own traditional and self-referential agenda and the instrumental agenda of those its serves. There is nothing essentially new in this, but architects must learn that being chewed over comes, as they say, with the territory. It's what designing is all about. The artistry of the designer's professionalism lies in winning through this contradiction. Charisma and an ability to win trust are as important as expertise and talent.

Dreaming

The illusion of 'total aesthetic control' was nourished . . . by the historical association of the architect's role with the absolute power of the state and the cultural hegemony of the court over the classes that could provide patronage.
Margali Larsen
And it lingers on as a dream of legitimate ambition.

3. A *creative* art such as that exemplified by designer's ability to problem-find.

4. An *intellectual* art characterised by the academic theorist.

Firstly, there is professional competence suitable to familiar situations, one founded upon facts and requiring the application of a rule governed, technical form of rationality. This is an art of implementation. *Problem recognition* is followed by instrumental action. Means are separated from ends and instrumental problem solving becomes a technical procedure whose effectiveness is measured in terms of success in achieving pre-established goals. Research in terms of controlled experiment is quite separate from practice. Knowing is separated from doing. Objectivity is of great value. A mechanic or computer programmer does this; a designer, too, must have this form of competence, especially in engineering.

Secondly, there is professional competence suited to less unfamiliar situations requiring rule-governed data gathering, diagnosis, inference, and hypothesis testing leading to some degree of *problem-framing*. This is a more *improvisational* form of artistry. Doctors, teachers and lawyers often practise it. They have learned forms of inquiry which enable problem-framing to link their general knowledge with particular cases of a relatively unfamiliar nature.

A third form of professional competence arises when existing knowledge does not fit every case, when problems do not have a right answer, or when indeterminate situations have to be transformed into determinate ones - perhaps when sense is made out of a unique, uncertain or conflict-full situation. It applies when usual theories of phenomena, strategies of action, and even ways of framing problems are insufficient and problems must be resolved by a form of creative reconsideration *within* modes of action (rather than apart from it). Problem-*finding* becomes crucially important. Means and ends now have a degree of inter-dependency. Coherence must be constructed and imposed. Knowing (academic research) and doing (practice) become inseparable. Familiar rules, theories and techniques have to be mediated through some degree of reflection within and during the action as an interactive process which becomes profoundly intuitional. Validity is now concerned with a mode of transformation, perhaps relative to some over-arching theory or concept and set of values introduced into the situation. Objectivity becomes a test of transformative effort (e.g. have we achieved the transformation intended?). Schon borrows the term 'worldmaking' for this form of professional behaviour, but one of its most important features is that it takes place *during* action. In a sense, it is that action or can hardly be separated from it. Architectural design exemplifies this form of competence - a form of it which is reflective (and intuitional) even as it is simultaneously dependent upon a rational understanding of how problems are framed and can be technically resolved.

There is also a fourth kind of competence that can be added to Schon's list: a value forming and *intellectual* competence e.g. that exercised by a philosopher or theoretical physicist. Rule governed knowing is once again of relevance, but it is a different order to the one we met previously (now, for example, subject to Karl Popper's criteria of falsifiability). Because this is not a form of professional competence concerned with direct socio-economic action (praxis) and hardly of direct relevance to the present discussion, I shall dare to ignore it.

It would be nonsense to suggest that different disciplines are locked within one form of competence or another. For example, the artistry of an architect clearly embraces all four. However, whilst new technologies and the forms of technical competence they engender might foster new issues, it is, Michael Brawne has pointed out (Brawne 1992), an improvisational problem-framing that is the platform of design innovation. This, rather than any new technology, is likely to be the basis of the brilliant and admired architectural insight. In realising such an insight, the designer works in such a way that design judgement and action become at once unified and interactive. The judgement and its result are experienced at the same time and proceed iteratively as the designer reflectively probes her way forward against the background of the situational-problematic. Thus a reflective competence is the essence of design, but it is, nevertheless, strongly dependent upon implementational and improvisational competences

Projectors and Undertakers

In 1784 the architect James Gandon found that a Dublin Grand Jury 'had a very erroneous idea of the profession of an "architect" as it stood in England. Some of them considered me as a contractor, or, as they termed me, "a projector and undertaker" not one of those able personages whose occupation it is to bury the dead, but to bury stones and mortor'.

(without which any creative artistry would be crippled). To the extent it inevitably has an intuitional content it is opaque to technical forms of rationality - forms such as those embodied in most project management theory. Project management competence is, undoubtedly, also a form of 'artistry', but its principal emphasis is upon implementational skills, e.g. in terms of the planning, monitoring and control techniques which form the basis of orthodox project management. Its intuitional content leans toward leadership and team issues rooted in motivation and human relations.

On Preparedness

Nearly all successful scientists have emphasised the importance of preparedness of mind . . . [this] is worked for and paid for by a great deal of exertion and reflection. If these exertions lead to a discovery, then I think it would be pejorative to credit such discovery to luck.
Peter Medawar.
Designers ignore the need for 'preparedness of mind' at their peril.

3 **The Tingle Factor.** An incidental scene in Adrian Lynne's 1993 Hollywood movie *Indecent Proposal* has the hero - an architect resurrecting himself from the despair of lost love - offering inspiration to his students whilst showing them slide images of great buildings. As skyscrapers, cathedrals and exciting architecture from disparate ages and cultures flash up in rhythm behind him, the architect picks up a brick, holds it before the class and speaks of Louis Kahn - a brilliant architect who died in the men's room of Grand Central Station and whose unrecognised body lay unclaimed for three days. The hero explains that Kahn had spoken of 'what a brick wants to be' - meaning that this humble artefact, made from the most common of materials, could be

Four Professional Competences

Forms of professional competence are by no means exclusive, but the different professions appear to emphasise one or another. Architects, for example, have to practise all four kinds, but there is a self-evident importance given to their creative skill without which they have little upon which to legitimate themselves and differentiate their profession from others such as builders, surveyors and engineers. Within the architectural profession (even within a single practice) there might be leanings toward one of the above sectors or another. Most firms have a more technical / production type possibly attuned to the ways of builders. They might also have 'signature' types who become design leaders. The seniors leading the firm and adopting a job finding role are likely to have to cultivate an improvisational and politic competence.

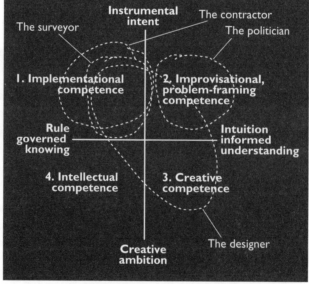

 Opposite the architects are the people they become reliant upon: those competent at implementation - a rule-governed mode of competence which, nevertheless, has to have elements of the other kinds of competence if it is to be successful.

 Surveyors arguably have more in common with builders than architects - except they wear suits and chose to determine policy rather than to execute it. Their expertise is again of a technical form and, as project managers, they can be good at applying a purposive, technical form of rationality. It is difficult to see much need for any improvisational skill.

transformed from its mundaneity into glorious architectural edifices. Like the buildings being illustrated, they might lift the spirit of man.

There are many fables like this: the sculptor who speaks of releasing marvels lying bound within inert stone, awaiting release into the world, given birth by the genius and dedication of the artist; the vernacular tradition of folk tales, such as the princess who has to be awoken from her sleep by the kiss of a prince who has fought through a seemingly impenetrable forest; and, especially, the alchemist who transmutes dross materiality into precious gold - the esoteric version of which is a person's attainment of self-knowledge or a spiritual condition. In these examples, sculptor, alchemist, and fairy tale prince are presented as figures of extraordinary talent, dedication, courage and, above all, vision. They win through whilst lesser mortals might fail or give up. They creatively challenge all that is heavy, dark, without spirit and victim to base instinct, transmuting it and irradiating our lives. Hollywood avidly consumes and recycles this mythic cultural content motivated or conditioned by the search for something not present, something lost, to be revealed or found again, to be reinvested and given a place in our lives. The teaching class in *Indecent Proposal* offers architecture students the vision that they, too, might become alchemists transmuting the ordinary into something extraordinary - something that can gratify by uplifting our spirits. Their eyes light up and they leave the class inspired. (8) How they might become alchemists and the extent to which the dross defines the gold (and vice versa) are not explained, but problem-finding and the art of problem-framing are crucial to such endeavours, to what Buckminster Fuller would, not doubt, have described as an 'anti-entropic' undertaking.

4 Sandwiched. Architects might dream of alchemy but architecture is - self-evidently - almost invariably prompted by mundane and utilitarian need. We expect our buildings to be useful, robust, practical, safe, and also economic, as well as inspirational. (From an engineering viewpoint, the value of an architecture is the degree to which it will deliver the product functionality for which it was designed.) And there might also be issues of vanity and the display of wealth, power and authority. Against such a background the architect's values have to be artfully *insinuated* into the client's agenda and programmatic requirements.

In terms of process, it is as if the alchemist has to make a saturated liquid out of which the something precious might crystallise, just as architecture must grow out of the situational context which gives it birth. This mixture is at once a rich, thick understanding of the situational-problematic and a skillful concoction. The architect is expected to exercise such an alchemical magic, transforming instrumental programmes into buildings which exhibit design skill and foster aesthetic satisfaction and emotive caring. Sent off on a design adventure with base material, the architect is expected to return with something precious, as well as useful. This is what commonly separates definitions of 'mere' building and architecture, what is considered to be design in the engineering sense and what is imbued with aesthetic and cultural appeal - that special ingredient product designers refer to as the 'tingle factor' and automobile designers identify as 'kerb appeal'. The method which gets the designer to the goal is principally a reflective artistry, and then improvisational and implementational.

To the extent that design is concerned with more than instrumentality, means/ends values, and the application of an implementational, technical competence (often no mean task in itself), it faces a difficulty at the heart of its alchemical undertaking: *there is no agreed Gold Standard.* One person's gold can be another's 'fool's gold'. And if neither the mandarins who serve as the guardians of public taste or professional standards, those who use and inhabit buildings, or the alchemists themselves can agree on the measure of quality, then how do architects give validity to their dreams and ambitions? How are their compelling commitments to be made convincing to others? How are clients to know the difference between the extraordinary design, what is merely satisfactory, and what is inadequate if their natural purposive-rationality and instrumental value system is deemed to be an insufficient basis upon which to found appraisal? The designer's reconstructive artistry denies justification on baldly instrumental grounds but it opens itself to the criticism of vagueness and arbitrariness (of which it is sometimes guilty).

Confronted by these issues, it is arguable that project management has little

On Design

Design is the conscious effort to impose meaningful order.
Victor Papenek

The opposite of design is chaos.
Buckminster Fuller.

Design is putting flesh on the spirit.
Art Kane.

Designers . . . should be market creators who can make new products by combining social trends and the inner factors of their own corporation.
Yasuo Kuroki, Sony.

Design is good business.
Thom Watson, IBM.

Architecture is the will to power.
Freidrich Nietzsche

choice but to subordinate design skill to strategic purpose. The architect then becomes valued for a professionalised competence rooted in technical expertise. Aesthetics and the values of the alchemist become something that can only be safely accommodated as *style grafted onto technical competence.* The form becomes appeal, sometimes specified as another performance criterion (and sometimes a cosmetic palliative), whilst the content remains soundly instrumental. The architect's service claims are sandwiched between two sets of potentially conflicting criteria which the skilled practitioner must *manage* to resolve: instrumental client criteria and design criteria that are at once vocationally and culturally oriented. Architectural practice and its project contribution becomes the meat in a sandwich between architectural and client agenda.

It sounds uncomfortable, but this is what design has always been about and it is arguably a predicament out of which worthy design sometimes grows. And, it must be said, the extent to which the project manager's concern with process is a contribution to a satisfactory project outcome should, in theory, be of considerable assistance to the architect. However, if clients desire to positively incorporate design values, the task of design and project management is to find ways of addressing the architect's value system and to appreciate the kind of 'artistry' being exercised. In turn, architects must find ways of validating their compelling commitments within the framework of project management criteria.

Schon, for example, has argued that the architect's artistry (described above as a mode of thinking rather than as an aesthetic agenda) is increasingly important to instrumentally-minded managers and other professionals confronted by the need to be creative - a topic otherwise confined to forms of 'brainstorming' and the copious use of 3M Post-its within 'stimulating' environments. On the other hand, the architectural profession is challenged to value the technical expertise it has progressively shed (currently maintained by self-interested professional specialisms and as a defense against liability), and to be at once less naive (the functionalist view) or cynical (the anti-commercial view) with regard to instrumentality. The survival imperative presses this upon them, but they must also seek to reformulate a contemporary architectural ideology of pride to themselves and genuine worth to clients and users which is not at odds with the latter's values. Set out in these terms, architecture is at the forefront of socio-economic interactions between what Jurgen Habermas has described as the values of the 'Systemsworld' and those of the 'Lifeworld', the latter being under continual intrusion from the former. The appropriate practise of project and design management are arguably defined by that interaction. To regard it as a something akin to portrait painting is not very helpful.

The remainder of this section looks at some of the ground-rules of effective project action which many architects are prone to forget: the management of available time, the all-important concept of the project life-cycle, the significance of a project's front-end, and the need to cultivate process values.

Similar Challenges

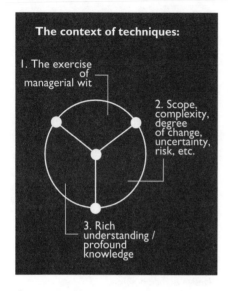

The context of techniques:

1. The exercise of managerial wit

2. Scope, complexity, degree of change, uncertainty, risk, etc.

3. Rich understanding / profound knowledge

Being a good manager requires as much inventiveness, skill and operational wit as being a designer. Three considerations stand out, each rooted in the pragmatics of effective action:

• The natural wit of the manager in the sense of an intelligent ability to assess, judge, decide and take action when circumstances might be changing, ambiguous, etc.

• The many factors which are intrinsic to the situation and form the context of action.

• The manager's understanding of the situation i.e what Edwards Deming calls 'profound knowledge'.

Paperback [] amzus_ch1 36 02+0.00 UV
Getting There by Design: An Architects Guide to Project and
Design Management - Allinson. Kenneth   **7,751**

One time, On time

Quality is no longer a stake to be raised. It is the ante necessary to enter the game. Time is where the stakes are being laid.
A Survey of Manufacturing Technology, Economist 5.3.94

Architectural services are profoundly concerned with the management of time. For that reason, it is worth placing this emphasis upon time into a wider context. The competitive post-modern business environment has engendered an emphasis upon the importance of time which has overtaken that obsession of the 1980's, quality assurance, and is becoming an equal to the consideration of costs. Time appears to become less available; it is in short supply; it must be used ever more effectively; it is increasingly the strategic key to competitive advantage. And current business ideology sees time as the key to better quality, market responsiveness, higher market share, production adaptability, and higher profit margins. All these considerations are evident in the construction market.

'Time-based competition' typically has three fundamental features:

a. *A focus upon customers sensitive to variety and responsiveness.* Products can be priced accordingly, often at a premium.

b. *The adoption of strategies which surprise competitors* by the achievement of a time-based advantage.

c. *Productive delivery systems* which are 2-3 times as fast and more flexible as competitors.

These ambitions derive from the claim that time compression strategies can produce a variety of counter-intuitive advantages, including low-cost variety in the production process and fast response times. Other advantages typically claimed include:

• *Productivity increases* - for every halving of process time or doubling of work-in-process, manufacturing productivity can increase 20-70%.

• *Time elasticity* - which means that customers will often pay high premiums for short-time delivery. With a response advantage, companies can charge 20-100% more than the average price.

• *Risk reduction* - reduced times equal reduced risk because of less emphasis upon the need for longer term forecasting. In the clothing business a lead time of 9 months can give a plus or minus on the forecast of 50%; this can reduce to 10% with a one month lead time.

• *Increased customer satisfaction and market share*

2 **Squeezing Time.** How is all this achieved? Time based companies - particularly those manufacturers seeking flexibility in production - aim to maximise *the time value is being given to a product within the process.* The organisation of work is important to achieving an optimal process the flow of work must be broken down and reassembled. Traditional factories, for example, are organised according to process needs (for shearing, punching, assembly, etc.), generating a time during which value is being added reportedly as low as 0.5 - 5% of total time in the system. Flexible, time-

Time Heuristic

The 0.05 to 5 Rule
Most products and many services are actually receiving value for only 0.05 to 5% of the time they are in the delivery system.

The 3 / 3 Rule
During the 95 to 99.95 % of the time a product or service is not receiving value, it is waiting for three reasons, each with about equal weight:
• completion of the batch of which it is a part, as well completion of the batch ahead.
• physical and intellectual rework to be completed.
• for management to get around to making or executing a decision to send the batch on to the next stage of the value-adding process. Working harder has no impact. Working smarter does.

The 1/4-2-20 Rule
For every quartering of time within a value delivery system, firms typically experience a doubling of the productivity of labour and of working capital. These gains can result in as much as a 20% reduction in costs.

The 3 x 2 Rule
Cuts in time consumption can produce growth rates of three times the industry average and twice the industry profit margin.
(Stalk & Hout, 1990)

The Time Elasticity of Profitability
(adated from Stalk & Hout)

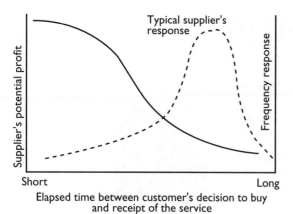

Typical supplier's response

Supplier's potential profit

Frequency response

Short — Long

Elapsed time between customer's decision to buy and receipt of the service

Too Little Time

Very few of the jobs we have at the moment have the generous design time Lloyds allowed us. Everything now is much faster. . . One of the things I lament is the very short design time allowed for a number of projects before they hit the site. One is also tailoring techniques for developing ideas, where one can telescope the design process into shorter time frames. . . What we enjoy more, and is happening now, brought about partly by the speed with which things are having to move, are less formal situations, where the design is developed with the client during the presentation.

John Young (Snr. partner of Richard Rogers and job architect for LLoyds of London): (Quoted in Robbins, 1994)

It's not so simple . . .

There is no direct correspondence between a simple criterion and its concretisation. Transformations in architecture are not as rapid and evident as might appear in compendiums and manuals. It is necessary to go through the whole design as well as the actual building process to attain normality.

The eminent Portuguese architect, Eduardo Souto de Moura. His point is often lost to view by both architects and managers.

based manufacturers organise according to product and each business is looked upon as *a value delivery system* (sometimes a *value chain*). While the traditional pattern is to provide the most value for the least cost, the flexible pattern is to provide *the most value for the least cost in the shortest time*.

Above all, such companies seek to reduce design and development times by a focus upon *process engineering*. They reduce complexity with modularisation, simplifying interfaces, minimising the number of parts, and designing for ease and simplicity of assembly. Instead of emphasising the installation of systems for achieving flexibility, smart production and assembly, they emphasise the employment of people who search for it as the result of smart design. For example, General Electric could not gain productivity increases in manufacturing its CF6 jet engines until they turned to design rather than manufacturing, eliminating valves, cables, tubes, etc., in order to simplify the engine and reduce its weight (a significant factor in aerospace engineering). Thinking that had chased the sexiness of that extra pound of thrust had to accommodate the realities of overdesign and costs. Toyota got its RAV4 from design to production in 43 months, with designers, engineers, manufacturing and purchasing people all working as one team. Value engineering was used to reduce the number of parts, nearly half of which were adopted from other models. Design simplification cut the costs of cooling-system pipes, indicators and bumpers, etc., by 20-30%. Similarly, in 1995 Compaq computers were using a 'design-for-manufacturing' concept which produced common components between models, snap-together fixings, etc., producing some models using one third fewer parts and screws than predecessor designs of five years earlier. Component suppliers were encouraged to locate very close by and some offered 15 minute. delivery times. As a result, Compaq's costs fell by 75% in two years and product life-cycles shrunk to nine months. In such examples, reduced process and development times go hand in hand with instrumentally motivated concerns for responsiveness to change, rapid innovation, quality as a reference to customer needs as well as minimum defects, and tighter cost control.

Time-based companies know that half the life-cycle cost of industrial products might be fixed by the original design; 80% may be set by the time production begins. They know innovation is more about improvement than invention and also seek ways of alleviating organisational rigidities as well as the cost burden of late (and inevitable) changes during design development. While traditional design procedures organise design and production as a sequential 'pass the baton' concept, time based companies have learned to adopt '*concurrent design*' procedures which fragment design considerations and involve as many people as possible as soon as possible in the process. The different aspects are developed in a way that cuts across functional boundaries and *brings together those people working on similar things*. Customers and production specialists will have a voice at the design stage ('listening to customers') - their in-depth needs are addressed at the beginning.

Another key tool is *Computer Aided Design*, which has been able to cut drawing times by up to 90% and provide 'digital pre-assembly' which simulates and tests component fit and performance. Large design and development time savings can result. With CAD/CNC processes, for example, information can be passed from CAD to Computer Numerically Controlled (CNC) machines to produce unprecedented actual, close tolerances (near perfect fits) - a technique used on the production of current Boeing airplanes. The same process can produce models and prototype configuration samples which have become vital to product development and the communication of ideas.

One of the oldest methods for focusing upon time are *experience curve* strategies, employed to both reduce time and costs. These were developed in the 1960's, although noted in the mid 1920's with reference to airframe construction. Typically, the costs of complex products and services, when corrected for the effects of inflation and arbitrary accounting standards, have been noted to decline by about 20-30% with each doubling of accumulated experience. For example, the fourth airplane that is built might cost 80%

as much effort as the second; the eighth costs 80% of the fourth, etc. (hence one of the business arguments for maximum market share).

In planning terms, there are two core concepts for time compression:

1. *Organisation around the main sequence* i.e. those activities which add customer value in real time - everything else is support, preparing for the main activity or is an 'off-line' activity which can be completed at any time (see later section on planning).
2. *Continuous, smooth flows* of work through the main sequence, without interruptions.

Once processes are structured appropriately, the time-based company *shares information* differently than the traditional company. Traditional business works to forecasts; a time oriented business avoids the planning loop problem, thus increasing its responsiveness and reducing time delays in the system. The company gets closer to its customer's needs, and serves them more quickly and effectively. By emphasising short time cycles the time-based company can employ shorter planning loops or avoid them altogether. Fast response times are founded upon techniques such as the use of small, empowered, self-managing, closed-loop teams which include everyone necessary to produce the flow and have everyone working toward the same objective. Even then, simply putting people from different departments together as a team is not sufficient - the work content must be fundamentally reconsidered. When such radical thinking is applied to an entire company and its operations we have what is termed business process re-engineering - a way of re-examining an entire business and its work flows (Hammer & Champny, 1993). This was hugely popular in the early 1990's and, although suffering severe criticism even from its own authors, continues as simply a variation on time compression, main activity planning and related concepts.

3 **Trading in Time.** *Effective architectural practice is fundamentally bound up with the economic employment of time.* Time is its medium of services dispensation, and the measurement of time (facilitated by the ubiquitous weekly time sheet) is the basis of competent practice accounting. The management of time's productive and effective utilisation is profoundly important to all practitioners. Practice *is* time in the form of hourly remuneration for services rendered, and it is time when fees - however calculated - are translated into manhours appropriate to the completion of the project in hand. Progress on a project is measured in terms of time: manhours already accounted for on time sheets and which remains to be undertaken as 'percentage to be completed'. Extra services that add value to the practice enterprise are measured in manhours applied and the income derived. Internal project portfolio management - allocating resources between projects - is dealt with in terms of a supply and demand of available manhours. In other words, the inescapable basis of the architect's offer is the effective utilisation of human capital within a temporal framework.

The argument against time compression concerns creativity and the need to reflect. Perhaps this is indisputable during scheme design, but the pull toward some conception of a reasonable maximum is unavoidable from any perspective that incorporates a purposive, instrumental content. After sign-off the architect is engaged with production realities which unavoidably require the confrontation of issues simultaneously addressing productivity, effectiveness, risk and quality in the context of a tightly framed, instrumentally-biased equation: a project phase when there is even less argument against minimal time expenditure. These pressures translate into productivity issues and raise fundamental practice questions. What is the actual process time during which potential value is being created, harnessed and realised in the typical architectural practice? What does this depend upon? How can we measure it? How important are decisiveness, focus and commitment, disciplined working practises and the overall cultural milieu? Such questions underly much of project and design management theory.

Just Do It . . .

"I tell my people that if we make 100 decisions and 70 turn out to be right, that's good enough. I'd rather be roughly right and fast than exactly right and slow . . . the costs of delay are vastly greater than the costs of an occasional mistake."
Percy Barnevik Chairman and ex-CEO of Asea Brown Boveri, a company of 217,000 people, 1000 companies and 5000 independent profit centres around the world in 140 countries. Quoted in Information Strategy, 12.96.

Traditional methods

• *Improve function by function.*

• *Work in departments, batches.*
• *De-bottleneck to speed work.*
• *Invest to reduce costs.*

• *Specialists create, then share with users.*
• *Managers build information bridges across organisation.*

• *Central processing, slow feedback.*

Time-based methods

• *Focus on the whole system and its main sequence.*
• *Generate a continuous flow of work.*
• *Change upstream practice to relieve downstream symptom.*
• *Invest to reduce time.*
• *Teams create and use simultaneously.*
• *Multifunctional groups build their own sources of information to do everyday work.*

• *Local processing, fast feedback.*
(Stalk & Hout, 1990)

The life-cycle concept

The concept of evolutionary progression and shifts as a project develops from inception to completion is described as a 'life-cycle'. Most projects have a basic, five-stage life-cycle:

1. a foggy birth when the project is formulated, followed
2. by build-up of resources and efforts,
3. a more active middle period, and
4. a run-down to project termination and, finally,
5. a return to normality.

The stages after the 'foggy birth' were presented in the previous section as a succession of design challenges addressing project potential - i.e. *envisioning potential as the formulation of a scheme design; harnessing potential in the form of detailed, co-ordinated specifications; and realising potential* in a substantial, built form. Each of these stages has a distinct project deliverable which provides the team with a focus and enables the manager to identify project *milestones* marking significant achievements (see page 56-7). These are also natural decision-points where progress and performances can be audited and stop / go controls instituted. A project life-cycle, however, is more than a linear sequence of events. It has within it a wave of effort that normally builds up and declines in a predictable pattern. This is exhibited by looking at life-cycle stages in terms of *team-working*. This perspective identifies three stages, with sub-stages within each of them:

1. First, a stage when the team is built-up, comes together and sorts itself out. The content of this stage is sometimes described as *Forming, Storming and Norming.*

2. This is followed by a stage when the main body of work is undertaken, the first accomplishments are celebrated, and when leadership has the task of maintaining performances as further conflicts arise, etc. This is sometimes described as *Working, Uniting, Performing and Maintenance.*

3. Finally, there is a *Run-down* or *termination* stage when team morale and performances have to be maintained whilst the project is wound-down to its hand-over and termination. This is when positive finishing skills are needed, especially if the previous project history has been problematic.

2 Divided Interests. It would be misleading to think of the contributions to an architectural project as a homogeneous whole. In reality, its overall life-cycle is made up of the efforts of many agencies and individuals comprising the discrete contributions of separate firms. The overall life-cycle is actually a whole series of individual life-cycles, each with its own pattern of development and internal reality. Or, to put it another way: the client's project can almost be considered as a number of different, subsidiary sub-projects within the overall parent umbrella. Somehow, they all have to be orchestrated.

To complicate matters further, each project agency is likely to be undertaking a portfolio of disparate projects, probably for different clients. A practice aims to be a lean and efficient, but people-centred enterprise that retains distinctive capabilities and corporate knowledge whilst undertaking project work necessitating a flexible attitude to staffing. Mutual professional loyalties have to be cultivated and capabilities maintained even though the nature of project work, paradoxically, demands a kind of adaptability requiring a constant readiness to hire and fire in accordance with workflows and the natural resourcing demand of project life-cycles. Firms have the problem of managing

---

A Project's Developmental Pattern

A. *A foggy beginning*

• *Build-up*
• *Forming, Norming, Storming*
• *Envisioning potential*

• *Main stage*
• *Working, Uniting, Performing*
• *Harnessing potential*

• *Run-down*
• *Realising potential*

B. *A fixed end*

A more cavalier view of these stages for getting from A to B has been re-presented as follows:

• *First, there is euphoria,*

• *Then, we progress to disillusionment,*

• *This is followed by chaos,*

• *Then by a search for the guilty,*

• *There is then the reward of the uninvolved,*

• *Followed by the promotion of non-participants, and*

• *Finally, a definition of project requirements.*

The enthusiasm and over-optimism of the initial stage is superseded by a disillusionment that, one assumes, follows from facing the real content of the project and knowledge of what it is all about. The chaos must come from a failure to cope with the issues, tasks and need for co-ordination. And the search for the guilty will be the finger-pointing that follows knowledge of delays and cost-over-runs. And so on.

possible conflicts in resource demand which can severely impact the generalised productivity presumptions made for each project, and which can affect the firm's capability and culture. Individuals might be readily available when the work-load is comparatively low, and over-stretched when it is high; from a skills and experience viewpoint, they might be in the wrong team at the wrong time and, since project management implies hiring and firing as necessary, a firm is faced with the issue of maintaining cultural continuity when who it is (in terms of the individuals in the firm) can vary enormously year by year.

The answer for most firms is to organise in a layered, hierarchical manner, as a series of rings around a central core (9). This will comprise those partners and directors who make the firm what it is and represent long-term continuity (and ownership). Around them will be a middle-management layer of senior professionals and associates who usually end up as the job-runners. Between them, these two inner groups will constitute the distinct capability of the practice with which others identify. Beyond them will be a ring comprising other, project personnel who are, in turn, linked to an outer sphere of external sub-contractors and suppliers. At times of economic pressure the firm will hope to reduce staff overheads by shedding people in the outer layers without affecting its distinctive capability. However, through good times as well as bad, the firm must always seek to optimise the fee-earning content of available time and to make certain utilisation is as productive and effective as possible. This economic logic applies regardless of project goals, practice culture and prevailing value systems.

In summary, the life-cycle concept does not help the managers of projects in any direct way, but its underlying reality is fundamental to all anticipatory planning and estimating. Acknowledging and conceptualising a particular project's life-cycle can be argued to be the basis of all project planning and its overall management.

project-oriented organisation

Peripheral project agencies and personnel outside the formal organisation (secondary stakeholders)

Lowest levels of the organisation (Stakeholders)

Middle management layer, comprising associates and key personnel (the *extended* team)

Inner core, comprising partners and directors

The Life-cycle Principle

Thinking of the history of a project in terms of its life-cycle is an important conceptual basis to project management techniques. The diagrams above simply plot effort against time and indicate how effort can be expected to rise to a peak, and then decline.

The lower diagram illustrates the point that an architectural project is made up of many discrete sets of effort, undertaken by the various agencies involved. The same point applies to an agency team within a practice when it splits its team in order to, say, produce a set of construction information, or people servicing differing stages or aspects of the project.

An executive project manager might adopt the upper diagram, but it says very little. Adopting the lower perspective on what is happening is more realistic and begins to suggest that attention must be given to the synchronisation of efforts. It is also important to acknowledge that each agency's effort is likely to be a part of another form of orchestration: other projects within the practice.

Common life-cycle problems include: truncation - when the project is halted; catastrophic stretchout - when a phase is delayed for one reason; chronic stretchout - when the cause of the stretchout is exacerbated until the condition becomes chronic. In addition, build-up, peaking, and run-down each have their own problems.

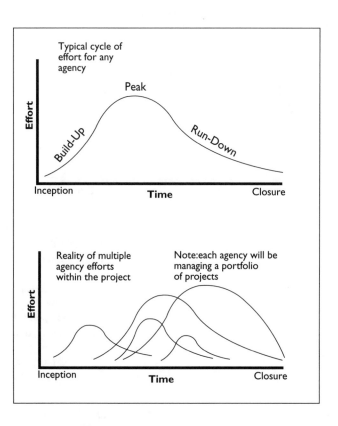

Typical cycle of effort for any agency

Peak

Build-Up

Run-Down

Effort

Inception — Time — Closure

Reality of multiple agency efforts within the project

Note: each agency will be managing a portfolio of projects

Effort

Inception — Time — Closure

Getting it right first time, up-front

There is a common tendency to underestimate the importance of not only moving quickly, but also appropriately and effectively at the very beginning of projects. This concerns the sponsor as well as the project agents, including the architect. What is often called 'the fuzzy front end' of a project is crucially important, but it is simultaneously the time when the identification of a project and the decision to act is most indefinite and subject to debate and procrastination.

Because relatively few people are usually involved at the beginning of a project, initial efforts will tend to have a low cost profile and be considered low priority in the context of other, more immediate claims on time and resources. The time at this true front end when a project is being crystallised into definition and before a full team is in place might comprise 40-50% of total project time and, once lost, cannot be recovered. As a project unfolds, so does a sense of urgency. The perceived opportunities which initiated the project might be slipping away or persistent difficulties will still be in place underscoring the need to realise change. The reasons why opportunities are lost vary enormously, from lack of salience to organisational lethargy, an inability to unlock and apply resources quickly enough, etc. However, the fact remains that lost opportunity nourishes the bitter fruit of hindsight. Organisations have to be ready to act and capable of getting it right first time, up front, with a minimum of hassle, i.e. efficiently and effectively.

Smith & Reinertsen (1991) see the situation as schematically represented above.

Even when a project has been identified and, if necessary, formally agreed upon, initial decisions affect the entire subsequent chain of events and the nature of decisions down the line. It is at the beginning of a project that parameters are defined and balanced in terms of reasonable performance targets relative to experience and industry bench-marks. Full account has to be taken of what appears to be common to such precedents and what is unique to the project situation. Many factors are involved, but an invariant rule applies: *problems at the beginning are hard to see but easy to fix; problems later on are easy to see but hard to fix.*

The beginning is the time for *problem-finding* as opposed to later implementational stages of *problem-solving*. It is the most creative phase in the sense of giving a fundamental configuration to the project structure, its content, direction and character. It is now that designers and other key team members must put in place the foundations of future success. The principal issues at this early stage concern:

- *A conception of what the problems and opportunities are.* This depends upon how the situational-problematic is 'framed' and aims are described, as well as upon self-evident constraints and stated criteria. The principal ambition is 'smart thinking' which accrues benefit to the client by conceptualising a means of harnessing project potential. The term 'feasibility study' implies an exploratory exercise, identifying and framing problems and opportunities. This is when creative artistry can be most effective.

The life-cycle principle

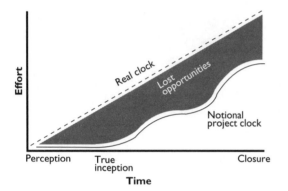

Leverage up front

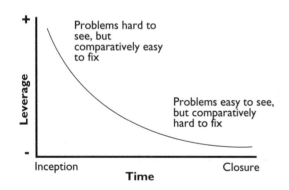

• *A conception of what temporal and budgetary capital are needed and how they might be optimally employed.* This implies consideration of the procurement route in the broadest terms i.e. what resources are needed to get there, what path is to be followed, etc.

• *A conception of what human capital will be required and how it will be employed* e.g. identifying the team and defining specific responsibilities.

Acts of conceptualisation within this process of problem-finding are accompanied by the formulation of a project scheme. The two are sometimes confused. The scheme, for example, should be a thoroughly worked out proposal ready for formal agreement and sign-off. It embraces every critical issue and project parameter. The conceptualisation is a stage on the way to the scheme's formulation and agreement. However, the conceptualisation is sometimes erroneously employed as a basis for sign-off. In effect, the foundation of the project might not have been fully explored before commitments are made. When omissions are discovered or faults in conceptualising are revealed, the situation might be more difficult to sort out (it might even be too late). To some extent such a predicament might be traced back to educational mind-sets which encourage architectural students to consider they have schematically resolved all crucial project issues when, in fact, they have only addressed issues of framing and conceptualisation. The exercise of wit and inventiveness in these terms is argued to be a sufficient basis for the more practical skills acquired in practice, but (apart from considerations of training and learned expertise implied by the notion of professionalism) the student is being encouraged into a mind-set which elevates intention above realisation. This has become a major issue with the architectural education system. What is incidental to the creative enterprise becomes an end in itself, implicitly devaluing the sphere of professional practice. It engenders an architecture of expressive gestures ironically reliant upon the instrumental values and problem-solving abilities of the 'practical men' it seeks to obviate. A properly considered and stated scheme design is more than this - it implicitly anticipates issues of design development, procurement and final construction.

2 **Now and Then.** A corollary of the rule governing up-front leverage is that as a project progresses, not only does leverage decrease, but the nature of the work content changes, becoming more routine, certain, fixed, and costly to change. Problem-finding becomes problem-solving, project emphasis shifts to scheme development, implementation and the obviation of risk. More tasks will be undertaken, more unavoidable cross-disciplinary coordination will be called for, and more devolvement of responsibility to middle and lower management will take place. This is the later project phase during which planned activities predominate and the instrumentality of actions becomes crucially important.

At the beginning, the team awaits the designer's formulation of a resolution to the situational-problematic i.e. a scheme design. Toward the end, the builders construct that design according to its detailed specification. At the beginning we have uncertainty but room to manoeuvre. Toward the end, when there is knowledge and understanding of what has to be done, we have no room to manoeuvre and lots of risk to potential success. At completion, we have hindsight and a full understanding of what should have been planned for. The shift from the early to the later project stages also sees a transformation of the meaning of 'conformance to customer requirements' - a much-used term in project management and quality assurance (see diagram above). Initially, this is the posi-

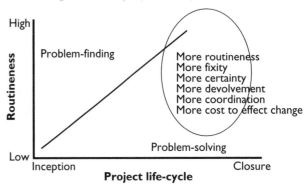

Change over the project life-cycle

High

Routineness

Problem-finding

More routineness
More fixity
More certainty
More devolvement
More coordination
More cost to effect change

Problem-solving

Low

Inception   Closure

Project life-cycle

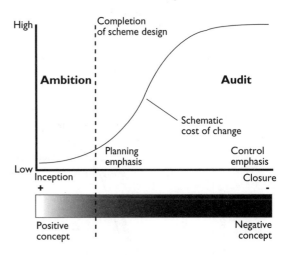

Conformance to requirement shift

High

Completion of scheme design

Ambition

Audit

Schematic cost of change

Planning emphasis

Control emphasis

Low

Inception   Closure

+   -

Positive concept

Negative concept

tive search for a design and project proposition appropriate to the perception of customer needs. Later - during design development and implementation - it becomes a concept aimed at constraining and controlling project content, enabling auditing to track progress as a programming issue. In parallel, project management's focus shifts from planning to monitoring and control. The approval of a scheme design is a crucial point where most of this changeover takes place.

3 **The Dangers of Missing the Boat.** Getting it right first time, up-front (or, 'one time, on time'), is probably the single most important factor in project management. Not to do so is to ensure that later project stages are encumbered with all kinds of unnecessary difficulties. This is more than an issue of the best possible scheme, project organisation, team set-up, etc. The later projects stages are a fulfilment of what has been determined in the initial stages and 'getting it right' is an attempt, by design as it were, to predict the project's own success during its later stages. The 'architecture' that is formulated at the beginning is more than a conception of the end product as a built entity. It is also a structuring, configuration and characterisation given to the developmental process, the organisational means employed, and the team who work on the project. Means and end become inextricably bound into an ongoing, developing conceptualisation that informs the situational-problematic in the most profound sense. In this scenario, that situational-problematic is not only the brief given to the architect, but the particularities of team chemistries and politics, the constraints and potentialities of the site, the budget available, the prevailing economic climate at that place and time, etc. The project is given a configurational architecture, as well as the building. Managers as well as architects get there 'by design'.

Disparate Project Life-cycles

The cumulative life-cycle on the left is common, sometimes tailing off rather slowly. However, some projects do not manifest completion until their final stages when 'everything comes together'. Meredith and Mantel (1995) give the example of baking a cake or editing a book, where successive stages of effort toward the end produce large increments of completion. Shop fit-outs and exhibitions are sometimes like this, manifesting cumulative progress from concurrent work efforts only in the last stage, after which no further work is possible. The former project life-cycle exhibits the opposite effect. This is typical of most building projects that can drag into extended snagging, final changes and adjustments, extended negotiations over the contract, and so on.

Which form of life-cycle to choose is a matter of managerial judgement, but has implications for project planning, scheduling, reporting, and also client management. The first curve implies a traditional 'snagging' opportunity at the end of a project; the second curve implies there is no opportunity for this and that everything must be more or less right upon installation (suggesting , say, prefabrication, off-site production, emphasis upon process values as a quality assurance check, etc.). 'Getting it right up front' has a different pattern and feel to it in the second curve, where it is all the more important not to be deceived by what appears to be the time available and by the need to sort out the basis of the project.

When risk is taken into account, project management might decide to build-in the contingency buffer that attempts to transform the second curve into a variation on the first (at least for some components of the team effort). This is a strategy in software development. At Microsoft, for example, it is common to build a 20-30% post-milestone, de-bugging contingency into the planning of all major project stages. No one knows how or why it will be needed, but experience suggests it will be required. Many architects are culturally averse to such a rigorous procedure, being enculturalised during training to have a woolly notion of project completion and of success criteria.

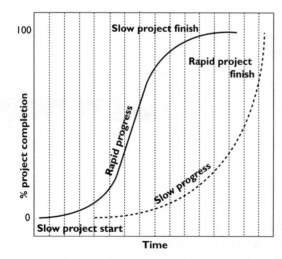

The later stages of a project are a *fulfilment* of what has been determined in its initial stages. Not to get a project right first time, up front, is to ensure that these later project stages are encumbered with all kinds of unnecessary difficulty that threaten project success. Not to get it right first time is not only to miss opportunity and fail to grasp potential, it is to court a walk across a ploughed field: perhaps of a discontented client and of what is possibly an inadequate scheme full of problems that are difficult to resolve, or of unreliable team members who are not truly committed, aren't good enough and who don't understand that a job isn't over until it's finished and that a failure to complete it properly means it was hardly worth doing in the first place! The list is almost endless. Getting it right first time is an attempt to avoid such typical project difficulties entirely, up front, in the broadest sense. It means, for example, not having to re-work elements of the project, not having to correct, to go over the same ground again, and compounding difficulties in the process. It means constructing the parameters of future project success. It means getting there, successfully and enjoyably, being prepared for inevitable difficulty and welcoming it as a challenge rather than a daunting prospect.

An Alternative Viewpoint

'Getting it right first time' is a limited concept. As Edwards Deming comments, "But how could a man make it right first time when the incoming material is off-gauge, off-colour, or otherwise defective, or if his machine is not in good order, or the measuring instruments are not trustworthy? This is another meaningless slogan, a cousin of zero defects." (Deming 1982) Deming is referring to the environmental context of action, to the systems of action or cultures within which people operate.

The Concept of Dominance Shift

Who leads? Traditionally it has been the architect. More recent concepts employ the concept of 'dominance shift'. For example, the architect adopts a natural lead consultant role at the beginning, but leadership in the sense of the dominant agency then shifts toward ostensibly more practical-minded people.

This is a 'pass the baton' concept of dominance which begs the question as to who is overseeing it all in the client's interests. The real shift is toward a purposefully-minded project manager orchestrating disparate overall efforts and a secondary level of shifting role dominances beneath that role. Apart from obvious political issues affecting practices, the principal looser might be design itself, relegated to a strategic role at the beginning, and a secondary role thereafter. 'Design and Build' procurement methods exemplify this approach.

Architects typically respond to such a scenario by simplifying their designs, making them more robust to the influences of the 'practical men' who will apply entirely instrumental criteria to the project and its content.

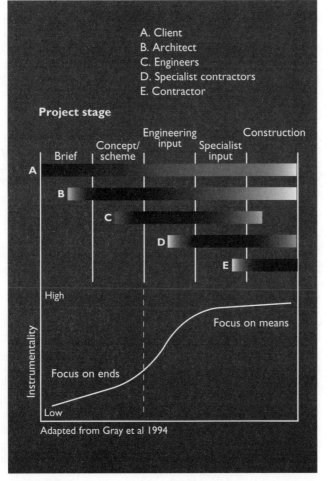

A. Client
B. Architect
C. Engineers
D. Specialist contractors
E. Contractor

Project stage

Adapted from Gray et al 1994

Managing design

Design management concerns itself with the design content of project outcomes and the effective management of the design process. In broader terms, it also concerns the beneficial 'capture' and effective utilisation of the potential to be realised by design expertise and skill. The term is widely used outside architecture in areas where product design, graphic design, corporate identity, packaging design and similar embodiments of design knowledge - areas where the managerial content of project undertakings is readily accepted more than it has been in architecture - provide service inputs to both business and state enterprises. Within an architectural context, design management usually wears an instrumental guise and is largely a spin-off from project management and its perception of design risk. In these terms it has three principal dimensions:

1. a concern with programming facilities.
2. a concern with constructional issues.
3. a concern with *inter-agency co-ordination*

Programming

Buildings are *programmed* to provide facilities suited to user needs (even the speculative building, targeted at a specific consumer market). The concept is very much a spin-off from space-planning, however its real concerns are broader and address every designed, performative aspect of a building considered from the client or user's viewpoint. The provision of hospital facilities is a good example. Programming will begin with the brief, follow a design through development, and ensure the facilities at hand-over are in conformance with requirements (in some people's eyes this is, by definition, a measure of quality). It defines what a building must *do*, and then attempts to ensure the realisation and delivery of that performative intent.

By its nature, this concept of designing facilities can easily be offered as a specialist consultancy. This might happen whenever expert consideration of user needs is separated from design competence. Even speculative office design has adopted this approach, using experienced space planners to ensure basic geometric arrangements are suited to market needs and possible modes of use. However, this can leave the designer in a fragmented and emasculated role, unable to provide a fully integrated design. Better designers will seek to adopt purposive programming as a basic feature of sound design practice and design management: at the very least, an underpinning of technical expertise; at best, the outer aspect of a consultancy service that is more culturally oriented.

Construction and Co-ordination

Managerial concepts anticipating the construction process, component modularisation and interface control have always been significant features of an integrated design development process. So, too, are concepts ensuring a coordinated, timely flow and transfer of information - which also concerns the quality and adequacy of its content. The two have always been linked. However, it is now argued that the construction industry's evolution away from the employment of craft-based materials and techniques has lead toward an ever-increasingly sophisticated employment of highly engineered materials, components and techniques on the building site. Innovation is producing more use of factory-finished building components and this affects the design process, often calling for improved managerial controls in order to effect optimal benefit and quality control.

Specialist contractors play a crucial role in this predicament and one design management argument seeks to persuade architects to acknowledge this dependency by allowing more managerial and political clout to be given over to these ostensibly more practical people who might serve as agents of purposive rationality (10). It deliberately seeks to develop strategies transferring decision-making responsibility to a more instru-

DBT's

When Boeing was developing the 777 it employed the concept of Design-Build Teams (DBT's) as a secret managerial weapon. Citing how it used to be when designers and engineers collaborated, one manager commented that, "I would love to have a building in which the entire organisation was within fifty feet of each other. With ten thousand people that turns out to be really hard. So you start devising other tools to allow you to achieve that - the design-build team. You break the airplane down and bring manufacturing, tooling, planning, engineering, finance and materiel all together in that little group. And they are effectively doing what those old design organisations did on their bit of the airplane." The 250 DB groups, each with a zone or sub-zone of responsibility and 10-20 members, used regular, tightly run meetings as a management tool. The groups included outsiders such as customers and engineers from foreign plane manufacturers, the aim being to get everyone's knowledge into the design. This meant going beyond sending the teams out to learn and, instead, to bring the expertise into the enterprise.

mentally conceived 'engineering' function as soon as possible in the project process. In turn, this function will coordinate with specialist contractors having an even more technical bias; finally, the contractor dominates the process. This amounts to a concept of *dominance shift*: a management of the project so that, as room for manoeuvre becomes constrained during project development, project efforts are increasingly dominated by 'practical men' (see schematic diagram). The intention is to marginalise the designer's influence - a common feature of design and build scenarios.

Inter-agency co-ordination.

The ideal form of design management would probably embrace all the necessary expertise within one person or, more plausibly, within a single agency. This would be rare and even the smallest project is likely to involve more than one agency. This will produce all kinds of decision-making and organisational disjunctures. The most obvious split is between designer and builder, but splits within the team formulating the design and specifications are likely to be more significant. Disparate agencies have to be oriented in the same direction and fully co-ordinated against the grain of quite separate portfolios of projects within each one. For example, information flows have to be managed - as the passage of more or less complete packages of information, or as the more continuous flow required by concurrent, time-compressed procedures - and efforts have to be synchronised and continually checked. There is a need for dialogue on the one hand, and clear, staged commitments on the other. Clarity, thoroughness and ease of communication become important - issues being improved by CAD drafting protocols and standards enabling what is, in effect, work on the same set of drawings by different agencies. Ensuring this takes place will require more than planning: there has to be a positive spirit of co-operation between those involved. This can be assisted by the proper management of, for example, meetings, their agenda, and decisions to be made.

2 **A Focus on Means and a Focus on Ends.** Such concerns are typical of a design management interest seeking to optimise specific issues of product selection, performance, value for money, life-cycle costs, sustainability, etc. - usually from an instrumental viewpoint. However, project managers should also be seeking to adopt a more holistic approach and to evolve action plans instrumentally framing the project content as a whole. Their ambition should be to ensure a *continuous process control* focused upon managerial ambitions embodied in terminology such as 'conformance to requirements', 'quality control', and 'management for improvement'.

Because design has the reputation of a potential wild card, it will be likely that such control will implicitly embody the notion that the architect provides a creative

Shifts as Values

This is another way of expressing a natural dominance shift within the project life-cycle. Initially, instrumental values will be present as an aspect of the project brief (whether this brief is to grab opportunities or solve problems is irrelevant to the idea of being purposive and goal-oriented); later, they shift to become an aspect of process management. Similarly, design values help to translate the client's brief into a scheme, and then need to infuse the development work. A design lead in the early stages shifts to a managerial lead during later stages (whether the architect manages these later stages or not is besides the point, just as one would expect managers on the project to have an input into the early design work). Of course, design values can mean different things (see later sections on practice culture). For example, instrumental 'delivery' values might dominate all sectors and this would result in a relatively low design content relative to the real potential (which is not to say these values are inappropriate to the project). On the other hand, 'signature' values might be desirable. Similarly, instrumental values can be weak or strong.

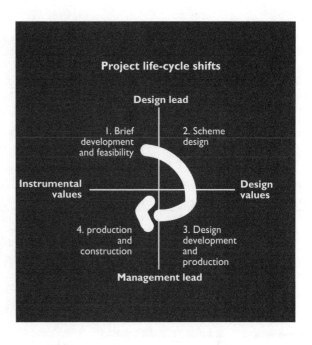

contribution that is of high value at the beginning and increasingly risky as the project develops. In the words of a book on the subject (Gray et al. 1994):

> As they become more sophisticated, clients will seek to limit their risks, particularly those caused by failure of the designers to manage their tasks properly, especially where the failure results in claims for delay. The aim is to focus the design team on to their responsibilities.

Astute contract agreements will be drawn up in anticipation of such project difficulties, clearly specifying the tasks and responsibilities different project agents undertake and allowing for those ubiquitous causes of delay: late information and changes originating with the designers. Typically, clauses are imposed allowing for the recovery of costs.

In other words, architects see projects in terms of *design* risk, reflecting their vocational commitment and enthusiasms. However, design management presumes adequate technical expertise and design talent (why commission anyone without such capability?) and translates their own sensitivities to risk into an issue of the *managerial* content of projects. Whilst the designer is focused upon a perception of ends (in terms of what it's like to be there), the manager is focused upon the process means which will ensure a successful project deliverable. The idea of appropriate and properly structured means is embodied in a *project action plan*.

3 Procurement. The most fundamental and important feature of a project action plan will be the identification of a 'procurement route' - something to be agreed early in the project process. Conventionally, the term has been applied to that phase of a project *after* the designers have completed their design work and sent information out to tender (the building is then 'procured'), suitable contracts being founded upon the idea of the development of all design information *before* handover to a building contractor. The argument in favour of this way of working is self-evident: know exactly what you intend to do before you commit to doing it. The principal argument against the procedure concerns the not uncommon divorce of design from specialist sub-contractors. But the real issue is the claims-oriented attitude of those contractors who accept construction responsibility and take full advantage of the supposed completeness and adequacy of specification information. Common difficulties include issues such as:

- the nomination of specialist sub-contractors by the architect
- design responsibility within specialist packages of work
- problems of coordination

Getting Ahead

- Get it right first time, up-front.
- Identify and manage the project-specific risks.
- Measure what you do and how you do it. Know those measures and use them advantage in project learning and planning.

Infusing the Project

Project management has to permeate the whole project. Organisationally, it can be thought of as a web spreading out from a strategic viewpoint. Each agency adopts the project management ethos, thus insinuating instrumental values into their work, harmonising it with other agencies. In turn, individual agency personnel must also adopt the same project management aims and values. Without this happening, project management, as an overview, will be both superficial and effete. Question: How does one infuse a project?

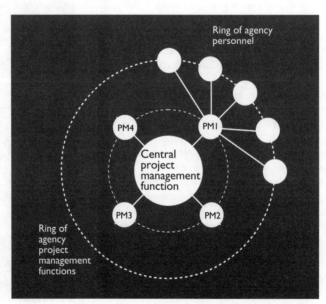

• problems of contractor's substitutions
• managing necessary change.

Contention is invariably rooted in the structural difficulty that relations are defined by divisive forms of 'classical' contract which not only specify in exact terms who is undertaking what and the nature of their responsibilities, but leave out and mitigate against the parts which cannot be legislated for: trust and willing collaboration.

Two coping strategies have evolved: the first has sought to find ways of bringing the builder into sympathy with the demand side, or to encourage a consultancy and specialist managerial role (as with construction management); the second has been to place designers and builders under the same contractual umbrella (design and build, in which the architect ostensibly moves over to the supply side). Both these strategies and variations upon them have had a profound affect upon architectural practice, the architect's traditional role, and issues of liability (and this includes a 'pass-the-parcel' attitude to liability which invariably ends with it in the designer's lap, even in design-build forms of contract).

We are sometimes told that change has been necessary because of the specialist technical nature of contemporary building techniques, the inability of architects to adapt, and their managerial incompetence. To some extent this is undoubtedly true. But the real issue is a hegemony of managerial values, means / ends thinking and the dominance of a purposive-rationality which strategically assesses all actions in terms of their instrumentality and rarely encourages consummate co-operation. Ambivalence toward design becomes accepted: valued, necessary, and yet, ostensibly, a wild card within the project equation.

Other industries are learning to by-pass some of these difficulties and proving that instrumental values and a spirit of collaboration at not mutually exclusive. For example, when Boeing was developing the 777 it had drawings signed-off by the manufacturer as well as the designer, the checker, the supervisor and whomever else had to formally accept responsibility. The message was clear: design and manufacturing were collaborating as a team, and the content of the design was producible as well as properly designed. This was unheard of before the procedural innovations introduced on the 777 project, previous to which engineers (like architects) proclaimed, "I'm responsible". (Sabbagh, 1996) There is no reason why similar approaches cannot be more successful within architectural design and construction, but all too often they rely upon architects adjusting a mind-set prejudiced against managerial concerns.

4 Management and Managers. A feature of the contemporary construction climate has been the need to promote a consistent, unified, project-specific managerial ethos throughout a project team, thus overcoming endemic organisational discontinuities.

From this perspective there has to be a differentiation between project *management* and project *managers*. The former is a subject concerning the issues that arise and have to be dealt with when managing projects. Project managers are the people who formally do this, but we again have to differentiate between two kinds of role.

1. E*xecutive project management* by a person appointed by the client to ensure the project successfully gets to the goal. These are the people who, on many projects, have replaced the architect as the friend of the instrumentally-minded client. These are the specialists who get the client from A to B. They are interested in the one-off process -engineering of the project undertaking.

2. The diffuse body of *project management representatives*: all the managerial roles within the various agencies comprising the team: architect, engineers, specialist sub-contractors, etc. Because they fulfil a managerial role on a project, they are, by definition, project managers.

The executive role is to weld the team together into a common purpose, to focus the team on their responsibilities and upon the idea of a large potential to be realised. In this sense, the executive has to be a project champion. At its best, the role is epito-

Roots One

1. It was Vilfredo Pareto, an early 20th century economist, who formulated the 80-20 rule that states 80% of the effort expended in a process is caused by only 20% of the input. Retranslated, this became the rule that 20% of a company's products or clients produce 80% of its income. The rule has become a widely used heuristic.

2. The founder of 'time compression' theory and the idea of the 'experience curve' is Bruce Henderson, founder of The Boston Consulting Group. In 1966 Henderson introduced the concept that the cost of value added, net of inflation, will characteristically decline 25 - 30% each time the total accumulated experience has been doubled. But it is not experience that causes this, merely volume - hence the importance of market share (experienced in architectural circles as the reality that, on both sides of the Atlantic, the larger firms increasingly take a larger slice of the overall cake). Applying Pareto's 80/20 rule enables one to see where a firm's experience curve is being applied to create unique competitive advantage. (See The Logic of Business Strategy, 1984.)

(Incidentally, this is one of those 'laws' which parallels Gordon Moore's rule that microprocessor power doubles every 18 months whilst prices halve. [Originally, Gordon's 1965 prediction was that it was every year; it has recently been upped to two years. He got the pricing slightly wrong as well. Moore was a co-founder of Intel])

mised by property development professionals such as Stanhope, who have a concept of *professional development* that goes beyond any mechanical interpretation of the executive role. Stanhope sees their role as that of a professional client, mediating between investors and users, welding an effective project team together - one that works in a fast, efficient, cost-effective way whilst still maintaining quality. The team is seen as a body of specialists brought on board as and when needed. In this way the project content is carefully orchestrated and engineered. But there is also an acute awareness of the need for a strong team spirit, for pride and commitment - engendered by induction courses and the like which seek to form a team that believes in its own collectivity and in the meaningfulness of achieving the project goals.

Most executive project managers have a far more limited idea of their role. But in all instances there is a dependency upon the notion of a project management function and ethos diffusely imbuing all team efforts - as something taking place at every level in the team and within each participating agency. Because most building projects involve quite independent agencies, the executive manager cannot directly interfere in their internal affairs. They have to encourage, cajole and, above all, *lead* by example. But there is still a limit to what they can achieve; some form of project management spirit is either there, within the various agencies, or it is not.

It is useful to think of a project being characterised by five possible levels or kinds of project management activity:

1. *An upper level represented by the 'professional developer', as described above. A variation on this would be the client who is very project oriented - an increasingly comon phenomena.*

2. *The conventional executive project manager, sometimes forced to use more stick than carrot, strongly dependent upon co-ordinative, planning, monitoring and controlling functions. The person in this role is at once coach, catalyst, and champion.*

3. *The representatives of project management at the agency level e.g. the associate or director in charge.*

4. *A bottom level embracing everyone else in the team - project managment as an attitude permeating team efforts, constituting an integral part of agency culture*

5. *A peripheral body of project 'stakeholders'.*

The two mid levels typically represent an irreducible 'core team' responsible for accountable for the project team's performance. Others participate to varying degrees, depending upon the project, its stage, etc. On the periphery of the project will be the 'stakeholders' who are affected by it, can influence it, or have a contribution to make. They can be within participating agencies or external to them e.g. state or municipal regulatory bodies. Sponsors are also likely to have stakeholders within their organisation.

Project management agents have to anticipate the politics of the overall project situation. Just because stakeholders are described as 'peripheral' and diagrammed on the edge of a core team does not mean they cannot play a strategic role in project affairs. All these managerial considerations amount to an emphasis upon a project's process as well as design and strategic content.

Roots Two

1. *The idea of 'value chains' and 'value systems' comes from Michael Porter, formerly an educator at Harvard business School. Importantly, Porter considered a firm's value system in terms of the activities that create value, rather than departments or functions. Porter also gave importance to the notion of 'focus' and popularised the term 'competitive advantage'. (See* Competitive Advantage, *1985).*

2. *Peter Drucker formulated MbO (management by Objectives) jointly with General Electric in a post-war period of expansion and growth which led to a 1950's policy of massive decentralisation within the conglomerate. The result was a series of targets or 'hurdle rates' which engendered a culture of 'making the numbers'. It was also a culture of mandatory systems, a hard-minded values, tough management set against workers and ruled by a financial elite. MbO is meant to be behind us, but it remains a significant managerial concept.*

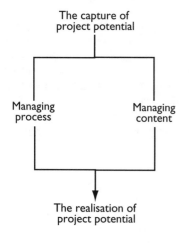

The capture of
project potential

Managing
process

Managing
content

The realisation of
project potential

Design Management Variations

Like design itself, design management is a multi-faceted subject. There are different and equally valid ways of approaching it, all of which are concerned with realising potential and avoiding risks.

Broadly speaking, there are three kinds of organisation who take an interest: Professional institutions, practices, and academia. Professional associations include the Design Management Institute in Boston, the Association of Project Managers in the UK, as well as other institutional representatives of the design professions. Practitioners are in commercial businesses and in consultancies (from the small Italian furniture company to the large corporate organisation desiring to consistently manage the design content of its operations, and other professional firms). Academic institutions and training agencies adopt four different viewpoints (see below). The boundaries between them blur, if only because of a professionalising tendency dependent upon the expression of a body of expertise and abstract knowledge in order to validate the claims of design managers.

Academics adopt four different approaches:

• The business schools adopt an explicitly business and instrumental perspective. They seek to apply a purposive-rationality to the employment of design within a business context and its expression of the profit motivation. The dominant paradigm is a managerial one. This concerns the design content of commodities, the design content of an organisation (such as its corporate identity), etc. The course at the London Business School - where design is introduced to experienced managers on an MBA course - is an outstanding example.

• A second kind of instrumental viewpoint comes from the engineering departments, who adopt a professionally oriented 'practical man' approach celebrating forms of technical rationality and expertise. The dominant paradigm is an engineering one. Construction courses at Loughborough University stand out; however, there are many kinds of product and industrial design departments who adopt an engineering interest in design management that - in automobile and aircraft engineering, mining, and prospecting, for example. Kinds of functionality tend to be the over-riding criteria.

• A third approach is the vocational and less formal, adopting a cultural and self-referential agenda, sometimes professionally mediated (seminars, CPD, etc.), often self-initiated, and caring little for instrumental viewpoints or in enhancing professional expertise as an end in itself. From this viewpoint, design management is a diffuse subject in which management exists in order to serve design values and end-users. All kinds of learning media are used. The dominant paradigm is cultural.

• A fourth approach adopts the professional designer's perspective on management issues (such as a product designer or architect). This is embodied in a growing body of university design management courses, such as that at Brunel University, on which graduate designers aiming toward a vocation in design management learn about management issues. Students are interested in the better management of design in order that its potential is more effectively realised. There is no dominant paradigm (the engineering, managerial and cultural each have a place). These kinds of manager have a design training and experience - they understand a designer's viewpoint and should thus be in a position to counter the professional designer's objection to be managed by managerial types without such a background. In effect, they become the advocates of process, just as designers have always tended to be the advocates of end-product.

Design Management variations

Practice

Academia — Professional Institutions

Academic viewpoints

	Instrumental rationale	
eg London Business School, exposing managers to design issues		eg Reading University construction management course, or those in industrial design
1. The business school agenda		2. The engineering department agenda
Managerial values (profit motive)		**End-user values**
3. The design school agenda		4. The social and art-biased agenda
eg The Design Management Institute; Brunel University, etc. aimed at training professional design managers	**Design rationale**	Self-initiated, using many informal media (such as books, TV, etc.)

A project recipe

Despite their intrinsic uniqueness, most projects follow a similar generic development path. There is no contradiction.

A. The Orientation Stage

Throw a gaggle of people together and say, "Do it!" Do what? How? On what terms? Clearly, the first priority of all projects is that they become properly oriented. Project inception and initial development through consultant appointments, brief formulation, and scheme design, are all ways of orienting the project and the efforts of those involved. This stage determines what it is that is going to be developed into a substantial form, by whom, when, with what resources, and according to what criteria. This when teams are formed.

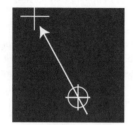

Beginnings

Project management starts with what it can know and what it can envisage. It respects the project sponsor's intent, the project prompts they are addressing, and the results they wish to achieve. It attempts to define project parameters by isolating crucial and critical elements and features of both the project outcome and the process of realising it.

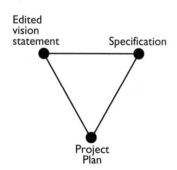

• The Vision Statement and its Editing (getting things 'right', up front)

Soundly founded upon their prompts, projects should begin with ambitious, exploratory vision statements striving to outline a project's ambitions and a vision of its potential. Without such an ambitious outreaching the project potential is already curtailed. Making and editing the vision statement formalises the defining project themes and begins, by design, to set up a project architecture in which the nature of the end product is already prefigured. Problems and opportunities have to be identified. Exploratory 'What if?' questions become significant. (Just *what* might be achieved?) Case studies and precedents are important references and bench-marks of achievement (and failure).

A vision statement should identify end-product features and anticipate their possible grouping and allocation to development sub-teams. Features should support activities and reflect crucial considerations. The statement should be explicitly end-user oriented (including the tingle factor), even daring to prioritise performative ambitions with reference to how the building will serve and facilitate the satisfaction of user needs and wants.

An ambitious vision statement might be balanced by vision editing exercises which seek to define what is *not* a crucial or significant part of the team's ambitions. This helps to focus the team on the *principal*, achievable aims and *critical* success factors. If attention is given to the benefit of end-users it is easier to sift and prioritise differing concepts of what the end-product is.

The vision should include process ideas for getting there as well as being there (at the project goal). This means many things: for example, who is involved, what they do and what contractural terms are anticipated.

• The Project Specification

Out of the push-pull of a vision statement and its editing the project team should be able to produce a self-validating outline specification (a scheme with its own architectural commitments).

Out of a thematic reconstruction of the project material there arises an architectural proposition and a range of specific features it supports.

An outine specification will describe the problems and opportunities which project features address; it will identify crucial interdependencies, risks and similar factors, and it will describe how a completed design is supposed to work.

As a communication tool, the specification confirms what is agreed and introduces new team members to a considered basis for further development. As a project management tool, it must include affirmations of project criteria and estimates of resources required to develop and realise the scheme. It must state who is doing what and by when as a confirmation of the agreement between those involved. Commitments are being made. However, at this stage the spec is still outline because it is to some extent provisional at the same as it is reassuringly plausible. Without this provisionality it would be too rigid and constrain the very creative development work it seeks to inform.

The project specification is a form of brief. This is initially formulated as something comparatively crude, but by the end of the orientation phase it has become a scheme description general and the basis of detailed development planning. By the *end* of the project a brief is a fully developed a statement that is simultaneously a complete definition of the problem and a description of its resolution. In other words a brief is a living, evolving document. However, there is a need to exercise progressive control and change control as the work progresses. While the team's leverage is progressively delimited, the inherent leverage promised by the developed project content should have correspondingly increased.

• The Project Plan

By the end of the orientation phase a project team should have an agreed direction and shared commitment - they know what it is they are progressing forward to implement. This will include a developed 'project plan' outlining roles, responsibilities, durations, costs and budgets, resourcing, staging, etc.

B. The Development Stage

Synchronising efforts, coordinating them and building periodic fixes into the development work are important features of the development stage that follows project orientation and agreement on a scheme (which includes the project plan).

A scheme design defines the underlying architecture of a product and its key features: what is fundamental, crucial, configurationally most important and bearing risk. The development stage now focuses upon the full range of secondary and tertiary features as well. There has to be a differentiation between making existing features work and adding new features, so that the agreed architecture does not become contradicted, confused or somehow begin to unravel. A range of 'freezes' has to be managerially imposed in order to shift a state of focused, developmental *possibility* to that of stabilised, resolved fixity. And this can only be achieved when development content has been fully co-ordinated and synchronised.

A thematic identification of project features allows for development work to be carried out by feature (or zone or systems) teams. Their members should be encouraged to consider their work as a part of the overall creative effort and not simply a production assignment that ticks completed tasks off a list. They need to be involved.

Inevitably, development work will produce conflicts resulting from change, reassessed priorities and even renewed vision. Professionals also suffer a tendency to drift toward their own self-referential agenda; end-users should have a voice. All of this - possibly engendering conflicts and trade-offs - must be *managed* toward final specifications which are the basis of the last project stage: construction and occupation.

C. The Realisation and Closure Stage

The final project stage is the developed scheme's realisation and a closure of the project. The project deliverable is put in place and the process of local change is completed with the users who initiated the project (if only indirectly e.g. as a targeted market) taking over.

Those involved in this final stage should have a voice during the first two stages so that, at least, their criteria are acknowledged and dealt with. In part, this is achieved as a collaboration between specialists and the architect. Some forms of construction management are also attempts to bring constructional experience and expertise on board in a front-end, advisory capacity.

From a project management viewpoint, this stage usually places the early development team into the background and allows its inputs to wind-down (although, even after hand-over to users, there is almost always some form of remedial activity to correct oversights). Some kind of review and formal closure is advisable (but rarely takes place). The cycle from prompt, through an unfreezing and application of resources, to the actual initiation of change, its realisation and a final refreezing is then complete.

Do it; Freeze it

When Boeing decided the 777 was to be made without mockups, entirely with computers, they had one model which thousands of engineers could work on simultaneously. In order to deal with component 'interferences' the design process was taken through six stages, at the end of which designs were frozen whilst interferences were reconciled. Microsoft have a similar concept for managing software design.

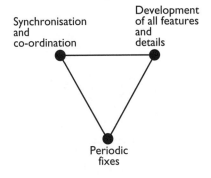

Development

Synchronisation and co-ordination — Development of all features and details — Periodic fixes

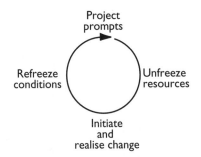

Project prompts — Unfreeze resources — Initiate and realise change — Refreeze conditions

A parable

This is a story of misfortune. It describes an architectural project with more than its share of problems and illustrates some of the points raised in this book.

Stage A:

The Situation. An experienced client in central London needed to commission a large building conversion. In essence, the project was to convert a large foot-print, seven-storey, basemented, air conditioned, steel-framed building less than 30 years old into office functions linked with an adjacent building. Its gross area was approximately 30,600 sq.metres. Each floor was different in plan and section (see diagram on left).

The client's first appointment was an executive project manager (PM) reporting to the property manager and a building committee. The PM then worked with the property manager to commission an architect, who was appointed as 'the lead consultant'; in turn, the PM and the architect interviewed quantity surveyors, engineers and prospective contractors (all of whom, particularly the contractors, emphasised the need for 'a team approach').

The Brief

The client's brief (prepared by the project manager) was as follows: to convert the building to its new purpose, including any necessary repairs and maintenance; to accommodate 500 staff and provide appropriate space-planning consultancy; to provide for staging of the work and phased hand-overs, allowing some internal occupancy and use of the building by staff during the works, including those from the new building. A budget and programme were given. The extended building life was expected to be 15 years.

In addition, a project sub-text was made clear. It stated, in effect: 'We have just finished one building and this time want everything to go absolutely smoothly, with no surprises and with us, the client, in full control'. (Hence the project manager's appointment.)

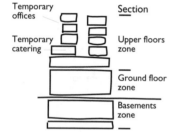

Temporary offices — Section
Temporary catering — Upper floors zone
Ground floor zone
Basements zone

The Conditions

• Whilst space-planning interviews were underway, a pre-contract demolitions contract was to be instituted (mostly in two extensive basement areas, one used for plant).
• Staff were to be quickly and temporarily housed on two upper floors, and provided with any necessary servicing. They would later be moved and those floors properly converted and rented out.
• The building was to be entirely reserviced.
• Executive apartments were to be provided.
• A new computer facility was required as soon as possible. A link had to be maintained through the works to the new building whilst general works were carried out.
• Some staff were using a third building at a high rent and on a limited tenancy. In part, the need to move them drove the project and engendered its completion date.

Stage A: Preparing a Scheme

The project got off to a good start with a feasibility study and preliminary proposal for dealing with all requirements, providing a fit, meeting tight budgetary constraints and schedule requirements, etc. The team was very confident.

Because of the complexity of the job the architects recommended a form of management contract. This was resisted by the quantity surveyors who considered it to be extra work for a fee already agreed. Other creative, multi-stage proposals were discussed which amounted to a mix of lump-sum and time-and-cost. Such approaches seemed the best options in the circumstances and within a heated construction climate of scarcity and inflation. The architects fought for the management contract but lost. It was agreed to go for an orthodox lump-sum contract based on a full specification and bill of quantities.

EUPHORIA

Meanwhile, the space-planning team found the client had over 800 staff, not 500 as stated in the brief! This altered all presumptions of fit, budget, sub-letting intentions, etc. The point was debated and researched in detail, delayed progress and sowed seeds of doubt about the client and project manager (who had set the brief and determined all goals and conditions). The Chief Executive Officer decreed that no more than 700 staff were to be accommodated in the refurbishment, parts of the brief must be omitted, and the budget and schedule were to be maintained; no allowances were to be made for expected expansion. (The aim was to be seen to exercise tight control.) This seemingly arbitrary decision further undermined confidence; it still blew most project presumptions away. Simultaneously, it was also being revealed that a client policy of extensive open-planning (which also suited the building) was being persistently resisted by staff departmental heads, each of whom were to 'sign-off' proposals.

The design team was thrown into very tight-budget scenario and had to already suggest major cost-cutting possibilities, even at this early stage. Costs were allocated on a proportional basis within the overall budget. A final scheme was prepared.

Meanwhile, the pre-contract demolitions and temporary works were initiated. Asbestos was found, delaying progress and inflating costs for the demolition work. This created a knock-on problem: available drawings were known to be inaccurate and a building survey could not be completed until demolitions were complete.

A final scheme was agreed which included major structural work to the ground floor, increasing the building's useable space. It looked good. However, because of space-planning indecision and pressures to continually revise a tight budget downward, the design team of architects and engineers were, from the beginning, behind schedule in putting together a tender package of specifications. The quantity surveyor was returning schedules of quantities now including basic items missing from the original cost plan which, upon reassessment always produced significant increases in cost estimates and yet further pressure to make changes. However, still confident of maintaining control, the QS recommended the client to end procrastination and go to bid on approximate quantities.

Results

By the end of the scheme stage, 'Get it Right first Time, Up front' was an dictum which had fallen out the window. It appeared as if critical success factors were being dealt with arbitrarily and new ones arose as fast as others were addressed and resolved. Risk had been compounded, not obviated, by the choice of contract and its subsequent compromise. The brief had proven to be incorrect; the budget was inadequate to the true needs; and both project method and required programme were naive.

Lack of accurate information and problems with the client's brief gave an unsound basis to the project which delays exacerbated. Lower level staff resistance to the CEO's and building committee's planning policy slowed the space-planning exercise (complicated, in any case, by the fact that the building had all kinds of spaces requiring three-dimensional thinking space-planners are unfamiliar with (even when they are trained architects). Specialisms manifested as closed, discrete mind-sets.

Leadership - skilled, experienced and among leaders in their

DISILLUSION

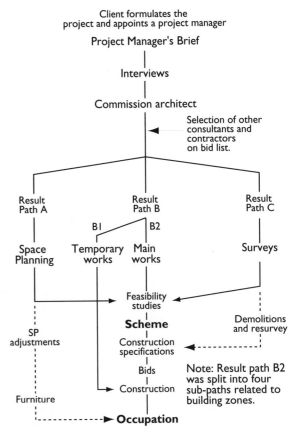

Project Intentions from formulation of the project through to occupation

Client formulates the project and appoints a project manager

Project Manager's Brief

Interviews

Commission architect

Selection of other consultants and contractors on bid list.

Result Path A   Result Path B   Result Path C

B1   B2

Space Planning   Temporary works   Main works   Surveys

Feasibility studies

Scheme

SP adjustments   Construction specifications   Demolitions and resurvey

Bids   Note: Result path B2 was split into four sub-paths related to building zones.

Furniture   Construction

Occupation

Typical Milestones content for the architectural team:

Result Path A: Space Planning, etc.
• Interviews
• Schedules of departments, staff, etc.
• Space Planning (SP)
• Sign-offs to SP scheme
• Adjustments during later construction
• Furniture selections
• Occupation

Result Path B: Architect's design work:

B1. Temporary Works
• Temporary offices works and fit-out
• Temporary catering removal and fit-out
• Final stage moves

B2. Main works
• Feasibility studies
• Condition surveys
• Scheme proposal and sign-off
• Tender packages
• Construction issue drawings and specifications

Result Path C: Demolitions and Surveys

• Initial surveys and plan checks
• Demolitions
• Selective resurveys

respective professions - failed to recognise the problems for what they were and to bring people together. This was true of both the executive project manager and within the architectural team - where personnel were led by a senior partner biased toward space-planing, a junior partner biased toward interior design; one associate biased toward space-planning and another associate biased toward design. Leadership was divided among itself and was not giving full or competent attention to the issues. Was this a real team?

Confidence among project members became eroded. The client remained optimistic but the team was not in harmony - it was about to enter the main stage having quickly moved from euphoria to disillusionment. It now hovered on the edge of chaos.

CHAOS

Spheres of Action

Design and project management refer to four spheres of action, criteria and value:

a. *The client's over-riding, dominant concern with instrumentality and value added, leading to a success-oriented, means / ends form of rationale applied to project considerations.*

b. *The concerns of disparate, professionalised project agents. More or less, these people address the situational problematic in holistic terms and formulate specifications for others to realise.*

c. *The concerns of disparate suppliers and sub-contractors who inform specifications as limited technical experts and who are concerned with built outcomes.*

d. *The concerns of project end-users who will use or operate the new arrangements realised by means of the project process.*

Each sphere has different criteria and differing concepts of what means and ends are. Each is valid. These can harmonise or be the subject of miscommunication.

Stage B: The Main Contract

During the stage of being out to bid, the job architect realised that general arrangement information from one of the zonal sub-teams in the architectural team was inadequate and could not be easily added to and issued to the newly appointed contractor as 'for construction' without significant amendment. The difficulty was compounded by lateness of the demolition programme which meant the main contractor started on site immediately demolitions were complete and already one week later than programmed. Survey information was especially pertinent to the problem area, but there was no buffer for surveys, checks and making adjustments.

Upon taking possession of the site, the main contractor complained about the state of the demolitions and argued their completion. Initial surveys taken after the demolitions began to reveal that pre-contract assumptions were incorrect, necessitating major design adjustments in some areas. After one week on site, a claim for extension of time was placed with the architect. A stream of letters began to move back and forth between the site offices, starting as a trickle and rapidly building a torrent, as each side of the team established entrenched positions.

More asbestos was being found, even after the building had been given the 'all clear'. The scope of work was growing but and had to be contained within the budget = more cost cutting. Meanwhile, the main contractor, realising the full potential for claims, began to procrastinate whilst protesting they were progressing as fast as possible. Arising contingencies delayed progress, but the main contractor was reluctant to quickly update their network and Gantt programme and adapt their schedule of dates indicating when information was to be released, generating controversy regarding whether it was actually late or not. Once released, packages of information were handled in a dilatory way, thus further delaying the work. More letters flew back and forth. The sheer bureaucracy of the job was growing and exacerbating the architect's managerial overhead.

Vested interests within the team, the client body and even within the professional agencies began to distort problem-framing and problem-solving. Delays in providing full and final information for construction resulted in the engineers and architects blaming one another. Existing client staff on the upper floor of the building began to complain about the noise of building works. The architects and engineers reluctantly moved on site in order to progress final specification issues; the site team was now split from its home base and felt themselves banished to metaphorically inhospitable territory far removed from the scene of initial euphoria. What appeared right for the job was not encouraging team motivation.

In order to enforce commitments, the project manager (not unreasonably) insisted upon a final information-issue schedule from the architects and engineers. The architects drew up a list but knew these were dates to work to rather than dates which grew out of a calculated work content and known anticipation of progress. As with all quota systems, pressure was applied to issue inadequate information in order to meet the scheduled dates. Estimates of percentage complete were always optimistic. The risk of going out to bid on approximate (i.e. incomplete) information was bearing fruit: not only was the contractor playing the situation for all it was worth, the design team was always catching up and fire fighting before it could get to an advantageous position. Extra resourcing hired on a crisis basis simply produced a larger managerial overhead and soaked available fees whilst failing to deliver an adequate productivity increase. The junior partner and the job architect began to argue about progress on the job, the former insisting information be issued, whether it was complete or not (in part, because he was under pressure to simply 'do it' from the most senior partner, a space-planner with little comprehension of project management issues in a construction context). The team became more demoralised as it saw authority compromised and eroded. Responding to the implied message that this was now a problem job without vocational reward, personal satisfactions or the likelihood of critical acclaim, the architectural team's motivation was drained. There appeared to be no fun and no profit, so what was the point? Only a refusal to be defeated, an inability to give up, and professional pride kept it going.

Matters of contractual principle arose, particularly concerning what might be deemed to be architect nominations within large joinery packages. With hindsight it was clear that the approximate form of orthodox lump-sum contract had been poorly advised. Lawyers and insurers began to be consulted. Meanwhile, fit-out mock-ups and presentations to future users was being enthusiastically received!

Results

The main contract phase was characterised by late information issues, continued cost-cutting, and recrimination from the top down. Collective leadership had failed and was characterised by any upper level accusing its subordinate levels of incompetence. In this way blame (in terms of an inability to instrumentally perform and deliver) was passed down the line without proper acknowledgment that responsibility lay at the top. It was also passed across agencies. The architects and engineers were particularly keen to cast blame upon one another. The job had fallen into chaos and a search for the guilty.

SEARCHES FOR THE GUILTY

Stage C: Run-down to Completion

Run-down was reached in terms of exhausted fees and an exhausted team. Even the main contractor gave up playing games and decided to complete the contract (too late: the building economy was now so over-heated they could not get the sub-contractors!). The project was completed much behind schedule and over budget, with adequacy substituting for excellence in workmanship. All agencies involved had fallen out and were glad to turn their back on the project. Senior architectural and engineering staff were pulled off and the job ended with contract staff attending to an endless snagging list. One member of staff was to spend months attending to the administration of mountainous piles of correspondence and the final accounts.

The irony was that the job was published and recorded client satisfaction - which meant the satisfaction of those using the building rather than those managing the project. Perhaps the former were those who, in Sod's Law, are the uninvolved people who receive the reward.

REWARD FOR THE UNINVOLVED

Lessons

The over-rising lessons of this well-intentioned project dogged by difficulties include the following:

• *A failure to establish a realistic brief.* The fact that it was so in error was misleading. Such a gross error is admittedly unusual, but it indicates how experienced clients and professionals can get it almost unbelievably wrong. Each key project dimension - purpose, budget and programme - was incorrectly stated. The project never recovered. Client and PM had failed to recognise the need to get the space planners and architects on board up-front, to help *describe* the problem as well as to *solve* it.

FINAL DEFINITION OF THE BRIEF

• *A failure to manage lines of authority.* Confusion between the executive project manager's role, that of the 'lead consultant' (the architects) and other consultants who held a direct contract with the client was self-contradictory, ultimately relying upon ambiguous 'relational' contracts and an optimism which disregarded the need for each agency to heed its own liabilities and to maintain professional autonomy. For example, the architects were expected to exercise authority over the engineers (a large, prestigious firm), but were entirely unable to do so. Such ambiguities were also seen within the architectural team, between senior and junior partners, and associates, all with differing interests to pursue within the context of the firm and its project portfolio. Project authority has to be in place, it has to be unambiguous and, if necessary, it has to have

Addressing the Design Predicament

According to IBM, 9 out of 10 software projects are delayed as a result of substantial redesign; globally, 7 out of 10 end up late. Consultants in this innovatory, rapid-development field offer project management advice like the following:

• Build the project on a business basis, not a technological one. Understand the action context of the project (e.g. business processes and what users need and want) and 'frame' the design and managerial predicament accordingly.

• Allow flexibility with regard to the product definition (the means), but not the business strategy (the strategic end).

• Focus on time-frame and functionality.

• Push the project through with rapid decisions, acted upon almost immediately. For example, brain-storm ideas with customers and clients one day and test them out the next.

• Establish executive support from above.

• Avoid inflexible systems which lengthen programmes.

• Break the project into small teams of 4-5 people, each team having specific tasks.

• Make problems visible.

• Use pre-tested building blocks with minimum risk attached. (The fast runner who wants to win a race doesn't use untested shoes.) Simplify interfaces. Test as you assemble.

Note: managerial heuristic can be looked upon as a kind of 'pre-tested building block'.

All this applies to architectural projects. The message is risk elimination, functionality, focus and goal-orientation. Advocates of moving fast are adamant this does not compromise quality - on the contrary, the need to move fast is often critically dependent upon quality. This has to embrace 'what it feels like', as well as 'what it does'. However, achievement and success are rooted in what situational contingency - where true wit and ingenuity flourish. This is the opposite of architectural design conceptually driven by an art-paradigm and obsessed with the notion of the expression of a personal, inner content.

real coercive power. To formally lead is one thing; to exercise authority is another.

• *A misconception about 'control'*. Fear of contingent change and the implacable conviction that plans, once stated, should not be varied amounted to a 'head in the sand' policy mistaking a high-handed, managerial obduracy for executive strength. Implicitly, it was considered that the professionals were some form of lower-breed, technical incompetents who should be instructed to deliver. The project manager could generate schedules and demand conformance, but their content was not validated and their publication did not amount to the elicitation of required performances. Similarly, performative demands within the architectural team were a naive attempt at coercion which begged a simple (if privately asked) question: 'Why should we?' (i.e. a motivational issue).

• *A failure to follow a suitable procurement path*. The presumption that the project was simple and an orthodox lump-sum contract was appropriate was manifestly poor judgement. The fact that key, experienced professionals were in its favour exhibited self-interested bias (conscious or not) in action.

• *Fire fighting*. Shifting and contingent critical success factors drew the team into a running battle in which they were unable, once behind, to get ahead. Additional resources appeared to simply add to the management overhead and produce a disproportionately small advantage. Implicitly, there was an inability to anticipate resource needs rather than plan resource allocations. Just how many manhours were required? Intuitive rules of thumb can go out the window in conditions of unprecedented and unexpected crisis.

• *Cultures*. The issue of disparate cultures was one of the problems across the project team and within the architectural firm. This is typical of many projects and is par for the course. Mutual respect helps, as does knowing roles and responsibilities. However, some problems within the architectural firm were engendered by a cultural triad of architects, interior designers, and space-planners. The job had a high architectural content but the firm had established its reputation within interior design an space-planning. The latter was the dominant culture and this gave the firm its competitive advantage. The result was a culture of research and consultancy in opposition to a culture of fit-outs, and both in opposition to a culture of concrete on shoes. The first tended toward flat hierarchies of professionals with intellectual pretensions; the second group felt intimidated by the architects who, in turn, recognised the need for a rigorous culture of production to support research and design propositions, but were culturally the weakest in the firm and resented that position. There should have been a condition of harmonious advocacy and mutual benefit, but crisis engendered a polarisation of positions. In the background was a project manager with a surveying background and a simple, instrumental attitude. Beyond him was the client's managerial representative, fearful of any symptom suggestive the project might be out of control (and therefore subject to internal criticism within the sponsor organisation).

The monumental but not uncommon problems of this project were all people-related. They all pertained to judgement, experience, and interpersonal skills, to cultures and mind-sets (and, yes, there was also a degree of predatoriness). Professional expertise and skill was crucially important, but of secondary significance whilst these other issues predominated.

A crucial mistake was the project manager's presumption that once he had framed and stated the situational-problematic, it merely required subordinate disciplines to technically execute the proper procedures and the project could be satisfactorily completed - perhaps with a few aesthetically tasteful morsels thrown in by those designer chaps! The client, fresh from a lengthy, prestigious building exercise which had not been without internal contention and even derision as well as critical acclaim, was all too ready to agree to this interpretation of the conversion projec as a mundane exercise in technical rationality and control. And the professionals simply wanted the work, the fees and the opportunities to practice what they enjoyed doing. .

Gateways Checklist

The idea of a project life-cycle and a passage from stage to stage suggests the concept of 'gating' - something to be discussed in the following section with respect to the scheme design. However, the concept has broader application in project management (see box on right).

Gating can be viewed in two ways: as a stage exit or as a stage entry.

• The entry gate is concerned with a simple, general question: *are we prepared for the work of this next stage?*

• The exist gate is concerned with another, equally simple question: *have we achieved what we intended to"?*

Four sets of criteria apply to these questions. With respect to an entry gateway, they might be phrased as follows:

1. Concerning fit with strategic aims and ambitions:
  • Do we have clear intentions and goals specific to this coming stage?
  • Are we clear about the relationship and fit of these goals relative to the overall, general project ambitions and criteria (i.e. the sponsor's business plan, etc.)? Are they valid? Has anything changed?
  • Has the client the team is to go ahead? Has the content of the previous stage been 'signed off'?

2. Concerning specific deliverables:
  • Do we know what the deliverables for this stage will be? Are we sure?
  • Do we understand the nature and timing of the audits, reviews and checks we shall apply? Do we know the criteria we shall apply?
  • Are we acknowledging the 'customers' of the deliverables and what they need and expect?
  • Are we prepared for the necessary co-ordination with other individuals and agencies?

3. Concerning the Project Plan and its components:
  • There is an full, valid, outline Project Plan, isn't there?
  • There is a detailed Project Plan for this stage, isn't there? We know what we're doing, who is doing it, when they will be doing it, and what our resource cost plan for this stage is? We know which performative, budgetary and delivery criteria apply to this stage, don't we? We are in sync with other agencies and have a co-ordinated plan, don't we?
  • Are we aware of the critical success factors, both for the project in general and with respect to this stage? Are we aware of specific risks and opportunities?

4. Concerning responsibilities and accountabilities:
  • Are personnel and / or agency resources in place for this stage? Have we accounted for scheduled vacations and the like?
  • Do we have single sources of accountability for aspects of the work and the deliverables?
  • Can our team be expected to deliver? What about evident commitment and morale?

Gates

Are gates exits or entry points? They are both, simultaneously, but different criteria are applied, depending on whether a stage is being exited or entered.

Exiting a stage implies tests of appropriateness, adequacy and quality of content. Entering a gate suggests criteria of preparedness: detailed plans of action and concerns with anticipated coordination, rework after consultancy, corrections, amendments, etc. before the stage being entered upon can be exited at its completion.

The concept of gates is applicable at all levels, to small discrete parts of the project as well as to passages from stage to stage. For example, information on the cladding, ceilings, roofing, etc. might be subject to gateway criteria as the work is undertaken (or partly undertaken) and passed on to other people. The key is that a gateways are in place and that they are either closed or open. Is what is coming through acceptable? reservedly acceptable? unacceptable? or so bad it suggests efforts should be aborted?

Both exit and entry gating can be a formal review., with stated purpose, agenda, key attendees, evidence to be presented, and comments to be made.

Management: It all Depends on Your View . . .

The manager has the task of creating a true whole that is larger than the sum of its parts, a productive entity that turns out more than the sum of the resources put into it. One analogy is the conductor of an orchestra, through whose effort, vision and leadership individual instrumental parts that are so much noise by themselves become the living whole of music. The manager is both composer and conductor. Peter Drucker

[The manager] is like a symphony orchestra conductor endeavouring to maintain a melodious performance in which the contributions of the various instruments are co-ordinated and sequenced, patterned and paced, while the orchestra members are having personal difficulties, stage hands are moving music stands, alternating excessive heat and cold are creating audience and instrument problems, and the sponsor of the concert is insisting on irrational changes in the program. L. Sayles

Power and influence make up the fine texture of organisation, and indeed of all interactions. Charles Handy

Men are thrown into conflict largely because they have seized or have had assigned to them specialised roles in a complex co-operative process in which many others must play complementary roles. Charles Lindblom

The underlying logic of the principles of excellence is a responsibility of the manager to shape the values of the subordinate in the direction of increased commitment to productivity and organisational excellence, all for the good of the team. Joseph Raelin

Project managers often lament that they don't have sufficient authority to successfully carry out their assigned project responsibilities. Often, the key is not the lack of support for their authority but their failure to motivate those who support their projects. Understanding personal power is critical for successful project performance. David Wilemon

Try to get people to do things differently. Once they do, attitude change will follow . . . intellectual training pales in comparison with the urgency created by pushing someone out of an airplane and telling them, 'The ripcord is in front; you should probably pull it!' Smith & Preston

An understanding of the human situations associated with the job will go far to solve the technical ones; in fact, such understanding may be a prerequisite of a solution. J.M. Juran

Quality to the production worker means that his performance satisfies him, provides to him pride of workmanship. Edwards Deming

The Bill Gates Guide to Managing Project Development

The following are the principles followed by Bill Gates in managing (software) product development projects at Microsoft (11). All the principles have direct relevance to architectural project management:
- *Use smart people and small teams (get the very best you can and place them in small, enjoyable team environments). Let functional experts define and hire for their own technical specialities.*
- *Have quick decision making on technical versus business trade-offs.*
- *Have managers who both create the product and make technical decisions (no non-technical management trying to make technical trade-offs, etc.).*
- *Have more than one person who understands the product details (spread understanding).*
- *Organise so that large teams can work like small teams. Establish functional specialities, but overlap and share responsibilities.*
- *Use large capital investments to support people e.g. giving people an office of their own.*
- *Develop product architectures that reduce interdependencies among teams.*
- *Keep product development on one site (promote face to face contact on an informal basis).*
- *People work on the same machines they develop products for (keeping in touch and taking responsibility).*
- *Promote the internal use of people's own engineering tools (use what you develop).*
- *People use a single main development language (consistency).*
- *Obtain an enormous amount of feedback from customers (be strongly customer-oriented).*
- *Deliberately learn from past projects (postmortems).*

The lifecycle of a Microsoft product typically develops through three stages:

- ***Planning*** *- during which a product is given a distinctive vision statement to guide its development, a specification (defining functionality, architectural issues, and component interdependencies, and described as a kind of cookbook for development, testing, marketing, etc.), a development schedule with milestones, and a feature description.*

- ***Development*** *- going through the most critical features first and the least critical features last.*

- ***Stabilisation*** *leading to release for manufacture - testing, reacting to customer feedback, debugging, etc. in three phases: internal testing; external testing; and release preparation.*

Each stage and the overall schedule has a 20 - 30% buffer element to account for unpredictable contingencies.

● Part Two:

Decisions and Techniques

A. Project Decision-making

Most project management theory is dogmatic in its advocation of planning, monitoring and controlling. But there are many kinds of projects involving all kinds of organisations, functional groups, skills, personalities and issues. What form of 'planning, monitoring and control' is appropriate to each project? What is most appropriate to architectural projects, particularly for those responsible for pre-construction phases?

Not all planning, monitoring and control requires project personnel to follow the linear 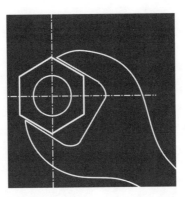 *'plan it out thoroughly before you do it - then do it' formula. Many creative and innovative companies are more concerned to escape this linear thinking and to promote kinds of concurrent work processes. The planning, co-ordination and synchronisation of efforts nevertheless remains crucially important to any economic and effective team effort.*

The mistake is to believe that techniques are a simple fix. Just as managers sometimes expect designers to turn on the tap of expertise as a form of technical-rationality, naive designers sometimes enthuse about project management techniques in a similar way. However, techniques are tools and managerial skill lies in their intelligent employment rather than their use as crutches.

Most managerial techniques are very simple. This is sometimes indicative of utility and sometimes of a misleading and illusory capacity. However, no matter how many good techniques are at hand to employ, the manager still depends upon strategy and judgement. Two aspects of this stand out: making appropriate decisions and effecting commitments. It is arguable that the management of design projects can be entirely distilled down to these factors. Getting to these decisions and commitments constitutes good design practice.

B. Designing Project Maps

A reliance upon planning, scheduling and monitoring is helped enormously by the availability of techniques that support such activities. The most outstanding of these are techniques concerned with project mapping e.g. networks. Architects will rarely use networks of any complexity at all, but the availability of computer programmes makes them very accessible. Try one. You will immediately see that their usage is dependent upon lots of mundane data and they do not do what you hoped for - give you instant answers to the planning and scheduling problem. Computers won't think for you.

But do not let this put you off. These techniques are worth grappling with because their real challenge lies at a conceptual level. What is the best way to 'image', 'picture' or 'map' the project effort? Should a range of maps be formulated? Can forms of mapping help with levelling resource demands within the team?

Shortage of space prevents me going into networking techniques in full detail. Many books are available that will do this and you will even find that the handbook for the computer programme you use will have lots of information. Instead, this section outlines these techniques and offers a way in to what they are about. The principal issues - and the interesting ones - are conceptual. Think of the planning 'map' as a kind of architecture that structurally informs the project efforts and enables you to identify crucially important factors (e.g. milestones) and use these to 'design' a secondary level of planning and effort. Considered this way, you will realise that - as in designing - you don't have to sort everything out at once and at the beginning. As in design, you are searching for the 'map' that is provisional and plausible. Then, on a rolling-wave basis, you'll add the detail that is increasingly committed, real and substantial.

Simplified decisions

What is management? The question is as difficult to answer as, What is architecture? And management has its Vitruvius, too, in the form of Henri Fayol (1841-1925), mining engineer, managing director and father of the classical school of management theory.

Writing in 1916 (*General and Industrial Management*) Fayol argued there were five basic managerial functions:

1. *Planning* - concerned with examining and drawing up plans for action. Fayol understood forecasting planning as a central business activity, enabling an optimum use of resources.
2. *Organising* - building up the structure, material and human, of the undertaking.
3. *Commanding* - maintaining activity among the personnel.
4. *Co-ordinating* - to bind together, unify and harmonise all activity and effort.
5. *Controlling* - to see that everything occurred in conformity with established rules and expressed command.

Similarly, Alfred Sloan (1875-1966), the famous Chief Executive Officer of General Motors from 1923 until 1946, considered that managers had three clearly defined jobs to undertake:

1. To determine a firm's strategy.
2. To design its structure.
3. To select appropriate control systems.
(Sloan, 1963).

In 1937 Gulick and Urwick extended Fayol's concept and gave management one of its first acronyms: POSDCORB:

- *Planning* - working out, in broad outline, what needs to be done.
- *Organising* - the establishment of formal structures of authority.
- *Staffing* - the whole personnel function.
- *Directing* - making decisions and embodying them in instructions.
- *Co-ordinating* - inter-relating the parts of the enterprise.
- *Reporting* - keeping the executive informed about what is going on.
- *Budgeting* - everything concerned with fiscal planning, accounting and control.

Such attempts to define the content of the manager's role parallel the development of a Modernist ideology within the architectural profession. In a similar way to which the latter has always faced criticism of its ostensibly rationalised, instrumentalist posture, the theories interpreting managerial action have also faced criticism, particularly in the post-war period.

2 **What Business Schools Don't teach.** Just as one might argue that architecture has always been defined by what architects do when they get out of bed in the morning (i.e. a focus upon the realities of praxis rather than theory), one might also argue that management is what managers *actually* do. (13) Among the questioning researchers in this field Henry Mintzberg stands out for his seminal examination of what managers actually do as opposed to what theorists suggest they do (Mintzberg, 1975).

Mintzberg's work began with a critique of POSDCORB and its like, arguing an analytical structure did not tell us what managers really do and probably distorted that reality. Tagging managers in order to monitor the truth, Mintzberg came to the following conclusions:

- *Managers prefer live action* - activities that are current, specific, well-defined and

Managerial Awareness

Management's genesis is linked with entrepreneurial enterprises operating in circumstances which required competitive efficiency within a progressive capitalist economy. The Industrial Revolution brought with it Adam Smith's division of labour and specialisation. This, in turn, required re-integration. Firms grew to be larger than a single proprietor or group of partners could supervise and a managerial profession started to evolve out of the body of 18th century clerks, especially during the later 19th. century, at which time the first business school was founded at the University of Pennsylvania in 1881(the Wharton school). Nepotism was to being replaced by merit.

We're Creative too

Management is, all things considered, the most creative of all the arts. It is the art of art because it is the organiser of talent.
Jean-Jaques Servan-Schrieber

non-routine. Reflective planning is rare. The manager's role breeds adaptable information manipulators operating in an environment characterised by stimulus and response.

• *Managers do a lot of work at an unrelenting pace*, the open-ended nature of the job always inviting them to contribute more. Their activities are characterised by brevity, variety, interruption and fragmentation. No matter what he or she is doing, the manager is plagued by thoughts of what else might be and must be done.

• *Managers prefer the verbal medium of communication*, disliking mail and lengthy reports. Scheduled meetings are the scene of formal information delivery and time-consuming events such as ceremony, strategy-making and negotiation take up a lot of their available time.

Out of this research Mintzberg posited ten roles for the manager to fulfil:

A. *Activities concerned with interpersonal relationship:*
1. The manager is a symbolic figurehead.
2. The manager is a leader offering guidance and motivation - among the most significant of roles.
3. The manager plays a liaison role, dealing with a web of relationships.

B. *Informational roles*
4. The manager must be a monitor to what is going on (internal operations, external events, analyses, ideas and trends, pressures.
5. The manager must play the role of disseminator.
6. The manager is a spokesperson to the outside world.

C. *Decisional roles*
7. The manager is an entrepreneur acting as the initiator and designer of controlled change within the organisation. This role particularly concerns projects seeking to utilise opportunities or solve problems, over which the manager acts as delegator or supervisor. As Mintzberg notes, the inventory of projects changes continually as new ones are added, old ones reach completion, and others wait in storage until the manager can begin work on them.
8. The manager is a disturbance handler, reacting quickly and dealing with conflicts between subordinates, difficulties between organisations, or resource losses.
9. The manager is a resource allocator - a role at the heart of strategy-making. Time must be scheduled, work must be programmed, actions must be authorised. Decisions are inevitably referred to models in the manager's head which describe how the organisation works.
10. The manager must act as a negotiator, responsible for representing the organisation.

Above all, Mintzberg concluded that managers undertaking these roles rely upon *intuitional* judgement - the one thing business schools (obsessed with the rational-deductive ideal and ambitions toward what was called scientific management) do not know how to teach (a theme later taken up by Donald Schon).

Intuition is commonly used to refer to a less rational basis for influences upon decisions which are counter to models describing a pre-eminent scientific method - traditionally considered to be rooted in inductive empiricism (the notion that observation leads to generalisation and hypothesis). The Viennese philosopher Karl Popper has been immensely influential with a counter proposal arguing for the provisionality of all knowledge and its basis in systematic attempts to refute hypotheses: those which cannot be falsified are accepted as true. How we creatively arrive at hypotheses remains opaque, but Popper argues for an incremental progress rooted in our perception and formulation of problems we desire to resolve - a notion which is analogous to the design process and its need to address the question, '*What is the problem here?*'

Schon has argued the uniqueness of the design method's way of probing and

Getting On With It

There are some people who won't leave home in the morning without an umbrella even if the sun is shining. Unfortunately, the world doesn't always wait for you while you try to anticipate your losses. Sometimes you just have to take a chance - and correct your mistakes as you go along.
Lee Iaccoco.

addressing such questions, but it is important that architects should be capable of framing their answers in terms which seek to touch upon a note of *authenticity* embracing felt human need, and not in terms of a narrow technical and instrumentally conceived expertise (which, nevertheless, has its place). How they proceed with their enquiry involves intuition, but it also employs a skill lying somewhere between the vagueness of intuition and a more explicit, rational understanding embodied in the use of *heuristic* - a term dealt with below and in the following section.

3 **Methodological myths.** *Both management and design practise share the concept of actions which are not only competent and involve timely decision-making, but are also strategic and purposeful. From this instrumental viewpoint, rational action is argued to rely upon a model of decision-making rooted in ways of thinking which proceed according to a rationalised deductive method which has little place for intuition or anything other than a technocratic form of judgement.*

The idea of proceeding deductively has a long history, originating with Plato and, in the modern era, featuring in the work of important figures such as Immanuel Kant, John Locke, and Jeremy Bentham. In essence, the deductive method proceeds from known values to action in particular cases. Kant, for example, taught that *a priori* reasoning could lead to the test of every moral judgement; Bentham aimed for a comprehensive, utilitarian calculus founded upon the principle of the greatest good for the greatest number. More latterly, this became a part of the social policy-maker's welfare function: the idea that decisions on principles and values can further the selection of options by a form of technical calculus (Braybrooke & Lindblom, 1963). This translated into the concept of rational action derived from fundamental aims, of a rational-deductive method which emphasises comprehensive analysis and is intended to proceed with a consideration of ends and means as follows:

• *First, define the issues, problems and opportunities. In other words, know what it is you want to do and what your criteria are.* This includes the proper identification of values, aims, and the applicable criteria. In policy-making, these considerations (in their most generalised form) are sometimes referred to as a 'mission' statement, from which programmes of action are derived.

• *Second, apply facts and analyses to the issues so that the conditions are known and understood.* This should include a relative weighting of the criteria that are identified.

• *Third, systematically generate a range of alternative policies or solutions* (the determination of possible means). Different ways of 'framing' the problem will suggest alternative solutions. Each alternative is to be provisionally assumed to be a feasible and viable proposition. Ideally, *all* possible solutions should be identified.

• *Fourth, compare, contrast, evaluate and choose (the optimal means).* The alternatives are to be evaluated against stated criteria; that which provides the best satisfaction of criteria is to be selected.

• *Fifth, proceed to implementation.* The selected alternative is effected with the confident expectation of instrumental success if execution is competent.

The model is extensively employed in all kinds of literature dealing with decision-making, including project management. But do Fayol's and Mintzberg's managerial decision-makers actually proceed in this way? Is decision-making such a procedural calculus, involving choices between synoptically considered alternatives? Does this model of goal-oriented instrumentality foisted onto designers have credibility?

Such questions are important because Schon's notion of 'reflection-in-action' described earlier is difficult to appreciate, especially from the viewpoint of disciplines more familiar with the exercise of an implementational competence and the employment of professionals as instrumental aspects of policy formulation or execution. Managers look upon designers as technically proficient, professional *problem-solvers* who

Planning Enthusiasms

Enthusiasms for planning derive from post-war accounting and budget planning in business which, after World War II, came to be founded upon a range of military techniques transferred from the Cold War effort to civil government programmes and the commercial sector. The key is to be strategic in the sense of thinking in terms of the goals upon which efforts are focused, to consider alternative possible futures and choose between them. Programming Planning Budgeting System (PPBS), rooted in wartime planning controls, stands out among postwar techniques used to deal with such issues. It was used by the US Federal Government to manage the military machine and its relations with civil corporations. Its concept of missions, programmes, and projects cutting across traditional budget boundaries filtered through aerospace industries from to major construction projects, eventually becoming 'activity-based' accounting methods at the local level. Computers, systems theory, operations management, game theory and similar thinking had made such considerations possible, initiating an era of strategic planning accompanied by the maxim that, 'If it can't be measured, it can't be managed'. Computer models and simulations became increasingly popular, in parallel with an optimistic belief in a future of rational, scientific management utilising ever-cheaper and more powerful machines. Although fraught with difficulty and complexity, modelling often enables implicit assumptions and features of the real world to which it is sensitive to be exposed. But there are economic limitations imposed by a law of diminishing returns when ever more data has to be compiled and utilised in evermore complex (and clever) models founded upon difficult value judgements at the policy-making level. Because of this - and criticisms of the rational-deductive ideal - more conceptual heuristic began to supplement planning methodologies, offering new planning frameworks to managers and initiating an era of managerial thinkers as conceptual gurus enthusiastic about a variety of concepts such as MbO, excellence, quality, teams, re-engineering, time management, etc.

should be following the rational-deductive ideal everyone ostensibly acknowledges to be the proper method for exercising technical forms of competence. The designer's artistry becomes perceived as aesthetic concerns skillfully grafted onto expert technique.

However, whilst it is true that design situations are intrinsically problematic, the truth is that designers rarely work in accordance with the classical model held up as a policy and decision-making ideal. Mintzberg, among others, would argue that, in reality, managers do not do so either.

Even given a useful definition of a form to the problem, there are limits to understanding that constrain the synoptic ambitions of the rational-deductive ideal. The Nobel prize-winner Herbert Simon (1957; also, March & Simon, 1958) was among the first to articulate the idea of limits to rationality, suggesting that it was 'bounded' and that managers searched for satisfying solutions rather than optimal ones. He called this *satisficing*: a person doesn't search for the sharpest needle in the haystack; they search for one sharp enough to sew with (14). Similarly, Henry Mintzberg's research (1975) also suggested that managers limit efforts and investigation: in the real world everyone avoids comprehensiveness and refers the issue at hand, not relative to the whole world, but to a specific (and implicitly limited) background or framework (15).

James March (16) went so far as to discuss such organisational behaviours in terms of a *garbage can model of organisational choice*. This can contains an interplay of independent problems, solutions, participants and choices. Decisions result from coincidental 'temporal proximity' which attaches solutions to problems, problems to choices preferred by participants who are there at the time.

But it is Charles Lindblom (17) who stands out among the critics of the rational-deductive ideal and the advocates of simplified decision-making. His comments have formed the criticism that post-war scientific-management thinking - so fundamental to orthodox project management theory - stands as an emperor without clothes. Typically, he focused upon three themes, each of which rationalises the real world and has relevance to design practice:

1. *Means and ends.* Practically possible options (means) affect the selection of policy (ends). This is different to the method of freezing goals and then selecting appropriate means according to the principle of technical rationality. It implies that the consideration of means and ends is a continual dialogue, and that the means selected are incrementally progressive from those already in place and familiar to policy-makers. The value-ambition of 'good housing for all', for example, means little until concretised as action options; in this process value becomes indistinguishable from policy.

2. *Options limitation.* The principle of bounded rationality necessitates that a restricted variety of options are considered. In parallel, a restricted variety of consequences of options are dealt with i.e. the crucial *margins of difference*. This involves the risk that some factors will have been overlooked but it makes the decision-making situation manageable.

3. *Incrementality.* Decision-making is focused upon the incremental (or marginal) difference between options and between the status quo and what options can achieve. It is the incremental differences between choices that is important, not their place in some comprehensive calculus. The resolution of a conflict is not achieved by resort to principles or ranking methods, but by stating how much of one value is worth sacrificing to achieve an increment of another. Costs are automatically considered because they enable incremental differences of outcome and choice to be compared.

4 **Finding and Solving.** Both designers and managers approach situational-problematics by gathering and utilising information in an *interpretative* and *interested* sense, rather than in the disinterested, synoptic sense put forward by the rational-deductive ideal. A designer's initial data gathering (identifying facts and defining conditions) is selective, not comprehensive. It has to be thorough, but the objective is to find

On Problems

In a wholly pure art . . . all problems are self-imposed. A large part of art will then consist, not in the solution, but in the creation of problems.
Roger Scruton

On Clean Slates:

Projects never begin with an entirely clean slate. Learning from precedent and experience is important. The basis of Chrysler's hugely successful Mustang (1964) was existing engineering onto which a new body was strapped. When the Cardiff Bay Opera House committee were formulating a competition brief in 1994 they toured similar buildings all over Europe. When Boeing were deciding upon the huge investment which might result in a plane taking them forward for the next 25 years (the 777, available in 1995)), they started with modifications of existing models. Learning from precedent and experience is important.

ways of framing the situational-problematic in design terms. To some extent this is a translational exercise, but it is also a form of *problem-finding*. For example, a 'site analysis' is important to most building projects, but the point is the search for a correlation between project aims, criteria and the analysis (an attempt to understand the conditions) which, in any abstract, *a priori* sense, is meaningless. What facts are relevant? What data should be gathered? How is the researcher to know when enough data has been gathered? What is salient? What is insignificant? There is no simple answer to these questions, no expert-system that will be effective. Framing the problem, examining the conditions, and conceiving a way forward are inextricably linked. The key point is the very *uniqueness* and *ambiguity* of the design predicament that designers have to creatively address.

The designer aims to deal with the situational-problematic by *reconstructively translating* it into significant *themes of concern* - a multiplicity and fluidity of values that will now include values deriving from the designer's agenda. Requirements, conditions and criteria can then be dealt with imaginatively. Conceptions of value on a given issue can be changed, extended, combined and recombined in relation to the facts affecting them - so long as the underlying sponsor goals are respected. This is the essence of 'getting there by design' (the reconstructive and reflective artistry which addresses means and ends simultaneously).

By reconstructively translating (or transfiguring) the brief into significant themes of concern - a crucial step in simplifying the situation - the designer is able to inscribe a blank sheet of paper with a creative proposition embodying some appropriate ordering principle for the project design. Inevitably, this proposition will be rooted in knowledge of architectural possibility and precedent, reinvented for a specific context, allowing for uniqueness and *inventively* capitalising upon its potential. A budgetary and programme framework will be similarly constructed from collective experience modified according to particular circumstances. And, typically, the constructional means selected might be novel, but are unlikely to be new. Ostensibly radical forms of constructional innovation are likely to be characterised by technology transfer from other industries whose expertise and skill is drawn into the project. This forms an incremental progression in the use of the technology, even though it might be put forward as a radical architectural innovation. (The work of the English Hi-Tech school has been characterised by this strategy.)

The analogy with a managerial process is again worth making. One commentator had the following point to make about government policy-making: "The kinds of problems encountered in analysing public policies stand high on the list of problems requiring simplification. Here, even the form of the problem is difficult to discern. *One has, as it were, to find the game - to decide upon a form for the problem.*" (13. My italics.) This notion that a suitable form for the problem can be considered as a kind of game-construct is quite important. It results in the perception of a kind of *gamesmanship* that characterises the design and how the project has been handled (the two are indivisible), lending it meaning, coherence and potential significance.

The process amounts to the search for a coherent ordering principle - a conceptual 'coat-hanger' upon which the design will be hung (and accommodative needs satisfied). This does not depend upon a comprehensive problem-definition, but upon the wit with which the designer frames the situational-problematic upon the basis of an adequate problem statement. This framing is simultaneously a tentative solution and a statement of the problem it confronts. Prioritisation is implicit.

This suggests the need for a brief stated as the client's perceptions of whatever has prompted the project and their goals. A statement in design terms is already arguing a solution, but this is the necessary translational step forward which is sometimes overlooked and sometimes over-formulated. Some competition briefs are examples of the latter. Sir Norman Foster's success at winning the Shanghai and Hongkong bank commission, for example, was in spite of the client's incomprehension at why they might want to talk to Bank staff and the way in which they reframed the brief stating the issues facing the architect. This reframing was fundamental to their solution.

Project reality is that a problem cannot be comprehensively stated (in terms the rational deductive ideal would prefer) before the problem is tackled, and it is more fully defined as the project unfolds. At any one time, understanding will be limited and crite-

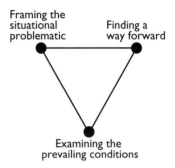

Getting Started

Framing the situational problematic

Finding a way forward

Examining the prevailing conditions

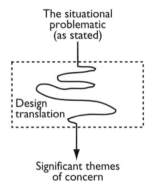

The situational problematic (as stated)

Design translation

Significant themes of concern

Deciding on a way forward is founded upon defining or constructing an kind of architectural game in terms of significant themes of concern i.e. to give a form to the situational problematic (which might be to address a problem or to grasp an opportunity). This form inherently bears the seeds of a resolution to the problematic i.e. means and ends have become inter-dependent - at the very least, it is the formulation of an ordering principle with which to develop the design.

ria will be stated as a basic set of critical success factors rather than a comprehensively considered and weighted listing. This begs the issue: what are the critical success factors and what is an appropriate, strategic way of addressing them? Generic solutions to generic problems (such as floor plate geometries) are obviously relevant, but their generality and abstraction is the root of their limitation.

Another fallacy derived from the rational-deductive ideal is the idea that designers should generate a comprehensive range of real alternative proposals. This is sometimes attempted, but it is comparatively rare. For one thing, time and/or money will almost certainly be in short supply (in terms of professional services, sometimes the same thing). It is also probable there will be a need to condense many considerations and criteria into a few strategic moves which will bear future development and which promise success. Real alternatives suggest genuine reconceptualisations of the situational-problematic - and designers rarely work that way. It is the single criterion problematic that is more likely to produce many variants. Typically, only a single thematic posture will be adopted, risked and used as a reference and bench-mark against which promising alternative possibilities will be assessed. For example, Foster appears to have examined many variants of the Hongkong & Shanghai bank's structure, but all bore a thematic resemblance. The choice between options is not a matter of ascertaining a function and choosing among a comprehensive, open-ended range of significantly different alternatives so as to maximise it, but amounts to a focus upon the *increment* or *margin of difference* between limited alternatives or variations - which, inevitably, are likely to have an underlying family resemblance. This strategy enormously *simplifies* the situation and is a common problem-solving and policy-making strategy.

In any case, the synoptic ambition built into the rational-deductive ideal fails to say *how genuine* alternatives are to be generated. Creativity remains a mysterious subject - even experienced designers have little knowledge of how ideas come to them. As Karl Popper argued, neither do scientists - they formulate a hypothesis and set about testing it by an attempted refutation. However, both Popper - and Einstein, who agreed with him - could offer no explanation as to how the scientist arrived at a hypothesis. Similarly, the designer is also hardly aware of how he or she arrives at a design proposition. Certainly, the notion that a veritable range of viable, exciting propositions might be made by one designer is somewhat preposterous. The many entries to a competition come near to the ambition, but they risk superficiality and not infrequently have to be radically reconsidered once the designers have entered into a discourse with client and users and details of the situational-problematic are properly investigated, understood and thematically reconstructed in terms of a more thorough understanding. The aim of most designers is always to *simplify* uncertain and potentially complex situations so as to find a way forward. This doesn't mean being simplistic - intelligence, skill and a mature, sound judgement are called for. No one wants this to result in designers in the guise of witless technocratic experts mechanically cranking through endless possibilities in a search for the rational ideal. The better designer (certainly in the eyes of peers who know what is going on) is someone who has a professionalised, sagacious knack of quickly homing in on solutions which demonstrate a promise and potential appearing to be, at least, the plausible basis for commitment and investment. In getting there it is, above all, strategies of *simplification* that stand out as a key to decision-making and fulfilment of the aim to 'get it right first time'. The result can be clarity and coherence, often of the kind which can be formulated as conceptualisations and diagrams which the non-professional can comprehend. The following section takes this principle and explains the concept of 'heuristic' as an alternative to the rational deductive ideal for planning projects.

Heuristic

There are two approaches to planning: bottom-up and top-down. The *bottom-up* approach assumes all relevant information concerning necessary and anticipated activities is synoptically available and simply has to be rationally organised: know what it is you have to do; plan and schedule it; then do it, closely monitoring and adjusting in order to be on target. The availability of such understanding is rarely the case. In fact, the full understanding of a problem is the perspective of hindsight, achieved *after* one has solved the problem. In architecture, certainty is reached when the project deliverable is realised. Prior to this the designer has to be satisfied with reasoning that is not final and strict, but provisional and plausible, making the certainty upon which planning is ideally founded difficult to attain. *The provisional solution precedes the final one.* Most planning proceeds *heuristically* i.e. it employs rules of thumb derived from experience which *simplify* an otherwise complex planning situation or one which incorporates a high degree of uncertainty.

Heuristic is defined as a branch of study concerned with the methods and rules of discovery and invention. It is both an adjective and noun which the Oxford dictionary describes as 'serving to discover; proceeding by trial and error'. The word is from the Greek 'heurisko', to find. Heuristic describes human behaviour when faced with the need to discover the solution to the problem at hand. Because it is rooted in experience, it engenders 'rules of thumb' (which can be mathematical) that work well enough and serve as guides to action when no precise algorithm exists.

The synoptic planning method of the rational deductive ideal is a search for the sharpest needle in the haystack. The heuristic approach is the search for a needle sharp enough to sew with - it accepts that information, time and resources are limited and looks for a solution that appears to work rather as an alternative to a prolonged search for the optimal solution that is logically available. For example, it adopts a 'rolling wave' approach to project planning which details subsequent stages just before they begin and when sufficient knowledge is available. This necessitates skill in discerning the most crucial issues to be dealt with, an ability to differentiate between significant and merely meaningful information, and to discard irrelevant and unnecessary data. This applies to both overall project planning and to planning within each agency.

2 **A method.** When solving problems we must first have a certain amount of experience and previously acquired knowledge (Polya, 1945). We are also dependent upon bright ideas - what Aristotle called acts of sagacity ("Sagacity is a hitting by guess upon the essential connection in an inappreciable time."). Polya's advice was to address problems in stages, asking three key questions: *Where should I start? What can I do? What can I gain by doing so?* (18) He outlines four stages to follow:

1. *Understanding the problem* (decomposing and recombining, framing and reframing): deal with the question, Where shall I start? by understanding the problem. It's foolish not to understand the problem or solve the wrong problem.
What is the unknown?
What is required?
What are we seeking to do?
What are the data?
What is the condition?
Can you name the parts of the problem?
Is it possible to satisfy the condition?
In other words, problem-solving begins with problem-finding, by asking: what is the form of the problem? In Lindblom's terms, what is the game? (a question that comes near to how designers deal with a situational-problematic).
2. *Dealing with the data* (devising a plan): link the unknown with the data in

Engineering Precision

Everything the engineer does . . . is under the control of heuristic. Engineering has no hint of the absolute, the deterministic, the guaranteed, the true. Instead, it reeks of the uncertain, the provisional, and the doubtful.
B. Koen

order to obtain an idea of the solution, to make a plan. We have a plan when we know what has to be done in order to solve the problem. This requires formerly acquired knowledge, good habits, concentration of the purpose, bright ideas and good luck.

Can you restate the problem?

Do you know a related problem?

Do you know a familiar problem having a similar unknown?

Did you use all the data?

Did you use the whole condition?

Can you imagine a more accessible but related problem?

Can you solve a part of the problem?

3. *Carrying out the plan*: work patiently and consistently. As work develops we need to shed what was provisional and deal with strict arguments. We need to work in an orderly way, relating the detail to the whole, checking each step.

4. *Checking the result*: look back on the solution, review it and check it.

Did it work?

Could you have got there differently?

Can you use the result for some other problem?

Achieving and constructing the idea of an argument or plan of action is crucial (equivalent to a designer formulating the conceptual coat-hanger mentioned earlier). The problem-solver must ask questions such as: *Have we seen the same problem in a slightly different form? Do we know a related problem? Have we taken into account all essential notions involved in the problem? Have we visualised the problem as a whole (and ignored details)?* The problem-solver is mobilising by extracting relevant elements from their memory. They then construct an argument i.e. they organise (adapt and combine) and, as they progress, they foresee (project) what has to be done - not with certainty, but with plausibility.

Focus Shifts

The importance of having a thoroughly explored scheme is sometimes underrated. Agreeing a scheme is to say', 'Yes, we're looked at all the issues and this is what we agree we're going to do'. There has to be a trust that all the critical success factors have been identified and dealt with, that the scheme bears within it the promise of its own success. Of course, the scheme can never be synoptic in its search,and entirely exhaustive in its examination of the issue, and generation of options. But to have done so sufficiently is all important. All too often, schemes are enthusiastically swept

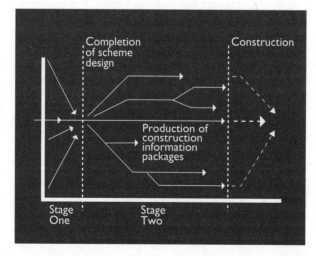

through approval without the degree (or kind of) consideration they should have received. This is always a danger.

The importance of a properly validated scheme is immediately evident when one's focus shifts to the next stage of commitment and development. Of course problems will be uncovered, but they should not threaten the presumptions implicit in the scheme. In project management terms, leverage has been deliberately curtailed by a scheme agreement. After that point (during Stage Two), development work fragments and diversifies, but always under the holistic umbrella of the scheme. In effect, scheme agreement constitutes a gateway. It should not be opened unless (other things being equal, which includes temporal pressures) all aspects of the project have been anticipated and dealt with. There is a convergence upon the scheme gateway, a divergence into scheme development aimed toward a set of specifications, and a final convergence again aimed at realisation of the scheme as am actual building.

Judgement and Bias

Heuristic assists decision-making in complex and uncertain situations but, under pressure and with limited information, opinion-forming heuristic can entail significant biases when used to assist judgement. This can result in an abbreviation and distortion of the exploratory stage of problem-solving. Ideas of our professional experience are riddled with bias. The lesson is that decision-makers need to be aware of how bias can close the door on creative strategies and solutions. (See Bazerman, 1990 for a full discussion of these points). Examples include the following:

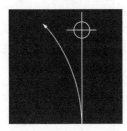

• The availability heuristic. This is an assessment of the frequency or probability of an event founded upon the 'availability' of memory recall. What is most salient, vivid, easily remembered, imagined and specific will be more available to memory and judgment will be biased accordingly. We are too ready to presume that available recollections are representative. For example, frequency of occurrence can be overestimated because of the salience of an event in our minds (even because of the discussion of its likelihood or, as in advertising, its presentation to us). Employers will base appraisal of employees on recent and most salient experiences (good or bad). Decision makers should be ready to extend their search for strategies and solutions beyond the short-hand of what they can easily recall as being successful.

• The representative heuristic. This founds an assessment of the likelihood of an occurrence upon the similarity with stereotypes of similar occurrence in our mind. Our expectancies of another person, for example (clients, employees, etc.) will be judged upon the category of persons to which they belong and of which there is experience. The base rates formed by sound statistical information will be ignored. In addition, people will be insensitive to small sample sizes when making a judgement; they will ignore the fact that extreme events tend to regress to the statistical mean on subsequent trials (a small sample cannot be generalised to the large group). They will misunderstand the randomness of an event outcome when previous events have resulted in a particular pattern (gambling is rife with this bias).

• Anchoring. This is the setting of a reference value, a kind of benchmark against which we set our judgement. Managers make assessments and adjustments relative to this 'anchor'. For example, on being told a person's salary is unreasonably low we will offer only an increment above that known salary; this is not cynicism, it's anchoring. First impressions will stick, regardless of a later need for reassessment.

• Adjustment. Individuals will overestimate the likelihood of conjunctive events (those that must occur in conjunction with each other) and underestimate the probability of disjunctive events (those that occur independently). This affects project work, dependent - as it usually is - on the simultaneous occurrence of many events (such as on time, to budget, and to the required performance standards). Over confidence in our estimates is also common. This can relate to our familiarity with the subject - unfamiliarity breeding over confidence (no adjustment is made) and familiarity breeding no over confidence or actual under confidence.

• The Confirmation trap. This is when we search data for confirmation rather than refutation regarding our decisions. Disconfirming information is often neglected.

• Hindsight (the 'I knew-it-all-before' effect). This bias suggests that people are poor at recalling or reconstructing the way things were or appeared to us before finding out the results of a decision. One implication is that it would make more sense to evaluate individuals on the quality of their initial decisions (even if they end up being wrong) rather than the outcome.

Bias is notoriously difficult to deal with. Experience is not enough and frequently underestimates its inherent prejudices.

Ideally, experience should be informed by expertise or what has been called 'strategic conceptualisations' that attempt to be rational and avoid bias, being without reliance upon uncertain, uncontrollable feedback and delayed results. Such experience will also be transferable, assisting learning (both corporate and individual).

***Within a project management context**, Forsberg et al (1996) note some typical negative biases that project participants can bring to their work: misperceptions based on weak project management experience; bad experiences resulting from flawed processes; misinterpretations of prior failures; little training or none at all; and fears about tight controls.*

Strategies of Simplification

• *Heuristic. Rules of thumb derived from experience that enables a person to tackle an otherwise complex situation or one suffering a high degree of uncertainty i.e. a method or rule of discovery and invention which can be used to tackle such situations.*

• Satisficing (a term employed by Herbert Simon) - *the search for acceptable levels of achievement. This limits costs and ensures feasibility, but it is a concept tempered by the need for being 'on target' in the sense of addressing the right problems, realising project potential, and being economical rather than verbose.*

• Remediality - *the removal of problems and obstacles to success (locally moving away from identified problems rather than toward generalised ideas). All architectural project management has remediality as a fundamental feature of its concerns, especially post-scheme design. Both business and practice management progress on a remedial basis toward better performance.*

• Incrementalism - *a focus upon policies which are only incrementally or marginally different. This places attention upon familiar, better-known options; it reduces the number of alternatives to be dealt with; it reduces the number and complexity of factors to consider and analyse. To be effective, the strategy must be rooted in a reconstructive dialogue between available means and possible ends, redefining preferences and goals as a continually shifting (and ambitious) programme. In product development and marketing, the incremental game is to complete the development cycle as many times as possible over a given period. (19) Note: a danger faced by incrementalism is a focus upon symptoms rather than causes.*

• Bottleneck breaking - *a focus upon obvious and likely problems. Critical Path analysis in project management is implicitly focused upon a search for bottle-necks. Efforts focused here pay dividends. Related tactics include a focusing upon Critical Success Factors and organisation around an identified main sequence.*

• Typological thinking *which orients the situational-problematic and initially frames it in terms of known strategies, precedents and solutions.*

• Looking for a second chance *in order to lessen the criticality of the first chance. This strategy is severely limited on projects, which implicitly offer one overall chance to get it right. Every effort has to be made to produce a climate which facilitates getting it right first time.*

• The employment of heuristic - *the methods and rules of discovery and invention based upon experience.*

Leverage Shifts

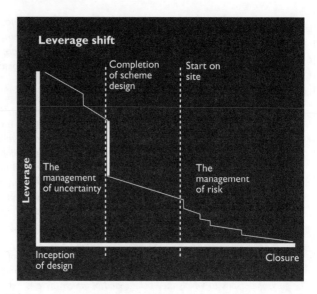

The leverage available at the beginning of a project does not decline uniformly as the earlier schematic suggests. It is more likely to decline in discrete steps corresponding to the passing of major project milestones. The most significant of these is the agreement to a scheme design. By that time, conceptual work is essentially complete (say, 80%) and a scheme has been described and signed-off in terms of of what it is, what it does, what it will feel like, how much it will cost, when it will be available, and how it will be realised. Everything will be in place for progression to a phase of planned design development and construction. Penalties are now likely to be incurred by change. The project is into a more instrumental phase.

At this point there has to be a presumption that the scheme will not be wilfully or arbitrarily amended and that the brief is frozen. The extent to which this is not true is the extent to which a scheme remains provisional and uncertain when the true ambition is to shift from the management of uncertainty to the management of risk. Clients, for example, should freeze their requirements. Otherwise they should attempt to clearly state what is and what is not frozen, and what will probably change. In software development at Microsoft, for example, it is common to deliberately keep the content as loose as possible and to 'harden' it strategically and incrementally - it is simply not true that the best project and design management freezes the brief at the beginning. However, after sign-off, project leverage will further decline in progressively, incremental steps, in conjunction with the commitments incurred - especially as forms of construction. Within this context the quality directive to achieve 'conformance to requirements' assumes an instrumental identity. At the up-front project stage it is a positive concept oriented toward customer needs and market requirements; after scheme approval, it shifts toward a negative performance check and attempts at developmental risk limitation.

Scheme sign-off gateway

During initial project design, the client's statement of need is translated thematically, so that a scheme design can be produced. In the *design development stage* it is the scheme itself that which now serves as thematic content. This change-over is an important aspect of project management.

The conceptual coat-hanger employed by the designer must be at once satisfying and potentially successful, in detail. However, at scheme design this is a matter of expectancy and promise rather than firm predictability. The designer will have no time to develop alternatives in meaningful depth and there is no way of knowing that a proposition will withstand the sustained testing of design development. Progression to design development and implementation will be founded upon informed 'best guesses' and confidence that design development can be pursued consistently and without surprises. It's risky.

Testing the conceptual coat-hanger as a developmental exercise will not be achieved by dealing with it synoptically - in terms of check lists for all stated criteria - but in terms of salient and demanding considerations and criteria. To some extent, propositions must be *made* to work and the designer initially has no real way of knowing whether unconsidered, unknown or unanticipated factors will arise and invalidate the idea. As Edison famously put it, this is a process of 99% perspiration and 1% inspiration. The less able designer (or practice) will get it wrong. The more able one will hit the soft spots early.

With relatively few notable exceptions (e.g. Sydney Opera House), design propositions normally present few serious implementational difficulties that have not been considered during scheme design. What is usually now at issue is the importance of a sustained vision penetrating through to the detail of design development. However, it is at this very point that an executive project manager will want to impose an instrumental rationale, perhaps by passing the design over to others such as a 'design and build' contractor. The assumption is that *uncertainty* has become comparatively negligible and that it is now project *risk* that is at issue. This is what planning, monitoring and control intend to address. There is a need to accept the dominance of instrumental influences, partly because the project has to develop to the point where problems are becoming easy to see but hard and costly to fix. The project is passing through a sign-off gateway, from top-down to bottom-up thinking - a vulnerable stage in the project history.

At this point two issues stand out. First, many people would argue that an instrumental project engineering function acting in a technical role cannot make developmental decisions except as an surrogate for good architectural design that integrates scheme intent and detailed design specifications. The issue is unavoidable and is a significant aspect of many design and build jobs in which the spirit and intent of the scheme design is easily lost in an enthusiastically instrumental attitude toward detailing and implementation. However, going forward into the next stage involves significant responsibilities.

The second issue to be dealt with derives from this move and the acceptance of its ensuing responsibility: in particular, contractually and legally defined design liability. English case law appears to lean to the position that the architect enters into a contract with the client for design services and is in no position to delegate the responsibility to anyone else. However, contemporary building methods almost invariably involve a sub-

The planned life-cycle

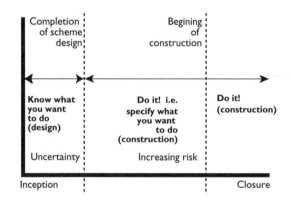

Completion of scheme design | Begining of construction

Know what you want to do (design) | Do it! i.e. specify what you want to do (construction) | Do it! (construction)

Uncertainty | Increasing risk

Inception | Closure

Projects within Projects

Like it or not, there is a sense in which the beginning of construction marks the start of an entirely discrete stage of a project - it is almost a separate project in its own right. The reference for this stage is the set of construction specifications. How they got to be that way or what their intent is in larger terms (i.e. with reference to initiating prompts) is hardly relevant to most builders, whose up-front consultancy (if there is any) is focused upon down-stream construction, not up-stream issues. Designers are in the middle.

contractor design content. Forms of nominated subcontract agreement and contract management attempt to cope with this problem, typically by warranties and the formation of direct contracts between the client and the specialist contractor. But the issue remains an ambiguous legal area. Architects have to be careful. From our viewpoint the significance of a scheme sign-off gateway is underscored.

2 Knowing and Doing. Project management's theory for rationally and instrumentally getting from A to B utilises a simple theory of how to go about the undertaking:

• **First know what it is you want to do:** i.e. undertake activities that bring a team together in order that the project can be properly formulated and a scheme agreed. This will be a fully described project content stating desired ends in terms of agreed means i.e. in terms of three fundamentals: a building form and accommodative content (performances); an agreed programme of *what* will be realised *when* and by *whom* (schedules); and a statement of anticipated costs, described as a project budget within which a detailed cost plan can be defined and expenditures controlled.

• **Then do it:** undertake activities that develop and implement the agreed scheme, leading to project run-down, handover, closure and occupation.

The design inventiveness that reconstructed and transformed basic project material into a design proposition presumed to bear within it the potential of developmental and implementational success has, after scheme approval, to be reinvented. It must attune itself to offering the scheme design as a dissected, analysed and detailed set of discrete specification packages. The holistic solution must become many products, each carefully coordinated across agency and disciplinary boundaries.

Project planning seeks to identify what has to be done so that it can then be implemented as a form of technical rationality, methodically monitored and controlled toward its goal. Literature on the subject almost invariably begins by suggesting the planner schedules all necessary activities and tasks (as in a Work Breakdown Structure). The discussion then shifts to the nuances of networks, charts and schedules. Criticality is expressed in terms of time, costs and precedents. What motivated the designer during Stage One has little place in these schedules.

Architects dislike thinking this way - it appears to reduce the creative and inventive content of their professionalism to the implementation of technical competence. The holistic meaning of the design is always in danger of becoming eroded or evaporating. They prefer to deal with the process of making constructional design decisions as something which bears within it the same motivations which informed the scheme

Special and Recurring

*Stage Two breakdowns of a scheme such as a Work Breakdown Structure (WBS) have two dimensions: **special** development areas which, by definition, make the scheme what it is and constitute the features of its architecture; and **recurring** considerations which cut across a number or all of the work packages. This is not only a matter of the finish, for example, which has to be dealt with within otherwise separate zones of the building, but also considerations of a managerial nature concerning quality, conformance, job administration, studio standards and disciplines, checks, etc. design and project management have to address both sets of issues.*

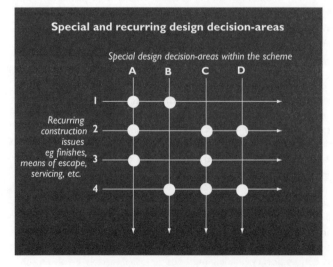

Special and recurring design decision-areas

Special design decision-areas within the scheme

A   B   C   D

Recurring construction issues eg finishes, means of escape, servicing, etc.

design. However, this is an increasingly threatened ambition. In order to maintain credibility, many designers have to turn inside out, now prioritising technical and implementational competence over the competences highlighted during Stage One.

3 **Translating**. When a project moves from an orientating Stage One to its developmental Stage Two (i.e. after scheme approval), the designer's holistic viewpoint should move from being explicit to being implicit within the project content. Ideally, the design concept will inherently predict its own success i.e. it will be without latent defects and will not need to be revised. At the beginning of Stage Two the scheme must be reformulated in such a way that its work content can be broken-down, planned, co-ordinated, monitored, and controlled.

Stage Two development work should be imbued with an understanding of the scheme design that penetrates through to the detail in a natural, logical and consistent way. The alternative is that the designer will be in two states of mind - still conceptualising the design and confusing the ground between Stages One and Two. This is rarely a good position to be in. On some projects it will, to some extent, be unavoidable, but some architects have an unhealthy predilection to argue that it is legitimate to revise the design at any stage, much in the manner of some Edwardian gentleman-architect telling the brick-layer how to lay the bricks (an attitude inculcated at architecture school, where students are frequently encouraged to believe designs can be continually revisited). However, reconsideration of fundamental or crucial matters at a stage which should be devoted to other issues (and enjoying another perspective on the project) mixes managerial 'keynotes'. It is hardly helpful. Revisiting, reconsidering and reconceptualising might be a commitment to design values, but it makes for absurd project management and is unlikely to be in the project's best interests. It is simply a waste of time. Literally. One has to infer from this that the original scheme design must be thorough, distinctive, robust, and capable of being championed throughout the 'engineering' phase of design development and, at the same time, that such an advocacy must not compromise an instrumental handling of the work. A translation has to be effected between differing modes of thinking as a shift takes place from a commitment to scheme design and its subsequent design development.

4 **Breaking Down the Work.** Assuming the completed scheme design fits our criteria, the designer faces the managerial problem of how to organise the work content of Stage Two. The bottom-up approach presumes everything can be identified and organised as a plan of work. A Work Breakdown Structure (WBS) can then be drawn based upon groups of similar work packages, expertise and responsibility (a modularisation of content).

The principles - and some of the conceptual difficulties - of setting up a WBS diagram are discussed in the following section. The technique adopts a rather mechanistic and strongly hierarchical approach which institutes an almost desperate reliance upon analysis and subsequent control. On the problematic side, it is a technique that will work best when everything is resolved and known at the point of planning the WBS, or when the unknown content is simply a matter of applying technical rationality within a temporal and budgetary framework that is predictable. Clearly, this is unlikely to be the case on many projects, not only those involving design. Such an approach is unlikely to deal with design ambiguities, and issues of *co-ordination* and the associated *synchronisation* of efforts (something that is literally in between the denoted delivery packages). Take suspended ceilings in most office buildings, for example, the suspended ceiling as an interface between a service void and areas of habitation is an integrated design concept. Such a ceiling system not untypically involves a whole array of specialist concerns: the ceiling framing and panelling itself; lighting fittings; the fire alarm and sprinkler systems; smoke detection devices and compartmentalisation; the PA system; the air conditioning supply and extracts grilles, and damper access; acoustic criteria; suitability for the partition planning grid; fixings for partition heads, etc. Discrete specialist responsibilities have to be anticipated, synchronised and integrated. The issue is more than simple design co-ordination - it is also a spirit of shared responsibility which aspires to the proper realisation of a design concept.

Another problem is that the analytic work breakdown technique might not pro-

Meetings as Tools

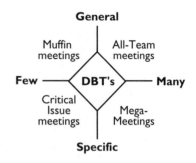

When developing the 777 Boeing used meetings as a managerial tool - the focus of co-ordination, problem resolution and agreement. Some of the most significant meetings were as follows:

• *Design Build Team Meetings - getting together for 2hrs about twice a week, for the many voices who had an interest in some specific aspect of the plane's development e.g. wings, doors, undercarriage, etc.*

• *Mega-Meetings - of all the Boeing chief project engineers, for about 6hrs.*

• *Critical Issue Meetings - when progress on critical issues was dealt with and crises were addressed.*

• *Muffin Meetings - weekly meetings when the 5 Vice Presidents on the project met to review progress and issues arising (and when the project chief offered muffins made by his wife!).*

• *Program Review Meetings - once a week meetings when about 70 people would meet to discuss general progress.*

• *All Team Meetings - when thousands of people met in one of Boeing's giant hangers.*

And in the background was Boeing's Board of Directors.

A concept of managed translators

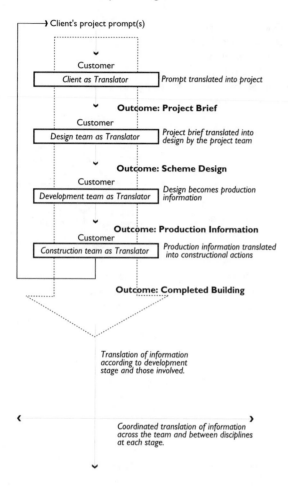

Client's project prompt(s)

Customer
Client as Translator — *Prompt translated into project*

Outcome: Project Brief

Customer
Design team as Translator — *Project brief translated into design by the project team*

Outcome: Scheme Design

Customer
Development team as Translator — *Design becomes production information*

Outcome: Production Information

Customer
Construction team as Translator — *Production information translated into constructional actions*

Outcome: Completed Building

Translation of information according to development stage and those involved.

Coordinated translation of information across the team and between disciplines at each stage.

Managing information requires a consideration of more than its linear development as a project unfolds. It has to be translated into forms suitable for those in subsequent stage. For example, the design scheme becomes a set of development tasks which, in turn, become a set of construction specifications. At each progressive stage, strategic leverage is being eroded and the information has to become more thorough, adequate and timely.

Two major points of translational difficulty stand out:

• from client needs and wants to a design scheme, and
• from constructional specifications to a realised building which satisfies requirements (all of them, including budgetary, temporal criteria as well as perfomative ones).

At both these points in a project's history misunderstanding can be exacerbated by exploitive attitudes seeking to realise maximum gain from the situation - an issue concerning designers as well as builders.

duce information (in the form of bottom-level work packages) which makes sense to builders and sub-contractors. To take a simple example, the architect and engineer will probably identify the reception lobby and the cafeteria as entirely different areas of design, but a specialist firm responsible for finishes will see them as different geographical aspects of a unified undertaking - a coat of paint in one area is likely to be as much the same as a coat of paint in another.

In addition, within a modularised design content, general themes will occur e.g. maintenance issues, cleaning equipment, security, fire escape, etc. Such issues are at the heart of the co-ordination and communication problem during detailed design development. The diagram above illustrates it as a matrix.

5 Multiple Translations. Answers to these issues are partly managerial and partly technical. Computerised drawings, for example, *technically* enable information to be filtered into specialist packages, although this can risk omitting crucial contextural information which integrates construction elements together (the planning example opposite uses the concept of an integrated set of working drawings). The traditional *managerial* resolution of the problem is the use of a general contractor, a management contractor, construction manager or similar who ensures the effective translation of design information into constructional contracts. This (sometimes unappreciated) role of the contractor completes a series of managed *translations* which see the initial project prompt finally realised as a completed building.

The notion of project content being taken through a series if translational stages is something that the more linear, hierarchical planning techniques such the WBS presume not to take place or not to be significant. In fact, nothing else could be more fundamental to the typical architectural project (and many other types). For example, the informational content of the production information given to suppliers and contractors is almost invariably a source of contention. But there are potential misunderstandings between any level and every other one.

This informational translation is not only progressive and developmental as the project unfolds toward completion: it is also *across* the team, between different disciplines, interests and perspectives. Agents, users, clients, funders, designers, engineers, statutory representatives and the rest have to be oriented toward a similar understanding and a shared goal. During the first stage of a project a climate of enthusiasm and optimism will dominate, easing any communication and orientation difficulties. After the scheme design gateway - during the developmental stage of the project - everyone involved will be far less tolerant of informational miscommunication and inadequacy. This is not just a matter of informational content in the sense of data, but of a presentational format and adequacy which suits the receiving agency.

Considering such a need for translations allows the introduction of the concept of 'internal customers' within the team - a concept that is important in contemporary process engineering and quality control. The inference to be drawn is that the customer's needs have to be respected and that this becomes a prime consideration at each level of 'translation'.

The WBS

Many project management commentators advocate breaking the project undertaking into a Work Breakdown Structure (WBS) - in effect, a form of project plan. This can be useful, but there are difficulties with the technique.

A WBS attempts to partition a large whole (the undertaking) down into a hierarchy of small, manageable parts. Like a fishbone cause and effect diagram (see later section) it is fundamentally a *Gozinto* tree-diagram that orders the project content into identifiable 'functional blocks', starting with the project deliverable and progressing to levels of more detail (from more to less generalised levels of information). The content can be be conceived in terms of project outcomes (events), tasks (activities) being undertaken, design functions or features. The point is to be consistent, seeking to be goal-oriented and aiming to identify logical divisions of the project that can be easily managed. For example, the whole might be broken into major assemblies and subassemblies, each with a cost-code allocation. The bottom-line would be functional aspects of the product which an individual would be responsible for designing (the 'task-owner', as they say). The aim is to develop a coherent basis for all kinds of work management scheduling and thus monitoring and control, defining bottom-line tasks in terms of a statement of work (SOW) which establishes responsibility, commitment and can even become a legal contract. The ambition is to have a bottom-up (rather than a heuristic-based, top-down) understanding of the project.

A full hierarchy might embrace the following levels:

• Mission.
This might be a simple statement. The most famous is probably, "To get to the moon by the end of the decade." (President Kennedy)

• Programmes within the mission.
Examples within the space program included: manned space flight; aircraft technology; space applications; supporting operations; unmanned investigations; etc.

• Project(s).
  • Tasks.
  • Subtasks.
  • Individual work packages.
  • Level of effort and responsibility.

Business organisations might also have 'missions' which help to identify who they are and what makes them unique. The programmes then become organisational, product or service divisions. Projects are discrete and specific vehicles of change which fulfil programme goals.

Each element of undertaking (project, task, etc.) is attached to a single level. The sum of work at one level should equal the work content of the next higher level. Each level and work package should be administratively meaningful, and can be given cost and time allocations so as to further the identification of milestones defined in terms of goals to be achieved. Each level is also denoted by a hierarchical labelling system which enables logical families to be easily identified. Once all this information has been formulated, it can also be presented as Gantt charts and network diagrams.

As a planning concept, the WBS presumes a reasonably full knowledge of content is available at the planning stage. This suggests the technique cannot be employed unless the project is essentially repeating former performances or until a full scheme design has been agreed. On the other hand, the WBS might be useful when used as a basis for conceptually understanding a performance brief and the hierarchy of undertakings that develop during early project stages.

WBS's are initially ordered in accordance with the natural, functional breakdown of what is being dealt with (for example, as a systems-derived perspective on the pro-

Three Ways

There are three basic approaches to constructing a WBS:

• The phase approach i.e. a temporal one, looking at the stages of a project.

• The objects approach i.e. looking at systems, components and similar hardware.

• The activities approach i.e. looking at the organisation, departments, individuals, kinds of activity, etc.

Disaggregation / Reintegration

Disaggregating a process into steps and checklists does not reintegrate it.
Henry Mintzberg

ject deliverable). However, most architectural projects naturally break themselves into *discipline* WBS's, and this might have little or nothing to do with naturally arising design interdependencies or sets of constructional undertakings. This can result in a fracturing of the holistic viewpoint and a resulting emphasis upon synchronisation and co-ordination between agencies. Knowing where cross-disciplinary interdependencies lie is not something the WBS can easily identify. Nor can it identify when these are critical or risky. This is because the WBS formally organises work in a Taylorist fashion. For example, contemporary team-working, with its cross-skill presumptions which enable individuals to swap around, take up each others tasks and share responsibilities is at odds with the WBS breakdown,

Another problem with the WBS is that it can be rigid and overly hierarchical in its ambition to achieve a tightly controlled development programme. For example, there is a tendency to presume that features at a *higher* level are always more *strategic* than those at a lower level. Designers know this isn't true and, in comfort with ambiguity, they concern themselves with all manner of relationships between detail and whole that is rarely constrained to a strict hierarchical relationship; they are ready to see when a lower level feature is actually critical and therefore 'strategic'. This focus upon crucially important success factors is a judgemental complement to the mechanics of a WBS, but one that a technocratic managerial perspective seeks to eliminate.

Some designers approach techniques such as the WBS as if it were an answer to the uncertainties which bother them as planners and organisers of efforts. However, the pitfalls noted above have to be taken into account.

Basic Planning Techniques

There are three fundamental things to consider in the planning method:
- *The critical success factors that inform the project medium.*
- *The content of the project being planned i.e. what has been undertaken.*
- *The process goals which the planning aims to realise and that define achievements. (This presumes the overall process or procurement route has already been determined during the formulation of a scheme.)*

The Gantt (Bar) Chart
A graphic monitoring technique which shows multiple activities on a horizontal time scale. Developed about 1900 by Henry Gantt. Useful and ubiquitous, but cannot show interdependencies.

Generic forms of network planning and control.

*• **Critical Path Method** (CPM) - activity oriented for use when the percent of completion of a task can be made evident. Developed by Dupont for construction project (1957). The critical path is usually the longest path through a network, and always the path with the least total 'slack'. Earliest/latest start and earliest/latest finish dates can be calculated for each activity, but these are single activity-duration estimates (not probabilities). Tends to be structured as activity-on-node (AON). Critical activities are commonly 10% or less of total; once identified they are targeted as possible activities to 'crash'.*

*• **Programme Evaluation and Review Technique** (PERT) - event oriented for situations where 'percent complete' is difficult to calculate. Developed by management consultants for US Navy research projects (1958). Uses three estimates of activity duration: most likely, optimistic, pessimistic. Tends to be structured as activity-on-arrow (AOA). Using simple statistical method the technique can provide statements of probability of completion in the estimated time.*
Precedence Diagrams
Activity-on-arrow allowing for leads and lags between activities (CPM/PERT require many sub-activities to provide for this). Developed about 1964 by IBM. Copes with split activities. Four times are used: start to start; finish to finish; finish to start; start to finish.

Computer programs are readily available to do all the calculating for network analysis, but the user will quickly find that they are dependent upon having sufficient information about the project (as a process and set of defined tasks), and about their dependencies, resource requirements and durations. The methods are ideally suited to programming the down-stream end of a design and development projects (i.e. their construction) or the programming of engineering projects with a known content. Design projects are equivalent to R&D ones, where probabilistic estimates start to make networks practicable. (21)

The concept of the Work Breakdown Structure (WBS)

The WBS is a hierarchical way of 'picturing' the work being undertaken. It seeks to map out work content in a 'tree-like' formation, each level generalising the level below it. To the extent it can be meaningfully and successfully done, the WBS furthers rational scheduling. It is undoubtedly useful, but the goal and the conceptual basis of a WBS have to be borne in mind when setting one up. You will find that the concept of 'partitioning' into 5/6 levels recurs in milestone and staging theory as a basic rule of thumb.

Making the WBS meaningful depends entirely upon the planner's goal. A systems view relates aspects of the WBS which work together, but the usual reason for doing a WBS is to schedule and plan scheme content development. This suggests a constructional or work tendering viewpoint has to be balanced against that deriving a WBS from the scheme and the need to develop its content in more detail. These two perspectives will often coincide, but not always.

❶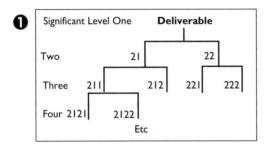

A WBS is likely to be partitioned into 5/6 levels. Each element of the WBS is a functional block, a work package and, at the lowest level, a set of tasks that cannot be meaningfully broken down any further. It should be possible to report against each element, regardless of agency responsibility.

❷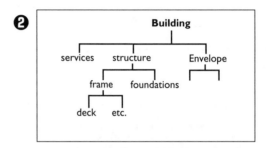

Each level and identified item has to be managerially meaningful. This means it can be assigned personnel, budgets and reporting responsibilities. Each can be then be planned, budgeted, scheduled, monitored and controlled. However, each level also has to be meaningul from a (detailed) design viewpoint.

❸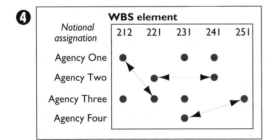

An overall WBS should should include every function resolved in the project, against which charges and responsibilites are allocated.

❹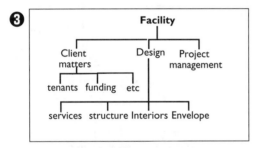

The WBS has difficulty with the interfaces between the functional blocks. It deals with the easy aspects of 'mapping' but might ignore what is crucial simply because it is difficult to map. This difficulty is twofold: the mechanics of mapping and, more importantly, identifying where dependencies are when the project content is to some extent notional and provisional.

❺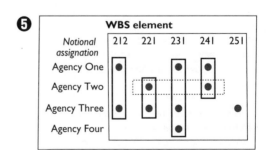

Because architectural projects are fragmented by agency and/or discipline it becomes important to identify shared responsibilties.

TREND Analysis

TREND is an acronym for Transformed Relationships Evolved from Network Data. *Despite this awful acronym it is a potentially useful project management tool (20). This utility derives from its attempt to cope with the 'softer' aspects of planning and management that a WBS cannot address. However, like similar techniques it is hardly intuitive and its expression of an understanding of content might be more significant than the benefits to derived from putting a large effort into employing it.*

TREND analysis deals with three factors: *interdependence* (between elements in the WBS), *uncertainty* (as to content, time frame, budget, formal reliance upon figures in authority,etc.) and *status* (of those undertaking the work, relative to others on the team, at any point in time or stage of the project). In other words, the method is an attempt to identify and map some of the organisational and managerial 'critical success factors' that the project is dependent upon when the project content is expressed as task groups working on the 'functional blocks' identified within a WBS. Problems not only arise from uncertain areas of the project, but also from one uncertainty being dependent upon another, for example when a higher-status group is dependent upon a lower-status group, etc. The aim is to then generate suitable managerial ways of addressing the identified area of risk. TREND analysis can be seen as another attempt to marry 'rational' technique with a manager's judgmental perceptions.

A notional development phase TREND diagram for a project's first stage of scheme design. Heavy blocks indicate an important function. Typical dependencies are shown by the dotted lines; arrows show the direction of dependency. Shaded blocks indicate high uncertainty in this circumstance; unshaded indicates low uncertainty.

During the second project stage of design development the game shifts and what was uncertain now becomes areas of relative exposure, risk and criticality.

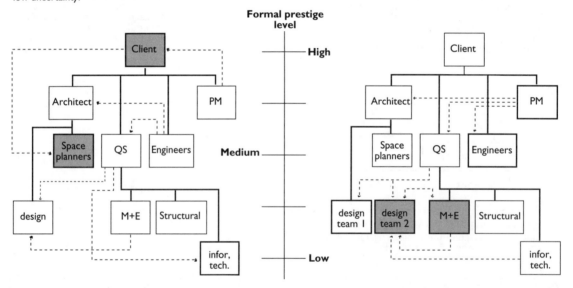

The example below adapts the concept to an architectural project indicated in terms of responsibilities. This kind of diagram can be broken down in the form of a WBS or even in terms of the conceptual basis of a design, in order identifying critical interfaces.

Note: *this example is entirely notional and each project will be different. However, the shifts that take place between key project stages will reflect generic changes in emphasis and team leadership shifts that will be a feature of most projects. The example presumes a client concerned with a fit-out project and a high-dependency upon information technologies. The later project stage presumes these issues have been resolved and that project development now shifts task uncertainty and inherent risk. In this instance it is presumed that general interior and furniture design is important, but that designing and managing IT installations remains critical. Identifying a critical interface and / or dependency between task groups will underscore items on the project's critical path, but it does so in term of organisation. In this instance, an area that designers might tend to neglect because of its high-engineering / low-glamour content should be given high-level managerial attention, particularly since it is being undertaken at a low-status / prestige level.*

Picturing it

act 5 scene 7

Planning techniques assist the planner with project control, but they are entirely dependent upon finding appropriate ways of 'picturing' what lies ahead. Henry Gantt's traditional bar charting technique - invented prior to World war One - is a familiar way of 'picturing' project efforts as discrete, scaled bars on a chart which places them against a time-line. Separate activities (or sets of them) are each denoted by a graphic bar. The concept is simple and useful, but it fails to do three things: show interdependencies between activities; show late and early starts in activities (and their implications), and the results of programme 'crashes', etc.; and show the inherent variability and durational probability of any activity. Addressing these considerations has led to other kinds of 'picturing' techniques, each of which has merits and demerits. The Gantt chart, however, remains in extensive use as a simple, valuable tool.

Activity, work flow, process, goal and network concepts - alongside associated scheduling techniques such as linear responsibility charts, drawing production programmes, information transfer schedules, organisation charts, implementation plans, and the rest - are all anticipatory ways of organising the future in terms of a plausible and useful representation of the undertaking. All these techniques embody particular concepts. In the words of Edwards Deming, the celebrated father of quality management, "A flow diagram, simple or complex, is an example of a theory - an idea." (Deming, 1982). Hopeful enthusiasms for techniques - grasped as if a life-belt - often ignore this fundamental point.

In using such mapping techniques, a planner is attempting to address and articulate a number of ostensibly simple questions:

- *What* are we attempting to *do*? (what is the content of the undertaking and what defines and qualifies its goal? what are the necessary activities? what are the crucial activities? where is the risk?). *What* needs to be *achieved*?

- *Who* is doing *what*? (how *many* people do we need? How many can we *afford*? Where does *responsibility* lie? How do we *organise*? What kinds of *co-ordination* with other agencies will be necessary?).

- *When* will we be doing what we undertake?

The initial aim is clarification - not as an end in itself, but as a managerial way of identifying goals, critical success factors and their relationships. Helpful techniques prompt both questions and answers to them. They then enable a form of 'picturing' or projective representation of what is intended. The example overleaf indicates some of the principles in terms of goal-oriented networks and the employment of event milestones as markers of progress.

2 **Being Goal-oriented.** An important ingredient of the employment of activity and process-oriented planning techniques such as the Gantt chart and networks is the concept of being *goal-oriented*. The contemporary guises this arises in are variations on Peter Drucker's influential concept of MbO, or *Management by Objectives* (Drucker, 1954). MbO aims to enable managers to choose among options and prioritise among variables; to focus business efforts and explain a whole range of business phenomena in terms of a small number of statements; to allow the testing of these statements in experience; to predict behaviour; to examine the soundness of decisions whilst they are being made rather than after the fact; and to improve future performance after an analysis of past performance relative to stated goals. Another significant ambition is to affect the motivation of individual managers. Clearly, setting goals necessitates some form of monitoring and measuring of performances.

The key to the goal-oriented planning concept in a project planning context is the identification and organisation of *milestones* - conditions (or events) produced by activities and marking some significant project achievement.

Gambling

If you schedule optimistically, the probability of completing a project on time has less chance of success than winning at blackjack in Monte Carlo.
Keszbom et al.

Milestone charts and activity plans - representing a process

1. Milestone planning is results-oriented, working back from project completion. As this simple construction example illustrates, it is easy to translate the activities of a critical path chart into milestones. Notice the mixing of trades and the implied splitting of trade activities.

2. The diagram has numerous 'result paths', but there are, in fact, at least six *sets* of results-oriented activities: a) foundations, frame, etc; b) external works; c) cladding and roof; d) principal installations ; e) second fix, etc.; f) finishes and finishing. The Critical path is indicated in a heavy line.

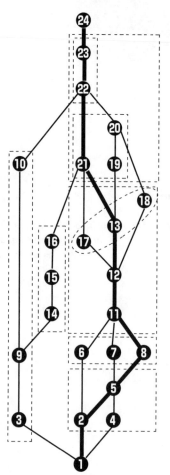

Notional simple timber frame house construction (with brick skin). Work is interpreted as conditions achieved. Times (in days) are notional but provide the Critical Path to the diagram. More goals can be noted (eg completion of the stud framing), but activities themselves are on the paths between the milestones. It is presumed that task precedents have been worked out. This is an Activity on Line diagram (events are on the nodes).

1. When work complete
(Implicitly includes all clearing up and snagging)
2. when floor sanded and varnished (2)
3. when external works are complete (5)
4. when electrical work is complete (1)
5. when interior painting complete (3)
6 when carpentry complete (3)
7 when kitchen fittings complete (1)
8. when final plumbing is complete (2)
9. when external grading is complete (2)
10. when storm drains for rainwater complete (1)
11. when flooring laid (3)
12. when p'board is fastened, scimmed and dry (10)
(Implicitly includes the stud framing, which could also be listed)
13. when heating and ventilating installed (4)
14. when gutters and downspouts complete (1)
15. when roofing and flashings complete (2)
16. when brickwork complete (6)
17. when rough wiring complete (2)
18. when rough plumbing complete (3)
19. when concrete basement floor poured (2 days)
20. when basement drains and plumbing complete (1)
21. when wood frame complete (4)
22. when foundations complete (2)
23. when excavation complete (4)
(Implicitly includes demolitions)
24. when work starts

Note: the Critical Path is the thick line
This is the irreducible, longest path through the network. A rule of thumb is that about 10% of tasks will be 'critical'.

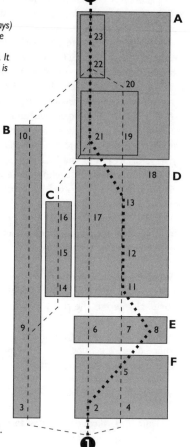

3. The diagram can be turned into a 'fishbone' chart to illustrate the contribution of sets of activities to the final goal.

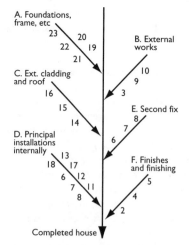

A. Foundations, frame, etc
23 20
22 19
21

B. External works

C. Ext. cladding and roof
16
15
14
3

10
9

E. Second fix
8
7
6

D. Principal installations internally
13
18 17
6 12
7 11
8

F. Finishes and finishing
5
4
2

Completed house

The intention is to focus project efforts upon *results* rather than *activities*, enabling managers to measure progress against the milestone plan and *not* against activities themselves. This keeps their focus upon ends (i.e. the milestones) rather than the details of means (specific tasks). Because the most significant milestone is successful project completion, the method usually works back from this final condition and asks about preceding milestones.

Milestone planning can be undertaken under the guidance of a number of heuristic, such as the following:

- *Consider the project as a series of hierarchical layers and intermediate goals* e.g.
  - at the global level (sponsor viewpoint)
  - at a intermediate goal level (PM viewpoint)
  - at an activity level (agency viewpoint)
- *Break major projects into sub-projects* (up to about 5).
- *Devise intermediate project goals (the milestones).*

Keep the overall number of milestones at about 15/20 maximum. If there are more than about 15, consider breaking into sub-milestones (a concept derived from the notion that a manager has a natural span of control over subordinates at about this maximum).

- *Work backwards from the end goal.* (This is not always possible, but this way of working reinforces the intention to be 'goal-oriented'.)
- *Ensure the milestones are meaningful, measurable and reasonably frequent.*
- *Involve the members of the team involved in the work.*
- *Organise the milestones into sets of result paths* which logically organises similar and related milestones together. Experiment with result paths as necessary, but expect there to be at least three.
- *Avoid a focus on the activities* which produce a milestone. Discussion of activities should be noted but kept aside.
- Later, identify activities (about 20 maximum) and tasks (again, maximum 20 per activity) for the paths leading to the milestones. Anticipate this, but finalise activity lists as and when necessary, otherwise attention is diverted and energy is wasted.
- When dealing with times, make reference to starts as well as durations and completions.

Note: *this method presumes that activities are on the arrows of the diagram, not on the nodes (the milestones).*

Of course, identifying what is critical is not just a matter of listing and relating activities and precedents, but involves issues such as lead-in times, organisational priorities, resource-levelling, problematic areas, other commitments agencies have, co-ordination, split work activities, interpersonal chemistries, and so on.

The three diagrams on the previous page suggest how a simple construction process can be 'pictured' or mapped in different ways, each offering different kinds of information. The first activity-on-arrow diagram (top left) provides a critical path and identifies 'result paths', but it fails to identify *sets* of results-oriented milestones or other considerations mentioned above. In fact, there appears to be six groups of milestone-related activities, four of which are on the critical path. These are seen in the fish-bone diagram (bottom centre).

A simplified milestone map (this page) also makes most sense when we plot starts for the activity sets as well as their completion. This facilitates the management of activities in these sets. The diagram on the right shows how the milestone diagram can be made even more simple, but it then loses information. In other words, it is important to consider why a network is being drawn and what the manager wants from it.

The diagram overleaf illustrates a fundamental aspect of all activity planning: efficient resourcing. It indicates the importance of precedences, and start and finish times and will indicate to some architects one reason why contractors appreciate full and timely information. The principle should also apply within a practice when job resourcing a portfolio of projects.

The fishbone diagram can be turned milestone chart indicating the principal goals. The starts for activities are indicative and a reminder of their importance.

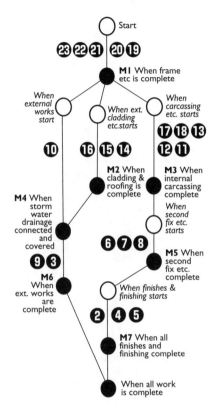

The diagram without starts is simpler, but it has lost information.

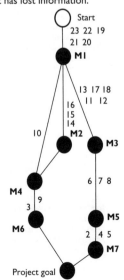

Simple networks, the issue of work splitting and resourcing

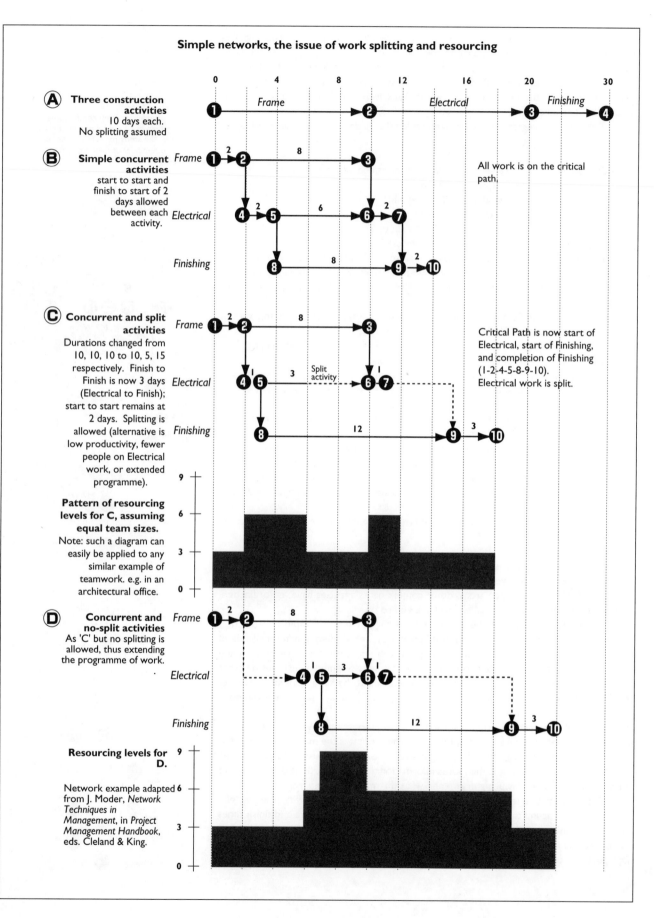

(A) Three construction activities
10 days each.
No splitting assumed

Frame / Electrical / Finishing
1 → 2 → 3 → 4

(B) Simple concurrent activities
start to start and finish to start of 2 days allowed between each activity.

Frame: 1 →2→ 8 →3
Electrical: 4 →2→ 5 → 6 →6→2→ 7
Finishing: 8 → 8 → 9 →2→ 10

All work is on the critical path.

(C) Concurrent and split activities
Durations changed from 10, 10, 10 to 10, 5, 15 respectively. Finish to Finish is now 3 days (Electrical to Finish); start to start remains at 2 days. Splitting is allowed (alternative is low productivity, fewer people on Electrical work, or extended programme).

Frame: 1 →2→ 8 →3
Electrical: 4 →1→ 5 → 3 → Split activity → 6 →1→ 7
Finishing: 8 → 12 → 9 → 3 → 10

Critical Path is now start of Electrical, start of Finishing, and completion of Finishing (1-2-4-5-8-9-10). Electrical work is split.

Pattern of resourcing levels for C, assuming equal team sizes.
Note: such a diagram can easily be applied to any similar example of teamwork. e.g. in an architectural office.

(D) Concurrent and no-split activities
As 'C' but no splitting is allowed, thus extending the programme of work.

Frame: 1 →2→ 8 →3
Electrical: 4 →5→ 3 → 6 →1→ 7
Finishing: 8 → 12 → 9 → 3 → 10

Resourcing levels for D.

Network example adapted from J. Moder, *Network Techniques in Management*, in *Project Management Handbook*, eds. Cleland & King.

70

The Gantt chart

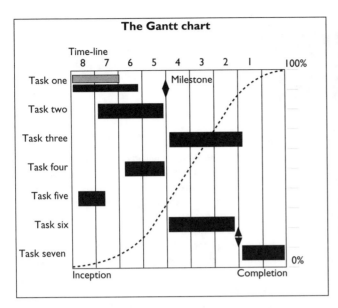

Gantt charts are very useful. The above example of a Gantt chart is set as a 'count-down' between inception and completion. Milestones can be indicated and there can be other Gantt charts within each bar. Progress can be simply indicated by colouring in the bars or supplementing them with other symbols on the basis of 'percentage of task completed' (see Task One in the diagram). The chart can also indicate which tasks are on the critical path - information derived from project planning software. By adding a 'percentage completed' bar down the right hand side, this information can also be added (shown cumulatively by the dotted line - which can be added to to indicate actual performance and any deviance).

Both Gantt and network charts can have the progress dimension enhanced by the employment of 'traffic signs', either as colours or, as on the left, in terms of three circles: an open circle for satisfactory progress; a half-circle for poor progress (a warning); and a black or coloured circle for unsatisfactory progress.

Note: see the Network Primer at the end of this book for further information on networks.

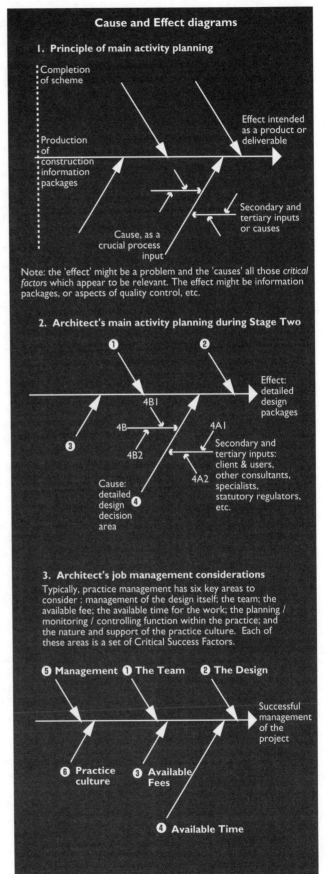

Cause and Effect diagrams

1. Principle of main activity planning

Note: the 'effect' might be a problem and the 'causes' all those *critical factors* which appear to be relevant. The effect might be information packages, or aspects of quality control, etc.

2. Architect's main activity planning during Stage Two

3. Architect's job management considerations

Typically, practice management has six key areas to consider : management of the design itself; the team; the available fee; the available time for the work; the planning / monitoring / controlling function within the practice; and the nature and support of the practice culture. Each of these areas is a set of Critical Success Factors.

Fishbone framing

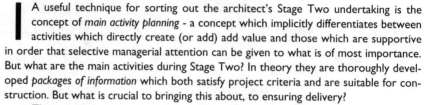

I A useful technique for sorting out the architect's Stage Two undertaking is the concept of *main activity planning* - a concept which implicitly differentiates between activities which directly create (or add) add value and those which are supportive in order that selective managerial attention can be given to what is of most importance. But what are the main activities during Stage Two? In theory they are thoroughly developed *packages of information* which both satisfy project criteria and are suitable for construction. But what is crucial to bringing this about, to ensuring delivery?

The principal activity is, in fact, making kinds of expert, appropriate and timely *decisions* about the details of the design. The actual production of information is a comparatively mechanical aspect of this process.

One way of 'picturing' decision areas is to use *'fishbone'* diagrams which seek to identify main activities in terms of effects and what causes them (see diagrams on previous page). For example, if the output is a detailed design expressed in terms of information packages of drawings and written specifications, the principal inputs are the decisions concerning the major aspects of the design. In turn, these will have their own inputs: from consultants, specialist contractors, user groups, statutory authorities, etc. (see diagrams on the right).

It is important to appreciate that a cause and effect diagram can only be developed from both a holistic and particular concept of what is at issue. It presumes some overall *framing* of the situational problematic, upon which the analysis is based. Whilst most buildings of any type will generate similar fishbones, the issue at hand is the identification of the *critical success factors in any particular instance*. A design must be analysed in terms of specific concepts and issues crucial to itself. Functionality will produce one type of specific fishbone, as will building systems, team responsibilities, etc. Fishbones are also useful ways of summarising as well as analysing. The diagram overleaf shows a speculative fishbone for the design of the Lloyds building (Richard Rogers Partnership, 1986).

However, whilst the focus will logically be upon *ends,* it is *means* which will determine success. From a managerial viewpoint, the crucial issue is the identification of *process* success factors and the work considerations (or variables) which affect them. This is a managerial concern. What process factors within the practice will significantly affect the success of the team's work on the project? The diagram to the right suggests some important project managerial considerations within a practice set out in a cause and effect format.

Design integration, co-ordination and synchronisation, and translation are three fundamental aspects of a project process during Stage Two. Fishbone cause and effect diagrams can be used to image each of these perspectives on design management. Similarly, a cause and effect diagram can be considered in terms of work packages that will result in information suitable for discussion and tendering purposes with specialist sub-contractors and builders. And a cause and effect diagram can also be considered in terms of construction activities - in which case design integration and co-ordination are assumed to be implicit and practical issues of realisation predominate as crucial success factors. A fourth basic fishbone might adopt a purely managerial viewpoint. The diagram overleaf illustrates how a manager in an architectural practice might identify crucial success factors relevant to successfully managing a project. In this example they are:

- Effective management of the design process:
    - a sound scheme design.
    - getting it right first time, up front.
    - few changes, from client or designers.
    - good internal and inter-agency co-ordination.

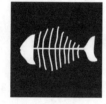

Issue:

What drives success?
What are the barriers to success?

Which factors derive from the project?
Which derive from the culture of production?

Which factors are critical?
Which are secondary?
Which are the primary value creating factors?
Which are supportive?

What are the drivers and barriers to decision-making?
What are the drivers and barriers to progress?

What are the drivers and barriers to less late change, error and rework?

How does management deliver the project maxim of 'one time, on time'?
By what means does management ensure effective integration, co-ordination and synchronisation?

Schematic design concept fishbone for the Lloyds of London building (Sir Richard Rogers Partnership, London 1978-86)

The situational-problematic was framed as the need for a highly adaptable building that would last 125 years. The architectural concept made a simple differentiation between the architectural frame, interior spaces, secondary support facilities, and services (basically, the served and servant concept), in the process acknowledging key dynamics of usage (everything from client culture to building maintenance). This idea had to be conceptually framed in terms of the site and the detail of specific client needs, formulated as a particular architecture. The clarity of the modularised concept was taken through Stage Two detailed design and helped to maintain design management control through an eight year project life-cycle and many kinds of change that had to be accommodated during the development programme.

The point about such a design fishbone is that it articulates the key concepts and hierarchically organises them. The difficulty (apart from the issue of hindsight) is that a holistic whole and an interactive set of considerations are fragmented. If this fragmentation has in mind a division of labour which will further design development and assist in the production of construction specifications, then it can be useful. Nevertheless, a holistic overview is crucially important. Managerial efforts have to work at both levels simultaneously.

Sir Richard Rogers, head of the Lloyds design team.
For a discussion of the history of the project (and that of the Hongkong & Shanghai Bank) see 'Lloyds and the Bank', the Architect's Journal 22nd Oct.1986. Also see Robbins (1994) for comments of the partner-in-charge (John Young) on using drawings on the project.

New building on site of original 1927 bldg.

I. Concept for building (adaptable served spaces and servant concept)

Restaurant — Kitchens
1.4. Podium level
Reception, cloakrooms, etc.
Retail — Security

1.3 Perimeter service towers
Prefabricated toilets
Lifts — Escape stairs
Roof plant & equipment
Services risers (data, power, fire, etc.)

1.2.3.Roof level
Roof plant
Cleaning & maintenance cranes, etc.

Basements

Podium level facilities
Captain's Room restaurant — Other
Atrium escalators
1.2.1.1 The Market
Lutine bell, information, displays,etc.
Underwriter's 'Boxes'
Galleries — The Room
Space planning

Concept for site
Rear service vehicle access to basement
Relation to existing (1958) building facilities
Lower level concourse accessible by the public
Retention of 1926 building entry porch
Main entrance on *piano nobile*
Secondary (Lime Street) entrance at podium level
Access

1.2 Simple stacked tower with central atrium, standard elements and clear floors

1.2.1.4 Chairman's Suite
Adam (board) Room
Fit-out
Furniture
Partitions
Finishes
1.2.1.3 Support staff offices
1.2.1.2 Services
Ceilings
Raised floors
1.2.1.Interiors

Stair towers
Other elements
Prefabricated toilets
Exposed services
Fixing frameworks, access etc.,

Atrium
Internal atrium walls
Maintenance

Main block exterior (Maison de Verre concept)

Claddings

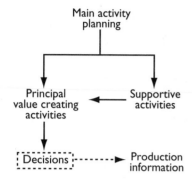

Main activity
planning

Principal
value creating
activities ← Supportive
activities

Decisions ┄┄┄┄→ Production
information

Why?

Western thinking has been criticised for its grasping at answers rather than a pursuit of problems (as in problem-finding rather than problem-solving). It has been argued that the better Japanese organisations avoid this failing. Toyota, for example, is known for asking 'Why?' five times, arguing that this will bring them close to the heart of the matter. Honda are similarly concerned with root causes, committed to examining alternatives without a built-in bias toward the most familiar or convenient solutions. (see Pascale, 1990)

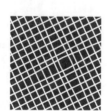

• low re-work rate.
• appropriate co-ordination.

• Effective management of fee income and expenditure:
  • fee-earning utilisation within the team.
  • the level of professional salaries.
  • overheads and support costs.
  • low team peaking / effective resourcing.
  • control of incidental costs.

• Effective management of available time:
  • client milestones / schedule.
  • selected procurement route.
  • information delivery schedules.
  • consistent productivity within the team.

• Effective management of the team:
  • participation (who is on the team)
  • motivation and commitment.
  • morale (*esprit de corps*).
  • participation in the planning process.
  • skill and professionalism within team.
  • leadership, and support from above.
  • sub-contract arrangements.

• Effective management of the job:
  • internal planning, monitoring and control.
  • client management e.g. agreements, changes to brief, etc.

• Practice culture ('the way we do things'):
  • facilities.
  • support / back-up.
  • people management policies and issues, including political climate.

The management and planning diagram overleaf illustrates how early planning for a typical large office building was conceived by its architects. The diagram is followed by a fishbone diagram for the project's stage to scheme approval.

2 Special and Common. In all the types of fishbone diagram already described there is often an underlying pattern of *special* and *common* (general and recurring) factors to be considered.

• *Special factors* are the more obvious considerations that are unique to the project, sometimes those which carry most risk. In negative terms, they are akin to acute disturbances.

• *Common factors* are more ubiquitous, tending to affect the whole project. In negative terms, they are akin to chronic disturbances.

The differentiation is an important one which can assist in managing the project and its design content. For example, each set of factors appears within three key areas of the project: within design decision areas; within design management areas; and within project management areas (see the diagram on page 75).

The special and unique factors have to receive focused attention. Successful resolution of the recurring elements is more likely to be the product of practice culture, the climate of professionalism, the project environment, the consistency of attention, etc.

The situation is similar to the quality control problems discussed by Edwards Deming, one of the fathers of quality management (22): process systems generate both special and common causes of failure.

The special causes of failure are the product of unique circumstances such as machine breakdowns, accidents, worker absence and the like. They happen, but as unusual, extra-ordinary events outside of the normal variations that can be expected within the performance range of a stable system.

Common causes are the random factors which lie *within* the expected statistical variations of a normal, stable distribution. If they are unsatisfactory, the nature of the whole system (the culture of production) requires attention in order that it can be reformed into a more appropriate performance norm. In Deming's words, one needs to appreciate that, "the type of action required to reduce special causes of variation is totally different from the action required to reduce variation and faults from the system itself" - a comment he follows with dire warnings about the consequences of meddling by adjustment, admonishing performances below the average achievement, etc., all of which are ignorant of system behaviours and basic statistics. Performance variation can only be corrected by the changing a system, not adjusting it. And change should be based on what Deming's called 'profound knowledge' - a rich, thick understanding.

This concept of special and common causes of failure, if inverted, also applies to the features and generators of *success*.

Within architectural practice the 'special causes' are likely to be the unique features of the project situation and the scheme proposal and thus an important creative aspect of what is being undertaken and dealt with. This is the opposite of special causes of difficulty in the production run seeking high performance from routine operations. Similarly, common generators of success are features of the distinct, underlying capability of the firm - the *cultural* equation which enables performance to be predictable and reliable, which embodies corporate knowledge, expertise and experience. In terms of heuristic, one might expect the 80/20 rule to apply: 20% of the project's features and considerations will contribute 80% of its success or failure. The remaining 80% is important, but not strategic.

Special Considerations

1. Design decision areas

Thematically unique elements e.g. in an office building these might include lobbies, office areas, conference rooms, plant rooms, toilets, etc. Other building types - such as a theatre - will be dominated by a few, large thematic elements.

2. Design management issues

Special elements e.g. identified areas with a higher uncertainty or risk content. User-programming needs will generate thematically discrete areas of concern. They might also focus interest upon critical long-lead time aspects of the design.

3. Project management:

Special elements e.g. specific areas of co-ordination.

General Considerations

Common concerns and features of a design e.g. maintenance, security, finishes, services strategies, energy issues, fire escape, specification clauses, rights of light, etc.

Mostly job planning and administration, but also including a managerial modularisation of the design effort, the adequacy and timeliness of information, etc.

People issues; design reviews, productivity, values oriented toward clients, general coordination, etc.

Special and General in Planning

The concept of Special and General (or Common) considerations applies in various ways throughout project management. In planning, for example, one can differentiate between Sequential events and Situational ones. The Sequentially driven considerations concern the logic of phasing and development; the Situationally driven considerations . Project needs such as risk analysis, configuration management and team building are recurring and situational. Those such as feasibility, scheme design and development are natural, sequential aspects of the project which supplant one another on the progression from inception to closure. Both have to be incorporated into the Project Plan.

Large central London office development (1) : early planning

Building approximately 60,000 sq.m. gross, with 34,000 sq.m. net of offices. Total height to 18 storeys (85m); floor plates 2500 to 1450 sq.m. Design plan undertaken at beginning of Scheme design.

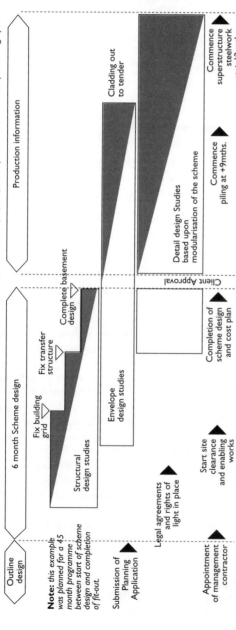

Note: this example was planned for a 45 month programme between start of scheme design and completion of fit-out.

Outline design | 6 month Scheme design | Production information

Submission of Planning Application

Legal agreements and rights of light in place

Appointment of management contractor

Fix building grid

Fix transfer structure

Complete basement design

Structural design studies

Envelope design studies

Start site clearance and enabling works

Completion of scheme design and cost plan

Client Approval

Detail design Studies based upon modularisation of the scheme

Cladding out to tender

Commence piling at +9mths.

Commence superstructure steelwork at +12 mths.

Hindsight: This project saw its original budget estimate climb to over 150%.

The project time of 45 months estimated at the beginning of scheme design went to 50 months and finally finished at approximately 55 months.

Problems were caused by an over-heated construction sector, a steel construction worker's strike, cost over-runs, etc.

Scheme planning : *In this example, the scheme design was considered in terms of three thematic design elements, each divided into interactive form studies and technical studies. Prior to scheme design, an outline scheme had been developed, during which time all advisors were placed.*

1. Building envelope:
Form studies
- Massing
- Solid / glazed curtain walling
- Exposed structure
- Roofscape
- Street level facades, Etc.

Technical studies
- Cladding / structure interface (the structural grid was frozen at this stage to cope with lead times)

2. Internal accommodation:
Form studies
- Space planning considerations (core and access logic, plan efficiency and flexibility, etc.)
- Podium and ground floor planning (entrances, retail content, housing layout, etc.)

Technical studies
- Internal structure (core, storey hts, services, etc.)
- Internal services (grid allowances frozen at this stage)
- Vertical circulation (lifts, stairs, escalators, etc.)
- Basement planning vehicular access, loading, plant, etc.)

3. Outline Building specification

In addition, there were a series of general and fundamental areas of investigation, including:

4. Accommodation, envelope and technical:
Briefs: shell and core offices; fitting out; retail and housing briefs
Surveys: comprehensive site and soils surveys
Legal agreements, rights of light, etc.
Fire issues (compartmentation, means of escape, fireman's access, smoke ventilation, etc.
Highways engineering

And some general and fundamental issues remained client-oriented:

5. Client matters such as pre-let negotiations.planning application, funding, agreements with inspecting authorities, planning application, etc.

Project planning at this stage anticipated a total of 342 scheme design drawings, ranging in scale from 1:500 to 1:10.

Detailed development : *Scheme design was aimed at fixing the brief and the design itself. The intention was that, after scheme approval, the architectural design team would be divided into six distinct groups, each addressing one zonal or crucial thematic part of the building design:*

- Building envelope
- Office development
- Podium and below
- Residential
- External works
  +
- Administration and management

Each design team was to undertake detailed form and technical studies before preparing tender information, issued in a work package format. It was these studies that were intended to be the vehicle translating the scheme design into the commitments of production information.

A management contractor was in place at an early stage, helping with buildability, putting administrative systems in place, organising a programme, consulting with specialist sub-contractors and generally helping to effect a translation between design intent and constructional requirements.

Information was produced as a master set of integrated, composite drawings, supplemented by detail drawings to make up sub-sets for specialist sub-contractors.

Large central London development office (2) : early scheme design fishbone diagram

It is important to note that this schema would be impossible without some agreed design basis. It is implicit that feasibility studies have already agreed an outline design and identified crucial features and concerns. These include the need to freeze all structural concepts and grids at this stage. Particular ideas, agendas and concepts are already strongly established – the nature of the beast has already been determined. For example, the idea of form studies and technical studies is a design management concept common to many large projects, but there is a particular agenda and set of values informing its conception on this project.

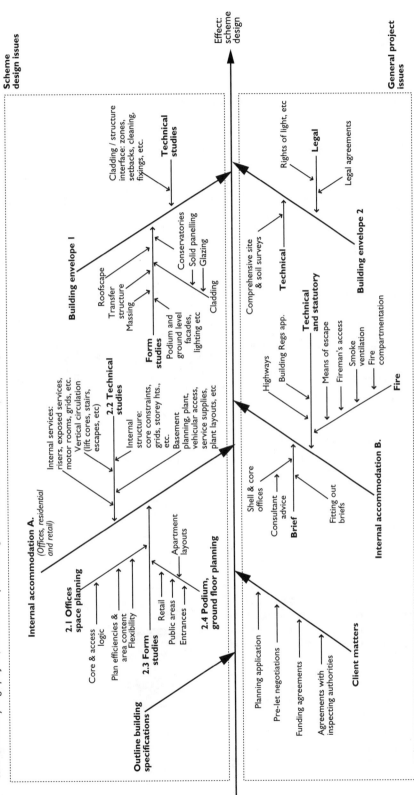

Note: after scheme approval, the architects for this project intended to break the design team into six distinct groups: building envelope (cladding); office development content; podium and below; residential content; external works; administration and management. Groups would issue information in work packages (see earlier diagram and outline programme for Stage One).

Matrix Activity Planning

Main activity planning and the idea of identifying Critical Success Factors has suggested the notion of a process prioritisation matrix (Brelin et al. 1995). The intention is that the list of CSF's should only include what is genuinely critical to goal achievement - the few factors that are necessary and also sufficient for the prediction of the desired outcome. The matrix is a simple variant upon the common evaluation matrix used as a device for comparatively rating, ranking and assessing products. In this case, the matrix is used to deal with the critical success factors and to identify where attention must be focused. The steps are as follows: first, the CSF's and key processes (the variables) are identified; these are then rated by being given a score of 1, 2 or 3 (1 meaning the process factor has little impact or threat to success, and 3 meaning it has maximum impact or influence). The total impact upon the range of CSF's is added. Next, each process factor is given an overall performance rating out of 10 (10 being a perfect process). The resulting 'performance gap' rating is then multiplied by the total impact rating. This enables the weakest process factors to be identified (and, as in all such techniques, it enables assumptions and values to be questioned).

This leads to an examination of each poorly performing process factors - perhaps even to a reconsideration of the whole process as a system.

This is what is done i.e. the activities and processes that affect or impact upon the CSF's.

These are the Critical Success Factors resulting from a consideration of goals and desired outcomes and what affects them. For example, successful fee management produces the outcome of good levels of remuneration and all that entails. The question then has to be asked, 'What are the critical media that produce this outcome?' These are the CSF's and they will vary from project to project and practice to practice.

Rating keys:

Process / activity impact
1 = low or none
2 = medium
3 = high

Process performance:
1 = inadequate
9 = very good

● **Key processes**

Critical Success Factors

EG: Successful fee management

Key processes	1. advantageous contract	2. productive team	3. milestone achievement	4. low overheads	5.	6.	Total impact score	Process performance rating	Process performance gap	Weighted gap	Identified Priority
1. progress and expenditure auditing	1	1	3	1	0	0	6	8	2	12	
2. achieved fee-earning utilisation rates	1	1	3	3	0	0	8	8	2	16	
3. staff skill / experience mix	1	3	1	2	0	0	7	7	3	21	●
4. change management	3	1	3	1	0	0	8	8	2	16	
5. proper work completion	1	3	3	1	0	0	8	9	1	8	
6. work planning	1	3	3	1	0	0	8	6	4	32	●
7. ETC.											

The essential difficulty to be overcome in order to use this technique is the identification of CSF's and key process factors impacting upon them. This is a conceptual problem. First, goals and outcomes have to be identified, and then the media that affect these desirable outcomes i.e. the critical success factors (another way of stating a cause and effect diagram). In turn, these media will be influenced by the process factors i.e. what people actually do. One way to approach these issues is in terms of cultural levels. Level One (Finders) goals will be different to Level Two (Grinders) goals, and so on. L1 and L2 will share some goals, just as L2 and L3 will share some goals - but, in most practices, L1 and L3 will rarely share goals. A matrix can be for sets of CSF's at each level. Some key process factors will, of course, be important at more than one level, increasing their prioritisation rating.

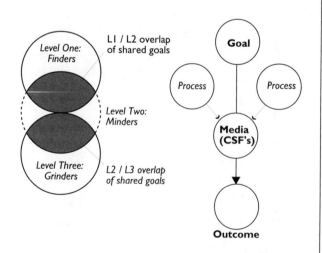

Synchronised efforts

1 The '*Know what you want to do, then do it*' approach to projects tends toward a sequential development concept sometimes called 'pass the baton', 'waterfall planning', or, 'tossing it over the wall'. It is rooted in the concept of the division of labour, Taylorist thinking, and its Fordist interpretation. As Henry Ford commented when describing his famous production line, "The man who places a part does not fasten it . . . The man who puts in a bolt does not put on the nut; the man who puts on the nut does not tighten it." In planning terms, this implies careful staging and task completion before moving forward, dividing planning from execution, design from manufacturing, manufacturing from performance and quality testing, etc. The ideal is to formulate a specification of need; freeze this spec; design to suit; build components; integrate these into a whole; test for conformity, performance and quality; and hand-over to the user.

There are problems with this concept for organising and co-ordinating efforts: a subsequent stage cannot begin until its predecessor is complete; process integrity is fragmented into functional interests, together with split responsibilities and accountability; and users might have only one stage at which they have a voice (at the very beginning).

2 **Running in Parallel.** As an alternative approach, *concurrent planning* seeks to speed up the project process by running functionally defined tasks in parallel or with significant overlap. A related concept is to *incrementally spiral* development, co-ordinating and checking on the run, providing *iterative enhancement* to the project content. Typically, development will begin as early as possible, even before user needs have been fully specified. Desirable features will be defined and prioritised, and work will move through a series of milestone targets which aim at balanced levels of overall synchronisation and stabilisation at each stage. This approach is highly dependent upon focus and a goal-oriented attention to critical success factors. It requires knowledge of what these factors are and a readiness (and ability) to shift efforts as the identification of CSF's evolves. And it requires an expert and motivated team comprising individuals who are tolerant of ambiguity. There has to be an *esprit* that is the opposite of the orthodox, mechanical concept of a team's internal workings.

Relay or Dash

Planning has traditionally adopted a 'relay' concept presuming one task is complete before another is started. However, it has become increasingly common to go for forms of 'concurrent' planning which run team efforts in parallel. Architectural 'fast-tracking' often presumes some form of concurrent process activity. Necessarily, there is a new emphasis given to co-ordination and synchronisation, to getting it right first time, avoiding change, errors and rework.

1. Sequential design concept

Complete information handed-over

2. Concurrent design concept

Information flows

Microsoft has evolved such a development process into a structured art - ostensibly messy, but rather effective. A starting point is sufficient structure for work to proceed, but enough flexibility for change to be accommodated. A rough specification or vision statement will be enough, but it will emphasise what the product is not, as well as what it is (a full specification is a part of the development output). And an important strategy is the 'continual synchronisation and periodic stabilisation' of the modular approach to content. As in any other development process resources must be controlled, milestones met and a progressive 'freezing' implemented that prevents further change unless absolutely necessary, and major phases have to be acknowledged: an initial stage during which features are defined, a vision statement is produced, criteria are stated, outline specifications are produced, and identity is given to the project content; and a development stage during which a series of milestones focus efforts and - importantly - test design content to ensure it is on target. Frequent tests and periodic progress audits and status reports must be instituted in order to ensure focus on the target and accountability. Businesses are being driven in this direction. However, there is an important implication of concurrent planning: the *managerial overhead* is likely to go up because interactions become more complex and more of them might become crucial.

At the heart of such strategies is the issue of project *duration* and attempts to reduce it. Various strategies can be attempted, but it has to be noted that those affecting the critical path can alter it and make new tasks critical. Examples include:

- Examining tasks and differentiating main activities from supportive ones, resulting in a focus upon the principal activities so that the support ones might be reduced.

- Increasing risk e.g. by reducing checking.

- Transferring resources from non-critical tasks to critical ones (but also avoiding counter-productive over-manning and increasing the managerial overhead).

- Increasing costs (usually meaning resources). This might be achieved by looking at the tasks on the critical path and accelerating them by adding people, beginning with those tasks employing having the lowest cost rates (so that the added resources are most effective).

Any overall reduction of project duration should still leave an adequate contingency which it is all too easy to eliminate. Also, the project leverage principle suggests attempts to gain time during actual team performances should be concentrated up front. In architectural practice management terms, it is common to hear it voiced that the fast-track project is preferred above other durational formats. The pressure means that people are more productive, making decisions and commitments, getting the job done. But fast-tracking does mean that a practice has to be capable and prepared to behave in an anticipatory way. Delivery systems have to run smoothly and the synchronisation of efforts will be a key concern.

 **3** **Synchronisation Across Three Fronts.** Synchronised efforts are particularly important during the development stage. This starts with a project plan describing milestones, gates, etc. This has already been discussed in terms of the need for *translation*, stage by stage (see p.61), but it is also necessary to consider the requirement for a similar kind of translation of the plan *across* the team at any point in time. For example, the principle aim at this stage is likely to be the production of a set of co-ordinated packages of tender and / or construction information. To achieve this three sets of inter-related, parallel considerations need to be anticipated:

1. *The need for a Project Plan*, describing agreements to be reached and signed-off, information packages to be released within the team and to contractors in a timely fashion, etc. This will probably be in terms of a set of discrete 'result paths', each defining related, significant events. (The concepts of 'gates' at exits

from stages and entry to subsequent ones will be relevant.)

2. *The need for decisions and commitments,* collaboratively realised within the project team and with other agencies such as suppliers and sub-contractors. For example, whatever has to be done in order to commit to the details of structural bay dimensions, floor to ceiling heights, window configurations, etc. Since this is now an issue across disciplines, between agencies and about component interfaces, the number of result paths might increase and boundaries might become blurred as decision-areas overlap. Getting to appropriate commitments will necessitate incremental freezes and a strategic focus founded upon the guide lines of the Project Plan but, in itself, this Plan will not be able to describe the realities of collaboration, co-ordination and team-work which has to be managed. Tight, anticipatory and light-footed orchestration will be required.

3. *The actual mechanics of drawing and writing, printing, etc.,* which incorporates and communicates a specification for tender or construction (i.e. the outcome of the Project plan and the collaborative efforts). A practice is likely to have rules of thumb to guide its time estimates (e.g. for a standard general arrangement drawing or detail drawing), but the list of itemised information and tasks concerned with co-ordinated research, selection, budget tendering, specification writing and issues of liability, can be shockingly long. The difficulty is to find an efficient production process in synchronisation with, on the one hand, the milestones of the project plan and, on the other, the process of collaboratively reached decisions. It is work that must follow the result paths of the Plan and the practice's project manager will be looking to avoid unnecessary change, errors, rework, split efforts and the like (exactly as on site).

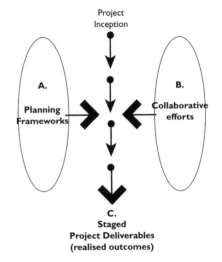

In other words the planning, often expressed in the short-hand terms of manpower resources and the number of man-days to produce a certain type of drawing, involves rather more than this. It is a managerial problem which must be informed by the motivated commitment of the production team - another reason to ensure the people who do the work are involved in its planning. The promotion of kinds of concurrency within the project will increase the need for a coordinated orchestration of

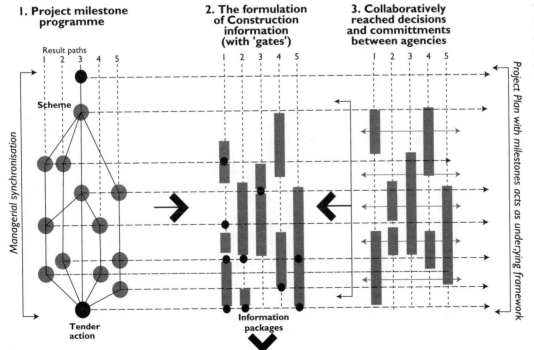

The managerial challenge of properly getting to the project goal necessitates different ways of looking at and 'picturing' the decision-making and productive efforts that must be synchronised, co-ordinated and orchestrated. A network is insufficient. Focus is naturally upon the outcomes realised stage by stage, resulting in the final deliverable, but process efforts must also be pictured and managed in other terms (see diagram above).

Monitoring and control

I No amount of planning and scheduling will be of any use unless *team efforts* and *progress* are monitored. The information produced by monitoring has to be evaluated (i.e. status is evaluated) and, if necessary, acted upon (the exercise of project control). The aim of such action will be to obviate any problems, to adjust and improve detailed forward planning, and to ensure the team is meeting client needs and continuing to realise the design potential that lies within the project. Adjustments will need to involve the team and draw forth their commitment. And realising design potential will depend upon the continued motivation of team members.

Planning, the monitoring of status, and project *control* are the three basic features of all project management.

Throughout this book there has been a distinct lean toward interested approaches to managing projects i.e. to the top-down, goal-oriented identification of critical success factors rather than the pursuit of a global, synoptic form of approach. This is more in tune with the designer's natural instincts than a technocratic, rule-governed pursuit of the rational-deductive ideal as a basis for the management of projects. It follows, that the first principle of monitoring is to be equally 'interested' and to monitor only the critical success factors rather than everything which can be monitored.

Monitoring the project action plan addresses *expenditures, progress, changes,* and *the quality of output.* The objective is to measure the current state of affairs as a part of the life-cycle dynamic and the project plan. Is the project team more or less on target? Are the critical variables shifting? Does it matter? What does performances to date tell us about future performances up to project closure? And such questions often come down to versions of the enquiry, 'Have you done what you promised to do?'.

By their nature, monitoring systems tend to be *after* the fact. If they can deal with indicative or statistical information, they can suggest future behaviours. On design projects, any *predictive* dimension of the data gathered is principally mediated by experience and judgmental appraisal. However, cumulative performance data is often used to indicate whether or not team performances are on target and, if not, what the deviation tells us about future performances (on the assumption nothing changes). For example, time slippage at any point in the project can be recorded as a deviation from what it should be; this might enable future goal achievement to be predicted. Translated into a cause for complaint, we have to assume the project plan was realistic (which, of course, it might not have been).

2 **Global and Local Monitoring.** Monitoring techniques on architectural projects are of two kinds: a *global* overview; and a more *local, itemised* review. These take place at the level of the project as a whole, at an intermediate, inter-disciplinary / agency level, and within the specific agencies involved with the project (such as the architect's practice). Each field of review concerns itself with similar factors: costs, durations, and - to use a term that has become all-embracing - 'quality'. To some extent, managers within each field will share interests vertically and laterally. This is especially evident at the mid-level.

• Global monitoring
Sponsor or executive project management perspective.

    Typical measures:
    • Earned value analysis.
    • Start / finish dates, meeting milestones, especially completion; progress with regard to critical success
    factors.

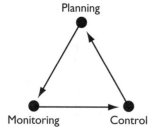

Planning

Monitoring   Control

Plan

Schedule

Act

Monitor status

Analyse data

Predict performances and outcomes

Control efforts

Plan

• Performance features of the deliverable. This is likely to include consultations with the staff
concerned, end-users, etc.,

• Inter-disciplinary / agency monitoring

Monitoring between disciplines and agencies is overwhelmingly concerned with synchronisation and co-ordination, and hand-overs of completed information packages (later, parts of the building).

> *Typical measures:*
> • Reporting against cost plans.
> • Meeting milestones; % complete.
> • Co-ordination of design content as an aspect of
> performance.

• Internal agency monitoring

(From our perspective, the architectural practice.) Although, in an overall project context, we are now at a local level, a practice will (because of its legal, organisational, and disciplinary independence) also effect 'global' to 'local' measures.

> *Typical measures:*
> • Fee expended / remaining; team resourcing
> • Time sheets; % complete / time remaining to complete; milestones met,
> especially as information completion.
> • Design reviews / audits.

3 Time for Sale. It should go without saying that measures and audits have to be undertaken in a timely fashion, analysed quickly and acted upon immediately, if necessary. However, there is no implied need to data gather for the sake of it. Some form of prioritisation is important. Calender regularity is arguably meaningless and weekly reports can swamp managers with meaningless statistics. Reporting relative to critical factors and *goal achievement* (milestones) is more pertinent. And, when it comes to control, it is worth bearing in mind Deming's advice: the drivers of poor performances have to be identified, but system tampering can often be counterproductive: there is a need to differentiate between normal variations in system performances, between special and common causes.

Apart from qualitative measures concerning design content and other measures which relate the design to the project's performative, budgetary and temporal criteria, the principal measure a practice must address concerns its own resource expenditures relative to its fee income. This is measured temporally, the weekly *time sheet* being the single most important document a practice produces. It tells managers how resources are being expended and it can be easily translated into a cost sum, enabling expenditures to be placed into the same language as what keeps a practice alive: its fee income. In effect, architects sell and manage time. Their talent and expertise is the content of this trade in time.

If fee expenditure in the sense of profit and loss is an aspect of practice management, then the agency's project management perspective is fee expenditure related to job progress and the quality of its content. The point at issue is simple: at any point in time, is the team moving toward its target (i.e. the targeted milestone) or away from it? How much of the work content is complete (i.e. the percentage completed)? How much is left to achieve (i.e. the percentage remaining to be done or time required to complete)? These two key measures of progress - what is complete and how much there is to do - might not add up. Presuming individuals have agreed to the milestone plan and 'bought into' it, *they* should be the ones reporting progress. But will they do it properly? Will they even do it honestly? (See page 84).

And then there is the quality issue: is the content of construction packages complete, consistent, and acceptable? (Asking if it 'conforms to requirement' is a familiar advocation, but it is a limited and negative concept unlikely to motivate any decent professional. Conformance is important, but quality is far more than that.)

Judging Deviations

The concept of critical success factors (or variables) appears to come from Dr Genichi Taguchi who developed the concept of the 'Taguchi Loss function' and won the 1960 Deming's Prize for his work on specifications in production. His theory states that a statistical deviation from the ideal causes a loss in quality and economy. However, not all system deviations are equal, some having more loss impact than others, independently of the degree of deviation. Some deviations were critical and attention should initially be given to these because they had the greatest impact on quality. The differentiation is important to project control.

The Humble Time Sheet

Every practice knows the problem: why haven't they all been handed in? Why aren't they in on time? Why are there errors and inconsistencies? Late and inaccurate information can be useless.

On the side of those individuals completing time sheets other issues arise: the practice pays me for a 37.5 hour week so why should I put down the extra hours worked? The practice doesn't pay me for them. It's overheads are built into the 37.5 equation. If they are charging on an hourly basis its clear profit to them and nothing to me. And if the unpaid hours go down, I'm criticised for over-spending or not being efficient. And so on.

Practices who don't analyse jobs and do post-mortems have little interest in learning from feedback so they don't need to know a package of information required all those extra hours over and above the 37.5 in order to be completed. Practices who want to learn will want all those hours worked recorded on the time sheets. However, whilst reporting overtime in terms of a charge against the job is reasonable from the point of view of a need to give feedback to individuals on their actual performance, it is a cheat when costs are charged against a project when they are, in truth, illusory. Such practises are disillusioning and alienating. At best, they are a hangover from the days when computers weren't available.

The flip side of this issue is reporting hours against a job when the individual concerned was actually doing something else. Sometimes employees feel the necessity to do this, even when bosses explicitly encourage them to spend a certain amount of time on non-fee paying activities (such as further professional development, seminars, etc.); this is another sign of distrust. Employees know that maximising fee-paying utilisation is important to a practice, especially in today's competitive climate. They sometimes read the time sheet as as a Taylorist device. Nothing could be more alienating to the motivated professional.

The answer to such problems includes the need for education, consultation, openness, honesty and shared rewards. Consultation begins with planning and the commitments an individual agrees to. Honesty must be two-way. Openness underscores and tests trust. Shared rewards are a kind of social justice within the practice. Every form of practice culture can operate with these criteria and standards in place. The humble time sheet - the basis of practice bureaucracy - can also serve as an important feature of a strong practice culture.

The typical time sheet is very simple: a matrix of projects and other time categories against days of the week. A typical format might be something like the one below (categories can vary). Time sheets provide a measure of utilisation. This has two dimensions: fee earning and non-fee earning (vacation, sickness and working on jobs that have over-run their fees). And, given, the hours many architects work, utilisation can reach well over 100%.

Acceptable utilisation will vary with individuals and their role or position in the practice hierarchy. Partners and directors will be normally expected to have relatively low fee-earning utilisations which reflect time spent on marketing and practice administration. Ordinary designers will have a relatively high target (e.g. 90-100% or even more) and middle range staff will be inbetween. Support and admin staff can also have their available time allocated in a similar way, but this is a matter of practice policy.

Notional time sheet			Week beginning							
		Job No.	Mon	Tues	Wed	Thurs	Fri	Sat	Sun	*Total*
Chargeable Time	Job X									
	Job Y									
	Job Z									
	Admin									
Non-chargeable Time	*Vacation*									
	Prof. devel.									
	Sickness									
	Time off									
	(in Lieu)									
	Totals									
Note: categories are notional									*Total*	

The available time calculation is simple, being the product of :

- *the number of working weeks in the year, allowing for 2/3 wks vacations, 1wk anticipated sickness and 1wk national holidays - typically 47/48.*
- *the number of hours expected to be worked each week - typically 35/45 (the latter being a true figure rather than the more politically correct 35).*
- *allowances for professional development, marketing, admin, etc.*
Note: software is available to assist in such calculations e.g. C•A•T, and Chronos, the latter having an architectural bias.

Utilisation - *i.e. the measure of fee-paying hours as a percentage of those available (or contracted) - is a measure of efficiency, but it is not a measure of productivity (or effectiveness, except in terms of fee expenditure). In this sense, it is one-dimensional. How is the manager to know that the fee-paying hours worked were employed productively and effectively, and were producing quality work? Auditing utilisation has to go along with auditing progress and content.*

Earned Value Analyses

A common cost method of project monitoring is the measure of 'earned value'. This is based upon two pieces of information:

• An expenditure / time-line profile. This is usually in a classic 'S' form and can be derived from a WBS and costings of the tasks to be undertaken.
• Measures of progress such as 'work completed' (alternatively, 'work to complete' or 'time to complete').

With these two sets of information comparisons can be made between the plan and actual performances. This generates five acronyms (two of which concern time, and three concerning budgets) and four possible variances:

• STWP - scheduled time work performed.
• ATWP - actual time used to perform the work.
The difference between these two is the time variance.
• BCWP - the budget cost to perform all the work.
• ACWP - the actual costs.
• BCWS - the budget cost of work scheduled.
The difference between these two generates a cost variance.
In addition, the difference between BCWP and BCWS generates the schedule variance.
Another variance would be the difference between the BCWS (what should have been spent to date) and the ACWP (actual cost incurred to date). This has been described as the resource flow variance.

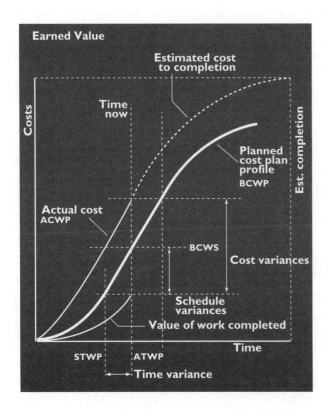

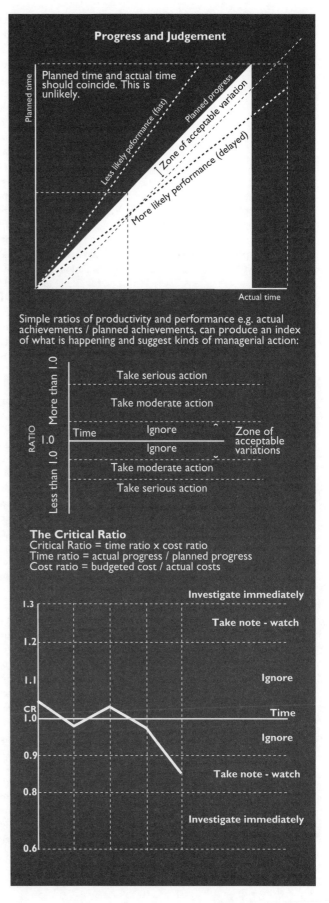

Progress and Judgement

Planned time and actual time should coincide. This is unlikely.

Simple ratios of productivity and performance e.g. actual achievements / planned achievements, can produce an index of what is happening and suggest kinds of managerial action:

The Critical Ratio
Critical Ratio = time ratio x cost ratio
Time ratio = actual progress / planned progress
Cost ratio = budgeted cost / actual costs

4 **Ratios.** Project *plans* are based upon an assessment of what is being undertaken: the scope, risks, critical factors, required progress, and the rest. They embrace arrangements for who will do what, how long it will take and, especially, some programmatic (or orchestrative) content. *Monitoring* and analysis give the necessary feedback on actual performances. *Control* will cope with deviance and any corrective actions called for as a response to change and arising contingencies. But is it that mechanical? Where does judgement come in?

Measures can assist judgement. On page 85 are diagrams illustrating the heuristic concept of *Simple Ratios* linking actual achievements to planned achievements. There will be variation. The question is, when is it worth doing something about the variation? Are variances significant? Are trends acceptable?

The diagram is self-explanatory. A key point is the creation of what is, in effect, a buffer zone of acceptable deviation. But it must be noted that it is still premised upon the validity of the original plan, of the validity and pertinence of the measures taken, and of when a measure of critical ratio becomes a matter of concern.

Another variation on this theme is a *Critical Ratio* which comments upon the crucial issue of costs as well as progress. It is a way of assessing the overall performance variation of a whole project or a set of tasks and is made up of two other ratios: one for *actual to planned progress*; and the other for *planned cost to budgeted cost*. The need for the critical ratio to be built-up from two other ratios is because poor performance, for example, might be off-set by lower costs.

A critical ratio of less than one is a cause for concern; a ratio of more than one indicates a healthy situation. (Once again, however, the ratios depend upon the truth and meaningfulness of the measures. The healthy ratio could result from poor measures or distortions.)

Simple Ratio One =
Actual progress : Planned Progress

Simple Ratio Two =
Planned Cost : Actual Cost

Critical Ratio =
Simple Ratio One x Simple Ratio Two

The Project
Plan

How?

Real team
performances

Those Tricky Architects

IBM project managers have been known to express a belief that the typical architectural firm can only be used three times. The first project involves the company in a lot of training, getting the architects into (for Godsake!) a managerial way of thinking. In the second project, founded upon sound basis, everything would probably go smoothly - the architects knew what was expected of them. A third project, however, would have the project managers less happy once again: the architects now knew the game and were quite capable of manipulating the situation away from an entirely instrumental agenda. They couldn't be used again. Lesson: architects can have it both ways.

5 **The Question of How?** Between a project plan and the monitoring that must take place lies the simple reality of team performances. It's all very well to put forward a scheme and lay down a plan, but managers - agency managers in particular - confront the issue of *how* to ensure appropriate and adequate actions that will produce success. Monitoring and analysis won't do it. And control is conventionally interpreted as a kind of programmed steermanship. Project management is sometimes adopted as a panacea when, in fact, it focuses an enormous amount of its concerns on planning, and monitoring and controlling against that plan. The real concern - content and economic, effective progress - remains shrouded in a managerial fog. Anyone can plan, monitor and steer. Can they also ensure an adequacy of content? Whilst an executive project manager can claim this is not his or her business (perhaps implying content is simply a matter of applied expertise and delivery), the project manager within an architectural practice has no choice but to marry the planning / monitoring / control triad with soft issues such as team motivation and leadership, practice culture, etc. For the latter, failure to conform to the plan cannot be met by simply bleating about or evoking a command requiring corrective action - it is entirely bound up with the mundane efforts which are not producing results and must be reformed. This is a realm of interpersonal factors in which corrective negatives have a limited effect. If a team is to get to its project goals successfully, then monitoring and control have to be components of a positive managerial setting.

Control has to be directed toward team members with strategic responsibility. Four aspects of such control have to be considered:

1. *Getting the key figures within the agency* to make a genuine commitment (not to play a passing role and pass responsibility on to a middle manager without sufficient authority to cope with fundamental problems).

2. *Getting the team as a whole to commit* or 'buy into' the project plan - they then become 'partners' in the enterprise, making a commitment and, it is hoped, taking responsibility. This is project management permeating down the layers to every level.

3. *Getting the team to contribute to and stick with the project plan* i.e. to use it as a

goal-oriented path toward principal project goals. This will include a co-operative spirit.

4. *Getting the team to respond to corrective directions* from managers and (more importantly), from its own awareness of what is going on, to initiate self-corrective actions.

These challenges are significantly facilitated if all members of the team are motivated participants of a project culture that it is the project manager's job to nurture. (This holds true at the agency level and should also be true at the level of the project as a whole, across disparate agencies, but the executive manager clearly has limited penetrative capability which stops short at the agencies themselves.) This presumes consistent team-playing - a project feature that is sometimes lacking among architects and similar professionals enculturalised into autonomous posturing.

Within the project culture there has to be a shared belief in the need for monitoring, audits, reviews of reports and subsequent controlling actions. Monitoring has to be on a regular, consistent and meaningful basis. A proforma spreadsheet might be used, one which not only indicates progress and work to be completed, but also task delays and their causes. This proforma might also include the prime schedule, so that actual progress can be compared with the plan. The aim is not to report on everything, but to highlight deviations from the plan.

The key factors such a spreadsheet should list (apart from the usual information such as project, date, milestone reference, person taking responsibility for completion, report date, etc.) might include the following:

- *Work estimated as complete* (percentage complete or man-days), for sets of tasks, on the relevant result path and with regard to appropriate milestone. The alternative is *Work remaining to be done*. Using both might underscore any over-optimism.

- Resulting estimated completion dates of the tasks.

- Quality acceptance at this point in time, as yes /no.

- Responsibility for the task (whether the responsibility plan is being kept to).

- Effects upon the milestone plan (easily observable if the proforma also includes the allocation in the plan for these tasks).

- Simple description of any problems, causes, possible consequences and suggested action (listed separately).

Reports will be of two kinds: those dealing with sets of related tasks leading to a particular milestone; and somewhat simpler, more strategic reports dealing with sets of milestones. If such information is properly considered and acted upon, the very ritual of report completion will itself assist in promoting managerial thinking, control and efforts to stick to the plan.

6 **All Change.** Another key aspect of monitoring and control deals with change. It is inevitable, if only as refinement of the plan, but it also arises in other ways. After the scheme design gateway, change can be progressively disruptive and has to be controlled. Three kinds of change stand out:

1. *Change arising out of development work* which has no impact upon deliverable parameters (more like the expected rolling wave of development). Whilst this is allowable from a global, executive viewpoint, local project management - within the architectural agency, for example - might have a different perspective (e.g. about the impact on resourcing and fee expenditure).

Barriers

Harnessing and realising potential might be the goals of design management, but change, error and rework are three fundamental barriers to success and symptoms of difficulty. How does the manager anticipate possible difficulties and obviate their effects when they arise?

Change Control:

Controlling change is partly about contingency, partly about choices, and partly about prevention and impact containment when the reference point is the project goal and its success criteria.

- *What was anticipated*
- *What should have been anticipated.*
- *What can't be anticipated.*

- *What is acceptable*
- *What is unacceptable.*
- *What there is no choice about*

2. *Change which requires adjustment* (for example, to the schedule and/or budget) and trade-offs, but can be contained within major project parameters. This is a common product of collaboration, and sometimes of client changes.

3. *Change whose impact cannot be contained* and must be addressed in terms of a major project reassessment affecting all three key parameters of programme, costs and design content.

A particular difficulty arises when the designer *proactively* sees way to improve the product. In principle, any significant reconsideration of the proposal will be disruptive; however, if it is early enough in the project, it can not only be tolerated, but might be accepted as an indicative feature of a creativity (or, alternatively, inability to get it right first time).

Another kind of change is *reactive* and contingent on circumstances arising. As a project develops, this will become the only kind of acceptable change. However, contingent change resulting from a failure to foresee something, particularly design development content, might be seen as a lack of professional competence. A scheme should bear within it the seeds of its own success; difficulties should not become strategic - this is what 'projecting' is all about.

Project managers attempt to formally control both these forms of change with what is called a *change control system* or a *configuration management system*. The point is to require all proposed changes to what has already been agreed to be documented and submitted for approval before implementation. This, in itself, prevents trivial change. It also enables the project manager to properly assess the benefit and impact of the change on costs and schedule. The key point, however, is that any form of change to the project plan is a hassle factor after that plan has been formulated in order to get through the scheme sign-off gateway.

7 **Typical Control Options.** Faced with difficulties which monitoring might have identified, a manager attempting to exercise control and bring the project back 'in line' might consider four options:

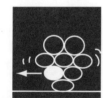

1. *Rearranging the workload content* so that a milestone target can be met - a kind of re-focusing as well as a rearrangement, perhaps by identifying bottlenecks and similar critical areas causing the difficulties.

2. *Adding to the resources*, although this might entail added managerial overhead, added costs, and the problem of delegation and teaching the new members of that team. Alternatives include encouraging overtime and a reassessment of team membership so that shuffling or replacement might be used to tune the critical area of work.

3. *Adjusting the milestone date* as an acceptance of delay (although this might feel like failure and also necessitate a reassessment of the whole project plan).

4. *Adjusting the work content* (which almost invariably means curtailment) and accepting this might mean a lowering of ambitions (another kind of compromise and possible perception as a failure).

Difficulties will normally arise as special causes (staff illness, client changes, and similar unexpected contingencies, for example) and the above tactics described will usually suffice. However, common causes might be at the root of the problem i.e. cultural issues which engender chronic difficulty. It might be revealed that staff simply aren't competent enough or have the wrong skills; seniors might be consistently failing to give the proper support and leadership; specialist capabilities such as specification writing might prove to be inadequate; internal communications might break down; poor relationships might turn into outright conflict, etc.

In most instances, there will be little choice but to live with such common (or cultural) causes and to deal with them 'on the run'. From the view of a practice running a number of jobs there is no alternative but to refine its culture in this way. It has to be underscored, however, that cultures do not change from the bottom up. Reforms attempted from the lower and middle levels of an organisation must, at least, have tacit senior level acceptance, if not explicit support. Partners and Directors are often so busy simply doing things and cultivating clients that they lose touch with the ways in which their behaviours, values and example affect the culture and performances of the organisation as a whole. Even when outsiders (such as consultants) are brought in to identify issues, the will and ability to act upon advice is sometimes lacking. (The seniors might even delegate change to middle management whilst they get on with seeking new jobs, etc., thus defeating initiatives before they have even begun.)

The same rationale applies within a specific project. It is also a classic problem in the literature dealing with the relationships between a project leader and a sponsor organisation - a common problem of the lack of authority which plagues some project managers in business and industry.

Finally, it has to be noted that attempts at control are subject to the law of diminishing returns (the effort / costs needed increase exponentially). It is not only complexity which drives up managerial overhead of a project, but also attempts to exercise a huge degree of control (perhaps including the measurement of unimportant features; a rigid emphasis upon procedures, possibly on the wrong things; adopting the 'if it can't be measured, it can't be managed' philosophy; etc.). Tight control cannot be justified as an end in itself unless we can presume the project plan is synoptic in its completeness and thoroughness. This is never likely to be the case. Control is therefore a form of balancing, a dynamic, continually adjusting influence which never seeks to over-exercise itself (to dampen all creativity into the mechanical implementation of technical expertise) and must be capable of trade-offs between principal aspects of the project content.

Change and Real Change

Do individuals change? Do cultures change? Of course they do, but how? What are the drivers of behavioural adaptation and learning? Special causes and common causes are similar to contingent adaptive change and deep behavioural change. Anyone can change their behaviour for a few weeks, but who can produce behavioural change of a structural nature? It's the same with organisations - it is the leaders who have the salience, power and influence to produce deep change; it can't happen from the bottom up.

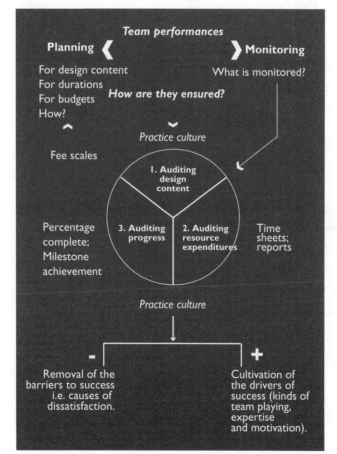

From Planning to monitoring

The absence of adequate planning, monitoring and control will almost certainly ensure project failure. But their presence will not ensure success. This paradox - that removing negatives is not the same as putting positives in place - is crucial to design and project management.

Planning without a monitoring of design content, resource expenditures (within the design and on fees), progress, changes, etc., is meaningless. But between what is planned and what is monitored lies actual team performances. How are these to be ensured? How are they motivated, coordinated, synchronised? Planning will not achieve this, although it might be of assistance. Monitoring is neutral. And controlling tends to be more concerned with push rather than pull.

Team performance is a *cultural issue* - at both the project level embracing many agencies, and within an individual agency.

A schematic proforma for reporting progress.

This might be co-ordinated with other reports and placed on a computerised spreadsheet to provide an overall view. If the project is simple, the report will be directly onto machine. The objective is to quickly highlight difficulties and exceptions to the plan. Forms should be designed to suit the practice culture and the project. Reports can be for major groups of tasks or by result path, individual task, etc., as appropriate. They should always be simple, noting only exceptions to the project plan.

Basic information:

Client
Project
Date
Partner / Director / Associate in charge
Person responsible for form completion
Package reference and description e.g. 2.3.3 interior fitout
(can be broken down by sub-group, as required)
Referent milestones (i.e. between X and Y)

Team
X = responsible for packages set
C = co-ordinates sub-package
T = executes the work
ETC.

Task or equivalent	work completed	work to complete	estimated completion date	Quality acceptance Y / N	Special problems Y / N	Allowance in schedule	Frederick Smith	Joseph Smith	Janette Smith	Mark Smith	ETC.
raised floor	7 mandays	9 mandays	June 3rd		Y	14 mandays	X		C	T	
carpets	5 mandays	0 mandays	June 10th	Y		6 mandays	X		C	T	
sus. ceilings							X			C/T	T
partitions							X	C/T			T
lighting							X				T
furniture							X	C			
user mock-up							X	C			
lighting							X			C	
ETC.											

Supporting information:

Package (or task) :   E.G. raised floor (or reference)

　　Problem   E.G. Delay to client deciding void depth

　　Cause   E.G. IT department reporting final specification

　　Consequence   E.G. Delay to finalising budget prices from possible sub-contractors

　　Possible action   E.G. Raise issue with client; report critical date.

Package (or task)

　　Problem
　　Cause
　　Consequence
　　Possible action

Project manager's comments

Disparate perspectives

I have outlined two approaches to planning: *bottom-up* and *top-down*. The former aspires to the ideal that all relevant information concerning necessary and anticipated activities is synoptically available and only has to be rationally organised. The top-down method seeks a short-hand, works heuristically and requires skill in discerning the most crucial issues to be dealt with, and an ability to differentiate between significant and meaningful information, and mere data. Both approaches have their place in project work, but the former has an established place in the mythology of how planning should be done and the latter is the reality of how it is done. The basis of this disparity of viewpoint has been touched upon - partly in terms of a confusion between kinds of artistry and competence, and partly in terms of the dominance of an instrumental rationale among managers.

These differences are evident in another guise: as *disparate assessments of why projects go wrong* - only in this case, there is a structural basis to the different perspectives, one which appears to be dependent upon position and role.

The common enthusiasm for formally planned actions enjoyed by *supervising* managers is not always shared by the *executors* of planning. The comparative observer thinks in the systems terms which can be adopted by an objective observer; the more active agent thinks hermeneutically i.e. from the relatively subjective and intuitive viewpoint of someone on the inside.

These disparities and their implications were noted in research into criteria for controlling projects (23) in which project managers cited and ranked 15 significant problem areas effecting poor project performance. Interestingly, their supervising managers had a quite different ranking of the same issues.

The project managers cited the following (numbers in brackets refer to the supervisor's ranking; only the first five are offered, but the disparity runs through the fifteen issues):

- Customer and management changes (4)
- Technical complexities (10)
- Unrealistic project plans ((2)
- Staffing problems (9)
- Inability to detect problems early (7)

Their general management supervisors gave a different ranking (numbers in brackets refer to the project managers' rating):

- Insufficient front-end planning (10)
- Unrealistic project plans (3)
- Underestimated project scope (8)
- Customer and management changes (1)
- Insufficient contingency planning (14)

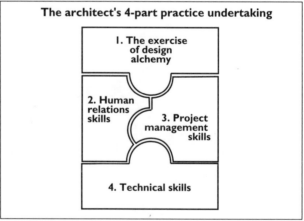

The architect's 4-part practice undertaking

1. The exercise of design alchemy

2. Human relations skills

3. Project management skills

4. Technical skills

Clearly, means/ends values and the notion of the project vehicle as a purely instrumental device were high on the supervisor's mind. He or she was concerned with what should have been done to obviate problems. They perceived change as having a negative affect only when the project was inadequately organised and managed. Problems such as sinking team spirit (ranked at 14), lack of commitment from personnel (12), priority shifts (11), and staffing problems (9), were low on their list of acceptable excuses.

2 **Subtle Causes.** The reasons for poor performance cited by project managers in the study were argued by the managers themselves (the subordinates) to actually be the product of more subtle issues. They suggested that, whilst insufficient front-end planning might have been a difficulty, the real culprit lay elsewhere. The researchers concluded that, *"Most of the problems . . . relate to the manager's ability to foster a work environment conducive to multidisciplinary teamwork, rich in professionally stimulating and interesting activities, involvement, and mutual trust."* These other, more subtle, factors were grouped by the researchers into 5 groups:

1. Problems with organising the project team
2. Weak project leadership
3. Communications problems
4. Conflict and confusion
5. Insufficient upper management involvement

These appeared to strongly correlate with a *poor* perception of performance; they are all to be avoided. The stronger and more frequently they were experienced, the lower was the superior manager's appraisal of the project manager regarding overall on-time and on-budget performance. This conclusion resulted in a list of *barriers* to high project performance:

- Team organisation and staffing problems.
- Work perceived as not important, challenging, or having growth potential.
- Little team and management involvement during planning.
- Conflict, confusion, power struggle.
- Lack of commitment by team and management.
- Poor project definition.
- Difficulty in understanding and working across organisational interfaces.
- Weak project leadership.
- Measurability problems.
- Changes, contingencies and priority problems.
- Poor communication, management involvement and support.

These problems have to be overcome by effective leadership and control. Suggested tactics include the following:

- *Attract and hold quality people*

- *Work out a detailed project plan, but involve key personnel, thus helping them to identify with the project.*

- *Define measurable milestones for team participants.*

- *Reach agreement on the plan with the project team and the customer/sponsor.*
    Break the work into phases and sub-phases.
    Define objectives, with full specifications, etc.
    Define specific results, performances, etc.
    Measure performances and achievements.
    Maintain senior management endorsement.

- *Obtain commitment from the project team members*
    Involve them. Use 'sign-on' procedures.
    Avoid threats, power struggles, etc.
    Provide an atmosphere of trust.
    Confront problems.
    Provide interesting and rewarding work.
    Provide proper leadership in every way.
    Show personal drive and involvement.
    Demonstrate acknowledgement and support.

- *Detect problems early.*
    - Institute regular reviews.
    - Allocate sign-off authority.
    - Define and implement a proper tracking.
    - Maintain good communications.
    - Ensure multi-agency involvement throughout the project.

- *Establish a controlling authority for each work package*

Architects who aspire to a better project management image have to simultaneously demonstrate managerial capability as well as the expert and 'alchemical' talents for which they have been employed. This results in a four-part equation: they must be seen to exercise project management skills; they must address the subtle issues rooted in human relations issues (as outlined above); and they must deliver the technical design expertise as well as the problem-finding and resolving 'alchemy' which is the legitimation of their design service.

Ways of Seeing

Professionals have a socio-economic role as experts: those who 'know better'. At the very least, they are expected to possess technical forms of expertise pertinent to their services. However, there appears to be something 'structural' in the relative perceptions of those involved - structural in the sense that it reappears in a similar form at different levels within project teams.

The problems perceived by senior management:	The subtle problems perceived by PM's:
• Insufficient front-end planning.	• Problems with organising the project team.
• Unrealistic project plans.	• Weak project leadership.
• Underestimated project scope.	• Communications problems.
• Customer and management changes.	• Conflict and confusion.
• Insufficient contingency planning.	• Insufficient upper management involvement.

Those in a supervisory, commissioning or similar role have a view of what causes poor performance which is somewhat at odds with those subordinates actually undertaking the work and delivering the service. The former emphasise kinds of technical rationality and expertise as a taken-for-granted, expected minimum. meanwhile, the latter are sometimes uncomfortably aware that life is not that simple and that the delivery of technical forms of expertise is often dependent upon elusive, vague and intractable issues e.g. people and their motivations, character, consistencies, etc.

Technical problems are fundamental to most design projects. However, 'technical' problems of a mundane or managerial nature can be very irritating. ("They couldn't organise a piss-up in a brewery! They do this sort of work all the time - why can't they even get the basics right?", or "What do they teach students these days - she hasn't the faintest idea about technical standards and regulations! And she has any conception of putting a package together and delivering it on time. I spend all my time holding her hand - I may as well do the work myself.") It follows that everyone has to be aware of this 'structural' characteristic of project work and what technical but strategic aspects of their work should be uncontentious. The executive project manager often met by the architectural agency will not expect to face incompetence in anticipatory planning, in resourcing and having the right kind of staff, in solving technical problems and so on. Within that agency, similar considerations will effect themselves. Support staff, for example (or anyone who plays such a role) will be expected to provide effective support in the sense of studio 'hygiene' (that which supports life and makes it viable). Much of this discussion is about removing potential causes of dissatisfaction so that the drivers of potential success can effect themselves without frustration.

Props and pitfalls

If the factors perceived to be associated with failure must be absent from a project, those perceived to be associated with success must be present (Baker et al., 1974) (25). However, even if they are necessary, in themselves, they do not guarantee success. The seven most important factors affecting perceived success concern:

1. *Co-ordination and relations.*
Team spirit, unity, human relations skills, enthusiasms, participation, etc. This factor is about four times as important as the seventh factor and about 50% more important than the second factor.

2. *Success criteria and salience.*
The importance of budget, schedule and technical performance criteria to parent, client and project manager.

3. *Initial over-optimism and conceptual difficulties* (negative impact).

4. *Adequacy of project structure and control.*

5. *Competitive and budgetary pressures* (negative impact).

6. *Project uniqueness, importance, and public exposure.*

7. *Internal capabilities build-up.*

It is worth noting that the seminal research by Baker et al., from which this list is taken, suggests that the variables associated with perceived *failure* do not include poor cost and schedule overruns. Those significant factors associated with perceived *success* also do not include good cost and schedule control. Most of the factors associated with perceived success and failure concerned poor coordination and human relations.

Much of this surprising conclusion, running against the grain of conventional wisdom and most project management ideology, is put down to hindsight, when schedule delays and cost overruns seem comparatively unimportant, particularly in the face of perceived satisfaction and good personal relations. Good cost and schedule performances were correlated with success, but were not among the most significant factors. Meeting technical requirements in the context of all-round good relations and perceived satisfactions was the basis of judging a project successful. Negatives associated with failure (as above) must be absent and other factors associated with success must be present.

The research team's conclusions are worth summarising:

• Project success cannot be adequately defined as completing a project on schedule; staying within budget; and meeting technical performance specifications.

• Perceived success can best be defined as meeting technical specifications and/or the mission to be performed; and attaining high levels of satisfaction from everyone involved.

• Technical performance is integrally associated with perceived success. Cost and schedule are less intimately associated with perceived success.

• Perceived personal and professional satisfactions are all important for perceived success. Good cost and schedule control mean little if the end result is technically lacking.

Arguing for Process

Getting it right and avoiding getting it wrong are the two sides of the same coin, but they aren't opposites. Project management effort (from executive to personal) has to strive on both fronts. Professional expertise and talent are not enough; a managerial content is important to project success. Teamwork is crucial, but this comes down to individuals making the effort and working well together. The successful outcome results from a successful process.

• After technical performance and satisfactions, effective co-ordination and good human relations patterns are the most important contributors to perceived success.

• Project managers have a significant level of control over the crucial factors involved in the perception of success, even under otherwise adverse circumstances. They can help achieve effective co-ordination and good relations, a salience of success criteria, and group consensus; they can make certain there is adequate project structure and control systems; they can avoid over-optimism, help with conceptual problems, building up resources, avoiding budgetary and scheduling pressures, etc. (26)

2 **Specific pitfalls.** Managing projects almost inevitably involves the anticipation of pitfalls. The following is adapted from various sources and embodies worthwhile advice on what to watch out for. (24) The list is by no means exhaustive.

Pitfalls at inception
• The project is poorly defined:
  • The project plans are not aligned with the sponsor's business plans.
  • The goals for the project are imprecise, sometimes because of a rush to possible solutions.
  • Scope limitations are not met, resulting in the wrong problems being addressed.
  • The principles and policies which define the climate of project work are not defined (responsibilities, resources, co-ordination, tools and methods to be used, etc.).
• There is insufficient support for the project:
• The project is underfunded or under-programmed.

Pitfalls in planning
• The planning level is too uniform resulting, for example, in too little detail at the operational (task) level and too much at the managerial (administrative) level.
• The planning tool is made unwieldy e.g. complex networks and schedules i.e. over-structuring.
• Complexity is underestimated e.g. because this is a new type of project.
• The planning range is psychologically unsound, focusing upon the end deadline and neglecting more immediate deadlines. The project manager needs to set short-horizon targets (goals which are manageable and achievable) for work completion.
• The planning method discourages creativity by being autocratic, avoiding democratic contributions from those involved in the tasks. There is a lack of team involvement in decision-making.
• The planning of time and cost are over-optimistic and therefore unrealistic e.g. they are cut back arbitrarily and unrealistically; there is insufficient experience against which to judge their content.
• The planning of resources overestimates their competence and availability.
• The plan omits activities.
• The project calender ignores lost time (illness, vacations, etc.).

Pitfalls in organising and co-ordinating
• Different agencies on the project are not welded into one team.
• The distribution of responsibility is unclear - this is particularly a problem in matrix organisations (where a project member will have two bosses e.g. the PM and a functional-line boss or one within a separate agency).
• The project has the wrong project manager
• The project manager's responsibilities and authority are unclear.
• The executive project manager over multiple agencies fails to champion good management within each one (attempting project management at the project level if it is not present within each agency will lead to difficulties).

Satisfied and Dissatisfied

It has to be remembered that the avoidance of dissatisfaction does not equal the perception or experience of satisfaction. The absence of dissatisfaction simply produces 'no dissatisfaction', not its opposite, satisfaction. In project management, many variables associated with success must be present and many variables associated with failure must be absent. However, presence or absence, in itself, is insufficient. For example, poor co-ordination and human relations - two crucial factors - must be replaced by sound coordination and human relations. This will eliminate failure but will not ensure success. For the latter, other factors - such as tight controls and commitments to them - must be in place.

Pitfalls in monitoring and controlling

• Lack of understanding of the purpose of control and confusion between monitoring and real control.
• Lack of integration between progress reports and the plan. The former should be written on the basis of the latter.
• Over control, which becomes an end in itself.
• Too much informality and lack of *formal* communications between the PM and team members.
• Inevitable changes to the plan or specification are uncontrolled, leading to a spiral of planning and replanning, cost overruns, etc.
• The PM has responsibility but little authority. It is dangerous to rely on personality (although charisma rather than position power might be a key source of authority).
• Poor co-ordination with the client, within the overall team, etc.
• Inability to freeze the design early enough.
• Inability to terminate the project properly.

Pitfalls in implementation

• The complexity of co-ordinating a variety of resources is underestimated.
• Activities are started out of turn, resulting in repeat work.
• Work is unfinished, sometimes because of an inability to close, sometimes when work is taken over and the new author ends up relearning and reworking.
• Time, cost and quality targets are unbalanced:
    • Team members seek perfection - the problem with professionals!
    • Quality control is inadequate, especially when left to the end of the project (it is no longer a process value and is too late to change).
• Pitfalls concerning human issues:
    • Getting different people to work together (chemistries, disciplinary differences).
    • Getting people to work to the same rules and procedures.
    • Lack of team spirit and sense of mission.
    • Job insecurity within team.
    • User representatives who do not understand the professional experts (and vice versa).
    • Inadequate project manager authority and influence.
    • Inadequate human relations skills within the team, especially with the project manager. Inadequate leadership skills.
    • Lack of *rapport* with the client.

Pitfalls after completion and closure

• Lessons are not learned. Experience is not candidly examined, recorded, and made accessible.
• Lessons learned are not passed on to other project teams, especially project managers and team leaders.

● Part Three:

Managing Costs and Fees

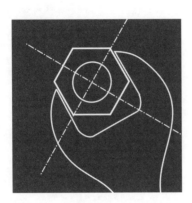

An instrumental approach to project cost management has two dimensions: estimating development costs and targeting product costs. From a practice viewpoint, the former concerns fee management and the latter concerns cost planning the product. These are the two topics in this section.

The aim of the sections on product costing is to set down the principles of cost targeting, as it is called, and to place the conventions of building costing in this context. It could as well have been entitled 'What the Quantity Surveyor Didn't Tell You'.

The aim of the section on managing fees is to outline the underlying principles which can help a practice estimator and planner in an era of deregulation, when formerly mandatory fees are advised with caution in trepidation of government accusations of restrictive practices, and competition, when practices are out to compete on price with one another and with related disciplines seeking to extend their professional jurisdictions. It is intolerant of the art paradigm which still influences many architects, leading them to presume a distinction between 'commercial' practice and other forms of (authentic, culturally oriented) practice. The distinction is illusory. An architect is either in business or out of practice. The basis of that practice is fee income and success depends upon its competent management. The famous few did not acquire helicopters and the like by being timid about remuneration for services rendered.

Change, understanding and risk

I *Risk* is an inherent feature of all project undertakings and has obvious cost implications. At its most basic, risk can be understood as a natural product of the degree of change being contemplated and the extent of *understanding* pervading a situation (see diagram on right). Such change can be *incremental* or *large scale*. Understanding of what is involved can be *low* or *high*. Combinations of the degree of change being contemplated and the level of understanding generate four decision strategies and analytical methods. For example, the best combination is a high level of understanding and a low level of change. This allows a relatively synoptic analytic method that could devolve into a rule-governed mode of decision-making. However, Few undertakings will combine genuine, large scale change and innovation with a high level of understanding. The opportunities are rare, the consequences radical, the uniqueness of the situation mitigates against full understanding and complexity generates unforeseen difficulties. On the other hand, a revolutionary or utopian undertaking might substitute ideological zeal and commitment for understanding and formal analytical method, pushing the undertaking through to success.

Another kind of large scale change is war or the grand opportunity where there is a low level of understanding and a high level of risk; formal analytical method will be necessary, but its efficaciousness will be poorly understood and hardly predictable. Strategies of incremental change combined with either low or high levels of understanding are more common. These allow more formal and predictable decision-making methods to be used. Decision-makers will learn from past strategies and build upon them, incrementally pushing forward on a broad front. They will tend to remedially *move away* from problems and unsatisfactory situations rather than *toward* ideals. Long-term change (which can be radical) will be achieved via a sequence of incremental, remedial moves (Lindblom, 1963 and 1968). This remedial approach is undertaken endlessly, becoming a strategy of 'disjointed incrementalism' i.e. it will take place simultaneously, continuously and disjointedly on many fronts.

Managing Risk

The key to managing risk is to identify it, appraise it, and do something about it. Know it, obviate it, and (if you're risk averse or risk is inappropriate) don't generate it and avoid it.

Since projects are about realising change, they grasp opportunities as well as confront problems - and risk is unavoidable. Risk management and opportunity management are arguably two sides of the same coin, but their motivations and consequences can be quite disparate (the difference between a fear of failing and a fear of not succeeding).

Risk Obviated by Understanding

Projects are about intended change. Change engenders risk. This can only be obviated by understanding. (which, it is presumed, is followed through with planning, monitoring, control, a motivated team and the rest).

Kinds of project risk can be stated in the three dimensions projects are usually considered: financial risk e.g. the project is over budget; temporal risk e.g. the project is finished behind schedule; design related risk e.g. the completed building does not perform as desired. Each of these kinds of risk have to be addressed during the key project stages i.e. pre-scheme; scheme development up to specification issue; and construction.

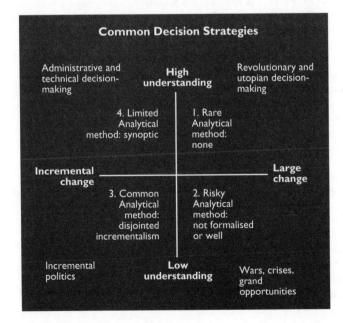

Common Decision Strategies

	High understanding	
Administrative and technical decision-making		Revolutionary and utopian decision-making
	4. Limited Analytical method: synoptic	1. Rare Analytical method: none
Incremental change		**Large change**
	3. Common Analytical method: disjointed incrementalism	2. Risky Analytical method: not formalised or well
Incremental politics	**Low understanding**	Wars, crises, grand opportunities

Profound Knowledge

What is real understanding (or, as Deming would call it, 'profound knowledge')? If you have it, you can anticipate and focus upon critical problem areas and sensitise yourself to particular kinds of risk. You know when feedback tells you a deviance from expected performance is cause for worry or not.

How do you check understanding and ensure its adequacy? You attempt to get right first time, up front, check as you go, but expect difficulties to be revealed by testing and inspection. You put buffer in the planning. You manage the risk.

A Risky Business

Concepts in risk management include the following:

• Scenario Planning
What if . . . ? Then what . . . ?
What could go wrong? What will the outcome be? What can we do? What opportunities are presented?

• Failure Modes and Effects Analysis (FMEA)
What could fail (go wrong)? What effects will failure have? How can set up a weighted ranking of the kinds of possible failure identified? Which of the possible / likely failure modes must be given attention? What can we do about the failures and subsequent effects?

• Hazard Analysis
What are the system hazards and what can be done about them?

• The example of other (similar) projects.

• Critical Path and similar network what if? analyses.

• Experience.

Where large scale change is attempted or is unavoidable, as on the Channel Tunnel project, we see that managers have to seek a high level of understanding if they are to obviate risk. However, in this case, the intrinsic uniqueness and scale of the project set itself at odds with this ambition. Managers confronted a high level of change with what they believed to be a high level of understanding, only to find this was not the case and, consequently, risks were inevitably large. This is not infrequent on large projects, sometimes producing huge cost and programme overruns. The tunnel, for example, was a highly managed project which came in behind programme and at over twice its estimated cost. Similar difficulties have been met in space programmes (NASA), the defence industries, software development, etc.

Because high risk undertakings are sometimes unavoidable, decision-makers must seek means of locating projects in less risky sectors. How can understanding be enhanced? How can large scale change be translated into incremental change? How can the consequences of risk be lessened? How can a dependency upon understanding be reduced? How can radical ambition utilise incremental strategies? (And, inevitably, how can risk be passed on to other parties?) The issue facing policy-makers, managers and designers is how to engineer themselves into low-risk / high success-probability situations. As Peter Drucker has noted, true innovators define and confine risks; they do not have the propensity for risk-taking popularly characterised as the typical innovator. They manage their way to success.

2 In design projects, four considerations are typically involved in minimising risk in order to promote success:

1. *Management* should properly organise, plan, control and lead the project, with the aim of obviating inherent risk, but without this taking the form of an excessive managerial overhead.

2. *Understanding* should be thick and rich, not thin and shallow. This will include intuitional and experiential understanding as well as analytical understanding. Areas of risk have to be anticipated, identified, localised and focused upon. This is where feasibility studies are useful.

3. *Complexity* should be minimised.

4. *Hardware design* should anticipate 'buildability'.

The logic of relating the nature of a project to 'procurement route' options is often neglected, even by the professionals involved. From the perspective of the experienced contractor, Macomber identifies seven kinds of risk (see Augustine, 1989):

1. *Understanding the types and phases of risk* i.e. budget; time; and design-related risk, found within each of the key project stages (pre-scheme; post scheme development; and construction).
2. *Assessing the risks of a particular construction project* (what are the critical success factors dealt with as critical risk factors?). The crucial issue is project complexity (see the comments on this issue in the section on fees and estimating).
3. *Matching risks with in-house capabilities and building a construction team.* An assessment has to be made of the the current and available capabilities for addressing the identified risks e.g. experience, specialists, availability, source, etc. Choosing the right people, together with issues of leadership, control, and coordination, are very important.
4. *Defining a building strategy.* A concentration of high-risk components suggests the need for contractors who are team players and produce results through cooperation. Low risk components suggest the price benefits of competition. There is a big difference between the new hospital wing and a warehouse shed. 'Fit' is important if risk is to be obviated.
5. *Picking the right kind of contract:*

• *Lump sum* (in which the contractor takes the risk and the owner takes none). The price is fixed, but so is the scope of work. Change can be expensive. Bids should be on the basis of full information in order to stay with the logic of this type of contract. It is no way to build unless information is available or complex content has been avoided.

• *Time and materials* (cost of work plus a fee) in which the owner takes all the risk - just the way lawyers and mechanics are commissioned. This form of contract can be appropriate when quality is all important (such clients do exist); when time is limited and extensive overtime is expected (as in shopfitting); or when construction information is incomplete. Trust is all important and the choice of builder should be on the basis of reputation (and some form of 'relational' contract).

• *Guaranteed maximum price* (cost of the work plus a fee, but with shared risk). Up to a pre-determined level, the contractor passes on all costs (and savings) to the owner; after that, all risks are with the builder. This has the benefits of both other types, however there will be a tendency for the bid price to increase. The contractor is being asked to become a team player without being given carte blanche; profit comes from good performance rather than cost-cutting. The choice of builder again involves trust, personal chemistries and the like; establishing the firm can behave professionally, as a consultant, is important.

A *turnkey contract* has the contractor providing financing and all construction services, turning the completed building over to the occupier/purchaser. *Design and build* links designer and builder together, ostensibly fostering cooperation, but at the cost of eliminating traditional checks and balances. Fee-based *construction management* is a form of consultancy.

6. *Choosing the right builder.* The choice should relate to the preferred contract type (see above).

7. *Monitoring the construction.* Again, the content should suit the form of the contract. Lump-sum suggests careful monitoring of what is delivered and installed. Time-and-materials suggests monitoring in order to see that the client's money is not wasted (waste rather than cutting corners is likely to be the issue). Guaranteed maximum price should have the checks built-in, but prudence suggests attention to workmanship and accounting.

Risk cannot be eliminated, but it can be managed.

Choices

Basic procurement route options can be expressed in terms of three modes of contract and the varying inherent risks they carry. Each is appropriate to different project circumstances and client / builder relationships. The degree of complexity, risk of change, adequacy and completeness of information, speed of the programme, experience and trust between the parties involved are typical considerations to be made.

1. Lump Sum Contract (ceiling)

Agreed Price — Actual Cost
Loss / Profit — Final Price — Actual Cost

Diagrams adapted from Augustine (1989)

2. Time and Materials Contract
(Price = cost + % fee)

Agreed Estimate — Actual Cost 8 10 11

Profit to contractor fixed % regardless of cost

3. Guaranteed Maximum Contract
Price (price = cost of work + fixed fee)

Agreed Estimate — Actual Cost 10 11
Loss / Profit

Profit to contractor varies.
Below est. = profit + fee
At est. = fee
Above est. = loss + fee

Costing technique overview

DTC best seller!
Baked Bean Can Architecture
A.N.Author

Perceptions of Value

The imperative to obtain value for money is independent of the budget itself (whether it is high or low). No on wants to waste money or to spend more than is necessary. Nevertheless, increments of cost will return different levels of value (hence the saying that 'the ship was spoilt for a pennyworth of tar'. All cost targeting has to carry within it a judgement that the target is not being set unreasonably low, at a level which will generate risk and increased overhead (for which it is implicitly unwilling to pay). But what is 'more than necessary' (or less than necessary)? What do we mean by necessary? Purely functional and instrumental criteria can be brought to bear, but buildings have a qualitative dimension as well. (When Boeing was developing the 777 it rejected one early design for, among other reasons, the fact that 'it looked wrong'.) On the other hand, measures of quality vary e.g. the stereotypical contemporary London banker still equates minimum quality standards in his or her office with hardwood panelling and leather, leaving other mind-sets to equally enjoy alternative aesthetics; when Lloyds of London was having its 1986 building fitted out it insisted on retaining an old fashioned and very uncomfortable seating design for the underwriters. Cost bench-marks often have to reflect qualitative and cultural criteria as well as performative ones.

One of the more significant concepts in project cost management is derived from US Ministry of Defence practices established in the 1970's in order to reduce cost uncertainty and defence budget overruns. This is called *Design to Cost* (DTC). It focuses upon costs during the early project stages in order to monitor and control final stage procurement costs. This covers cost planning and checking through a number of familiar project stages (27):

• The costs to be considered during the product planning stage (outline of mission,concept of the product, outline specifications,etc).

• Costs considered during the concept design i.e the formulation of main functional areas and the assignment of the cost target to the upper level functions.

• Costs considered during basic and detailed design, when cost planning is taken through to the middle, then the lowest functional levels, then to manufacturing specifications.

• Costs borne during the manufacturing stages assumed to characterise most product development (manufacturing specifications).

The initial task in designing to cost is to set an appropriate general cost target for a project. The intention is to set it relatively low, challenging the design and development team to meet the target. 'Low', of course, can range from very tight to average current practice. The target can be focused upon parts of a product where it is desired to reduce costs. It can also be dealt with in terms of tolerances and settings which relate the target to performance, specification or date of delivery. In any case, it is necessary to give voice to all influences and consider every discipline involved as well as the situational predicament, environmental factors, etc.

In commercial practice, a general cost target might be derived in the following ways:

• *Costs targets based upon known similar products*. This is a cost targets based on a possible selling price (or its equivalent), less profits, possibly based upon complex estimates of future market conditions.

• *Cost targets based on an additive, bottom-up approach* founded upon known technology costs. However this can produce an unrealistically high end figure.

• *A generic approach based upon design properties* such as engine size, building square meterage, cube, etc. This method examines the relationship between key properties of the product and expected costs.

• *Cost targets based upon a mixed approach*, using all the above methods and negotiating between the advocates of each.

Product designers in Japan use heuristic relating old and new properties, or the number of extra product functions. When the indications are very favourable for a product replacement, the new product might be costed at up to 50% of the old; when it is near to the old in design, a rule of thumb nearer to 70% will be adopted.

In addition to this supply perspective on cost targeting, there is the client or user's viewpoint addressing kinds of cost in use (for operation, maintenance, and disposal). These considerations can also be assigned cost targets.

2 **Assigning Costs.** Once a cost target has been established there is an issue of how it can be assigned so that it can be managed during the design and development process. Some typical methods include:

• *Assignment to functional areas* which combine to achieve the product's purpose. This allows the designers as much freedom as possible.
   • First, functions must be defined (e.g. by using a WBS form of family tree).
   • Second, the importance of each function must be evaluated e.g. from customer, design, and manufacturing viewpoints. This might involve weighting the importance of each function (usually to the customer) and breaking up the total cost accordingly.
   • Third, the target cost is divided and assigned to each functional area according to its relative importance.
The method allows designers to group costs relative to choices at higher levels of generality within the WBS.

• *Assignment to blocks of components* - deemed to be more inhibitive to radical innovation and therefore best applied to simple or mature products. The method works as follows:
   • Individual components are grouped into component blocks.
   • The importance of blocks are determined.
   • A cost target is assigned to each block.

Note: the assignment to functions and component blocks methods can be combined e.g one or several functional areas to one component or several component blocks.

• *Assignment to individual cost items.* This implies a simple or well-known product, allowing costs to be assigned to a detailed level. This, of course, can be quite restrictive to innovative product designers, but it is again familiar in building.

• *Assignment of cost responsibility to designers and teams.* This is done when specific functions or groups of components can be identified with one team (or discipline) who take responsibility for the costs assigned to them.

Tanaka et al. suggest that most Japanese product designers assign cost targets to the functions of products rather than blocks of components (as we do in the building industry). This is the basis of value engineering.

3 **Value Engineering.** This concept *of assigning costs to functions* is at once profoundly customer oriented and instrumental in orientation. Originally developed in the early 1970's, the concept is common in the USA and Japan. The idea is to use the functions of a product or service, rather than the physical product as a whole or its component properties, as the basis of cost management. For example, the major function of a knife is to cut materials; the function of a pen is to make a mark; and the function of a stapler is to insert staples. Such descriptions (always a verb and a noun) represent the product in terms of a service potential to the customer. It is on this basis that estimators can exercise the technique of value engineering (literally, the engineering of values).

The objectives of value engineering are to enhance the producer's profits, reduce its costs, lower the product cost to the customer, and to find a way of managing product enhancement or the introduction of new product features.

There are two kinds of value engineering, what is called 'first pass' and 'second pass', the former dealing with new products and the latter dealing with existing products. The method of value engineering might proceed as follows:

• All the disciplines and view-points concerned with the design, development,

Assigning Building Costs

Cost assignment should be a managerial issue rather than an accounting convenience, but this is by no means easy. The building industry assigns costs to blocks of components, and architects think in these terms because it suits their bias. But this does not aid an understanding of how budget allocations are serving aspects of the prompts which engendered the project in the first place. With regard to offices, for example, clients might commission a new building on the basis of a collectively considered set of facilities serving a broad range of activities. The building is a corporate overhead rather than a meaningful asset relative to particular activities being served. Costs are allocated simply on the basis of floor area used. And yet, within the organisation, the client might be employing more sophisticated accounting methods based on cost centres or specific activities.

manufacture and use of the product are brought together as a review team.

• Information will be gathered and made available about the product and all aspects of its specification, manufacture, etc.

• Functional trees. The product is analysed into its component parts, each of which is assigned a function. A transitive verb and noun are used e.g. a water-tank (part) stores (transitive verb) water (noun); the function is storing water. This analysis might take the form of a tree-diagram that proceeds from left to right in answer to the question 'how?' and is checked from right to left with the question 'why?'. The example of a pen might begin at the left with 'to make a mark on paper' and then proceed to identify sub-functions. These identified functions then have to be costed.

• Each function can be assigned a proportion of the total cost and might also be assigned a cost reduction target.

• Once the producer's costs are known, they must be related to the user's perception of value. These can be assigned relative (weighted) values. For example, the pocket clip on the pen might be given a low user value relative to the pen having non-smudge, quick drying ink.

• Finally, a ratio of customer value multiplied by actual cost might give an indication of where attention might be focused (a ratio of less than one being a cause of concern). Avoidable costs are likely to become a key consideration, suggesting elimination of some features or functions.

• Alternatives are examined, assessed and considered as possible substitution or innovation.

This form of functional analysis can be applied to services as well as products. Clearly, it's entirely instrumental orientation imposes limitations hardly acknowledged by the methodology. Aesthetic feel, for example, have to be dealt with in terms of 'esteem value' or something similar i.e. as another function.

4 Physical properties. Despite value engineering's emphasis upon functions, hardware design strategies also have an important role to play in cost management. For example, research by British Aerospace indicated that 85% of a products costs are determined in the early stages of design. Similarly, Rolls Royce found that 80% of production costs were attributable to design decisions. This figure has become conventional wisdom in engineering i.e. most costs will have been determined by the time a design is available for review i.e. at the equivalent of scheme design approval in building design. (28) There is no reason not to expect these findings to apply to architecture.

In terms of managing the technical content of the design, a number of coping strategies can be employed, such as:

• *Minimising the system content* (although this seemingly obvious principle should not be pushed to the point where a law of diminishing returns sets in, where simplicity becomes costly to achieve - it is well known that the elegant, minimal building is often the very expensive one).

• *Using known and proven technologies*, suppliers, components, etc., thus reducing learning curves (although this, too, should not degenerate into habit, laziness or refusal to make a paradigm shift).

• *Reducing overall system dependency* on any given component

Too Late

Architects are sometimes paranoid about value engineering's functional (i.e. instrumental) approach to costing. This is possibly because they confront the technique when it is being employed to cut costs and transfer allocations during a budget crisis. Typically, attention is then being given to local conditions because strategic allocations have already been made. Designers might see this as a form of 'tinkering' and spoiling of their architectural ambitions. Value engineering is best employed as an aspect of the design scheme, during the stage when 80% of costs are determined and prior to further development and constructional bids.

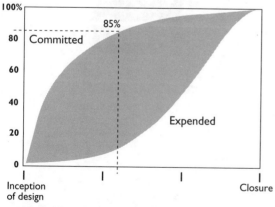

Typical gap between costs committed and costs expended

Adapted from Forsberg et al. (1996)

(whilst also avoiding excessive redundancy).

- *Reducing technical risk within the system (making it 'error tolerant':*
    - A system of ten modules, each with a 90% chance of successful performance, has an overall probability of success of 35%.

    A ten-module system with nine modules at 99% and only one at 90% has an overall chance of success of 82%.

    Similarly, if the tenth module's potential success is reduced to 80% the overall chance of success is still 73%. This is also likely to reduce co-ordination problems between disciplines and with specialist sub-contractors.

Note: this argument about chances of success also applies to predictions of lapsed time to undertake and complete a set of tasks.

- *Locating technical risk* where it has least chance of affecting the whole system.

- *Concentrating functionality* in one of two ways:
    - Within a module, thus minimising the overall number of modules. This has the advantage of integrated interfacing but might increase design time and co-ordination.
    - Across a number of modules, thus increasing the number of modules. This has the advantage of enabling design work to be split, but requires attention to interfaces. Another advantage is the possibility of adapting to change more easily.

- *Providing generous design margins* in order to lessen criticality of performance. (See earlier point about redundancy.)

- *Reducing or relieving constraints* on the components.

- *Minimising the number of interfaces* for each component or sub-system.

- *Making the interfaces stable*, robust, standard, and simple.

Such strategies profoundly affect costs but cannot, in themselves, be costed. There could be given a value but this would be extremely difficult. Nevertheless, they are points which any product designer should be considering as crucial (managerial) aspects of cost control.

5 **Estimation.** At the heart of managing any cost control system is the need to estimate costs as a project develops. As with planning, two approaches can be identified: the bottom-up, and the top-down.

The bottom-up approach to estimating aggregates all cost items into a whole, presumes all items are known and is best at the stage just before manufacturing (e.g. the bill of quantities familiar in British architecture). This means that it is less than useful at a project's front-end. In addition, when it is detailed rather than approximate, bottom-up estimating can be time-consuming and costly.

The alternative (top-down) approach to estimating is a quicker, cheaper and more convenient method based upon generalised data related to similar functions and products already in existence (e.g. the cost per sq.metre rate applied to a typologically characterised building or major part of it).

Clearly, the top-down approach (looking at total product cost) should evolve into the detailed bottom-up estimation, and they should harmonise. However, the detailed estimate can arrive too late to affect the designs upon which the former is based, leading to budget crises. For this reason estimating is usually approximate and founded upon faith that the team can manage its way to success.

This is the situation in building, where cost estimates progress from a generalised top-down approximation for the whole product, through to a more detailed approximation in the form of a scheduled cost plan, but real costs are not known until after specification and tendering, when bids indicate actual costs, in detail.

Mindsets

Coping strategies such as those described on the left, are alien to a system of architectural education which inculcates a mind set unsympathetic to product design values and methods. This mind set also permeates much of the architectural media and can engender peer group pressures and oppositions between academia and the media, and those in practice. To the extent the former define their position in terms of the art paradigm, the latter is made to suffer guilt about what it does. Calls to equip students for practice are countered by the argument that this panders to the needs of a commercial machine.

As Easy as ABC

Activity Based Costing (ABC) is, like many other managerial concepts reducible to some basic principles adapted for the problems at hand. In this instance, the key concepts include process engineering, *a focus upon* critical success factors, *and organisational cost centring. As a concept focused upon user needs, ABC helps to identify crucial product or service features . As a focus upon the delivery of those services or the management of a design process, it seeks to identify what is important to the delivery and what its cost drivers are (particularly overheads). The technique can also be used in cost targeting, working from performance to features.*

The basis of ABC is to relate services and products to activities which provide or deliver them, and to the consumption of resources. The 'cost drivers' will be at the final level, but they might be very different from one another.

Overall, there are four kinds of fundamental difficulty to be addressed:

1. *The difficulty of estimating costs at the early planning stage,* before detailed specifications have been established. Once an accurate estimate can be achieved, it might be too late to fundamentally affect the design.

2. *The designers do not estimate the costs of their own designs.* (The architectural profession has long since dumped any skill with a numerate base and rarely attempts estimating except on the most generalised basis; nevertheless, a minimum of knowledge is unavoidable and some journals still report cost analyses of the buildings they publish, providing designers with valuable information.)

3. *The cost of estimating specialists* can be high and they will aim to limit their reconceptualisations and repeated attempts at estimating. There will be a tendency to avoid costing alternatives. Similar difficulties apply to costing changes.

4. *Estimates tend to be based upon the costs of the physical product* rather than the costs of functions or design properties. These two perspectives can create tensions and conflict when a project begins on one basis and is later assessed on another.

A common basis of cost estimating is captured experience (precedent) in the form of *cost tables* and *databases*. These are sometimes sophisticated guides, especially in manufacturing. The equivalents in the building industry are relatively simple, listing items, trade rates by area, regional cost variations and the like. Industry cost tables can progress through to the kind of detail that might predict the full manufacturing and related costs of a product (involving materials, shape, finish, batch size, tolerances, time constraints, shipping costs, development, overheads, distribution, etc). However, the nature of the building construction project means that tendering bids from principal contractors, suppliers and sub-contractors remains a most important estimating stage (and sometimes an unpredictable one).

6 Costing Activities The institutionalised table of recommended fees published by the RIBA was a form of cost table. The shift experienced by the profession - from mandatory to recommended fees, then to advisory fees which everyone realises are out of line with market realities and current costs - has meant that practices now have to assemble their own databases and fee tables based upon what is actually done.

The principal difference in accounting practices between firms involves the identification and allocation of overheads either uniformly across projects of on a specific project basis (the later being potentially much more accurate, but also more difficult). In manufacturing, overheads have traditionally been attached to products in proportion to the direct labour and machine time spent on them, but contemporary techniques have left the approach inadequate, especially when labour costs reduce to a small proportion of production cost and production volume becomes less significant as the key factor to be considered. The solution has been to address production in terms of activities.

Tanaka et al. (1993) identify four kinds of overhead transactions in contemporary manufacturing:

1. Activities concerning the tracking and analysis of the order, execution, and confirmation of the movement of materials within the manufacturing process (logistics). *In architectural terms, are matters being progressed? Is the right thing being done at the right time in accordance with requirement?*

2. Activities ensuring the supply of appropriate production resources to match the work orders that logistical transactions reflect. *Architecturally, are the people available? Are the skills? Is the information or decisions?*

3. Activities concerned with the quality of output in relation to market need. *Is the service and product 'fit for purpose'?*

4. Activities concerned with all kinds of change in products design, work schedules, material specifications, etc. i.e. the continual efforts to ensure the firm is reacting effectively and efficiently to need, contingency and change.

These activities and their importance have parallels with experience in architectural firms, where the overhead going into competition work, promotional activities, training, internal auditing, practice and project management are not only different to practices before professional deregulation engendered a more competitive environment, but are more crucial to success.

One method used to identify and appropriately allocate overheads is called *activity-based costing* (ABC). Developed in the late 1980's in the USA, the concept seeks to find out what customers and end-users actually *do* with the design product. From it comes activity-based planning and activity-based costing - means of keeping design development on target and helping it prioritise commitments and resources by engendering a more holistic approach that can blend together individual perspectives of what is needed e.g. statements coming from departmental heads, specialist disciplines and interests.

Traditional accounting will allocate overheads as resources acquired e.g. salaries, stationery, telephone , etc., but ABC will analyse how these resources are used e.g. order taking, quotations and prices, customer liaison, etc. Management learns why costs are incurred and these are linked to causes and to the individuals who have responsibility for the consumption of resources.

ABC is based on two premises: *activities consume resources*, and *products consume activities* (in architectural practices, deliverables or outcomes consume activities). It begins with the identification of overhead activities and a cost attribution to them; these will often cut across department and discipline boundaries. The idea is to pool similar and related costs. The next step is identify the cost drivers to these activities e.g. quality control might be driven by amortising system set-up, auditing procedures, etc.

Cost driven

Tanaka et al. give an example of ABC in patient medical care where administrative costs had a per patient cost driver, nursing had a per clinical care unit cost driver (reflecting the intensity of care), and accommodation, meals, etc., had a per day cost driver. This assessment, now reflecting the use of resources by each patient, was in contrast to an averaged cost per day rate.
(Tanaka et al., 1993)

Activity Based Costing

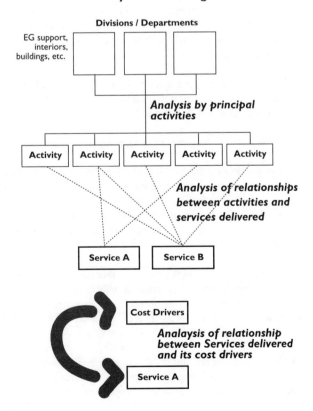

Three broadly defined kinds of activity stand out within the average architectural firm:

1. Those concerned with promotion, marketing, fee bids, etc.

2. Those concerned with administration, accommodation, equipment, back-up support, etc. i.e. those which are not directly earning fees and cannot be easily related to specific jobs.

3. Those directly concerned with fee-earning i.e. the core of architectural practice.

Each will have its own set of cost drivers. The point is to trace individual activities back to the source of demand (or, vice versa) and to understand the costs involved, including any hidden cross-charging between activities. This is a similar concept to seeking to identify the critical success factors (and identifying their costs and the drivers involved). The objective, of course, is to make service delivery as lean and effective as possible.

Cost drivers within an architectural firm will typically fall into two categories (these form basic considerations in the former RIBA fee scale) :

1. Those driven by work volume (which usually produces lower unit costs).

2. Those driven by the relative complexity or difficulty involved in servicing particular projects (job class and type) Increased complexity usually inflates the managerial overhead.

Of course, a managerial analyst would have to go into further detail to make the cost driver concept useful and they might find it becomes project-specific. In addition, some cost drivers will be 'soft' considerations and will include those whose common denominator includes economies related to efficient time utilisation and effective action. For example:

- *The cultures of project sponsors* e.g. an individual or a committee, the former being more likely to simplify decision-making and minimise multiple forms of consultation and the shear number (and length) of meetings to be attended. (See later section on cultures.)

- *The pace of project programmes.* Fast-tracking is often preferred because it pressures the team into making decisions (countering the Parkinson's Law, that work expands to fill the time available).

- *The preferred procurement route.* Is it, for example, design and build or orthodox?

- *Professional capabilities within the firm.* This is not just expertise in the sense of talent, knowledge and experience, but also as an ability to perform and deliver.

- *Interpersonal factors* such as motivation, team chemistries, lack of conflict, leadership quality and authority, etc. which act, as it were, either as oil or sand in the gears of a project.

To the extent a design practice self-consciously orchestrates its behaviours it is managerially 'getting there by design'. In effect, a designed 'architecture' has to be given to the project organisation. Its purpose is to remove potential causes of dissatisfaction and barriers to success in order that design creativity can flourish. Tactics the organisation might include the following:

- Use skilled, expert and inventive personnel - reducing learning curves; lessening risks; increasing potential productivity and inherent design potential (but note the dangers of specialists with limited project commitment).

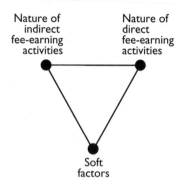

Cost drivers in the architectural firm

Nature of indirect fee-earning activities — Nature of direct fee-earning activities

Soft factors

A differentiation between cost-drivers affecting fee earning, and non-fee earning, supportive activities within the architectural firm is relatively simple to make. However, there are also a host of 'soft' cost drivers to consider which, in turn, split between those which are project specific (e.g. client, procurement route, etc.), those derived from project environment (e.g. an over-heated construction climate, planning issues, etc.), and those deriving from the culture of the practice i.e the way the firm does things.

5S's

Boeing attempts to employ the concept of 5S's:
- *Sorting*
- *Sweeping*
- *Standardising*
- *Simplifying*
- *Self-discipline*

In effect, these are parameters of an organised, disciplined studio culture which seeks to cut out the hassle of disorganisation, clutter, the unnecessary, etc. Hot-desking companies seeking the electronic, paperless office have to institute a similar culture e.g. 'either bin that piece of paper or send it to the library for electronic archiving (and back-up in a warehouse down the road)'.

• Maximising the time within the production process during which value is being created, harnessed and realised i.e. minimise wasted time and effort with focus, productivity, efficiency and a satisfied team.

• Learning by doing - maximising the beneficial learning curve that comes about from repeated production exercises and also gaining a broader, enriching experience.

• Intentionally modularising the development and production effort, by design.

• Exercising studio disciplines aimed at removing problems, hassle, bureaucracy, general entropy and, above all, error and the need to redo work of any kind.

Hourly Rates

Practice costs are usually averaged out and incorporated into hourly rates. There are different ways of doing this which amount to ways of accounting for overheads and attributing indirect costs to a project. Whilst the employment of global rates is a useful heuristic, it can obfuscate underlying issues. Just what are the drivers of costs? Some are intrinsic to projects; some derive from the practice context and are therefore 'cultural'. Some cost drivers are the product of 'special' causes and some of 'common' causes; some concern project problems being tackled, others concern people and how they work.

Managers have to give particular attention to understanding kinds of 'common' causes which drive costs e.g. prevailing cultural factors in a practice; people factors; overheads; and intrinsic project issues.

Special causes are, by definition, unique and unpredictable, even though they will account for a significant amount of time.

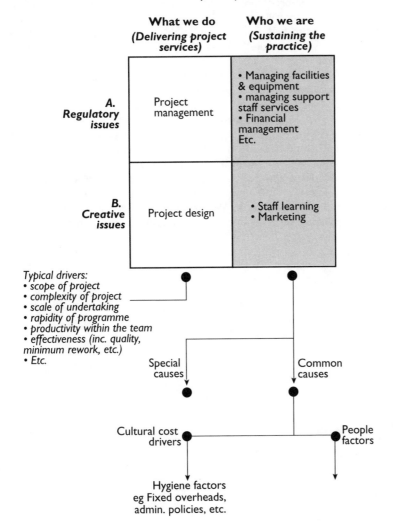

Activity Based Costing within an architectural firm

Each sector embraces sets of activities. Each of these will have cost drivers. Only examples are shown.

	What we do *(Delivering project services)*	Who we are *(Sustaining the practice)*
A. Regulatory issues	Project management	• Managing facilities & equipment • managing support staff services • Financial management Etc.
B. Creative issues	Project design	• Staff learning • Marketing

Typical drivers:
• *scope of project*
• *complexity of project*
• *scale of undertaking*
• *rapidity of programme*
• *productivity within the team*
• *effectiveness (inc. quality, minimum rework, etc.)*
• *Etc.*

Special causes

Common causes

Cultural cost drivers

People factors

Hygiene factors eg Fixed overheads, admin. policies, etc.

Dividing Labour

In 1776, Adam Smith published the Wealth of Nations *in which he argued that the successful capitalist enterprise was, as much as anything else, the product of structuring. The principle was already employed by such entrepreneurs as John Taylor, who had a button works employing seventy-two workers divided into seventy discrete operations.*

This same principle was the basis of a classic book on the subject written by Babbage in 1832 (and going into four editions in as many years) that described how the costs of producing metal pins had been halved by dividing the worker's efforts into numerous specialist roles.

By the time of Frederick Taylor and, later, Henry Ford, regularity, delegation and the principle of the division of labour were well established as the basis of the modern industrial economy.

The idea of the division of labour is, in managerial terms, profoundly bottom-up. It seeks to formulate an overall organisational structure aggregated from consideration of the best way to deal with each natural component of the process. The top-down element of the equation is the policy-maker's strategic viewpoint and goal definition for the organisation.

7 **What We Do and Who We Are.** A generalising examination of activities within the architectural firm suggests that it practises two sets of inter-related activities, each of which has a different underlying concern:

> 1. *What we do.* Those activities concerned with delivering specific professional design services through the project medium.

> 2. *Who we are.* Those activities concerned with sustaining the firm as a viable enterprise. These embrace both design practise and commercial issues.

In turn, each of these has a *regulatory* and *a more expansive, creative* aspect. For example, delivering professional services is not only creative, but also also includes some regulatory form of project management. Sustaining the firm as a viable enterprise embraces competitions, marketing, and staff training as well as regulating resources, support staff, contracts, finances and the like (i.e. culture in the sense of 'How we do things around here', a topic taken up in a later section).

Each set of activities also has cost drivers which, at any point in time, will tend to divide between those produced by *common* and *special* causes. The latter are dealt with as 'fire fighting', but the former are more intractable and are always in danger of being neglected or even ignored.

The latter is a contextural realm which will have its own set of cost drivers. These will be partly the product of basic considerations furthering the viability of the firm (in the biological sense of 'capable of sustaining life'): e.g. the need for premises, equipment, accounting procedures, capital investment, banking arrangements, support staff, etc., which are normally dealt with as comparatively fixed overheads (and which, by implication, need to be kept as low as possible). They will also be the product of 'soft' factors: e.g. who runs the firm and how capable they are at making appropriate strategic decisions.

From the point of view of managing a specific project, common causes within a firm (i.e. its culture) form a contextural milieu which imbues project work and mixes with factors deriving from the way the whole project team is organised and works (which is likely to involve other agencies).

In negative terms, project management aims to address and limit the effect of special causes and much of its energy is likely to go in this direction. But its positive role concerns the enhancement and refinement of common causes affecting how work is done i.e. how cultures are formed, sustained, and modified by learning and adaptation.

Techniques such as ABC attempt to avoid reducing these factors to an averaged cost e.g. global hourly rates, and to identify specific cost drivers that the manager can address. The principle is an important one, although it might be difficult to properly implement.

Variety and complexity

Inherent project *complexity* - generated by factors such as scale, scope or internal variety - is a key source of project risk and overhead inflation. For example, as each new element is added to the project or scheme content it has to interact with all other elements. Each new element can almost double the potential number of interactions that have to be managed. As internal variety increases (e.g. the number of components grows), each element has to be designed more carefully. If one assumes all elements interact with each other, the permissible error rate will diminish quite rapidly. Of course, this degree of interaction would be unusual, but the example proves a point. Similarly, if interactions are going to involve any risk of failure, then the overall risk increases rapidly with a growth in the number of elements. (Given ten modules, each with a 90% chance of successful performance, the overall chance of success falls to 35%; even when nine of those modules have their chance of success raised to 99%, the overall chance of success is still only 82%. The restriction of technical risk suggests a minimum number of design modules, each with simple interfaces. The same principle applies to the management of people and their organisation if excessive managerial overheads and the hassle factor are to be obviated.

So far as overheads are concerned, a typical industrial rule of thumb is that as *variety* doubles, costs increase at a rate of between 20 - 35% per unit of output. (29) This phenomenon is called 'the complexity slope'. For example, the design overhead of an engineering firm will be a function of project size. Typical slopes are given below (Stalk & Hout, 1990); figures are the percent increase in overhead per unit with each doubling of complexity):

• Hand tool manufacturing	154%
• Multinational construction company	139%
• Dairy product delivery network	137%
• Chemical processing	133%
• Detailed engineering design	121%

Similarly, typical complexity curves can be calculated in terms of *cost per unit* for each doubling of complexity:

• Computer programming	141%
• Advertising agencies	117%
• Custom software programming	108%

2 The offset to variety is *scale*. As the scale of production increases it can be expected that unit costs will decline 15 - 25% per unit with each doubling of volume.

Production managers seek to offset these two costs. because increasing variety means a more complex set of production processes which include managerial and set-up overheads, there will often be an attempt to reduce variety, particularly when costs are under pressure. Conversely, when the market is good, variety will tend to increase, even though this will drive costs per unit up. The counter to this rise will be the reduction that sets in with increases in scale.

Looking at the situation globally, managers have three key factors to consider:

• Scale in terms of the length of production runs.

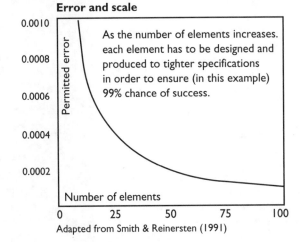

Error and scale

As the number of elements increases. each element has to be designed and produced to tighter specifications in order to ensure (in this example) 99% chance of success.

Adapted from Smith & Reinersten (1991)

Architects impressed by figures such as the 4 million parts in a Boeing 777 - most of which are rivets - might attempt the same calculation on a large building. The figure might be just as impressive. However, the effort put into a building's design and project management is rarely comparable with an airplane's simply because of repeated production exercises on the plane itself, the disparity in added value and the potential for revenue generation. Nevertheless, some of the potential is there.

• The organisational overhead associated with managing a process.
ª The complexity of scheduling procedures (30)

Manufacturing in small batches is both facilitated by and fosters means of production and managing processes so that kinds of complexity are reduced and simplified e.g. set-up costs, variety, component interfaces, the means of ensuring high standards, etc. (the reason firms do this is the need to rapidly respond to market forces). Maximising the time value is being added, just-in-time techniques, clever machinery and so on, are typical strategies of flexible manufacturers for whom economy of time is an important dimension of efficiency. Their scale-driven costs tend to remain fairly level, whilst variety-driven costs start at a lower level and rise more slowly as variety increases. Process capability, focus and teamwork are crucial skills. Hierarchies are flat, less time is taken make decisions between design and specification, to add process value and to get a job done. Time compression is the goal. It is arguably inevitable that service organisations such as architectural firms will have to exhibit analogous behaviours.

Scale, Complexity and Productivity

Lowest unit production costs (which can be translated into a minimum fee) result from the interaction of volume related and variety related costs. The former reduce with scale and the latter increase as variety and intrinsic complexity are enhanced. Manager's have to have the ambition of affecting this interaction so that the point of optimum (lowest unit costs) is shifted both down and to the right of the diagram opposite.

In architectural practice, volume is dealt with as construction value.

Design complexity is dealt with by classifying jobs into different categories.

Both design complexity and production scale are dealt with by the former RIBA fee scale which is still used as a bench-mark by many practices.

A third ingredient of the equation is comparatively hidden: productivity. In design practice this amounts to issues of speed, an ease of arriving at appropriate decisions, and an ability to efficiently and effectively produce construction specification information - i.e getting it right up front, first time, with minimum hassle. Talent and expertise are insufficient - these have to be effective. This, in turn, calls for the management of project inputs, at both the personal and organisational levels. Such considerations are closely allied to the management of both managerial overheads which normally accompany increased design complexity and increased production scale.

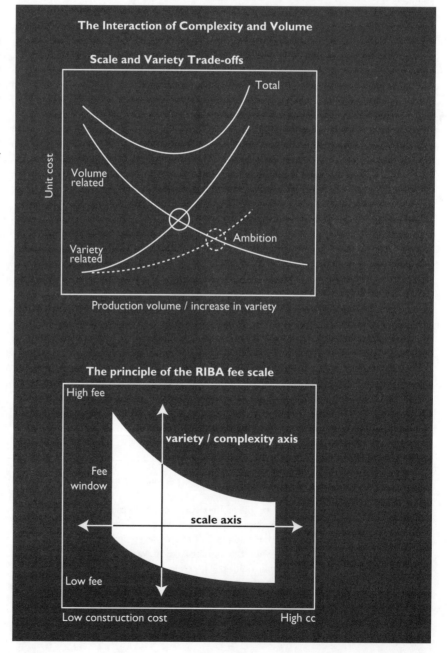

Practice cost benchmarks

Cost control within the architectural practice is epitomised by the problem of fee estimation and project budgeting when making competitive bids and planning a project. Until comparatively recently the architect on the end of a request for a fee estimate merely had to refer to the RIBA's once *mandatory* (Blue Book). Under deregulatory pressures, this became the later *recommended*, fee scale and, later still, an *'advisory' fee scale* (as the Yellow book, manifesting the then Director General's favourite colour).

As originally published in 1982 the fee scale offered a simple algorithm asking for the determination of four things:

1. a classification of the job which differentiated between building Types expected to be more or less complicated (therefore requiring more effort from the architect);

2. a secondary level of use classification within a Class category (e.g. the teaching hospital was expected to be more complicated than the clinic);

3. a determination as to whether the work was new build or work to an existing building; and

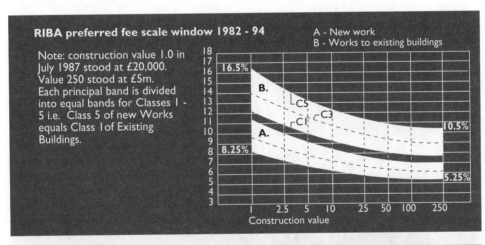

RIBA preferred fee scale window 1982 - 94

Note: construction value 1.0 in July 1987 stood at £20,000. Value 250 stood at £5m. Each principal band is divided into equal bands for Classes 1 - 5 i.e. Class 5 of new Works equals Class 1 of Existing Buildings.

A - New work
B - Works to existing buildings

Construction value

The former RIBA Fee Scale

Devised by true and good men who pooled the experience of generations and smoothed the outcome into elegant mathematical curves suitable for a rational era. It's principles embody basic industrial production considerations.

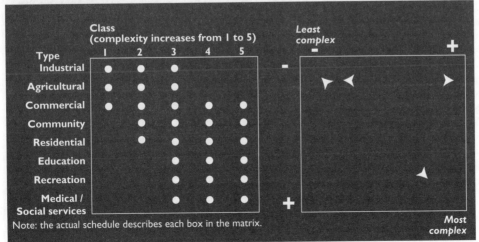

Class (complexity increases from 1 to 5)

Type	1	2	3	4	5
Industrial	●	●	●		
Agricultural	●	●	●		
Commercial	●	●	●	●	●
Community		●	●	●	●
Residential		●	●	●	●
Education			●	●	●
Recreation			●	●	●
Medical / Social services			●	●	●

Note: the actual schedule describes each box in the matrix.

Least complex

Most complex

Judging Complexity

Fee scale guides (such as the former RIBA Blue Book) begin with building types and classes, but are actually measuring complexity. Scale is the next component to consider. These are the two most significant criteria which form the basis of fee estimation.

4. an estimate of the construction value of the project.

The fee could then be quoted as a percentage of construction value (the key variable after job type and complexity are accounted for).

All practices applied this method. Whether you were a man and a dog in some remote country spot, or a large practice in the centre of a metropolis, the same logic and method applied. Whatever your skills, experience, practice culture, overheads, promotion costs, etc., the same calculus was used. Judgement rather than calculation was intended to be irrelevant, thus bolstering the institutional ramparts of the profession (everyone was on the same, explicit basis).

Clearly, the fee scale had to be significantly redundant so that, on balance, remuneration could guarantee a reasonable profit to partners (the usual organisational format at the time, later superceded by the permitted format of the limited company as the profession sought to allay the consequences of an increasingly juridified environment which boiled down to an increasing likelihood of being sued by the client).

Redundancy helped cope with the inevitable unpredictability of jobs so that, overall, practice accounts would stay healthy. In addition, the fee also had to appear to be reasonable to the client, but the need for such a perception was tempered by the market control implicit in the former mandatory status of the fee scale. When mandatory became recommended and then advisory, most architects were shifted to a competitive basis without an understanding of how the former fee scale worked. That remains the position to this day, when the old Blue Book is still used as a referential bench-mark

Deconstructing the scale

The RIBA fee scale dealt with both design complexity (or internal variety) and construction scale. These are the two key considerations in estimating the inherent scope within a job.

Complexity is dealt with in terms of Types and Classes of building (see page 114). Volume is dealt with in terms of construction value. These two considerations generate the two axis of the scale.

At any given construction value (horizontal scale), there is an inbuilt complexity relationship between the easiest and the most complex building type (vertical scale). The scale presumes that a Class 5 Work to Existing job is more complex as a Class 1 new Build job i.e at any given construction cost level, unit production costs are higher for the latter job type.

Higher by what factor? Since the fee doubles between a C1 Work to Existing job and a C5 New Work job, one can infer that the latter has twice the design content of the former. C1 Existing to C1 New has a 1 : 1.47 relationship. If there is an enhanced managerial content, this can also be inferred to have been taken into account.

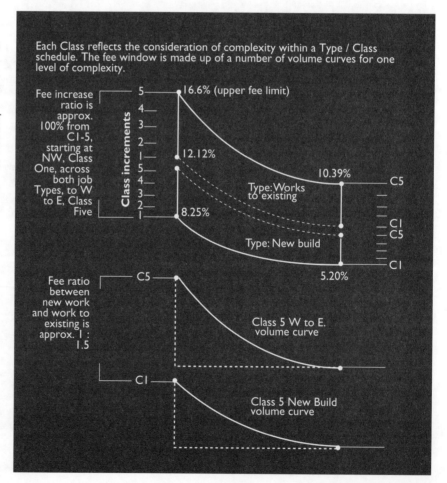

2 **A Common Estimating Heuristic.** Services delivered within the framework of the RIBA fee scale were divided between those considered to be *Preliminary* (inception and feasibility) and those that were *Basic* (outline proposals; scheme design; detail design; production information and bill of quantities, tender action; project planning (curiously late); operations on site; and completion. Preliminary services were on an hourly rate and Basic services were on the percentage basis. In addition, there was a list of services that were 'extras': surveys and investigations, development services, other design services, cost estimating and financial advice, negotiations, administration and management of building projects, etc. Services many buildings might be expected to need - such as engineering, interior design, graphics, furniture, landscape, etc. - were assumed to be provided by other consultants.

The dominant, underlying concept within the fee algorithm is that of a global, top-down service (i.e. the 'basic' service). It was certainly not intended or expected that an architect might provide an intermediate, isolated part of the possible range of services e.g. Stage E alone.

Once the fee was accepted there would be a simple system of allocating parts of the fee to the usual stages a project could be expected to progress through e.g. scheme design, tendering, work on site, etc. This suggested a way of invoicing for fees, of addressing the cancelled job, of invoicing for abortive work, and of managing the natural phases of a project.

As issued in a guidance format in 1994 (the Yellow Book), the overall fee scale was as set out as described below. As well as lowering the entry fees, stages C and D had been loosened from 15 and 20% respectively, to a range, admitting the front-end loading of previous scales (as practised among many disciplines, including builders):

Work stage	Proportion of fee	Total
Preliminary		
A / B (inception & feasibility)	(time rates)	
Basic		
C (outline proposals)	10 -15%	10 -15%
D (scheme design)	15 -20%	25 - 35%
E (detail design)	20%	45 - 55%
F G (information + bills)	20%	65 - 75%
H J K L (tender action, operations on site, etc.)	25%	100%

3 **Deconstructing the Calculus.** The RIBA fee scale set a bench-mark which remains in place, even though most architects have suffered drastically reduced fees over the last decade or more, especially during the period of recession from about 1990-94. (Incidentally, this is a global phenomenon not restricted to the UK.) The scale serves as a useful estimating starting point. However, the roots of the bench-mark are vague and this prevents its translation into a format useful to contemporary (and competitive) practice. How was the fee scale arrived at? Mostly by the pooling of informed common sense i.e. the accumulated wisdom of RIBA grey beards who, having considered a schema, could then apply mathematically elegant curves to their preferred range of fees and offer something that appeared manifestly rational and consistent. Given the comments about heuristic, intuition and judgement, this approach was sounder than one's imagination might suggest. The point, however, is that the presentation format suggests to most people a far more rational and technocratic basis for the scales than actually exists. What was not offered to the profession was an underlying rationale common in industry: a consideration of complexity and scale as the two fundamental variables to be dealt with when considering costs.

The diagrams on the page 112 to 114 illustrate the fee scale concept in terms of two, related axis (scale and variety / complexity) and fee scale windows (one for New Build and the other for Work to Existing Buildings).

The vertical scale accounts for complexity in terms of job Class; the horizontal scale copes with volume as a construction cost rise (a scale set at the 1987 figures of £20k to £5m i.e. from 1 to 250; after this, the scale levels off). The presumption is that jobs in a similar Class entail a similar level of work content and internal practice cost

Institutionalised fee scales represent the voice of the profession seeking fair and reasonable fees, but also protecting market interests through collective action - an undertaking accepted by most professional bodies (arguably their raison d'etre). The necessary presumption is that all members have the same expertise (implicit within the professional qualification) and bear similar overhead costs. Deregulation throws out this presumption and the professional institution (in this case, the RIBA) must legitimate competition between its members. In turn, those members are called upon to formulate a new basis for their fee charges and under-cutting naturally arises (especially in an over-populated profession such as architecture). Upon what basis is a firm to calculate its charges when generations of fee estimating heuristic are disgarded? How much does it actually cost to do this job or that one? How are disparities between expertise and overheads to be accounted for? How is market risk and commercial judgement to be incorporated into the calculus? Common sense suggests that the old fee scale should remain as a bench mark, but it is necessary to understand its reconstruction.

e.g. a purpose-built factory (Class Three) is the equivalent of offices, prisons, schools, or a clinic (also all in Class Three); a department store (Class Four) is the equivalent of a civic centre, a nursing home or a general hospital complex (also in Class Four).

Presuming the fee scale does not reflect special risk or similar factors, then, within any Class, the general ratio between fees for New Works and Work to Existing Buildings is approximately 1.5 reflecting anticipated increases in project content, complexity and demand on resources between these types of job. The overall fee range at any level of construction value is 1 : 2.

To the extent that the fee scale was proven to be useful and therefore valid, its internal mechanisms remain of interest. The actual level of fees attained is largely irrelevant. It is therefore worth deconstructing the scale in order to determine its rules for coping with complexity and scale. Note: this has to take the correspondence between jobs at the level of Class determination as entirely judgmental and the ultimate 'soft' basis of the scale.

History

Historically, architect's fees were often set at 5% - a level deemed to be appropriate by a Commission of Inquiry into the conduct of the business of the Office of Works in 1813 and, previous to that, used by English architects like Inigo Jones and Italian ones like Andrea Palladio. The first RIBA Professional Practice Committee of 1845 continued with this recommended fee, but in 1862 it published a document called 'Professional Practice and Charges of Architects, being those now usually and properly made'. The rules and general principles within this document were amended in 1872 and were later revised in 1898. In 1919 the recommended fee was upped to 6%. This later became more variable after WW II, eventually leading to the recommended fee scale of 1982 (the Blue Book).

4 **Accounting for Design Complexity.** The Type / Class schedule within the preliminary part of the scale (see page 113) accounted for the level of variety or *design complexity* engendered by different types of project. A set of declining volume response curves dealt with *scale* (in terms of the construction cost estimate).

In presuming that some kinds of job are inherently more complex than others and deserve more fees two kinds of consideration were implicitly taken into account:

1. How demanding the design work is upon the expertise of the practice, e.g. initially, the difference between a medical building and an industrial *Type*, the highest fee for the latter being the same as the lowest for the former. This is the design complexity of the job. Secondarily, degrees of complexity within each *Class* e.g. whether it is a clinic or a teaching hospital.

2. Complexity in terms of whether the job is new build or work to an existing building (the latter being presumed to be more complex).

The product of the first two considerations was a matrix with eight types of job (industrial, agricultural, commercial, community, residential, education, recreation, and medical / social services) set against five Classes of increasing complexity. For example, the 'commercial' type of job (the denotation already tells a story) is presumed to range from single storey car parks to high risk research buildings, TV studios and the like. Each Class was then used within the graphic scale to determine an appropriate fee. Taken together, the ten Class *curves (five for new build and five for work to existing buildings)* accounted for the complexity factor. All that remained was to allow for whether the job was Work to Existing premises or New Build, the former being presumed to be more complex. In effect, this generated ten classes of job for which, at any given construction value level, the fees double between the lowest and highest. It is being suggested that, across this range, a New Build Class 1 industrial storage shed is twice as easy to design as Work to Existing premises on a Class 5 teaching hospital.

5 **Accounting for Job Scale.** If we knew the implicit *volume response curve* built into the RIBA fee scale we would have a basis for translating the entirety of the RIBA scale into a format suited to the unique circumstances of each practice. The bench-mark we use would be *internal* (within the practice) and not external (institutionalised). Each individual practice culture could generate its own, true fee scale - a fee estimating and job budgeting calculus that was *practice-specific* and capable of fine-tuning.

With the goal of building a calculus in mind, we can infer that the RIBA fee scale implies *eight* incremental doublings of job content between the lowest and highest construction values for any Type or Class (i.e. between the lowest and highest given construction values, at which point the scale levels off). Over this range, there are bands of advantage gained by an increase in scale. The average volume slope is 190% across the entire range.

In other words the fee scale presumes that, in either Type category and for any Class of building within those Types, the average value of required inputs (e.g. manhours) increases by

The RIBA Fee Scale in terms of Volume Response Curves

I. The RIBA recommended fee scale, first published in 1982 and subsequently revised, can be simplified into heuristic **volume response** and **complexity slopes**.

The scale can be analysed into a break-down of three project **construction value bands** of three-fold doubling e.g. Band One from £20k to £40k, to £80k and £160k (at 1987 construction values), Band Two from £160k to £320k, to £640k, to £1280k; and Band Three from £1280k to £2560, to £5120k, and then to £10240k. In summary:

Band A: £20k to £160k construction cost
Band B: £160k to £1280k
Band C: £1280k to £10240k.
(At 1987 values. If 1985 = approx. 100; 1987 = 120; 1995 = 160. Nominal in 1997 figures for the range are approx £36k to £18.5k)

2. Complexity is dealt with by a schedule which deals with Types and Classes and presumes three doublings of complexity across the entire possible job range (i.e. C1 New Work, to C5 Work to Existing). For example, starting at a 8.25% fee, this moves to 10.31%, to 12.89%, and to 16.11%. This equates to a 125% curve for each doubling of complexity (see discussion of complexity curves).

3. Scale (or volume) is dealt by breaking the the 'fee window' into three **volume response curves** (VRC) bands. Each band accounts for a threefold doubling (e.g. 1/2/4/8; 8/16/32/64; 64/128/256/512).

4. The complexity and volume response curves are set out on the right in the three vertical (Class) and horizontal (construction value) bands between £20k and £10240k. These resulting nine sectors fall into a pattern that redefines the bands into three averaged volume response slopes, as follows (the inbuilt complexity curve for ten Classes is given in '3' above):

Band One: 182% (an 18% improvement)
Band Two: 190% (a 10% improvement)
Band Three: 198% (a 2% improvement)
That is, for each doubling of scale, unit costs increase only at the above rates.

Note that scale can be expected to bring with it an increase in the managerial overhead. This suggests that the actual rate of normal design productivity must increase at higher (compensating) rates than those indicated.

See page 193
for an expanded version of the diagram on the bottom right.

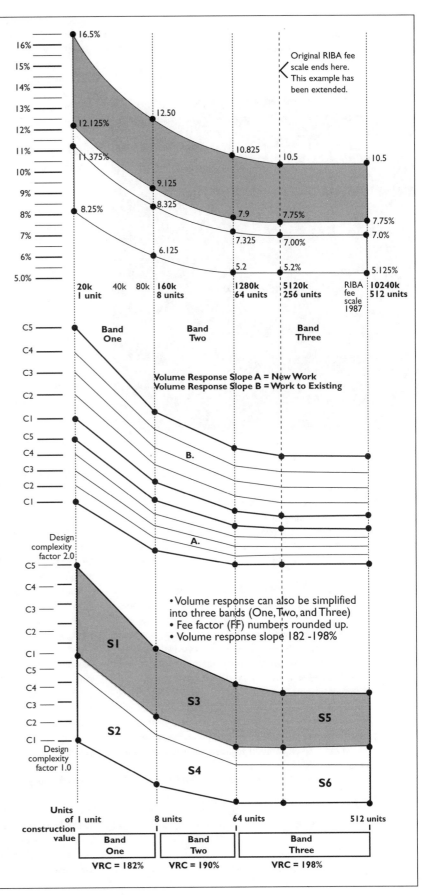

117

RIBA Fee Scale
Inbuilt Volume Response Curves

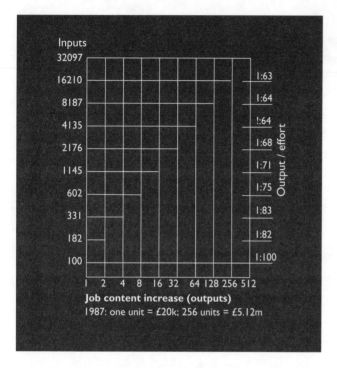

Inputs

32097
16210 — 1:63
8187 — 1:64
4135 — 1:64
2176 — 1:68
1145 — 1:71
602 — 1:75
331 — 1:83
182 — 1:82
100 — 1:100

Output / effort

1 2 4 8 16 32 64 128 256 512

Job content increase (outputs)
1987: one unit = £20k; 256 units = £5.12m

The RIBA fees scale has an inbuilt structure accounting for both complexity and scale. The latter is dealt with as an increase in construction costs across a scale ranging from 1 : 256.

The above diagram sets units of effort (vertical scale) against doublings of scale content.

The units of effort required decreases as the size of the job increases. This applies to all Classes at the same rate i.e. Class 1 and Class 5, as Work to Existing or New Build, are subject to the same rule

At the upper constructional value level the level of effort required is approaching three times less than at the lowest constructional level. No explanation has been given for this phenomenon, although conventional wisdom accepts its validity. Far too many project variable actually determine project costs and productivity to make more precision worth estimating and managing. In principle, it is scale alone enhances the productivity gain.

The diagram is based upon an analysis of percentage fees relative to construction value. It indicates that a response curve of approx. 190% operates for each doubling of presumed volume i.e. increasing volume relative to some base by 100% necessitates a 190% increase in the amount of inputs required. (In fact, the actual rate varies - see page 120.)

approximately 182 - 198% for each doubling of job volume measured in terms of the fee income derived from eight equal increments of construction value.

Knowing a volume slope, an estimator can use actual project histories to establish what is, in effect, a relationship *in that practice* between job type, practice culture, complexity, effort required (productivity) and fee income (construction value). The practice will have knowledge of how much 'complexity' of a given type can be dealt with by a unit of effort. By extrapolation, using the volume response slope, this knowledge can be applied to other jobs of this Type and Class, and also to other Types and other Classes. For example:

• Situation One: *New Work. Class Three*
Construction value: £2.5m. Normal job; no special difficulties; reasonable profit element, etc.
Manhours required to complete: 3360
Job used as bench-mark.

• Situation Two: *same Type and Class; also new build.*
Construction value: £5.0m (double the previous example). Similar conditions.
Manhours required at 190% complexity slope: 6384

• Situation Three: *Work to Existing, but still Class Three*
Construction value: £3.3m.
(2.5 / 3.3) x (3360 mhrs x 1.90) = 4836 mhrs
Allowance for extra complexity relationship of NW/W to E = 1:1.46
4490 x 1.46 = 7061 mhrs relative to bench-mark required to complete the job.
(Adjustments for Class are at a 108% multiple of the lowest rate for Type NW, Class One).
Etc.

The key to such an approach to job estimating is an appropriate bench mark (or a set of them). The former RIBA fee scale can be used as a bench-mark and each practice can establish its own, unique heuristic basis to fee calculus, allowing for special factors, commercial judgements, etc.

6 **Compensating for the Managerial Overhead.** The fee scale's volume response slope - brought into effect as job value increases - presumes some form of advantage or learning curve as the content of jobs inflates i.e unit costs of production must respond positively to increases in scale. And defining jobs in terms of job Classes appears to account for the inflation of design complexity. However, the concept of a complexity curve, as used in industry, applies to one class of production rather than many. It seeks to identify the inflation of an inherent managerial overhead which can be expected to accompany growth in production. It will also be present as an aspect of the disparate design content of jobs. However, the RIBA fee scale makes no mention of this factor and one has to infer that it is 'built-in' both dimensions of the fee scale.

The increased scale of larger jobs usually brings about an relative *increase* in the managerial overhead For example, as the number of personnel on a project increases, the managerial overhead will also increase. This is a common phenomenon and counters the benefit of larger job volume. Stalk & Hout offer a 121% complexity curve for an example of detailed engineering. In other words, unit costs increase by that rate for each doubling of job complexity (or internal variety) i.e managerial overheads respond negatively as the scale of an undertaking increases, even though the increase in scale is lowering unit production costs. The rule affects organisations as well as production. Increasing the range of services offered, for example, will inflate the managerial overhead. Managers often aim to identify the root causes which drive complexity curves and to tackle them directly rather than eliminating complexity as such.

The scale advantage in industrial production must, to some extent, also apply in building design, even though architects aren't producing widgets. Ten units of suspended ceiling cannot be ten times as difficult to design and detail as one unit, even presuming the larger building has more variants to cope with. The scale accepts this principle. On the other hand, the larger number of personnel, drawings, checks, meetings, etc., for the larger project suggests the managerial overhead (defined in this broad sense) will, at least, remain constant or, more likely, inflate. But is it going up *pro rata*, or is it (as in industry) increasing at something like a 120% rate quoted by Stalk and Hout?

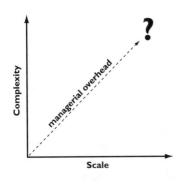

One has to include that the issue of managerial overheads affects *both* construction scale and design complexity, and that these are dealt with implicitly within the RIBA fee scale.

If it is assumed that the *base* managerial overhead is 5% of costs per unit of output and that this increases at the rate of 120% with each doubling of scale (a not untypical figure in other sectors), then this managerial overhead quickly increases from 5% to over 25% of the available fee across the fee scale. A higher content and more rapid complexity curve quickly has a dramatic effect (see page 120). This suggests that the volume response (to the extent it reflects productivity gains) must actually be *better* than the figures quoted earlier (see panel on the right).

Behind such figures lies a question: *what is the content of the 'managerial overhead'? What are the cost drivers?* Clearly, design complexity has to be carefully managed and, in effect, kept in check. The advantages of scale must be protected. But at the heart of this issue is an opaqueness with regard to the internal job mechanisms and the real cost drivers. These will always be a mixture of project-specific and practice culture factors i.e. to some extent they are the product of the nature of the job, the client culture, the preferred procurement route, the content of the negotiation at the level of contractual 'small print', the success of co-ordination, etc. They are also a product of the practice culture and how effective and competitive it is.

Fee Setting

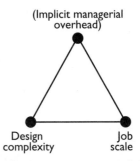

The presumed inherent design complexity of a job type sets the fee at a certain level. This includes whether or not it is work to an existing building or new work.

The construction value of the job is a modifier of this initial level.

The managerial overhead is dealt with as an implicit consideration built-into both design complexity and job value, but this is a fundamental cost driver.

When the managerial component, grows at 120% with each doubling of volume it reduces the percentage remaining for design work. This requires an enhancement of the VRC to compensate.

	%	%	VRC	True VRC
1	5	95		
2	6	94	182%	179.5
4	7.2	94		
8	8.6	91.4		
16	10.4	89.6	190%	184.5%
32	12.5	87.5		
64	14.9	85.1		
128	17.9	82.1	198%	191.5%
256	21.5	78.5		
512	25.8	74.2		

The ostensible VRC suggests that the input / output ratio ranges from 1 : 100, to 1 : 63. In fact (presuming a 5% management overhead increasing at 120%), it ranges from 1 : 100, to 1 : 47 across the range. Large practices are, by definition, able to operate at these levels of productivity, but they have to manage themselves carefully if the advantages of scale are not to be eroded.

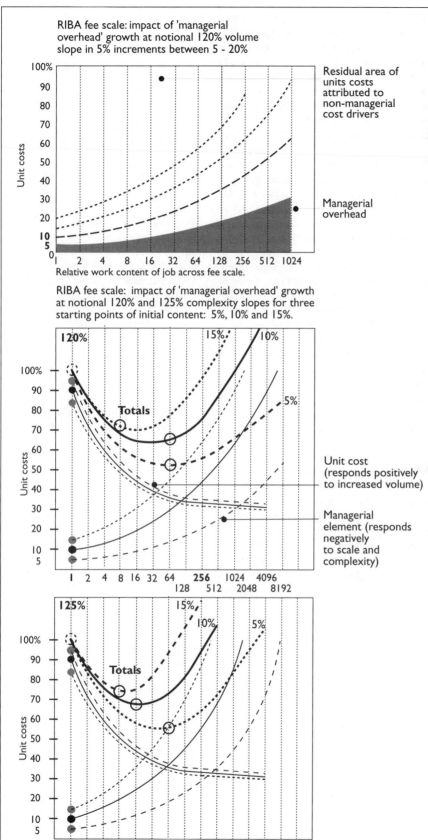

RIBA fee scale: impact of 'managerial overhead' growth at notional 120% volume slope in 5% increments between 5 - 20%

Residual area of units costs attributed to non-managerial cost drivers

Managerial overhead

Unit costs

Relative work content of job across fee scale.

RIBA fee scale: impact of 'managerial overhead' growth at notional 120% and 125% complexity slopes for three starting points of initial content: 5%, 10% and 15%.

120%

Totals

Unit costs

Unit cost (responds positively to increased volume)

Managerial element (responds negatively to scale and complexity)

125%

Totals

Unit costs

Alternative 'managerial overhead' growth at reducing rate in parallel with the volume response slope.

The Managerial Overhead

Because a job's managerial overhead reflects the inherent growth of complexity, it increases as a percentage of output as projects grow in size and complexity.

Many factors drive complexity and some of these are already accounted for in the Type / Class categorisation; however, other factors such as type of client, number of meetings expected, the speed of the contract, etc. will all influence 'complexity'. There is a split between what derives from the project and what derives from the way a practice goes about doing its work. Either way, these are managerial considerations.

Clearly, management has to aim to keep the managerial overhead low and to obviate the cost drivers which generate the managerial complexity slope.

The examples on this page illustrate differing rates of growth of the managerial overhead accounted for in simple terms relative to job scale. The changing volume response slope is built in i.e. a slope which starts at 182% and flattening out at 198% through three stages (as described on page 117). The managerial content is shown at three levels: 5%, 10% and 15%.

The middle diagrams illustrate the effects of a 120% complexity slope across the range. The lower diagram slows a 125% rate. This, of course, makes a significant difference to the managerial content. The lowest point on the Total curve is the lowest unit cost rate.

Behind such diagrams are important questions about the content of the overhead and what its cost drivers are.

Overall interaction of RIBA fee scale complexity and volume response curves

Assumes 5% management overhead at point of smallest job / largest fee, increasing at 125% rate.

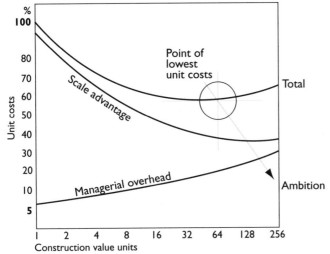

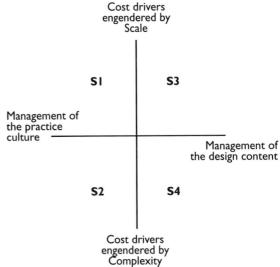

In many production sectors scale-driven unit costs are expected to decline at the rate of 15 - 25% with every doubling of volume. The complexity slope which is a component of scale increases might vary between 115 - 150%. Stalk and Hout (1990) give a figure for the Percent Increase in overhead cost per unit within engineering design of 121%. They suggest a figure for the increase in total cost per unit with each doubling of complexity in advertising of 117%.

'Complexity' can mean a range of things: e.g. the number of components, considerations, range of services, etc. Design overheads in engineering will be a function of project size (as in architecture); other business see complexity as a function of the number of delivery routes, the number of programmes offered, the number of departments in the organisation, etc.

The effects of complexity and scale work together, producing an optimum point of lowest unit costs.

The planner seeks to shift the lowest unit output cost (the lowest point of the Total curve) to the right. This can only be achieved by enhancing the productivity gain of scale, or containing growth of the managerial overhead.

The latter has two cost drivers: that deriving from the project, its client, the speed of the programme, etc.; and those costs which derive from the culture of the practice.

Fee negotiation is often implicitly concerned with cost drivers which increase the managerial overhead and need to be remunerated. Similarly, unit output costs can also be contained by agreement on the 'small print' of contracts, for example as a limitation to scheme content as one scheme and two revisions, or a limitation on the range of services. The Standard Form of Agreement is set up to enable firms to carefully frame their fee bid negotiations so as to keep rates competitive whilst also containing thew content of service.

The diagram above polarises four aspects of the discussion regarding the management of overheads.

The horizontal axis differentiates between managing the design content and managing other sources of overhead generation.

The vertical axis differentiates between issues of scale and complexity.

Four sectors of interaction are identified. Typical questions which might arise in each sector include:

S1: What are the cost drivers within a practice that are driven by scale? This includes size of jobs, size of all jobs together, number of personnel (fee-earning to non-fee-earning, utilisation, etc.), number of disciplines and services offered, etc.

S2: What are the cost drivers which come from the complexity of how we do things? Can we simplify our culture of production? Is it too simple and not complex enough? What about decision-making, change and re-work?

S3: What are the cost drivers deriving from design complexity? Which cost drivers are engendered by job Type and Class? Procurement route? Client culture?

S4: What are the cost factors deriving from issues of scale (i.e. the construction value of the job, or the overall size of all the jobs in a practice)? Number of systems? Interfaces? Some jobs are too small?

Bottom-up

The former RIBA fee scale's top-down, global assumptions and its implied redundancies covering a wide range of circumstances have been superseded by an attempt to offer architectural fees as a bottom-up aggregate of partial services, rather than a global core plus special additions. This is the basis of the RIBA *Standard Form of Agreement*, adopted in 1992 as a new form of agreement with clients. This is an entirely different basis for offering architectural services, shifting the architect toward a sub-contractor mind-set.

The SFA argues for itself in terms of the demands arising from a consumer, market-led economy; conditions of competition; legislation protecting the consumer; the impact of quality management; and a need to "negotiate realistic and firm conditions of appointment" (to quote the document itself). The new format was argued to be more logical, comprehensive and adaptable, enabling a "clear match between what the client requests and what the architect undertakes to provide".

The core of the SFA and the basis of fee estimating is a series of three schedules as follows:

- **Schedule One**: information to be supplied by the Client.

- **Schedule Two**: the services to be provided by the Architect:
    - Miscellaneous services provided by the architect:
        - Design skills *e.g. interior design, presentations, etc.*
        - Consultancy services *e.g. applications for grants, expert witness, rights and easements, etc.*
        - Buildings / Sites *e.g. selection of site, surveys, etc.*
        - All commissions *e.g. advise on other consultants, etc.*
    - Services specific to building projects, by Stage:
        - *A-B Inception and Feasibility*
        - *C Outline Proposals*
        - *D Scheme Design*
        - *E detail Design*
        - *F-G Production information and Bills of Quantities*
        - *H Tender action*
        - *J Project Planning*
        - *K-L Operations on Site and Completion*

Hard and Soft Bidding Considerations

It's useful to consider bid issues in terms of interacting 'hard' and 'soft' factors: practice capabilities and the job procurement route, and the project team and client culture respectively. Interactions between these considerations produces a series of questions which are important to understanding the project.

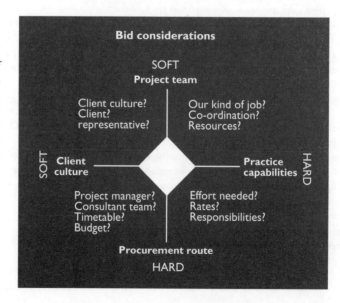

• **Schedule Three**: the explicit way payment for services is to be calculated, charged and paid.

Listed items in Schedule Two, for example, are deleted or added to, as required. Some of the services - listed as Basic - are conveniently grouped for a single selection; items within these groupings can be deleted, as necessary. Typical Additional Services are listed, for selection; these can be added to.

Aiming to be more specific about what the architect is doing and to remove possible misunderstandings, the SFA offers services as a shopping list. What was presumed and global now becomes a carefully negotiated and *aggregated* list of what is allowed for by the fee. The *demand* side presumption has changed to a *supply* side posture - usually accompanied by all the small print that can be expected in a subcontractor agreement. The fee bid has become a *strategic* document with an eye on changing project content and extra costs that can be imposed on the client.

It can be argued that all this, ironically, places even more emphasis upon the need for an executive project manager! And so far as the average architectural firm is concerned, the SFA offers little guidance on how a bottom-up, aggregated fee might be calculated. In fact, it implies continued reference to the former global fee basis, broken down into the stages of the RIBA's Plan of Work, now referenced to what is diplomatically offered as a fee survey, instead of an advisory schedule (now at about 70/75% of what was being advised in previous scales, although the figures come from a five year period between 1985-1990 when inflation was comparatively high, making percentages a very poor guide relative to construction values).

The real challenge is for a firm to know what has to be done, to be able to predict its productivity, and thus to accurately estimate its costs. This is the only way to look at the bottom-up posture adopted by SFA.

2 **Estimating Heuristic.** In line with the sub-contractor position implicitly adopted within the SFA format, it has become common for an architect bidding in competition to offer a complete schedule indicating who will do exactly what and when - what is ostensibly an 'open book' policy indicating instrumental project management thinking and pretending to a 'nothing to hide' offer. The implication is that this project is like any other of this stereotype and that project uniqueness has a relatively minor role. Design ability is taken for granted (addressed in the interviews which select a short list) and the bid is effectively on price and a demonstration of project management thinking. On the basis of some heuristic such as 'number of general arrangement drawings per sq.m., or £1m of anticipated contract value, etc., a schedule can be assembled. A similar heuristic can be used for resourcing (e.g. number of manhours per general arrangement drawing) and names can be placed against the schedule. The message is that the switch is ready to be thrown and the delivery mechanism will enable all to fall into place . . . This is not entirely sleight of hand, but it probably exaggerates instrumental project content as an act of ritual reassurance.

How does the estimator arrive at the fee itself? In theory, they identify what has to be done and simply schedule it all out on a bottom-up basis, using previous job histories to inform judgement. In fact, the key ingredient is judgement.

The estimator's approach commonly has three principal aspects to it: a feel for what the appropriate fee might be; the identification of key qualifying issues; and an estimate of the effort required to service the job.

Many practices will not use project histories. These will often be incomplete, inconsistent and - something intrinsic to project work - necessarily unique. Circumstances change, as do people on the team, clients, the procurement routes, etc. - jobs are rarely the same. In any case, most practices have neither the time of resources for post mortems and analysis. Instead, estimators rely upon 'live history', upon impressions, and questions such as the following:

• What is the client culture? Is it a power culture where one person will make all the judgements, or is it a consensus culture necessitating attendance at lots of meetings with lots of presentations, subsequent changes and possible delays to the project timetable? (Sentiments may lean toward th latter, but commercial

Fee Bid Estimating Considerations

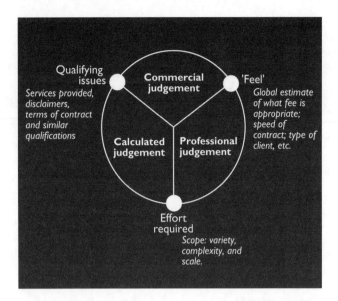

It would be naive to presume that fee bids were simple calculations. Three kinds of judgement underly most fee bid estimating:

• Judgements informed by calculation, resulting from estimates of the manhours considered to be necessary, and the terms of the contract.(which often have to be shrewdly stated). This might include an assessment of the firm's cultural capabilities and any advantages or disadvantages the firm has at that point in time.

• Professional judgements informed by experience and 'feel' of what is appropriate set against the effort estimate.These considerations include client type, speed of the job, etc.

• So-called 'commercial' judgements which weigh up the softer, more subjective considerations and which includes a risk assessment.

An Example of fee Research

Many practices are overly optimistic regarding the rationality of their job estimating methods and neglect historical records which could provide important information. This was indicated by research which asked the MD's and Senior Directors of a number of significant London practices (some American) about their current fee estimating and resourcing practices. (31)

Interviewees not only put a heavy reliance upon experience and intuition which Henry Mintzberg would recognise and probably approve of, but they tended to ignore historical records and neglect any systematic analysis. The history that mattered was an alive one: the memory and opinions of colleagues who had worked with this client, on similar jobs, etc. Recorded history was of secondary importance.

This was puzzling, especially when it was invariably claimed that historical records were complete, consistent and readily accessible for analysis. Interviewees argued that no two projects were the same, that the people involved differed, that circumstances varied, as did project criteria, etc. And some argued that, in the early 1990's, computers had finally delivered their promise and that this alone invalidated former production heuristic. In any case, who had the time or could afford to keep analysing records, especially in a competitive practice climate?

In other words, recorded histories were not valued - a reality underscored by the researcher's difficulties in obtaining detailed project histories, even when the practices were being co-operative to the point of letting him examine the files (these weren't consistent, nor even complete, as claimed; they were just dead).

What heuristic were employed? Firstly, they used a variety of heuristic rather than a single one. They also asked network colleagues for advice. Typically, they started with a globalised percentage fee and then worked from the bottom-up and compared the two results. Key considerations in a fee estimating calculus included client culture, the time given to the project, the other consultants, the key players (the most important project personnel, bearing responsibility and decision-making roles), and the proposed form of procurement. All were 'soft' (judgemental), qualifying factors rather than 'hard' (analytically derived and quantifiable) ones. Sometimes the fee was negotiated on a percentage basis with other consultants on a 'share-the-pie' basis, before making an offer to the client. A practice then had to work within its portion of the group fee (whatever was considered to be the going market rate). The shorthand of a global, top-down fee was reverted to whenever possible.

It was all common sense - which is exactly the point. But, from a formal viewpoint, it was a dangerously uneducated and potentially biased common sense also at odds with current managerial ideology.

sense leans toward the former.)

• Is the client experienced, understanding what will take place during the project, what the opportunities and problems will be? Have they already organised themselves? Are they prepared to support all the itemised services we see as necessary?

• What is the preferred procurement route? Traditional or design and build, for example? Will there be a construction consultant assisting with 'buildability' issues? Is this useful or problematic?

• How long is the project timetable? Shorter projects might produce management and productivity pressures, but they are likely to be more profitable and possibly with less hassle. (Fast-tracking is often preferred because it spurs the team into action.)

• What are the risks (of not delivering the service, of losing money, of getting it wrong, of being liable, etc.)?

• What are the opportunities and benefits?

• Are we in a good position to do this kind of work? Is it our kind of work? Are we experienced? Do we have the expertise and / or talent?

• Who is the competition?

• Who is on the team? Do we know them? Do we know someone who has experience of this client or project manager? What is our team? Can we work well with them?

• What kind of remuneration conditions will apply? What is the client's reputation in this respect?

• What liabilities exist and warranties might have to be undertaken?

• What fee will the job bear? Do we have to think of a global sum and then divide up the cake?

These are 'soft', judgemental questions, but they come out as hard, quantified decisions and commitments. Gossip with colleagues and fellow professionals will be as important as market intelligence and an understanding of one's own production culture and costs. Typically, firms will adopt the following strategies and exhibit the following attitudes when making fee estimates and bids:

• There will be a reliance upon multiple heuristic, both top-down and bottom-up.

• There will be a reliance upon judgemental and intuitional considerations, as well as hard facts.

• Relevant considerations will be 'live' rather than historical.

• Client culture, procurement route, and other members of the team (if known) will be important considerations.

• There will be fee-enhancement awareness, particularly as a result of change, client delays, etc.

• Bids will be qualified, explicitly and implicitly.

• Contract terms and conditions will be important.

• Disclosure will detail costs and might include an explicit profit element.

• The internal production culture will be important.

Heuristic trapezoids

Trapezoidal graphics are a simple technique for imaging the project life-cycle in terms of employed resources set against a time-line (32). Conversely, the trapezoid can be used in estimating and resource planning when some of its dimensions are known (or can be reasonably guessed). The technique is founded upon the fact that almost invariably, teams will develop through three stages: build-up, a peaking, and a run-down. This forms the basis of the method, countering any implicit assumption that required resourcing is simply a matter of fees divided by averaged manhour costs.

If team size is set against a time-line, a trapezoid becomes a geometrical shape representing the scope and pattern of activity - the total of a team's manhour input - over the project life-cycle (or, that part of it being considered). The diagram to the left is adapted from James Bent's paper. It shows how a post-conceptualisation stage of engineering development and procurement is made up.

In order to properly construct such a trapezoid the following has to be available:

- the scope of work in manhours
- the effective hours per month that are available
- the % of the overall life-cycle given to build-up and rundown.
- the appropriate peaking (in construction, this is sometimes the viable number of men per sq.m. doing a job).

If key information is missing, it can be extrapolated from what is known, especially if rules of thumb are available. For example, a duration of X is simply calculated from such data using a formula such as:

Trapezoids

The trapezoid concept seeks to translate the base realities of the project life-cycle (build-up, main stage, and run-down) into something easily mapped.

It can also be a reminder that productivity is also unlikely to be uniform across the life-cycle. It will vary with these same stages.

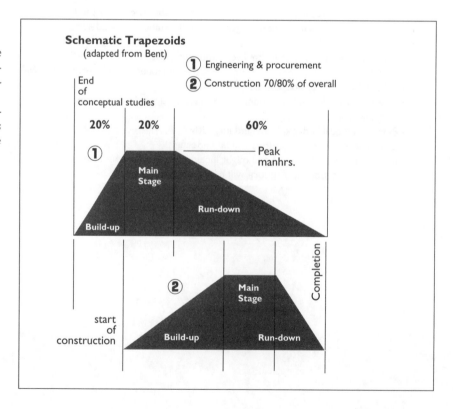

Schematic Trapezoids
(adapted from Bent)

① Engineering & procurement
② Construction 70/80% of overall

End of conceptual studies

20%   20%   60%

① Peak manhrs.

Main Stage

Run-down

Build-up

Completion

② Main Stage

start of construction

Build-up   Run-down

Resource planning and trapezoidal estimating

The effort contained within the life-cycle of a project can be expressed as an area on a graph that sets effort in terms of people (or manhours) against time.

However such a graph does not represent the realities of a life-cycle as a three stage process: build-up; main stage; and run-down. If these are drawn, we begin to see a representation of the peaking - shown here as a trapazoid whose area is equal to the effort required.

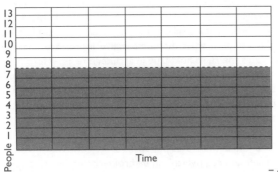

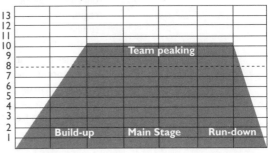

The RIBA fee scale guidance tells us what the architect should expect to charge for the different stages of the overall service, but nothing about the concept of build-up, peaking, and run-down, nor about productivity changes within these stages.

The relevant RIBA stages and their stage equivalents are as follows (i.e. the % charged stages) :

Build-up
  C   Outline proposals
  D   Scheme design
Peaking
  E   Detail design
  FG   Production information
Run-down
  HJKL Tendering, Planning, and Operations on site

This is for a conventional procurement path does not properly address issues arising with concurrent phasing.

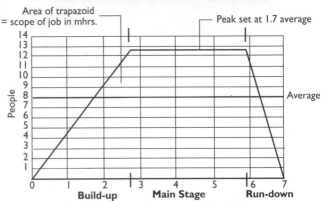

Example: total manpower effort required = 56 units
Build-up, RIBA stages CD = 25-35% of the total fee = say, 19.6 units
Peak main stages, EFG, = 40% = 22.4 units
Run-down stages, HJKL = 25-35% = say, 14 units
Average manpower units = 8
Assume peak of 1.7 x average = 8 x 1.7 = 13.6
Build-up = 56 x 35% = 19.6 units of manpower = A x 13.6 /2
Therefore build-up stage is 2.88 time units. ETC.

This is a real example of a complex refurbishment and fit-out project to an existing building, with staged hand-overs, clients on site, etc., undertaken over three years from iinterview / appointment to full completion. It illustrates various special problems, but still conforms to the general trapazoid pattern. The project required about 800 drawings. The pattern is for the manhours input within the architectural practice.

The high early peaks are a feasibility / scheme proposal, and a major report and scheme presentation covering every aspect of the project and concluding a large series of space-planning interviews. This was followed by delay to a scheme agreement. Demolition works followed internal moves and revealed new issues to be dealt with. Tender information was 'approximate' and final information dealt with concurrently with works.
Run-down after drawings completion was at first accelerated, but this eased to leave a site supervision and administration team.
The inflation adjusted average (inflation was comparatively high at the time) brought the peak team size to 1.7 of the average.

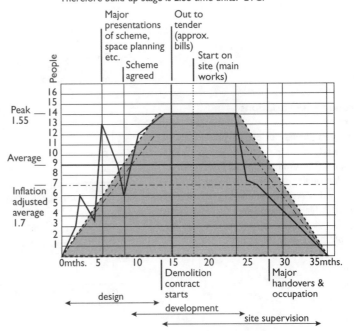

Project duration = scope in manhrs / effective monthly manhrs i.e.
((buildup / 2) x peak men) + (X mths. x peak men) + ((rundown / 2) x peak mean)

In other words, the area of the trapezoid is calculated. Where manpower is not restricted - for example, to a site density or what can be managerially accommodated - then it is easy, using a similar method, to calculate peak team size (assuming a given duration). On the kind of projects Bent was familiar with, peak team sizes were in the region of 1/1.65 for the engineering, and 1/1.45 for construction. It is surprising that similar information has not been made available to architects. A comprehensive survey by the RIBA could quickly establish what the comparative figures are; meanwhile, my personal information indicates the rules hold true in architecture as well.

Another heuristic employed by Bent would also be useful in design estimating: the number of manhours per sq.m. of building. This could use the RIBA job Types and Classes to suggest a base heuristic which can be adjusted for other factors, thus enabling a leap from complexity/scale to manhours required in one step.

- Type / Class / size = manhour rates per sq.m.
- Project size = manhours req.(which can be broken down by principal grades)
- Hourly rates x manhours = minimum fee required.

Bent also discusses productivity (inputs / outputs) over the life-cycle, noting that in engineering construction it is worse by about 10% at the beginning, improving considerably at the peak stage, and deteriorating rapidly during the last 20% of the project. Presuming their applicability in architectural practice, these are significant differences in productivity which any practice manager should be aware of when job planning, especially when planning the larger project. (Admittedly, there are real problems in measuring productivity.) In addition they might want to apply other factors to the productivity measures e.g. favourable or unfavourable circumstances.

Experience shows that practices cannot rely upon their professional institutions to provide this data. They must be proactive and undertake their own research and analysis. However, there is a limit to learning from one's own practice experience. There is also the contradiction that a firm can miss opportunities and even go out of business whilst it learns. One has to conclude that professional institutions should be gathering, analysing and sharing information so that the individual firm can adapt this data to its own experience. Nothing less is acceptable in a pervasive climate of deregulation and competition.

Productivity variations

Managers should not expect productivity to be constant. It can vary by significant amounts. This example derives from construction, but similar problems can be expected in design - they are engendered by the nature of life-cycles for the project and for team-building. The difficulties of winding down at the end are particularly problematic.

Construction stage productivity example
(adapted from Bent) E.G. value of manhour inputs / value of work completed.

● Part Four:

Cultures as Action Systems

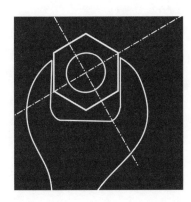

Architectural practices are action systems.

What practices do and undertake, and the manner in which they do it is a rich matrix of many factors in relationship. This is 'culture', which simply means 'the way we do things around here', in that colloquial sense which embraces values as well as mundane activities and decisions.

The way a practice does what it does, the way it acts out who it is as a collective body with a history and ambitions, with unique capabilities and flaws, cannot be divorced from issues of design, quality assurance, competence, professional reward and all the many considerations which can be abstracted out from a deconstructed, once-holistic whole. However, despite uniqueness in terms of capability and character (often born and sustained by default rather than design), practices tend to conform to a range of stereotypical identities. Politically and hierarchically they are fashioned in accord with similar structural issues and difficulties, among which are the realities of project work and the need to ensure that kudos and competence stick to the core members of the organisation.

This section looks at cultural types and goes on to deal with other, (ostensibly) more practical aspects of managing projects within a practice context.

Commitment as action

1 One of the most exasperating issues to confront an architectural manager needing to plan design efforts is obtaining simple answers to questions such as: *How long will it take?* When the process involved is a simple matter of the application of technical expertise the question should be relatively simple to deal with. When design issues of uniqueness and uncertainty are concerned, it is more difficult. In either case, designers simply don't know. How long *does* it take to exercise creative competence and produce satisfactory results? Such as question lies at the heart of productivity issues in design practice.

Earlier sections have considered how the problem can be dealt with by translating the question into a form of technical rationality and the exercise of technical competence. If designers could adopt an entirely precedented, typological approach, requiring only for the exercise of rule-governed technical competence, then the 'design' process would be relatively easy: remove the angst and simply do it! Activities and results would be fairly predictable, entirely dependent upon the initial problem definition.

But the point about design is its reconstructive, creative content and its ability to deal with uncertainty and ambiguity. Such an approach necessarily ignores the creative motivations and competences that produce the desired outcomes. It also leaves the core issue undealt with: *what* is going on during the design process? how can the manager begin to *understand* it? In pragmatic terms, how can it be *managed*? how *do we ensure results - i.e. get the work satisfactorily done in the available time?* How do you know that the institutionalised rules of thumb work, or apply to your practice, or to the project in hand?

One could measure productivity by outcome. However, after-the-fact measures are, by their nature, too late; after-the-fact on a very frequent basis would become bureaucratic and over-bearing. All that is left is to read performances symptomatically - does it *appear* as if work is being effectively performed?

2 **Actions.** The fundamental issue at stake in the design process is that of *decision-making* and consequent policy and action *commitment*. Without commitment a project cannot progress - it can merely degenerate into 'wasting' time. The design team has to quickly *focus*, apply its capabilities and make commitments. These can then be followed up with dependent and co-ordinating commitments until, with concrete being poured, an ultimate level of commitment has been reached and change is materially and (to all intents and purposes) irrevocably realised.

The common denominator is *action* within the temporal framework of the project i.e. the time given to make a proposal, coordinate and agree it, and specify it for action by others, resulting in the desired change of conditions the project aims to realise. Commitments are kinds of action. As the clock ticks away and commitments are made, available funds (resources) are expended, room for manoeuvre is slowly eroded and project leverage is reduced. Given the need to get things right first time, up front, these actions are not only intentionally irrevocable, but must be *increasingly* irrevocable as the project develops.

In these terms, we can describe design management as the purposive manipulation of a project content dealt with as a set of interacting, dynamic considerations, efforts, decisions and commitments made within the context of a valuable temporal resource (and in terms of other, budgetary and performative criteria). Four basic issues stand out. These concern:

1. *The informants of decisions*: goals, values, ambitions, criteria, risk, crucial success factors, etc.
2. *The appropriateness and 'fit' of decisions*. This includes differentiating between

Valuing Action One

"Problems . . . are not just hassles to be dealt with and put aside. Lurking inside each problem is a workshop on the nature of organisations and a vehicle for personal growth. This entails a shift; we need to value the process of finding the solution - juggling the inconsistencies that meaningful solutions entail. . . . Getting grounded is essential because it draws us into experience. . . It is easier to act ourselves into a better mode of thinking than to think ourselves into a better mode of acting. . . Realizing our possibilities as persons isn't about knowledge or information - it's about our own potential. . . Most people are at their best when they are in a relationship with what is going on. . . . None of the ideas work unless we do."
(Pascale, 1990)

To do list

• design a masterpiece ✓

• build the masterpiece ✓

• get the fees in ✓

131

architectures that are performance-driven and features-driven. The focus - either way - is upon end-user activities (activity planning) and experiences.

3. *The quickness and* timeliness *with which appropriate decisions can be made.*

4. *The* time *required to turn design decisions into reliable, descriptive design specifications for others to act upon.*

It would be unrealistic not to acknowledge that it is quickness and timeliness which are of crucial importance. The informants are contextural; the 'fit' is an outcome; and the production time is relatively mechanical. Design skill is not just a matter of being able to home in and get it right - it is also an ability to do these things in the time that is realistically available. Good design is its practice, not its just promise. The *actors* making decisions and consequent commitments not only have to be theoretically and potentially capable, but have to *act* accordingly and deliver results. However, it is difficult to see how time estimates for many design tasks are anything other than an establishment of plausible parameters. It's not that the task takes the time (especially near to the front end of projects), but vice versa: the time available appears to drive the decision-making. Whilst such a conclusion still leaves us in a fog with regards to making time objective estimates, it becomes clear that the planning requires the full engagement of those involved, a full appreciation of what is going on and an ability to identify crucial issues, and a quality of leadership able to manage efforts toward a satisfactory conclusion. There is a mass of literature commenting upon aspects of means-ends thinking, but no researchers appear to be tackling this more pertinent issue.

3 Well Behaved Cultures. When action commitments are being made in a multi-agency context it is necessary that the proposed commitments are understood, discussed, co-ordinated, agreed, and accepted by those all involved and taking responsibility. Your decisions have to accord with mine. If they don't - if there is a mismatch or we are out of synchronisation - then there will be misunderstandings, conflict and wasted time. Not unnaturally, some team members will be convinced of the rightness of *their* proposed commitments and they will not only seek to persuade, but will act politically and strategically in order to win. It follows that promoting and negotiating

Eastern humour

Honda - who attempt to set up a work environmental triad comprising enduring values, trust and empowerment - have a way of encouraging innovation by setting up a balance between set tasks and loose controls. How these are managed is interesting. In the words of a Honda executive discussing how task groups work: "We put them upstairs, remove the ladders, and say, 'You have to figure a way to get down.' Then we set fire to the first floor. I think human beings display their greatest creativity under these circumstances."
(Quoted in Pascale, 1990) Architectural practice can be like that.

Design Commitments

The key to job progress is commitment to appropriate courses of action. Until social actors (as they are called) make decisions which results in consequent policy and action commitments, a job cannot make progress. Timeliness is obviously important, as is proper consideration of the relevant informants of the situational problematic being confronted. When these have been formulated and acted upon as a decision, the result is an outcome in the form of commitment which moves the job forward.

Inability to make the decisions which produce commitment is a major cause of procrastination and delay.

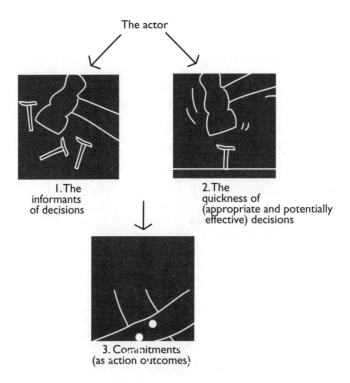

The actor

1. The informants of decisions

2. The quickness of (appropriate and potentially effective) decisions

3. Commitments (as action outcomes)

design commitments are crucial ingredients of inter-team politics. The corollary of this is that team members have to take willing responsibility for shared commitments - they have to 'buy-in' to joint undertakings, becoming stakeholders in the overall success of the project.

Project managers have to accept working principles entirely dependent upon a managerial kind of problem-finding before problem-solving. This has to penetrate through to every level of the team. It has to be accepted that all planning - no matter how good - is dependent upon the team's motivated engagement, full commitment and effective decision-making skills. Project management must ensure this take place at all levels. Planning must be as shrewdly as possible, always identifying 'critical success factors' and anticipating those of the next stage. Commitments must be real, but always working toward a progressively unfolding, 'rolling wave' approach to milestone content which, by implication, is always goal-oriented in the sense of homing-in on getting to where it wants to be. And buffers must be allowed for contingencies, although work must be aimed at the milestone *less* the contingency, 'freezing' commitments to the specification of architectures and features in a timely, progressive manner.

When such considerations are brought together within an architectural firm as features of its behavioural capability they are statements of 'who we are' and 'the way we do things around here'. And, in interaction with its environment, these behaviours are either more or less successful. This is the *culture* of the organisation. Understood in this sense, organisations become *places* to be: the actor is on the inside.

It is important to understand that culture is a behavioural actuality, not an ambition, a set of values, beliefs or, worse, some self-delusion. It follows that most project cultures are a resultant - the compound product of the disparate, participating agency cultures. Since every project and its team is unique to some degree or other, each project culture is similarly unique. The managerial components of the project - at every level and in every aspect of the project organisation - have to contribute to forging an effective project culture from the day of inception, on the run, whilst performances are enacted, commitments are made, and services are being delivered. From this perspective, planning becomes a form of contextual programming, one that is dependent upon the sources of leadership within the team.

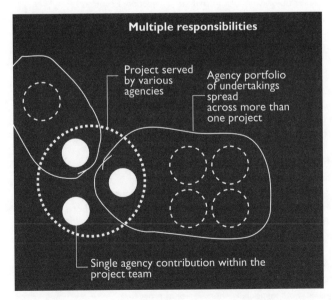

Multiple responsibilities

Project served by various agencies

Agency portfolio of undertakings spread across more than one project

Single agency contribution within the project team

Practice Management

Project planners within architectural practices have to deal with a number of questions e.g.

- *what are we seeking to achieve and deliver? (what is the undertaking?)*
- *what must we do? (what are the necessary activities? what are the crucial ones? where is the priority? where is the risk?)*
- *who is doing what? (how many people do we need? where does responsibility lie? how do we organise? who reports to whom?)*
- *when will they be doing it? (how do we monitor progress? how do we audit it?)*
- *what kinds of co-ordination with other agencies will be necessary? (how do we ensure co-ordination and synchronisation? how do we monitor and check it?)*

Whilst considering delivery schedules and available fees for one project, they will will also be aware of similar questions pertinent to other projects the firm is dealing with. The implication of portfolio interests is that a practice might have to carefully manage its resourcing in an attempt to level peak demands and even 'out-source' project servicing - familiar problems to construction contractors. The aim is a balance between over-stretched or redundant and under-utilised human capital. In a broader sense, it is to orchestrate having the right people, doing the right things (in the right way), in the right place, and at the appropriate time. The reality is that this isn't going to happen, certainly not all the time and there has to be a constant concern with maintaining the quality of service.

Contractual relations

There are three basic forms of contractual relation, all working externally between agents and internally between an organisation and its staff (33). The first contract is the simplest: *the spot contract.*

You have. I want. We can exchange. Examples include buying a taxi ride; buying vegetables at a market stall; purchasing a newspaper or magazine, etc. No written contract is involved. Extensive, formal negotiation is unnecessary. Trust is irrelevant. Usually, if the purchaser is cheated in some way, they don't repeat the transaction although, in the background, there might be generalised state legislation intended to indirectly govern spot contracts and protect the consumer. A firm engages in spot contracts all the time e.g. when purchasing stationery.

The second form of contract is ubiquitous but formal: *the classical contract* (offer / acceptance / consideration).

This is the opposite of the spot contract. It is context-specific and is founded upon a precise and stated set of relationships between the parties involved. No trust is asked for or offered. If you undertake to do this and that, I accept and offer this consideration on agreed terms (the offer / acceptance / consideration equation). Exactly what, when, and for how much will be crucial, as are conditions, criteria, arbitration procedures, payment arrangements, etc. This is a common form of contracts and is a boon to lawyers, especially when a dispute arises.

The third form of contract is ubiquitous but informal: *the relational contract.*

As the term implies, the relational contract is based upon trust, commitments, honour codes and the like. In a cynical world, they work because they are necessarily rooted in the prospect of repeated relations over time. Employment is often characterised as a relational contract - 'work to rule' being an example of what happens when the relational contract degenerates onto a classical basis. Marriage contracts exist, but they undermine the very spirit of co-operation they are intended to underscore and the intended shared benefits the parties seek i.e. the pursuit of a bigger cake for both, rather than the maximisation of one party's share.

Any business organisation uses all three forms of contract and is confronted with the need to ensure their consistency, i.e. to establish that planned outputs can be achieved with the use of available, planned inputs (labour, materials and capital, both monetary and human). In fact, a firm is defined by the contractual relations it forms. Classical contracts will define a project commission, but it is the web of relational contracts that will be so important to capturing these commissions (by offering quality of service as well as quality of work) and establishing a corporate capability for dealing with them. If added value is to be created - in any form - it is dependent upon the firm's success in organising and effecting these contracts, especially the relational type.

Formalised professionalism is a concept seeking to avoid the need for classical contracts or to supplement them with a relational contract. Clients talk of 'their' lawyer, doctor or architect. Professional codes of behaviour and enculturalisation are intended to suggest that classical contracts are unnecessary - this is someone or a firm that can be trusted to behave in accordance with ethical codes of conduct that have personal disinterest at the core of their services - a disinterested expert service being

Offer, Acceptance and Consideration

Contracts normally have three elements:

• An offer i.e. an indication offered by one party to another of a willingness to be contractually bound in certain terms are accepted.

• An acceptance i.e. an unqualified acceptance of the precise terms of the offer.

• A consideration i.e. an act r counter-promise (e.g. a payment) by one party in return for another's promise.

Contracts can be oral or written, express (the full terms are set out in written documents), or implied.

offered in return for tolerance of self-interested market closure and self-regulatory control - what sociologists call the 'regulative bargain'.

2 Architectural Contracts. The managerial client naturally seeks an optimum instrumental advantage by finding the best talent and strongest commitment for the lowest fee and minimum risk on a one-off basis - hence competitive fee bids, free design pitches, collateral warranties, penalty clauses and the like. These instrumental strategies move architects from the demand to the supply side of the project equation, making them simply another sub-contractor executing a classical contract. But the price to be paid is erosion of the professional ideal (including its relational dimensions) and its reduction to kinds of expertise without any expectancy of trust other than that which can be given in law and specified in the contract. Professional codes of conduct are becoming a hollow anachronism. And the architectural contract becomes ever-more dependent upon the small-print which can both self-interestedly exploit the classical relationship and give protection against its exploitation by others.

On the other hand, both client and architect will desire a relational contract which, if nothing else, establishes a less 'mechanically ordered' bond between them and which not only engenders an enjoyment of the project process, but also makes their relationship viable. Client, architect and builders can all expect to be constantly torn between a desire to construct an informal, realistic working relationship rooted in emotive aspects of human relations, and an equally realistic relationship rooted in 'classical' behaviours. However, relational contracts suffer from attempts to be too specific about the nature of the relationship (as the marriage example indicates). The key to their success is the prospect of repeated relations and aspirations toward that end. Consequently, unequal relations, lack of trust and poor prospects for a repeat contract pull the nature of the relationship apart, toward kinds of selfish action (at least, toward ambiguity and even contradictory actions). On the architect's side, the possibility of a repeat appointment or the indirect client referral are aspects of repeat relations but, on the client's side, there is sometimes little to reinforce the relational dimension except committed professional service whilst the project is in progress (or immediately afterwards). This will be especially true of corporate clients, where staff can be expected to move on, leaving only a residual classical content to a project's history.

The presumption of a strong relational element to contractual relations was the basis of the traditional architectural fee: a team leader's basic percentage of construction costs, intended to cover a broad, generalised service that does not have to be spelt out in exact detail. Mandatory fees shift contractual issues toward those of ability, personal chemistries, service, etc. - what can be key issues in a relational contract.

Conversely, fee competition becomes especially important when it is presumed that a short-listed group of firms under consideration are equally talented and expert. It follows that changes to the relational contract between architect and client, and in the agreed form of remuneration are two sides of the same coin.

Scepticism toward the professional ethic, the rise to hegemony of managerial values and its purposive-rationality, and the

Repeat relations

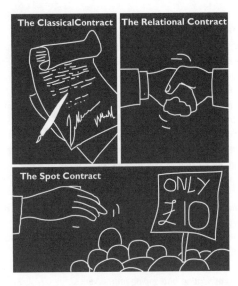

Thinking about a firm (such as an architectural practice) as an organisation is of limited usefulness. It engenders charts and similar means of 'picturing the relationships between those who have power and influence. This way of thinking has to be balanced against a consideration of the firm as a culture, as a set of behaviours which it is only half-conscious of determining - it's 'the way we do things around here' (and, the way we don't). These behaviours are characterised by a large variety of contracts. The most obvious are formal. The least obvious, but most important, are subtle and hard to define. These - the so-called 'relational' contracts within a firm and between it and outsiders - are rooted in the expectation of return relationships.

The types of prevailing contract also affect service delivery. There are possibly two kinds of job which an architect will work on: those where some form of repeat relationship with the client might be expected or is hoped for, and those which are unique, one-off projects which are unlikely to be followed by a return pattern of relationships. Both are common. An example of the latter is the unique exhibition contract between a sponsor / curator and an institutional venue in which shared vested interest in a successful might not be enough to avoid conflict and mutual game-playing aimed at realising advantage with regard to other interests. Once the event opens it is too late for change; the outcome might be a fait accompli by one or another of the parties involved. In this situation, only some form of classical contract will ensure agreements are respected. However, this might be inappropriate or deemed to betray ostensible trust and good-will. There is a natural tendency to avoid classical contracts - in which case, the expectation of a repeat relationship needs to be encouraged by the weaker party.

3 A's: Aptitude, Attitude, Achievement

There is a large body of psychological research indicating that measures of intelligence are not predictors of socio-economic success. Similarly, in design, talent is not sufficient. Aptitude must be mediated through an appropriate attitude if achievement is to result. For example, the reliable, supportive project team member who is able to socially blend with other team members and is oriented toward task completion is arguably of more usefulness than most prima donna who appear to have a wealth of talent. Daniel Goleman (35) has called termed such kinds of social success a different kind of smartness - one he terms emotional intelligence. Academic and instrumental definitions of talent, skill and intelligence are severely deficient to the extent they leave out consideration of this dimension of IQ.

A definition of emotional intelligence includes abilities in five domains:
• self-awareness - recognising a feeling as it happens.
• managing emotions, especially negative ones, depression and lack of optimism and hope.
• marshalling emotions in the service of a meaningful goal - including delaying gratification and stifling impulsiveness.
• having empathy i.e. being able to recognise emotion in others.
• an ability to handle relationships with others.

Emotional intelligence is crucial to the success of project teams. Those who possess it are able to harmonise with others and help to produce a kind of group intelligence. Without this quality, a group is merely an aggregate of talents and abilities that remain forever in potentiality rather than realised effectiveness.

Emotional intelligence in the group is an ability to harmonise, to realise the potential performance of the team. This has been seen to be hampered by those who are too eager as well as those who hold back - in other words, behavioural aptness and a sense of what is appropriate. Research at Bell Laboratories indicated that star performers cultivate informal networks of complex social ties that pay dividends when difficulties arise. Three kinds of network appeared to operate: who talks to whom; expertise networks based upon who is turned to for advice; and trust networks of those people confide in. Other skills possessed by stars in the labs included an ability to co-ordinate their efforts within the team context; being leaders in consensus-building; being able to see things from another's perspective; and an ability to be persuasive and promote cooperation whilst avoiding conflict. They were also self-motivated and able to regulate their time and work commitments.

shift from a generalised agreement to a negotiated and formally classical one (as the RIBA's Standard Form of Agreement, based on a commodified shopping list of services) are symptoms of profound changes of a structural nature. Other symptoms of structural change include attempts to affect internal self-regulation, educational programmes and the nature of the profession's expertise by imposing external constraints and performance standards. Examples include quality assurance and auditing, value engineering, continued professional development programmes, health and safety regulations, etc. Most of these are initiatives from *outside* the profession which informally redefine its regulative bargain with society (34).

Some professions - such as estate agencies - are a poor breeding ground for relational contracts and the lack of expectancy means that, on the contrary, economic opportunism is expected and accepted. Reputations rarely suffer because of it. However, architectural culture is deeply rooted in the importance of a good reputation. The dilemma can only be resolved by splitting service values: on the one hand, the tradition of design expertise and excellence; on the other, a commercial attitude to remuneration and the exploitation of opportunity. This is now accepted behaviour, but it is rarely commented upon in the architectural media or within architectural education. The only indication of attitude change is that the appellation 'commercial practice' - once a familiar way of dismissing a firm as unworthy, devoid of traditional practice concerns with design and liberal- humanism, and too concerned with monetary reward and managerial values - is now rarely heard. However, self-evident prejudices still linger, indicative that the architectural profession still stands on unfamiliar ground.

Games People Play

The nature and character of relational contracts can be illustrated by simple game theory.

The Prisoner's Dilemma:

Two prisoners are taken in by the police and face serious charges. There are three possible outcomes, depending upon how each prisoner deals with the situation. If **A** confesses and **B** does nothing, **A** gets off free and **B** gets 10 years (and vice versa): however, if both confess, they get 7 years each; if neither confesses they still get one year each. They can't communicate. Confessing becomes the dominant (best) strategy. This remains true regardless of what the other person does and no matter how many times the game is played. Even knowledge of what is happening makes no difference.
The business equivalent is the prices war: both parties have an interest in avoiding it, but both have a self-interest in undercutting the rival. The parties involved should co-operate, but this requires trust and commitment as well as communication. Another parallel is fee competition between architects and the constant calls for common action (mandatory fees closed the client's game). In the game, the dilemma is that it is other prisoner's interest to say they will cooperate, and then to renege on the agreement! Experiments suggest that people do co-operate, but on a tentative basis which enacts tit-for-tat reactions to infringements.

The Prisoner's Revenge

A variation on the Prisoner's Dilemma is when A confesses, B gets ten years, but then B's friends beat A up very badly (the equivalent of, say, 5 years in jail). As in the PD, the best outcome depends upon what the other prisoner does, but the best strategy also now depends upon the actions of the other prisoner. There is an implied benefit in co-operation and, if one prisoner has a dominant strategy, this can be calculated. It is in the interests of each prisoner to second-guess the move of the other (resulting in 7 years each, or one year each).

These two games illustrate the equilibrium resulting from the best thing to do given the other party's preferred action. In both games there are two positions of equilibrium. Sometimes the best choices producing equilibrium are not obvious or easily resolved. An illustration of this is another game: the Battle of the Sexes.

The Battle of the Sexes

In this game two players want to do the same thing but can't communicate. For example, a man and a woman want to go out together, but have to make separate decisions about where to meet. He wants to go to restaurant A and she wants to go to restaurant B. Is the best plan to be selfish, hoping the other person will not be selfish and meet at the first's preferred venue, or is it to be unselfish, each turning up at the less preferred venue? In which case the risk is a wasted evening without the partner and at the less preferred venue? His best outcome is to go to restaurant A and find her there; her best outcome is to go to restaurant B and find him there. How are they to choose? The two choices producing equilibria have the same value. The symmetry can be broken easily if one person imposes commitment or hierarchy. For example, he has an invitation to a free dinner at restaurant A, or both know that this time it's her turn! Hierarchy plays an important role in project leadership. Someone is needed simply to decide (what is decided is arguably less important).

In the PD it is important that both parties reach trust in each other's commitment. If A gets B to commit to no confession, it is in A's interest to renege on that agreement. Holding back is a natural dominant strategy. However, gain comes not only from the commitment of the other person, but also from the manifest and credible commitment of oneself. The classical contract produces what is termed *perfunctory* cooperation. The relational contract produces what is termed *consummate* co-operation. It is the latter that everyone is looking for, especially in building contracts

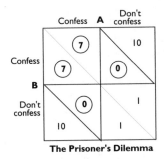

The Prisoner's Dilemma

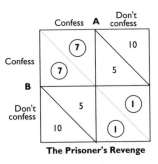

The Prisoner's Revenge

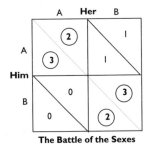

The Battle of the Sexes

(These examples are adapted from John Kay's book on corporate strategy, Foundations of Corporate Success, 1993.)

Cultural architectures

In the context of project and design management culture is very simply the collective behavioural characteristics of an organisation, summed up in the notion that 'culture is the way we do things around here'. Culture is what outsiders experience - a way of objectively labelling a characteristic pattern of services, values, decisions, performances . . . but to understand it, we need to enquire about formative influences.

In an earlier section we discussed the importance of relational contracts and the importance of their rootedness in the expectation of repeated relations between people. It is these relational contracts that form the 'glue' binding people together into an organisation. Their significance is illustrated by the 'work to rule' tactic sometimes adopted during industrial conflicts - a resort to the 'classical' contractual terms that formally define relations. Relational contracts are also the glue between a firm and those with whom it does business: its suppliers and customers. The nature and structure of the web of relational contracts forms an organisational *architecture* and helps to define the distinctive character and capabilities of the firm.

Relational architecture - just like the architecture of a building - is configurational and advantageously manifests itself both as a co-operative ethics and as organisational knowledge affecting behavioural routines, The ability to reproduce services from project to project, an ability to innovate, to exchange information in an easy and open manner, etc. On the inside, it is hermeneutically summed up as 'who we are', but clients know that firm by what it does i.e. the manifest cultural behaviours that are the product of who it is. What differentiates one architectural firm from another is not generalised professional expertise as such, but its specific, manifest form as a feature of distinctive organisational capability and character i.e. the firm's competitive advantage.

2 Culture as Control. The organisational architecture of a firm's relational contracts is often subtle and, by its nature, hard for competitors to replicate. At its best, this architecture enables ordinary people to achieve extraordinary results within the context of the organisational framework and its cultural behaviours (its organisational structure, routines, style of doing things, etc.). The histories of the British Raj, IBM during its heyday, Marks & Spencer, or Liverpool football club (maintaining its position despite many team changes) are classic examples. However, a key issue is the difference between those firms ostensibly unreliant upon any individual and those for whom individuals are clearly fundamental to an ability to offer services, e.g. advertising agencies, architectural firms and the like.

Because of their diffuse relational underpinning, organisational cultures can be rather intractable - at once the product of individual member's values, commitments and behaviours, yet simultaneously elusive and difficult to actually locate and manipulate. Frustratingly, individuals can be rather helpless in influencing overall cultural behaviours except in the most local and short-term manner. Ideally, culture is changed from above, where leadership can exercise example and maximum leverage; influenced from below, change must be forceful and is likely to be the product of crisis.

Nothing is a better illustration of this than the futile attempt of the established but creatively impotent firm to buy in young talent in the hope of transforming itself - a beneficial result will be short-lived unless it is sustained from the top and indutibly imbues and amends organisational culture. The reasons are structural and political. Whilst it is individual professionals who create the added value and realised potential which differentiates a firm's distinctive capability and competitive advantage, what sustains the integrity of the firm is its ability to ensure that added value accruing to the firm sticks to the organisation rather than any individual member. This is the only way the firm can enhance its reputation and long term capability independent of individual pro-

Three kinds of service value:

1. As a creative alchemical act that mixes aesthetic, social, and utilitarian ingredients from which - by design - something precious is realised from project material.

2. As creative consultancy aiming to realise maximum benefit to the client from the project situation i.e. as smart thinking accruing value to the client. This is sometimes a strategic, up-front service whose benefit derives from defining the design ambitions and content of a project, or it can be the exercise of specialised technical expertise anywhere in a project history.

3. As technically-biased, project development and implementation, embracing the avoidance of possible dissatisfactions as well as the realisation of design and constructional potential.

Value of these kinds is created by a firm's success in putting relationships and contracts together. Ensuring intended service outputs is dependent upon the consistency as well as the quality and distinctiveness of these contracts. In behavioural and experiential terms, the medium of service and value realisation is practice culture.

fessionals who, on the other hand, self-evidently make it what it is. The firm will seek to prevent opportunism and check overly-individualistic behaviour by linking professional and social life. In addition, the firm will encourage a corporate ethos which plays down the importance of the *prima donna*, encourages team-playing, enhances corporate intelligence as a distinctive knowledge base, promotes its corporate reputation with media publicity and portfolios emphasising record and achievements, and by cultivating an extended 'architectural' network of external contacts with associated professionals, trade associations, clients bodies, etc. Everyone must work as part of a collective to exercise the firm's distinctive capability and realise added value.

Firms with acronyms such as SOM, DEGW, HOK, BDP, etc., are deliberately depersonalising the corporate image and emphasising an identity which utilises individual talents whilst remaining independent of them. Behind the acronym are the directors and shareholders who influence the firm's policies and behaviours. An alternative strategy is to keep the firm trading and offering services under the banner of its founder's name, even though everyone knows the real work is done by a broader spectrum of staff.

An essential aspect of these arrangements is that the seniors of the firm will channel, gate and dominate the work of individual professionals so as to ensure it (and they, as partners or directors) control the derived flow of benefits. Without such strategies a firm would fall apart, its members making off with project cudos and the firm's clients. And this sometimes happens. On the other hand, individuals must be allowed a sense of personal satisfaction - which returns to the need for relational contracts and their basis in the mutual expectation of *repeated* relations.

3 **The Logic of Professional projects.** Without a strong internal relational architecture classical contracts will necessarily predominate and it is difficult to imagine how these would help a firm cultivate creative responsiveness to the unique potential of client's projects. The corollary of this is that classical contracts will be a stronger feature of employer / employee relations when the project content is more repetitive and predictable in terms of challenge and expected outcome. Cultures characterised by classical job descriptions, tightly defined roles and 9-5 behaviours will be biased toward perfunctory rather than consummate contractual relations. However, given the uncertainty of most architectural projects and inevitable calls upon staff to provide extra, non-routine effort, such a culture is likely to be relatively plodding and creatively unresponsive. It will possibly be anathema to the vocational and creative

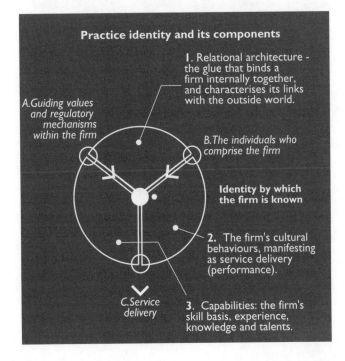

Practice identity and its components

1. Relational architecture - the glue that binds a firm internally together, and characterises its links with the outside world.

A. Guiding values and regulatory mechanisms within the firm

B. The individuals who comprise the firm

Identity by which the firm is known

2. The firm's cultural behaviours, manifesting as service delivery (performance).

C. Service delivery

3. Capabilities: the firm's skill basis, experience, knowledge and talents.

Practice Identities

The 'architecture' of a firm is what literally informs the services it provides. Its expertise, skills, experience are married to kinds of cultural behaviours which characterise how jobs are handled, and both are infused with the relational contracts which give the firm its uniqueness. Specific individuals, guiding values, studio disciplines and similar regulatory influences in the firm all contribute to characterising an entity which is very difficult for anyone to replicate. They can learn from example, but this still has to be absorbed into their own organisational architecture. All this can be distilled down to the perception of identity - the acronym or logo, the short-hand by which people recognise and acknowledge the underlying complexity.

instincts of staff enculturalised into a mentality thriving upon unique problem situations and suffering a slow death when confined within a bureaucratic environment where mechanisms of planning and control are likely to be fundamental to the delivery of technical expertise and corporate control. In any case, a professional's commitments lean toward loyalty to peer groups rather than employers. For these reasons classical contracts tend to be restricted to support staff who, in any case, are likely to be more concerned with the specific content of the employment contract than most professionals, especially young ones.

The vocational commitment that is at the heart of the better architect's endeavours goes hand in hand with a relational contract. This suggests flat hierarchies and remuneration structures, informal human relations, openness, trust, consummate co-operation, and information sharing together with an awareness that the firm's performance benefits everyone in the firm. Such an idea is somewhat at odds with the need to accrue benefit not only to the firm, but to the individuals who own it, control it or give their names to it and accept legal liabilities. The result of this tension is a limit to the realities of a 'family' spirit, an engendering of internal politics and the formation of internal hierarchies.

In any case, the logic of project work is that it is hire and fire business, people being taken on as and when needed, and discarded when the project winds down. This entails the difficulty of ensuring employment continuity and produces consequent strains upon the both the firm's organisational architecture and its distinctive capabilities. This logic again reinforces a hierarchy that differentiates between a tight core of job-getters with managerial and creative control, a body of trusted associates aspiring to the inner core but with limited real benefits, and a third layer of employees and sub-contracted workers who are employed on a hire and fire basis depending upon the work flow. The middle layer is especially important to project and design management, to ensuring delivery and the minimisation of risk. Strong, reputable firms are almost invariably organised this way. They have strong cultures but they are also tough and can be ruthless. They astutely manage the contradictions between the need for robust internal architectures made up of loyal and committed individuals, and the nature of project work. They form one of the standard stereotypes of successful practice: the power culture (see the following section).

Relational architecture, Power, and Practice Culture

The diagram above relates the four cultural stereotypes to relational architectures and to power structures.

A 'Thick' relational architecture is strong and present throughout the firm. A 'Thin' relational architecture is weak and diffused. A 'Diffused' power structure is evenly distributed, suggesting each individual concerned has a voice. A 'Focused' power structure is concentrated and suggests weak away from the central source of power.

		Power structure	
		Diffused	Focused
Relational architecture	Thick	**Task** (thick and distributed) Accrued benefit shared	**Power** (thick and local) Accrued benefit controlled
	Thin	**Role** (thin and differentiated) Accrued benefit indirect	**Person** (thin and specific) Accrued benefit localised

Cultural stereotypes

Stereotyping is sometimes misleading, but often useful. Organisations can be characterised in terms of four predominating cultural stereotypes (36), all of which can be found in architectural practice. Each type describes a power structure as well as professionally characteristic behaviours. Relational architecture, power structure, and behavioural culture will tend to form a consistent entity and inform the practice's service output. However, at the heart of this equation will be the core issue of the control and management of accrued benefit

• The first type is the *task culture*. This is a consensus-seeking culture of individuals often operating in teams or as a matrix organisation. The type is a common aspiration of architectural practices because it implies reasonable professional autonomy, allows the individual voice, and offers flat hierarchies and consultation within an organisational climate imbued with expertise. Multi-disciplinary and multi-team practices are often task cultures. At its best, such a culture is co-operative, expert, good in a variable environment, and characterised by strong relational contracts between mutually respectful colleagues (described as 'thick' in the adjacent diagram because they are uniformly distributed through the organisation). It is not a natural risk-taker. Ideally, it will be transparent and accrued benefit will be equitably shared. At its worst it tends toward excessive navel-gazing and can also become a disingenuous front for the reality of an underlying power structure of another type (accruing distinctive capability to the owners). In a crisis, task cultures quickly revert to the power type (see below) - if only temporarily.

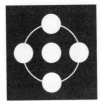

• The second type also has strong and 'thick' relational contracts, but it operates on a different basis - the contracts are localised rather than uniformly distributed. This is the *power culture* - often centred around a strong individual at its centre who legitimates organisational behaviours and is surrounded by a politicised web of reliable individuals who think in a similar way and act out of fear as much as respect and loyalty focused on the centre. Empathy at the centre must be strong. There are few formal rules and little or no bureaucracy, but the organisation will be inherently disciplined. Setting policies, making decisions and dealing with crises is the strength of this type. Decisions will be made quickly and unequivocally. Consultation will be limited. People will be judged on the basis of effectiveness and results. The hierarchy is obvious and with little ambiguity. Promotion will result from 'fit'. Accrued benefits will be tightly controlled from the centre and middle management will probably be swamped in machiavellian politics. At the lower level, accrued benefit will be mostly professional cudos.

Property developers often appear to be power cultures and the type is common among architectural firms. In fact, it is arguable that the best, strongest and most consistent firms are invariably of this type. Examples proliferate: Foster, Farrell, Hopkins, le Corbusier, Aalto, Mies, Frank Lloyd Wright - all have had the reputation of operating disciplined power cultures. Outputs are readily identifiable - not as stylistic idiosyncracity, but as a distinctive capability and commitment - so that the type sometimes becomes a 'signature' firm. The Foster practice, for example, is repeatedly quoted as an exemplary contemporary model and is renowned for simple, coherent and instrumental building solutions executed with rationality and focus (as well as flair).

• The third cultural stereotype is the *person culture*. This is a minimum-culture organisational type, created from a cluster of individuals who have banded together for specific mutual benefits but wish to remain as independent and autonomous voices. The organisation is loose, decentralised and networked. Examples include barristers chambers, communes, specialist consultants in hospitals, some teachers and similar groups, as well as architects. Many professionals like the person culture because they naturally feel more allegiance to their profession than to any employer or strong organisation. They work for themselves, see the organisation as a base to spring from and are difficult to organise and exercise power over. Being expert, they are slow to acknowledge the authority of management; being autonomous specialists, sometimes with tenure, the exercise of power over resources affecting them might have little influence; position power is something they are inherently suspicious of (and, in any case, it is lacking in coercive ability); and personality will have a limited ability to influence them. For all these reasons, we can say that the relational architecture of such a grouping is thin and specific. Benefits accrue on an ad hoc basis to those individuals involved, not to the networked organisation as a whole. Academics and the large body of sole practitioners in private practice - manipulating professional status but allied to few - exemplify this type.

• The fourth stereotype is the bureaucracy or *role culture*. It also has a thin, hierarchically differentiated relational architecture and is characterised by kinds of classical contracts binding the individual members of the organisation together. Formally defined roles, rules and procedures characterise this organisational type. Job descriptions and authority definitions will abound, power will come from position rather than charisma (as in the power culture) or expertise (as in the task culture), and individuals might hide behind their roles. These cultures seek minimum risk and maximum efficiency and effectiveness, although they will suffer from rigidity and a slow responsiveness to change. Systemised co-ordination will be accompanied by a high degree of interdependence, close monitoring, supervision and control. At best, the role culture is reliable and takes pride in process. The type has become rare in architectural practice, although it was once common among local authorities, where accrued benefit is not meant to exist except in the diffuse sense of the community at large and in the indirect sense of job security and 9-5 routines.

2 **Dominant Themes.** All practices will have elements of all four stereotypes - the issue is one of dominance, consistency and how cultural behaviours are structured and informed. In turn, this will necessarily have to 'fit' the kind of projects the practice undertakes and the kind of clients its serves. Architectural power and role cultures, for example, share a concern with managerial control and hierarchy, but in entirely different ways. Similarly, professionalism is a common background to all four stereotypes, but it will be handled in different ways. The task culture and the person culture share a self-evident professional orientation in the sense of the autonomous professional ideal, although the former seeks cohesion and the latter seeks limited interdependency. Power and role cultures are more dependent upon (formal or informal) organisational hierarchies.

Staffing will also be affected. The more esteemed power structure is likely to be staffed by employees who are there because of their youthful talents and enthusiasm rather than their professionally enculturalised expertise. They will enjoy enlightened patronage under the domination of a politicised staff of finders and minders who form the core of the organisation or represent it, and will conform and perform with dedication, obtaining, in return, the experience of excellence and an esteemed name on their c.v. Typically, remuneration will be low for the majority and high for those at the centre of the web. And 'nights of the long knives' will be decisive cost-cutting exercises as the core sheds its redundant, replaceable peripheral assistance.

Multi-disciplinary types of practice will tend toward a reliable, consensus-seeking culture of relatively autonomous and equal professionals, lending such firms the ability to handle larger, more complex projects (as task cultures). However, an appetite for consensus will have to be tempered by the need for principals to balance democracy against the need for organisational consistency, purposefulness and effectiveness between multi-disciplinary teams. Staffing policies might lean toward older, more experienced professionals who can develop a knowledge-base of expertise, and strong organisational routines and support systems will be needed to enhance capabilities and provide an instrumental orientation focused upon cost-effective service.

The knowledge-based consultancy is likely to be a variation on the task culture and will be even more dependent upon apparently flat hierarchies. The practice might model its aspirations toward current best practice in business, occasional weekends will be spent navel-gazing and the consultancy element will generate a proliferation of support staff. However, to the extent that such a practice also has to deliver a design service it will also find itself incorporating elements of the role culture and an instrumental, delivery-oriented culture with a natural power-seeking base. Younger, consultancy personnel, possibly of an intellectual background, might find themselves at odds with a production culture tending toward pragmatism and a more pyramidal hierarchy of older staff.

Overall, an underlying power culture retaining distinctive capability in the hands of a few is likely to be the norm for most architectural practices, whatever the pretensions are.

3 **Type-casting.** Such considerations lead to the notion that practices can usefully be type-cast. The model on the previous page has three elements: the power structure of the practice; its problem-orientation; and a characterisation of practice type. Power cultures are divided between practices tending toward being consensus-seeking, as exemplified by the task culture of a multi-disciplinary firm, or those tending toward a more centralised power-seeking web. Problem orientation is divided between problem-finding and problem-solving (as the concepts have been earlier described).

The resulting four types of practice culture are: *the expert practice; the signature practice; the consultancy; and the delivery firm.* Each characterisation will be reflected in differing behaviours and policies, dealing with such issues as, for example:

• The practice's project operating and managing strategies and methods.
• Where project decisions are made in the practice (the balance between finders, minders, and grinders).
• Staffing policies at middle levels and below (recruitment of minders and grinders).
• What the practice sells.
• The best markets for practice services (who to target).
• What the practice can charge, and best profit strategies.

• *The expert practice* is the one with the grey beards and expertise. Its hall-mark will be a broad capability. It will be skilled in a thorough, problem-framing, improvisational artistry and will seek to ensure sound delivery practises tempered by long-term considerations (such as 'green' issues, conservation, life-cycle costings and the like). The expert practice will pursue considerate, mainstream aesthetics reflecting capability without the gestures or idiosyncracity that might come from a 'signature' firm, the sacrifice of constructional common-sense or public acceptance. It is probably the most stand-alone practice culture, often multi-disciplinary and well managed. It will seek to acquire and develop the skills and specialisms it requires as need arises and markets change, although it will, by its nature, safely root itself in a sound knowledge-base and established good-practise. Sometimes there are 'signature' pretensions, possibly as a hangover from a former reputation or a sense of inferiority. Consequently, such firms might resort to buying-in talent which they believe will transform their image. Led from the top, by new leadership, this might even work. By nature, it will tend toward a task culture structure.

• *The signature practice* is more or less expressive and idiosyncratic, sometimes characterised as the 'ideas' practice who are the brightest dudes on the block (age is irrelevant). The output of this stereotype represents a practice ideal, flattering and attracting publicity, although rarely a consensus about the worth of its output (which almost always has an emphasis upon form). Aesthetic and intellectual criteria will be important. Means/ends thinking will be admitted only in the form of specialist inputs from other, expert professional consultancies - otherwise it will be frowned upon as inappropriately philistine. There will be an emphasis upon ideas and innovation, and upon arguing that intelligence, wit and inventiveness - as well as technical expertise - are required for the exercise of creative competence (although such firms can be as disparate as Sir Michael Hopkins and Terry Farrell). The service will seek to range across both problem-solving and finding. Delivery will be important, especially for commercial or speculative projects and younger firms of this type might have to join with others with an established reputation in order to obviate perceived risk and secure work.

A consultant is an ordinary person a long way from home. An expert is someone with no elementary knowledge.
Anon.

• *The consultancy* will emphasise a comparatively narrowly defined, in-depth, professional knowledge base that can be brought to the strategic benefit of clients. This can be broadly or narrowly defined, but it will always be focused; analysis, research and report writing will be important. Specialisms such as space and facilities planning for offices, historical conservation, energy conservation, and even litigation are examples. Orientation will be toward instrumental problem-solving and might be focused upon the front-end of projects where managerial leverage can be maximised. At other times the consultancy might be an aspect of another architect's more holistic design considerations. However, since few practices of any scale can support themselves entirely upon such a specialised basis, the consultancy can also be expected to offer other services. For example, the space planning practice might get involved in interior design and fit-outs, and even in new-build offices. Typically, an hourly-rated consultancy service will be supplemented with a percentage rated design service. Good design will be expected, but it will rarely be of the 'signature' type. These supplementary services can produce an internal cultural conflict between the job-finding, leveraged consultancy and the weight of a production culture.

• *The delivery firm* is the opposite of the consultancy. Procedures and execution are their hallmark. This is the 'trust-me-we'll-get-you-there' practice exercising implementational artistry. They tend to standardise their services and products within a familiar framework of technical expertise and problem-solving. Originality will not be essential or important, but purposive internal management will be. These people understand the statutory and regulatory environment as fact rather than principle. They get the job done and set a bench-mark of instrumental delivery service. Staffing will be reliant upon para-professionals.

4 Dominant Types. We now see that the earlier diagram offering the identity of a practice as a mix of relational architecture, cultural type and capability can be rephrased. Cultural type is now one of four stereotypes informed by a particular power structures, and capability partly derives from problem-orientation. Any particular practice can be expected to attempt to mix these cultural stereotypes. This might not be easy and there is an opinion that cultural consistency is important to success. However, it is clear that there are three dominant types: the Ideas (or Signature) firm, the Expert firm, and the Delivery firm, with the consultancy firm as a lesser example. The professional identities of these firms becomes more clear when the stereotypes are described in terms of scope of service envelopes and schematically placed upon a project life cycle (see diagram opposite). No one of the above stereotypes is completely filling out the project potentiality. It would be unrealistic to expect this; however, each will be seeking to supplement or complement its essential distinctive capability. This can only be achieved if the firm's relational architecture and its culture make it feasible.

The *Expert firm* will seek to serve a project from inception to completion, and to appropriately broaden its depth of service to compete with the kinds of knowledge-base offered by Consultancies, the flair of the Signature /Ideas practice, and the effectiveness of the delivery firm.

The *Signature firm* is best at formulating a scheme and setting up its key features. Its ambition must be to stretch this capability into a broad design development and an instrumental delivery service, shifting its internal value system and project-orientation as it does so. Being biased toward a design agenda it is unlikely to be involved in formulating the project in very fundamental terms (i.e. the brief).

The *Delivery firm*, reliant upon an implementational skill, will be seeking to be instrumentally effective between scheme design and the completion of construction.

The *Consultancy* can serve the project before or after scheme design, but it is limited to an in-depth and otherwise narrow focus.

There is a theory that cultures tend to evolve, that there is a natural tendency, for example, for the signature firm to develop an expert role and also experience a pull toward enhancing a delivery role. The ageing process will account for some of this development, but its affects are probably exaggerated. Grey beards can still have the mind-set which is oriented toward the fullness of an more purely architectural agenda (motivations and behavioural patterns tend to be very resistant to change) and it is the maturing of their clients and markets which will really effect manifest change. However, it is likely that the firm's founders will be reluctant and rather unhappy by the time they reach the delivery stage and it is generational change which will further the developmental process - in this sense it is the culture that is maturing, not the individual members.

To the extent consultancy is a specialisation, it can sustain itself without other kinds of capability; however, most should expect their specialisation to be supplemented by the fullness of service provided by expert and delivery cultures if the firm is to be economic and viable on a larger scale. In this sense, consultancies (as in space-planning) tend toward an Expert identity. Similarly, the Expert culture might expect to learn enough to become a specialist consultancy in some areas.

Delivery cultures can also evolve, although the type's unglamorous identity both hides examples and suggests development to other types is unlikely. Or it it? Cultural change is affected by a variety of factors. Three stand out: the ageing of the firms founders or controlling influences; the ageing of the markets the firm serves (see below); and - if the firm survives - generational change which sees control and client management pass into new hands (and mind-sets). The problem, of course, is that someone enjoying a more purely design agenda is unlikely to be within a Delivery firm. Another version of 'generational change' is when a firm is taken over or comes into an alliance. This is not uncommon and can effect significant change.

Overall, one has to conclude that stereotypical cultures can be described as undergoing stereotypical change, but the realities (i.e. outside of the limitations of stereotypical descriptions) will be more complex.

5 Firms and Market Evolution. A common feature of almost all firms appears to be the way in which both they and their markets evolve - in one sense independently; in another, they appear almost organically linked.

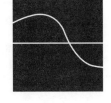

Bright young things will seek to establish themselves and, despite talk of 'It'll never happen to us' and 'We will always remain small', they will inevitably welcome the opportunities of new clients, larger, grander jobs, bigger conversations, more photo opportunities and the potential of congratulation. A larger practice will seem like a small price. They will grow and, in the process, they mature as the partners or directors get older and more experienced. The firm is then likely to become an expert practice undertaking a range of more or less complex jobs and ensuring the capability to handle them is there. Some firms manage to stay at this point (Sir Norman Foster's firm is an example), but this is heavily dependent upon middle management politics, the quality of leadership and an ability to win a range of job types which successfully spread the image of success across a comparatively broad front. In Foster's case, there is a sense in which the firm has almost become its own market niche. Other firms lose the personality element and renew their inner capability from within (perhaps painfully), changing and adapting in line with market circumstances. Those (usually larger firms) who survive major recessions are good examples, even if their organisational success goes unnoticed and uncelebrated.

On the other hand, there are firms who are more tightly linked to specific markets. These markets never stand still and can even change at a rapid rate. An example is the way public housing in post-war practice in the UK evolved through the heady years of the welfare state and government subsidies, through to an era of professional deregulation and a corresponding change to a market economy. Initially, housing was a field of experimentation and architectural prestige, a market in which many architects established a good name for themselves. Then it became a sphere of expertise, handled by firms who were not only bright, but could handle the regulatory side of the project

How can a Firm Transcend the Four Cultural Stereotypes?

Stereotypes are, by their nature, generalised pigeon-holes. How can an ambitious firm transcend them and mix capabilities and cultural features? In brief, it becomes exceptional:
It must become both simple and complex. It must orientate itself to both problem-solving and problem-finding. It must foster consensus and operate as a power culture. It will be simultaneously expert, ideas oriented, reflective and focused upon delivery.

The key is to become smarter. This means employing smarter and more expert personnel, and effecting a rewarding, smarter management system. The problem is cultural.

The relatively dumb culture will neces-  *sarily generate more rules in order to regulate its cultural activities. Smart people - especially professionals - will resist such a rule-governed culture and demand an ability to take the initiative and bear responsibility. What will tighten the culture and prevent it disintegrating is a power culture - in other words the culture ends up as at once centralised and decentralised, seeking flat hierarchies yet precisely organised, having defined authority yet keeping this low profile and rather blurred. None of this can be achieved without intelligent and expert personnel who are motivated, dedicated and hard working professionals. They also have to be co-ordinated and synchronised into a coherent culture entity. Rules must become guidelines. Rigidity must become flexibility. Bureaucracy must become a culture with esprit.*

A firm of this kind will have a culture emphasising technical competence and delivering a highly respected and valued service. These ambitions will be valued above sticking to rules and regulations, respecting formal job and role titles, and cultivating political aptitude.

This kind of firm is also likely to be characterised by challenge and a perceptible cultural dynamic. Members of the firm will believe in who they are and what they do. They will want to get on with it

Management consultancies are organisations of bright managers jealous of their autonomy. Individual enterprise has to be balanced with collective purpose. Some agencies attempt what is called a tight-loose technique of management - meaning a strong common culture rather than tight supervision. The slogan at McKinsey (one of the most famous and successful of consultancies) is 'one firm' with a single profit centre. Skilled staff are grown on the inside in a 'move or move out' culture. Perhaps architectural firms could learn lessons here.

Paradigm Shifts

Forms of continuous, incremental change are normal, but they risk being locked into particular paradigms which habituate ways of 'problem framing' and action. The result is kinds of crisis, sometimes the failure of a firm, sometimes a necessary and radical attempt to achieve a 'paradigm shift'. The maintenance of order - an implicit predicate of much organisation theory, including most project management theory - produces familiar concerns with monitoring and control systems. A counter theory to the search for order and coherence accepts that disequilibrium might be important to longer term survival (because it engenders learning, renewal and change). This produces an evolutionary view of organisations in terms of periods of tradition punctuated by occasional periods radical change (project management features significantly at both levels).

Research in manufacturing has suggested the theory that firms in that sector go through four stages (most don't make it to the last one, or slip back): being reactive; being competitively neutral; being a strategic contributor; and being a source of world-class competitive advantage. Companies often hold and inflated view of their position, but rarely skip a stage. This theory supports the incrementalist view but, there appears to be an 'invisible wall' between stages three and four requiring radical action in order to break through (see Pascale, 1990).

Pascale - concerned with an anatomy of revitalisation - argues that firms need to address four characteristics which drive stagnation and renewal:

• *Fit - pertains to an organisations's internal consistency and coherence. (Unity)*
• *Split - describes the way the whole is divided into a smaller units, each with a strong sense of ownership and identity. An an architectural practice this might be the separate project teams and the support staff. (Plurality)*
• *Contend - the presence and value of constructive contention, an aspect of organisational life that should never be entirely resolved and must be managed. Contending is harnessing the positive aspects of contention. (Duality)*
• *Transcend - fit, split and contend entail complexity; to transcend is to accept disequilibrium and use the tensions between opposites in order to form new mindsets.*

Pascale is concerned with a contradiction between the specific ways a firm services its customers and the way it can simultaneously renew itself and cites examples of firms whose management not only had to face crisis or go under (as at Ford), but some who constructed crisis in order to foster change and renewal (as at General Electric). His comments are not a million miles away from Judith Blau's conclusions (Blau, 1984) concerning the way architectural firms succeed and survive recessions. The nature of 'fit' , split and the management of the 'contend' factor relates directly to how architects' offices are organised and run. (See Robbins, 1994, for comments on this subject in terms of using drawings.)

equation. Finally, the housing market became one in which delivery criteria became dominant. It became more competitive and the budgets became tighter, and the fees hit such a low level that being able to afford to do such jobs became the nature of the expertise! Firms found themselves in strong competition - generally at first, together with many kinds of practice; later, as one of a few able to compete well in such a market. Problem finding is forgotten in favour of problem solving. The game becomes one of emphasis upon delivery and those firms who desire to stay in it have to become thorough delivery cultures. Good design is still possible, but the equation is stacked against it. Sometimes firms can't or won't adapt, leaving room for leaner, hungrier practices to move in.

The same thing has happened to practices in the health sector and also in offices design. In the latter example, some firms at the leading edge came to possess real professional expertise but, somehow, slipped into slick delivery. It is a common phenomenon, with market forces and natural evolutionary patterns often working together - their interaction exacerbated by the speed of contemporary change and the experience of markets which appear to enjoy quick lead-ins and shorter lives.

Leading practices can sometimes survive change and maintain a hold on the more prestigious element of markets (the research-led consultancy firm DEGW is an example in the office field), but most get swept along. Some get swept aside. Reversing this developmental pattern is impossible.

Market forces argue for a necessary specialisation, but how does a firm ski-jump from one niche to another? It is still those firms who are able to serve a broader range of projects who have the opportunities to survive and evolve.

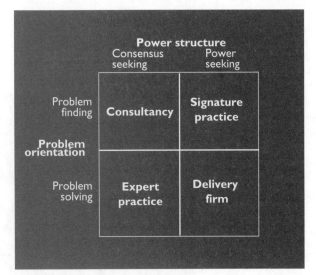

Architectural Cultural Stereotypes

The four architectural types identified can be arranged in relation to prevailing power structure and to problem orientation, as above. Of course, positioning somewhat depends upon the job and the firm. Specialist Consultancy, for example should be problem-solving (as in most space-planning), but is, more properly, architectural problem-finding. Expertise should be problem-solving (as in historical restoration) but will sometimes effect itself as problem-finding (as in brief-writing).

Hair-shirt or pinstripe?
High Street or Designer?

Another way of looking at cultures is in terms of their orientation toward older professional values and newer managerial values. A differentiation of this kind was a feature of a cultural model developed by Coxe in the USA (Coxe et al., 1987). Taking the idea of cultural type as a 'technology' driving the firm, their model generated a matrix of three technologies (delivery, ideas, and expertise) and two value systems (practice or business). This 'super-positioning' model is perhaps flawed, but the book is nevertheless an excellent discussion of the implications of such modelling on staffing, decision-making, marketing, staffing, etc.

The notion of a stark orientation toward either practice (a vocational commitment and therefore a way of life) or business values (a concern with commerce as a way of profiting and thereby making a living) has been a significant feature of professional life, but it is arguably becoming less important as the profession adapts to the prevailing climate. The truth is that all practices have to be 'commercial' to some extent, otherwise they would be bankrupt! One also has to be aware of firms who declares their devotion to artistic values, yet practise a tough fee remuneration attitude with glaring discrepancies of reward within the firm - organisations, like individuals, can live with plural value systems and will 'turn face' as necessary. Many important firms admired by their peers and celebrated in magazines maintain this artful duplicity.

A differentiation can be made between kinds of explicit posturing e.g. vocation or business. Another notable differentiation is between firms who appear to be cosmopolitan and those appearing more parochial. The former have a broad, international, sharper view; the latter enjoy a more parochial view. Each has is advantages and disadvantages, depending upon the situation. For example, the large, international, delivery-culture firm such as SOM will be in sector one below; it is manifestly biased toward delivery and commercial values. Sir Norman Foster, another international firm, declaring older practice values, would be in sector two. Each is quite different to firms having a more parochial outlook (and advantage) because they operate in local markets.

Cultural Stereotypes: Capability and Change

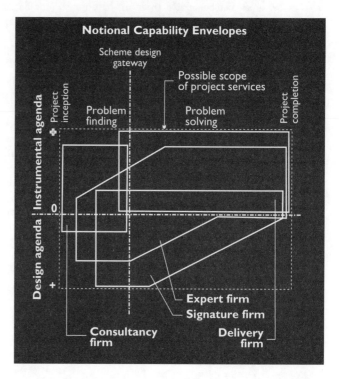

The idea of cultural bias and of stereotypical firms implies different capabilities within the framework of the project and its potential. The diagram above differentiates between an instrumental and a design agenda in relation to the project life-cycle and the four cultural stereotypes.

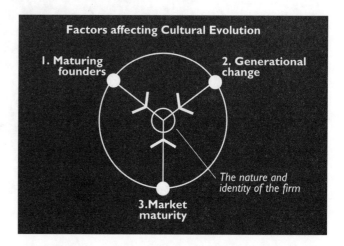

A firm's culture is unlikely to stand still. Its evolution will be influenced by three factors: maturing of the founders (and their retirement); generational change as control passes to new people (usually younger); and a maturing of the firm's markets. This evolution is unlikely to be straight-forward. For example, new blood might shift an agenda from, say, Expertise to Ideas, but they will have to fight a maturing market.

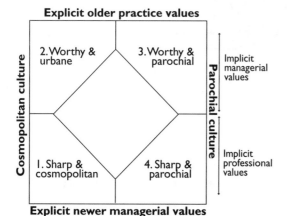

Cultural layers

I Project planning must take account of cultural architectures. For example, for a goal-oriented milestone concept to work properly it is necessary to appropriately locate its elements within the framework of an organisation's hierarchical layers. This usually means inbetween an executive top-down view of the project and an activity level, bottom-up view. This places the milestone plan at a natural level of administrative control. Three levels need to be considered (they are, of course, never quite as distinct and separate as descriptions suggest):

Upper Level:
This upper, executive level is where the project must be 'globally' aligned with business needs. In marketing jargon this is the *Finder* level (i.e. of the business senior who represents a firm and finds work). People at this level determine major policies, for planning, organising and controlling the practice, thereby setting a context for the project. They are also likely to be involved in doing the same for the project (probably dependent upon the practice size). Their time-span perspective is very long-term (even beyond the project life). Typically, there will be more than one senior executive level involved (e.g. Chairman and Partner or Director-in-charge). The executive project director (the most senior project manager) is usually placed at this level.

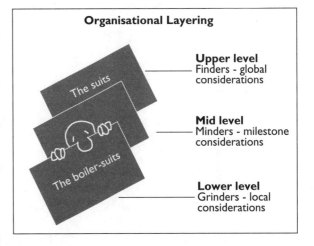

Organisational Layering

The suits

The boiler-suits

Upper level
Finders - global considerations

Mid level
Minders - milestone considerations

Lower level
Grinders - local considerations

Mid-Level:
This administrative level is where intermediate goals for time, costs, and quality are formulated and administered, both by more senior designers and project managers. In marketing jargon this is the *Minder* level (e.g. the associate in an architectural firm). The relevant time-span dealt with at this level will typically be weekly or monthly and people at this level have a major say in who does what. They play a crucial role in organising a scheme design into system components, planning practice efforts and co-ordinating the work programme with other consultants and specialist contractors. However, they will also be expected to have a committed, long-term relationship with the project.

Lower Level:
This activity level operates on a daily or weekly time-span of review and the perspective is likely to be local. This is the *Grinder* level, where the actual method of achieving work is determined - typically, by technicians (para-professionals) and/or junior designers.

The relationship between these levels forms the architecture of the firm's culture. The implicit tension between controlling partners and lower level professionals seeking autonomy, challenge and voice is very important.

2 **Finders, Minders and Grinders.** Project managers sometimes enjoy the illusion that architectural practices carry out conceptual design at Level One and delegate execution to lower levels. In fact, it is common for responsibilities to significantly overlap as forms of consensual dialogue within a practice and even for most conceptual work to be undertaken at Level Two. This is especially true in medium to large practices.

Whilst the larger architectural firm can be expected to have an unambiguous formal hierarchy of architects and others, smaller practices blur roles and combine levels in a flatter hierarchy (although the underlying power structure might be similar).

It is argued that inter-organisational communications (between the agencies involved on a project) should be matched, so that levels correspond, alleviating the pos-

Planning Principles

The project management view of planning and its implementation has two fundamental principles:

• Planning itself should be democratic.

• The implementation of plans should be autocratic.

sibility of misunderstanding. It is a notion that has implications for meetings, assumed responsibilities and formal decision-making. For example, if we take the typical staff grades found in many architectural cultures they sort themselves into the three levels as set out below. Although crude, the Finder / Minder / Grinder concept is arguably more realistic and useful than the (more bureaucratic) grading.

Finders

• *Grade Five* - most senior roles in the organisation. Ambassador of the firm e.g. chairman and/or chief executive officer (CEO) responsible for strategic policies affecting the firm. View is beyond each project. This level corresponds with the client level and Finders in other agencies.

Minders

• *Grade Four* - partners or directors with responsibility for sections, departmental budgets, large projects or portfolios of projects. This can also be a client level of correspondence and is equivalent to the Contracts Manager in a contracting organisation.

• *Grade Three* - associate partner / director responsible for a project team and its performance. This is equivalent to the site manager role or the account handler in an advertising culture. Grades Three and Four will often work together as a pair, with specific project responsibilities.

Grinders

• *Grade Two* - experienced designer or technician role. detailed design and production drawing work is carried out at this level.

• *Grade One* - junior designer or technician role.

3 **Planning Participation.** Without formally described and assigned responsibilities, project roles can become ambiguous, especially when a practice is carrying through a portfolio of projects and individuals play separate roles on different projects. A bottom-up, instrumentalist logic requires that all tasks can be clearly defined and a responsibility matrix drawn up that describes who does what, reports to whom, signs-off, etc. The roots of this rationale derive from the tradition of Taylorism (see later section) and are somewhat at odds with a contemporary emphasis upon teamwork and consummate forms of co-operation.

Team members with a project management responsibility play a crucial role in motivating those they associate with. In order to avoid alienation resulting from high-handed planning, those doing the work should be involved in its strategic planning. They will often know best, they are able to contribute ideas, they become involved, their motivation is enhanced and a sense of team membership and mutual dependency is increased. The strategy should aim to avoid swamping the individual with too much information, but to focus their efforts whilst also offering a strategic overview.

Without this form of participation team members are likely to feel uninvolved and might feel reluctant to accept the demands placed upon them by the plan. This is especially true of professionals, who do not like being managed and prefer to act autonomously (thus having voice and being accountable for their contributions). This consideration is an important aspect of the relational contracts within the project team. However, as a corollary to participation (and at some risk of indicating lack of trust and an exploitive attitude), team members might be asked to enter into a formal or ritualistic classical contract entailing their literal 'sign-on' to the plan bearing their contribution. Individuals then work on activities described in the action plan within the framework of the milestone concept and they are held to their agreements - an application of the *Management by Objectives* concept conceived by Peter Drucker in the 1950's.

Taylorism

The most notable exponent of purposive rationality in management was the engineer and management consultant Frederick Taylor (1856-1917), who maintained that antagonism and inefficiency within industry could be reduced by the development of a true science of work, thus increasing productivity and the size of the ultimate profit workers and managers could share. Taylor laid down four principles:

1. The need to develop a true science of work. This was the concept of 'a best way'.
2. The need to scientifically select and progressively develop the worker - people were to be matched to tasks.
3. The need to bring together the science of work and the trained worker in order to effect a revolution in management. This depended upon the notion of supervision, reward and punishment.
4. A constant and intimate cooperation of management and workers - based, however, on staff planning and controlling the workers.

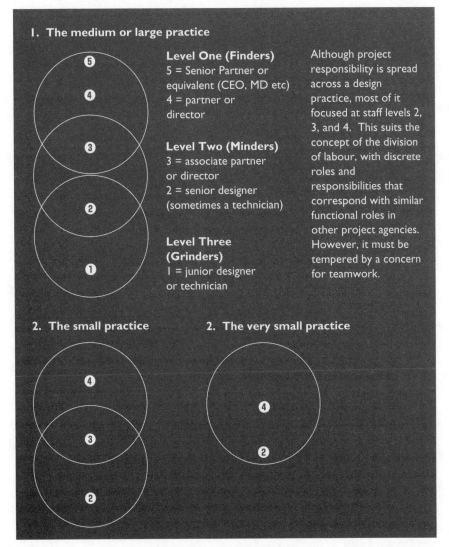

1. The medium or large practice

Level One (Finders)
5 = Senior Partner or equivalent (CEO, MD etc)
4 = partner or director

Level Two (Minders)
3 = associate partner or director
2 = senior designer (sometimes a technician)

Level Three (Grinders)
1 = junior designer or technician

Although project responsibility is spread across a design practice, most of it focused at staff levels 2, 3, and 4. This suits the concept of the division of labour, with discrete roles and responsibilities that correspond with similar functional roles in other project agencies. However, it must be tempered by a concern for teamwork.

2. The small practice

2. The very small practice

Hierarchies

Practices organise themselves in different ways, with varying numbers of levels, but the basic principles always apply. Medium to large practices can be expected to have up to five levels - more when non-professional administration and support staff are taken into account as a subsidiary hierarchy.

A key point in a firm's evolution is from the 'man and boy' equation where there is no intermediate level, to the scale of organisation which can support an associate level.

The design of the overall organisation and its inherent relationship of parts, and the design of each discrete item of work were all important. The latter principle was to be objectively established by the application of systematic observation and measurement; the former were to be characterised by 'the 'functional' management of specialists. Within this framework, an organisation could maximise productivity by continually reducing jobs to minute and specialised tasks. These were to be objectively observed, measured, assessed and specified in terms of 'the best way' of being performed and subsequently undertaken by systematically trained, highly paid workers. Both worker and manager would be subject to the same discipline of instrumental 'scientific management'. The various 'best ways' should be aggregated into an appropriate organisational form in order to facilitate their management and integration.

Taylorism became the philosophical expression of purposive time and motion studies, cost analyses and an assembly line mentality that was to take hold throughout business and industry (and in Russia too - apparently Lenin and other revolutionaries were keen fans). Implicit within its philosophy was not only the old concept of the division of labour, but also the notion that all workers were inherently lazy, insecure, selfish and that in all work conception (by managers) should be separated from execution (by workers).

Taylor argued that once a rationally designed organisation puts the 'right man' in the 'right place', then an industrial process should work smoothly, without inherent conflict and to the potential benefit of all concerned. If conflict was present, then either the organisation of tasks or the kind of people employed were inappropriate. New rules, improved procedures, and better training were to resolve such difficulties.

The functionalist logic of Taylorism was reinforced by later systems theory and became important to the rationale informing project management, particularly when expertise has to be co-ordinated and made both effective and productive. *Plan what you want to do, then do it.* This Taylorist, bottom-up maxim lies at the heart of the orthodox project planning mind-set.

2 Challenges. It has been noted that 'Taylorism' has four secondary assumptions (Rojot, 1991) :

1. *An analytical assumption:* scientific study of the tasks at hand will establish the correct, 'best way' and an appropriate organisational design for the fulfilment of identified production goals. This, in turn, will eliminate industrial conflict.

2. *A bureaucratic assumption:* the only kind of legitimate power is the authority which derives from position in the organisation.

3. *A personnel assumption:* people are the skilled products of training and should be allocated to a place in the organisation as required, in a manner appropriate to the goals. This concept built upon the Victorian notion that wealth, position and authority were a product of merit and superiority; the workperson's position was due to a lack of 'character' (appropriate attitude), and the virtues of industry, reliability, ambition, religion, thrift, regularity, and sobriety.

4. *An economic assumption:* it is assumed that individuals are motivated by monetary reward (to be scientifically determined, of course).

Each assumption has been questioned. For example, the *analytical assumption* of an objective best way is contradicted by the fact that organisations appear to rarely work entirely to rules - in fact, 'working to rule' became a common disruptive tactic in labour relations; it also counters needs for flexibility and innovation.

The *bureaucratic assumption* is contradicted by the realities of social relations and influence deriving from charisma, leadership qualities, respect, and similar sentiments.

The *personnel assumption* is contradicted by the rich complex of social relations which research has found to characterise any work group and considerably determines its productive capacity (see *Human Relations Movement*).

The *economic assumption* has been contradicted by all kinds of motivational research and related theory - from the human relations work of the 1920's, to Maslow's concept of a hierarchy of needs, McGregor's Theory X and Theory Y hypothesis put forward in the 1960's - people are motivated by many factors besides monetary reward; and Maslow's subsequent Theory Z - the notion that human relations must transcend all other principles.

Even Taylor's assumption that conflict can be eradicated has been questioned, using the counter-argument that the pervasive need for negotiation is a fundamental feature of organisational life: conflict is unavoidable (is even desirable) and can only be managed, channelled and contained, rather than eliminated (Pascale, 1990).

Despite such criticisms, Taylor's instrumentalist logic became a part of the spirit of the the so-called Machine Age which has straddled the end of last century and penetrated deeply into the 20th. As implementational practice, Taylorism became Henry Ford's production line: "The man who places a part does not fasten it . . . The man who puts in a bolt does not put on the nut; the man who puts on the nut does not tighten it", was how Ford put it. As socio-economic ideal, it was also expressed by men like H.G. Wells, who favoured a society run by a small elite of rational beings.

Whilst Taylor's concepts have been undeniably influential and useful, it can also be profoundly alienating and has at times become a part of the mythology of work and poor industrial relations (in for example, the famous British post-war movie starring Peter Sellars, I'm All Right Jack). The contemporary business world still employs the Taylorist mind-set, but ideas confronts a post-Taylorist reality which modifies and even reverses the polarity between planner and executant. In the professional realm, the class-ridden era of the aloof architect and his technicians has been superceded by accessibility to the profession (even though gender-bias remains an area of contention), by its massive growth, egalitarian values, and an ever increasing rate of change experienced as deregulation, increased competitiveness, the blurring of disciplinary boundaries, and the enhancement of productivity at the prosaic level by advancements in desktop computing. Even the profession's aesthetic ideology, celebrating instrumental values, has had to move on. However, from another direction, the ideal of a rational, scientific management has been experienced as a long series of reports which have repeatedly called upon architects and the construction industry to 'modernise' and increase their effectiveness and productivity. The underlying drive is economic; its implicit values are purposive; its consequences are instrumental forms of rationality. The net outcome is contention and tension which some commentators have argued is fundamental to the contemporary management scenario and which should be positively embraced as the principal feature of a paradigm shift (see Pascale, 1990).

It would be naive to blame Taylor for the establishment of an instrumentalist rationale within management. To do so would be to ignore history and the army of others who have promoted similar values and managerial concepts. It would also be in danger of underestimating the extent to which Taylorism has been symptomatic of deeper structural forces in society. From this perspective, counter-forces to Taylorism have argued for worker empowerment and demonstrated its potential in the post-war success story of a Japanese economy which has been noted over and again as a cultural phenomenon founded upon people and teams rather than (or, as much as) technology. At a higher level, the collapse of state-planned economies and the promotion of market forces are counter to the centralist planning ideal advocated by taylor (and people like Max Weber). Every organisation - large and small - is seeking ways of coping and continually renewing. Architectural firms and individual architects face this same challenge.

It's an Old Story . . .

Taylor's attitudes were hardly new. They are fundamental to the Industrial revolution and transformations in the manufactories of the 18th century. For example, William Sutherland's 1726 report on Britain's naval dockyards commented that 'the efficiency of the yard . . . depended not only on its equipment but also on its organisation, and particularly on the control which could be exercised over the workmen' (quoted in Linebaugh, 1991). Samuel Bentham - inventor of the panopticton (not his brother, Jeremy) and Inspector-General of the Naval Works from 1795 - was a radical manager in attempting changes which might break a link between the process of production and the forms of worker's self-organisation. These were combinations which Taylor was to deal with, as were the researchers of the 1920's Hawthorne Experiments and later members of the 'human relations' movement. It;'s an old battle that still continues.

Professionals on the job

Perspectives

The twentieth century is not .. the century of the common man but of the uncommon and increasingly professional expert.
Harold Perkin

[In a capitalist society] the definition of professional roles and the alternatives open to professionals depends neither on the state or the market, considered separately, but on the control of the one over the other and on the manner in which state control has been achieved - this is the crucible in which professional differences among nations are formed.
Margali Larsen

The '60's marked a watershed in sociological writings on the professions. Whereas most had earlier emphasised positive functions and achievements, recent writers have been consistently more critical.
Eliot Freidson.

Architecture never escapes the initial relationship of patronage to create a controlled market. Its dependence on wealthy and powerful sponsors, be they private or public, is simply more accentuated than in other professions, which were able to use sponsorship for their project of market control.
 Margali Larsen.

There are few sociological examinations of the architectural firm. One of the most notable - a book called *Architects and Firms*, by Judith Blau - is almost fifteen years old, but it has conclusions which appear as if they have withstood the test of time (Blau, 1984).

One of Blau's more interesting observations concerned motivation and personal satisfaction. For example, there is an interactive chemistry between job structuring and personal motivations: "How content, egotistical, alienated, or satisfied architects are can be explained by the ways in which their jobs are structured and the opportunities they have in the firms in which they work". A number of things are important, but three stand out:

1. *An ethos of egalitarianism* i.e. the belief that equal voice in professional affairs is just and proper. This is supported by collegiality - the extent to which goals and a set of common conventions are shared.

2. *An ethos of voluntarianism*, the professional principle that individuals have the skills and good sense to act more or less independently when they can, consult with others when they cannot, and to organise their own work and carry it out.

3. *A value attached to artistic and professional autonomy*, which embraced the concept of a link between creativity and this autonomy. This arises from the exercise of judgement and a freedom of expression.
(Similar these points are noted by Raelin in his examination of professionals and managers together.)

Blau noted that, "Situational alienation, evident in specialisation and powerlessness in organisations, is the source of low commitment among architects". This was often the result of an absence of opportunity for personal expression. As a result, most employed architects sought residual satisfaction from other related sources: voice (the power to influence decisions) and diverse responsibilities.

It was consistent feature of Blau's research that, other things being equal, complexity of organisation was associated with innovation and that large firms were held to achieve higher quality work than small ones (they have advantages which size and complexity confer). In fact, of the many factors correlated with winning awards, size (which relates to complexity and similar factors, such as computerisation, strong personnel policies, rules, the routinisation of work, etc.) was the most significant. However, when size was held as a constant, it was found that these factors were not statistically significant - in which case factors such as the percentage of architects in the firm became significant. In fact, bureaucratisation appeared to have little or no affect upon the achievement of excellence, although the large firm could achieve high quality work and could be highly profitable. On the other hand a curious logic of eccentricity applied: when a small firm acquired the characteristics which are normally associated with the advantages of size (complexity, affiliation, incorporation, personnel regulations, consultants, and government clients), then that firm became peculiarly advantaged i.e. the structurally advantaged small firm was likely to be an award winner. The acquisition of a rationalised capability, when mixed with open communications and a broad range of employee responsibilities, enabled the small firm to become a winner.

No logic of eccentricity applied to large firms, who were neither advantaged or disadvantaged by eccentricity. Size produced centralised decision-making and rationalisation along economic and organisational lines. Sheer complexity - the product of size and the range of services on offer - was negatively correlated with winning awards and reduced individual voice (only partially compensated for by the rewards of specialisation and the higher remuneration it sometime brought). Overall, Blau's research confirmed some conventional wisdom: that the more complex an office, the less noteworthy its products; and that the small office is advantaged by differentiation. In Frederick Herzberg's terms, the removal of potential causes of dissatisfaction (the hygiene factors which bureaucratisation tends to address) did not mean that the causes of satisfaction were in place (Herzberg, 1966).

A key to employee fulfilment was found to be a diversity of tasks which promoted both professional fulfilment and voice within the organisation. Firms enjoying a wide scope of services and less specialisation found they could promote voice - in principle, one can have comprehensive services and diverse tasks. However, the former were associated with the large firms and the latter with the small ones. The larger firm also tended to p;lace its employees in specialist roles (which tended to produce dissatisfaction and came with less voice). Smaller firms offered less scope, more diversity and voice.

During recessionary times large size gave a buffer against collapse. Small firms could foster a helpful entrepreneurial posture, but this was equally likely to produce failure of great success. The larger firm can become enfeebled as its stable markets collapse - in effect, they are in need of some form of paradigm shift. When better times return, one finds the profession restructured. This is exactly the experience in the UK during both the recession of the early 1980's and, especially, that of the early 1990's. By then, the successful small, eccentric firm will be well on the way to becoming the medium or large normal firm.

Other interesting points in Blau's research concerned client returns and referrals. High peer evaluations of project quality, repeat client rates and the completion of higher cost projects was associated with the number of organisational positions filled by those with direct client contact. High evaluation, client repeat rate and staff commitment were correlated with the likelihood someone other than a principal was in charge. The percentage of high-cost projects completed and the client repeat rate was improved by more individuals sharing responsibility for a project (but the likelihood of an award went down). Client referrals declined when someone other than a principal was in charge.

Professional Types

Professionals are a form of human capital (as opposed to landed and financial capital). Their origins and development parallel the Industrial Revolution. Their proliferation and ubiquitous presence accompanies the evolution toward large service sectors in the developed economies. This also comes with a certain dymystification of professionalism and outright deregulation (a battle fought within the architectural profession over the last 25 years)

Professions such as architects developed in the 19th century from loose associations to ones enjoying a social contract with the state. In the case of architects, this has meant state patronage and protection to the name 'architect'. Justification is in terms of some value to society, in the larger interests of social efficiency and well-being. As with other professions, the name of the game is access to a flow of income and protection of what becomes a jurisdictional field of practice. Status is important to realising this ambition. However, at the boundaries to their mutual interaction and when new fields develop (as with project management), different professions fight for jurisdictional control.

The behavioural characteristics of professionals include:

• A drive toward autonomy.
Supervision should be general rather than close and superiors need to focus upon results rather than means (avoiding day-to-day supervision). Controls need to be strategic rather than operational, allowing the professional a degree of self-management. Against this background, the group is considered a resource.

• A pursuit of vocational job challenge.
Job enrichment, authority over one's own work, and responsibility are sources of satisfaction. Jobs should tap creative and entrepreneurial instincts.

• A reluctance to be managed by non-professionals.
Job descriptions and bureaucracy are anathema. Standardised procedures are resisted.

• A leaning toward the service ethic
For example, as a contribution to social welfare. New knowledge is published and shared.

Professionals harness and market their own capital (i.e. themselves and their expertise). Managers address financially capitalised markets and deal in commodified exchange values in order to maximise those two great media, power (for their own organisations and themselves) and money (ditto). The instrumental mind-set is crucial to realising theses values and ambitions.

Of course, these stereotypical descriptions belie two contemporary truths: we're all professional now and, simultaneously, professionals have been called upon to nurture and exercise managerial skills. deregulation - fostering increased competition within a profession and between professions - has become a strong instrument of the latter.

Quality

Edwards Deming - one of the fathers of quality management

Three Reasons for Pursuing Quality (Away from Problems; Toward Opportunities)

• *Professional pride (the motivation to do better and satisfy clients and users).*

• *The fear (and various kinds of direct and indirect costs) of liability and therefore the ambition to remove it's causes.*

• *The ability to attract more clients and win more work in a competitive practice environment.*

I . . . must be one of the most abused words of the last decade. The almost universal concern with it derives from economic competition, the success of Japan in the '60's and '70's, and all kinds of concern with end-users and consumers once manifested by activists such as the American, Ralph Nader. Despite sometimes hair-splitting attempts to define the term (almost invariably reducing the notion to meaninglessness) the subject, in essence, is about the rectification of lost potential, waste, low service aspirations and the power of the consumer or end-user.

The fathers of quality management - Edwards Deming and J.M. Juran - would argue that addressing the quality issue is about *people* and, above all, the attitudes of management. Everyone agrees on the quality ambition, but the reality within the construction industry is that quality has fallen into the grasp of technocratic mind-sets and become subject to technical forms of rationality enshrined in BS and ISO documentation (e.g. ISO 9000), and the belief that quality is to be achieved procedurally. The outcome of this approach has been a 'certification' industry seeking to structure processes into procedures meant to reassure consumers and customers that an audit would reveal there truly are mechanisms in place to ensure 'quality'. What they mean is conformance to a specification stated at the beginning of the process, a lack of defects or the ability to significantly criticise. The presumption is that systems need to be rule-governed and that people need to be carefully guided in what they do. The adumbration of Taylorism and what became known as 'Theory X' overshadows the proceedings (see the section on motivation), all of which appear to be wilfully ignorant of the advice of people who have fathered quality management. Deming, for example, comments on the suggestion that someone might install quality: "No. You can install a new desk, or a new carpet, or a new dean, but not quality control. Anyone that proposes to 'install quality control' unfortunately has little knowledge about quality control." (Deming 1982)

There is, of course, a place for rule governed behaviours within any process, including architectural design. But it should be self-evident to even those with limited experience that, whilst this might constitute a useful framework for process actions, it is no substitute for a *culture* of quality that might inform people's attitudes. The moment concern, care and motivation are introduced into the equation one realises that rule-governance (and the implication of regular audits, constant monitoring and control) is insufficient, producing a hollow kind of quality concern entirely focused upon avoiding causes of dissatisfactions rather than engendering kinds of satisfaction (the two are not opposites). The avoidance of defects and a negative concept of conformance to specifications (or requirements, as it is sometimes stated), is an environment ruled by mild fear. The avoidance of defects is important, but not the same as ensuring the quality ambition has become a cultural attribute.

Deming was scathing about the 'zero defects' concept and its implicit ignorance of statistics as applied to processes, about quotas, bonus systems and a focus upon those who perform above or below a measured average. He was fond of demonstrating how 'average' is a statistical mean and, by definition, one can always expect half of performances to be above and half below that mean. His emphasis was upon the system of production itself, upon a distribution of outcomes which form a stable system, on differentiating between system causes of problems (usually over 90%) and special causes, on a strategic focus and on the drivers of difficulty and success. Typically, Deming would demonstrate that 'good' results and 'bad' results were both the product of a stable system; improvement would come from system changes, not looking at specific faults and attempting to correct them - this was a form of tampering which could make the system unstable and matters worse! He was adamant that quality was a *management* issue and that workers sought pride in workmanship. What managers needed was what he

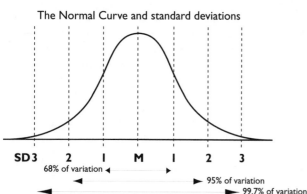

The Normal Curve and standard deviations

The 'standard deviation' of a distribution indicates a kind of 'average' amount by which all the values deviate from the mean.

called 'profound knowledge' of the system. As leaders, their job was to improve on many positives: quality, pride in workmanship, man/machine performances, etc. In negative terms, this amounts to removing the causes of failure.

The bottom line to the quality issue in a service business such as architectural design is simply people, the culture they form when they act cooperatively, and the way the organisation they are a part of is managed.

2 How? In the same way that project management must infuse all levels of the project team, quality ambitions must similarly be ubiquitous throughout the project endeavour. The question everyone's wants answered is: How do we achieve it?

The very intention of achieving quality - or, more likely, quality assured certification - will, in itself, promote the kinds of organisational and process-system examination that will further the cause. However, experts in the field argue there has to be obsessiveness. No practice will go this far unless there is a pay-off - such as quality assured status and resulting increased work-load.(37) The latter, lets face it, is a crucial reason any architectural practice will go through the effort, the changes, the pain and expense - that, and a more generalised professional motivation to perform well, together with a fearfully motivated ambition to avoid problems and the liabilities which might result in being sued. As with further professional development and training (CPD), practices will all advocate support of the worthy ambition, but more often than not fall short of initiating action.

Both Deming and Juran advocate that achieving quality is a continuous cycle of effort running through planning for quality, establishing quality control and monitoring, and pursuing continual quality improvements. This sometimes described as a "Plan (What do we want to do?) / Do (Carry out the change) / Check (observe results) / Learn & Act again (What did we learn?)' cycle.

This advice is really only applicable to circumstances that repeat. However, the very uniqueness of projects as predicaments - as a potential to realise and as a team of people dealing with these considerations - obviates against anything but a kind of learning cycle which comes to *infuse* a practice culture ('the way we do things around here') by moving from particular examples to the general lessons which are learned, absorbed, and applied almost invisibly. A firm moves *toward* quality because of a positive motivation, but it sustains quality assurance mechanisms as studio and practice disciplines and constraints - kinds of safety nets remedially initiated and motivated by the concern to *move away* from lack of quality or anything which will engender it.

The bottom line to the quality issue in architectural practice is that everyone wants its benefits in terms of being on target and fewer errors, hopes to avoid its direct costs and the managerial overhead involved, and desires quality assurance mechanisms to be unnoticeable, like the air one breathes, so that attention can be given to issues of project potential. The visible part of this equation should be outcomes, not bureaucratic procedures. It says volumes for the wholesale way in which we uncritically subscribe to instrumental, means-end thinking that the worthy ambition of quality assurance has become such a monument to technical forms of rationality.

Checking Quality

Addressing the quality issue during a project results in four principal concerns, each fostering procedures for promoting, auditing and checking what is going on:

• Managing quality
This has been a general concern throughout this book. Deming would throw the issue straight back at management and ask how it was engendering a system with quality inherent within it. In effect, this is what design management is all about, in the broadest terms. How might management audit itself? Of course, this rarely happens except in the sense of an indirect fallout from the audits and reviews of the kind listed below, but there should be the occasional attempt at an objective stand-off review (e.g. the weekend workshop, perhaps involving external consultants).

• Assuring quality
This is a more familiar and easily dealt with aspect of quality. It results in formal audits of two kinds (usually related to certification):

• the system (or process) audit which asks, Does the quality 'system' instituted within the practice satisfy the criteria of ISO 9000? Is everything in place?

• the compliance audit asks how that instituted system is actually working and being complied with.

The game is a demonstration of capability to the outside world, thus validating certification. In itself, this hones a practice's self-examination and improves processes. But, of course, only procedural issues can be dealt with.

• Checking quality
This amounts to kinds of control checks upon work that has already been completed (looking for defects). The RIBA has them, but they are very tedious. Nevertheless, they are valuable, especially with regard to co-ordination.

• Design quality
Design quality is usually reviewed, but it can also be audited in the sense of 'programming' i.e. checking that there is compliance with specification requirements and that the design is offering the desired performances. A review would look at all aspects of the design. This might embrace 'fitness for purpose' buildability, life-cycle issues, safety, costs, etc. Is the design feasible? Is it viable? Is it being developed properly? If a broad range of people are involved it is likely that the difficult aesthetic issue (the 'tingle factor') will be short-circuited as a hideously difficult territory.

Image makes the sale. Quality holds it.
Don Osman.

The Limitations of Technique

'Quality is, above all, 'about care, people, passion, consistency, eyeball contact and gut reaction. Quality is not a technique, no matter how good.'
Peters and Austin.

Professionals have a difficulty with this concept because its self-evident truth runs against the grain of professionalism as a form of technical expertise characterised by the administration of proper procedures. The outcome is that the genuine search for quality is often enshrined in bureaucratic standards which, mechanically implemented as an aspect of instrumental thinking, mitigate against their objective. On the other hand, properly applying technical forms of expertise and following procedures can be an important aspect of delivering quality (e.g. party wall agreements, planning applications, dealing with building regulations, properly given architect's instructions, etc.). A balance has to be struck.

3 **Profound Knowledge.** The key to moving forward in the quality game (apart from motivation, positive or negative, time and funds,etc.) is a willingness to make commitments. This comes back to practice management. Unless the leaders of the firm are fully backing the ambition - which means more than being willing to say, 'Yes, let's do it' - the ambition will not become a real initiative or realistically get to grips with the important issue: practice culture. Quality improvements will not come from isolated bottom-up efforts.

A starting point might be an overview ('helicoptering', as it is called). Many practices will appreciate what is wrong, but lack the political consensus, will and ability to move forward. A peer group review linked to the insider's knowledge which can identify the crucial factors to be considered is one way forward (everything that can be addressed does not have equal weight). Still, most practices find it incredibly difficult to institute and sustain a momentum of reform which authentically transfigures their culture as well as instituting the comparatively superficial measures which regulate behaviours.

The key to progress has to be an *opportunism* which builds steadily and *incrementally* on the basis of work in hand. In other words, a concern with enhancing quality has to grow out of the context in which it is set, just as a design project similarly grows out of its own, unique situational-problematic.

It also has to be the acknowledgement that 'quality' is a relative concept, even within the project life-cycle. Managing quality is managing a dynamic issue, not something programmatically fixed in terms of a technical rationality. Quality in terms of envisioning and harnessing the project potential prior to a scheme agreement is different to quality after going through the scheme gateway into a phase when 'conformance to requirement' changes its nature - becoming an attempt to conform with the agreed plan, as opposed to the prior stage of formulating the content of that plan. Quality also becomes a matter of compliance with procedures instituted in order to provide assurance. A quality that is initially a creative response shifts to being, in part, a (necessarily) negative control mechanism.

A third key is to accept the dual nature of quality: both a move *toward* the realisation of potential (opportunities) and a move *away* from problems. The positive and negative motivation are the two sides of the same coin. However, given that a generalised, positive, professional motivation exists, it is hard to see how a practice can do anything other than address self-evident problems and inadequacies.

In addition, each project within the practice has two contexts: *relative to the organisation* which handles many jobs at once, and *relative to project sponsors* and the larger project team outside the architectural agency. Improving quality in the latter sense is a matter of specific deliveries; with regard to the former, it is a matter of enhancing the firm's more generalised, distinctive capability. The first kind of quality benefits a one project; the second serves many. In other words: since practices are necessarily project-based, their generalised capability has to arise from addressing specific, one-off opportunities as they arise; however, they have to be ready to grasp such opportunities and institute change whenever they can, meaning they must be primed and ready. Such preparedness is, in effect, a 'profound knowledge' of the culture of service and production, as well an ambition to do better.

Features of a Project Quality Plan

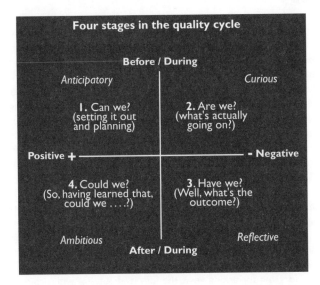

Four stages in the quality cycle

Before / During

Anticipatory · *Curious*

1. Can we?
(setting it out
and planning)

2. Are we?
(what's actually
going on?)

Positive + ———————————— **- Negative**

4. Could we?
(So, having learned that,
could we ....?)

3. Have we?
(Well, what's the
outcome?)

Ambitious · *Reflective*

After / During

---

*Four reiterated questions - Can we? Are we? Have we? Could we? -
express the notion that quality is a continual, progressive effort
which starts with an ambition, goes through implementation and
checking, to a final point of learning, before repeating the cycle.*

There are probably three levels at which this takes place:

*• Within a specific project, dealt with from an executive overview.
Quality at this level is formulated in terms of ambitions and criteria,
the brief, and the selection of a suitable team which will realise the
quality ambition.*

*• Within the culture of a practice. This is the milieu of action which
must be more important than the project itself. However, each, specific project gives a firm the opportunities it needs to apply and
develop its culture. It is in this sense that the firm acts opportunistically and incrementally in managing and effecting quality, perhaps
within the context of a quality assurance intent
or promise.*

*• Within a project, dealt with as a specific agency's responsibility.
Quality at this level is focused upon that project's unique problems
and opportunities, seen in terms of that agency's project role and
responsibilities.*

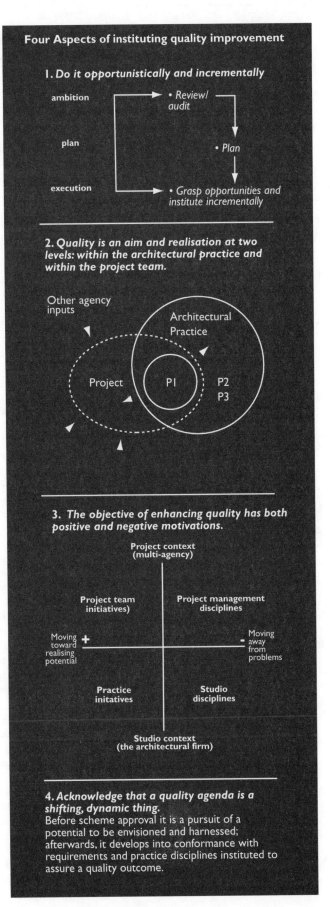

Four Aspects of instituting quality improvement

1. *Do it opportunistically and incrementally*

ambition

plan

execution

• *Review/
audit*

• *Plan*

• *Grasp opportunities and
institute incrementally*

---

2. *Quality is an aim and realisation at two
levels: within the architectural practice and
within the project team.*

Other agency
inputs

Architectural
Practice

Project

P1

P2
P3

---

3. *The objective of enhancing quality has both
positive and negative motivations.*

**Project context
(multi-agency)**

**Project team
initiatives)**

**Project management
disciplines**

Moving
toward
realising
potential **+**

- Moving
away
from
problems

**Practice
initatives**

**Studio
disciplines**

**Studio context
(the architectural firm)**

---

4. *Acknowledge that a quality agenda is a
shifting, dynamic thing.*
Before scheme approval it is a pursuit of a
potential to be envisioned and harnessed;
afterwards, it develops into conformance with
requirements and practice disciplines instituted to
assure a quality outcome.

Teams

Just as commerce has discovered the project as a business tool, it has also discovered *teams* to be a major organisational innovation. A common manifestation of this is the concept of 'cell-manufacturing' in which teams of 2-50 workers are grouped around the manufacturing equipment they need, each cell making, checking and even packing its products, each worker performing several tasks and each cell responsible for the quality of what it produces In effect, this a version of process-engineering. Harley-Davidson, for example, introduced teams, reduced cylinder-head production from one week to three hours, reduced factory floor space by one third, learned to turn over stock 40 times per annum rather than 4.5 times, and has reduced inspectors significantly because of quality improvements. WL Gore, the Gore-Tex people, cut the production of specialist cables by a half, reduced stocks by a third, shrank the space taken by plant by 25%, and increased delivery-on-time from 75% of products to 97%. Lexmark, the computer company, changed to cell-based production, saw productivity shoot up 25% and changed the manager-worker ratio from 1:20 to 1:100. Other variations on the theme include the cross-departmental team that brings design, marketing, production, sales, and similar functions together in a form of institutionalised co-operation. The secret to these teams is said to be simple: *worker satisfaction*.

Architects would be forgiven for asking what the fuss is about - as with projects, they have always worked in teams. However, many professionals are poor team-players and an awareness of how teams work does not stand out as a natural strong point. Professional status is considered to bring a entitlement to full determination of the work agenda, free from constraining interference and, enamoured with autonomy, professionals like to choose their own work, implement it on their own and work without the interruption of day to day supervision (especially a manager's efforts at control). They tend to use the group as a resource rather than the unit which does the work, even when that group is readily consulted or even acts as a professional referent providing direction. Managers, on the other hand, will more naturally refer to the group as the work unit and will look upon the individual as a resource.

In fact managers and professionals can make poor bed-fellows. In brief, professionals can usually be stereotyped as follows:

- They enjoy long training periods in order to master professional skills. Entrance exams monitor standards and gate access to professional associations. Surmounting such gates amounts to a rite of passage.
- During training, the norms and values of the profession are inculcated. Figures of respect are identified. Ethical values are internalised. Peer group values become a standard reference. Most friends are other professionals.
- During employment, skills and values are sustained by continued professional development. Professional associations represent and protect collective interest, maintain educational standards and gating procedures. For the real professional, loyalty develops with regard to the profession before the employer. Autonomy becomes a sought-after feature of work. Supervision has to be general rather than close.
- Over-professionalisation is always a danger, self-esteem resting upon professional expertise. Job challenge is very important. Supervision by non-professionals is reluctantly accepted, if at all. Transition to management status is difficult, appearing to entail a denial of professional commitments.

Managers are different. Their belief systems tend to refer back to the 1950's, when enthusiasms for rational administration and a true professionalisation of management got under way (although few sociologists would accept managers meet professional criteria).

- Managers usually enjoy a multi-disciplinary background of relatively short duration. Some might take a post-graduate management course, when education is

There's Nothing New . . .

Teamwork . . . is the problem we face in the twentieth century. There is no 'ism' that will help us to a solution; we must be content to return to the patient, pedestrian work at the wholly neglected problem of the determinants of spontaneous participation.
Elton Mayo.
Mayo's words still apply in the late '90's and undoubtedly will in the 21st century.

focused on pragmatics and the employment of case studies. The most prestigious qualification is a Master of Business Administration (MBA). Alternatively, business is taught in a general way at under-graduate level.

• Managers learn their craft on the job. This will be concerned with general problem-solving, kinds of interpersonal and organisational development, and conflict resolution (much more so than professionals).

• Managers adopt a career ethic. They will subordinate learning and suppress curiosity in order to advance their careers - work promotes a better quality of life (for the professional, vocational commitment tends to be put before career development). The corporate employer forms the home base, not a university or a professional referent organisation. They do not subscribe to any ethic of 'disinterestedness'.

• The manager's role will articulate organisational goals. Procedures will be met to meet these goals. Work is not an end in itself, but a means of serving group interests, and of serving their personal success. The group is seen as a work unit, with individuals being used as resources (the opposite attitude is held by professionals). They are probably less concerned with solving problems than impressing the boss - this team player is a game player.

• New knowledge is considered to be a corporate property and managers are loathe to share it. Being 'disinterested' is alien to business practice; serving social interests has only recently impinged upon the managerial mind-set and the corporate agenda.

Whilst professionals trade in human capital and are strongly motivated by vocational reward, managers address a financially capitalised market with the principal ambition of dealing in exchange values in order to maximise the accumulation of the two great media of modern capitalism: money and power. (See Allinson, 1993) If professionals and managers are to share team membership, they must overcome this disparity of outlook and establish a common basis for their project endeavours.

2 Drivers and Barriers. Teams are purposeful and goal-oriented. They are structured, knowing who is doing what. They act in concert, sharing goals. And they are led, possess a strong, co-operative spirit and a shared vision. *How do they get this way?* Is it by formulating the team instrumentally and with classical contracts describing everything that has to be done, by whom and when? Is it by carefully orchestrating membership so that each member is a carefully chosen personality / skill mix?

The question pin-points an issue at the heart of managing the project team: the planning / scheduling / controlling functions of orthodoxy are important and useful, but they are, in themselves, useless in creating a high performance team. They might provide orientation, direction and offer audit checks, but they will never generate the *esprit de corps* needed in a high performing team. Hans Thamain, an authority in project management research, claims research suggests project success in creating a high performance team is determined by the strength of *driving forces* and *barriers* related to the job content, personal needs, the general work environment, and leadership. For example, the strongest driver is a professionally stimulating team environment, and this is characterised by:

• interesting, challenging work
• visibility and recognition for achievements
• growth potential
• good project leadership

A stimulating environment leads to the perception that the team has:

Aspects of team management

Provision of satisfiers
(promoters of success)

E.G. quality management

E.G. cultivation of motivation, mentorship

work orientation of leadership — people orientation of leadership

E.G. assuring and checking quality; looking after the team by ensuring 'hygiene'.

E.G. conflict resolution; removal of poor team members, etc.

Removal of dissatisfiers
(barriers to success)

The Nature of Teams

Teams don't exist without a broad, orienting purpose and specific performance goals. The require complementary skills. They foster roles. They engender individual dn mutual accountability. But they only work if there is sharing, commitment and a common approach.Out of this can come success, reward and enjoyment.

- low levels of conflict; high levels of commitment;
- involved personnel; good communications;
- a positive attitude to innovation; and
- offers on-time and to-budget performances.

From these considerations we might conclude that there are three issues of paramount importance to team members:

1. Potential sources of *satisfaction* are enhanced. The successful team pays attention to human issues i.e. the work itself engenders creativity and innovation, it is challenging, allowing for recognition for achievement, responsibility and personal growth. Job challenge is offered in terms of the intrinsic nature of the work rather than competitiveness among team members. Professional and personal goals are aligned, engendering purposive, relational contracts and consummate forms of co-operation.
Of course, the reality is that jobs are never quite like this. Some degree of uninteresting work is inevitable and unavoidable. But if satisfaction cannot be guaranteed, at least team managers can attempt to remove causes of dissatisfaction.

2. Potential sources of *dissatisfaction* are removed. These are largely environmental factors concerning the conditions of the job and the avoidance of unpleasantness. They can include the physical environment, the terms, conditions of employment, supervision, status, remuneration, company policies, etc. (38) Removing these potential causes of dissatisfaction paves the way for sources of satisfaction to be addressed.
Whatever the satisfaction / dissatisfaction equation, it is not, in itself, sufficient to keep a social group - especially a goal-oriented project group - sustained as an effective team. There has to be a third element:

3. *Leadership.* A winning team has good leadership - individuals who dare to lead, championing the project and the motivational interests of team members. This can also be looked upon in positive and negative terms, even as 'good' leadership. For example, a positive orientation includes cultivating motivation and providing mentorship; a negative orientation includes removing sources of conflict, checking work content, etc.

The motivational points about satisfaction and dissatisfaction derive from Frederick Herzberg's research that suggested the sources of dissatisfaction, when removed, do not produce satisfaction, but rather *no dissatisfaction*. Satisfaction itself derives from those factors concerning job challenge, personal growth, etc. Because of this differentiation, Herzberg called the sources of dissatisfaction *hygiene* factors i.e. factors that, in the medical sense, were conducive to physical health and well-being, but not happiness.

It is arguable that *planning and scheduling* are aspects of project work that function as hygiene factors. In themselves, they do not create satisfactions and ensure success, but their absence will certainly cause problems and dissatisfaction! Similarly, the right kind of classical contract will not ensure consummate co-operation (satisfaction), but the inadequate classical contract will

engender discontent (dissatisfaction) that militates against forms of consummate co-operation. Contracts can support (service) motivation indirectly (e.g. as remuneration to spend on whatever thrills you), but is more important as a removal of potential dissatisfiers; they cannot, in themselves provide motivation.

Project management theory tends to be weak on these points, suggesting that goal-oriented actions, properly planned, scheduled, monitored and controlled are all that is required. This does not appear to be true even on a non-creative production line using the cell-manufacturing team concept, and it can hardly be expected to be true on an architectural project! Technical rationality does not adapt itself to human relations problems very easily (if at all). It is happier generating plans, schedules and checks which are all necessary, but insufficient, aspects of project management.

3 Building the Agency Team. What is the team-building reality in the architectural field, where project teams are formed *between* agencies as well as *within* agencies, when the over-riding reality is that the agency is effective because it is a successful, internally bonded family before it is an effective member of the project team?

The 'many minds, one heart / one firm' principle is the ambition of many professional organisations who realise they must be alert, expert, a learning organisation, adaptable yet well disciplined, strongly motivated, and closely bonded. But professional employees as team members need a positive family identity to relate to, one deemed to be successful in the eyes of peers. A strong common culture and loose forms of supervision is an ideal, but this suggests intellectual muscle as well as organisational commitment.

As always, it is easier to move away from problems than to set up ideals. Whilst Thamain's drivers of success include the motivating factors mentioned above, it is the *barriers* that will confront the team-builder and will have to be addressed. These include: unclear project objectives and directions; insufficient resources; power struggles and conflict that are not confronted and resolved (this might go together with lack of mutual acceptance and trust); poor job security (although this is in the nature of project work); shifting goals and priorities; uninvolved, disengaged upper management (leadership, example, and leverage for change).

Some of these barriers can be tackled directly; others are removed indirectly, by dealing with their causes. At the heart of these considerations lies a crucially important point: team building does not take place in a vacuum. The project enterprise, in its purposive, ambitious, goal-oriented sense, is the milieu in which team-building takes place. Team leaders must grasp that dealing with the project and forming the effective team are necessarily one and the same thing. Project management literature often misunderstands this point, telling us we should plan and then act. The fact is that 'planning' *is* the action. The crux of planning is the *process* of planning. Forming an agenda and acting upon it become one and the same thing. Commitments are made. Team members become involved and interdependent. Planning intent becomes programming action, which becomes policy and strategy. *In the process*, meaningful team-building can take place. Team-building is rarely prior to goal-oriented project action. It is difficult to see *how* it can take place outside of the context of the project as a situational-problematic the team is formed to deal with.

The qualification to this remark is that an architectural agency has to be a viable organisational and service enterprise which sustains itself outside of any particular project. The basis for project team-building has to be in place, even though the practice cannot sustain itself in isolation from the projects which give it meaning and viability. The problem is a bit like that of the bicyclist: is it being upright or keeping moving which is the real trick?

Bearing this in mind, making an effective team requires three things to be undertaken by those who form and lead it.

Content i.e. *having the right team members* - something that is often set up as an ideal or a basic requirement, with much talk in the literature about having the right psychological types within the team. On the one side is the need for appropriate skills and experience; on the other is the 'chemistry' between team members. However, the team-builder / leader rarely has full control of team membership in this way. It is not just a matter of availability and resourcing at any point in time, but also *over* time, as the project life-cycle develops from one stage to another. The reality is that effective teams usually have to be forged from mixed material - there is no such thing as the perfect team. Firms are likely to have more than one project to service and people usually join the firm as members of the practice family before they become members of any particular project team. In the favour of such a mix, research suggests it is the diversified team rather than the more homogeneous, high-profile team that is successful.

Collaboration. Forging a good team means *having the team work together as an effective cultural entity.* The aim has to be an optimally effective group who get it right first time, up front, even as the team is being created, reformed and then run-down over the project life-cycle. When a group collaborates the concept of an individual winning is irrelevant and possibly counter-productive. Collaboration is about the understanding that success will be a team quality and derives from the endeavours of more than one mind.

Commitment. Forging a good team means *sustaining group morale.* Teams can work well without dominant leadership, but only on the basis of a shared vision, mutual respect and co-operation. A key source of team effectiveness will be the commitment that comes from authentic involvement and job satisfaction. Other things (such as some form of organisational discipline) being equal, it is this which will produce the co-operation and appropriate, decisional action commitments that take the team toward its goal.

More than anyone else, it is the leader who must forge both creativity, co-ordination, and productivity, and the co-operation and mutual supportiveness that are a crucial features of motivation and work satisfaction.

The Team: an interaction of multiple factors

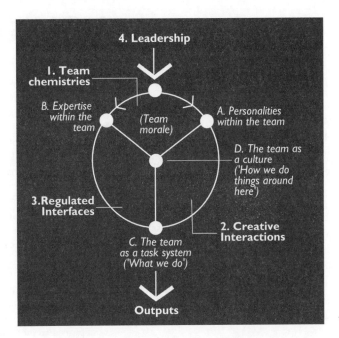

If a project team is fundamentally made up of the people and the capabilities within it, and the tasks it has undertaken, then the key features if team life are interpersonal chemistries, creative interactions (envisioning, harnessing and realising), and a host of regulative mechanisms (from studio disciplines to project procedures and even personal ethics). Leadership is vitally important - whatever form it takes (autocratic, consensus-seeking, contingent, situational, etc.) - and is always, to some degree, an overview of what is going on i.e. it is always both objectively outside of the team as well as subjectively a part of it. Put together, all these factors constitute the team's identity and culture. From this equation comes the team's outputs (what it achieves and what it is judged by).

The term' team chemistries' is a crucial area of the diagram where one arguably sees the application of personal motivations and commitments, and the formation of team morale. A poorly motivated team usually means a team with low morale or esprit de corps, low commitment, divisive politics and poor performances.

Me manager; you ox

'No, but . .

*You can no more 'motivate' someone than
you can . . . volunteer them.'*
Baden Eunson
*Perhaps, but the manager or leader can
surely awaken motivation, lend it orientation
and or give it the possibility of flourishing.*

The issue of motivation has always been a key management concern. The 18th century legislators and capitalist producers of the Industrial Revolution who were important to the formation of an industrial labouring class confronted the difficulty of transforming the attitudes, motivations and behaviours of a formerly agrarian workforce who, more often than not, reluctantly adapted to new socio-economic roles. Owners had the task of developing businesses ready to find ways of entrusting non-family assistance at a managerial level and a disgruntled workforce which often had to be coerced into cooperation on the other. It was a background and tradition against which Frederick Taylor almost appears as a profound humanist. Different sentiments which, whilst not entirely serving the workforce, reforming management's adversarial posture or its instrumental concern to enhance productivity, quality and profit by whatever means, did not appear until after World War I, but remained contentious even after WWII.

The most notable landmark in what was to become known as the Human Relations Movement was a series of productivity experiments carried out in the 1920's by Elton Mayo, an Australian psychiatrist, at a factory of Western General Electric in Hawthorne, Illinois. In brief, the Hawthorne experiments noted that worker productivity appeared to increase independently of varying conditions i.e. it was the experiments themselves and the attention they gave to the workers which was the crucial factor. Whether the lights were turned up or down, productivity went up! The conclusion was that organisational sub-cultures and similar aspects of informal social relations were crucial factors in controlling productivity. It was as if, to use Herzberg's language, hygiene factors (such as conditions, reward, etc.) were being manipulated, but that it was the 'soft' ones of human relations that were most significant, not the 'hard' ones of lighting levels and the like.

In 1960, Douglas McGregor published his Theory X and Theory Y contrasting Taylorist presumptions with their more socially sensitive opposite: i.e. the notion that workers were, in fact, motivated, could be trusted, liked work, can change, want their parent organisations to succeed, etc. The argument was that management can make a massive difference to a team's success simply by changing its own mind-set - a notion claimed tom have been vindicated by Robert Townsend at Avis cars (see Townsend 1970 and 1984), who turned a loss-making enterprise around by retaining workers whilst changing their morale. It is a contention which lies at the heart of much debate about Japanese production and the comparative attitudes of Eastern and Western management. In that light, for example, it is accepted that the Hawthorne experiments continued the smug, parent-to-child assumptions manifest by Taylor's presumption of the 'ox-like' nature of workers.

One of the most significant figures in this field was Abraham Maslow (1908-70) who, in the 1940's, developed a theory of human motivation which has been profoundly influential. Maslow argued for a hierarchy of needs and wants which began at a basic, physiological level and evolved through to a higher level of what he called the need to 'self-actualisation' i.e. a need to satisfy that most far-reaching of human motivations: the desire to find and become 'oneself'.

The notion of a hierarchy - its components only partly fulfiled at any point in time or in any given situation - was important to McGregor. It was also important to Frederick Herzberg who, in the 1950's and '60's, researched causes of satisfaction and differentiated between what he called *motivators* and *hygiene* or maintenance factors - the latter being equivalent to the lower levels of Maslow's hierarchy, and the former equating with the upper, actualising, levels (see box on the previous page). Other theorists have considered factors such as a deep-rooted triad of predominant needs for either *achievement*, *affiliation* or *social interaction*, and the need for *power* (David

McClelland). According to this theory the affiliators will prefer unskilled friends to skilled managers; the power motivated person might be more concerned with politics and being manipulative than with getting things done.

Victor Vroom is a figure who added to the so-called 'content' models of Maslow, Herzberg et al by considering 'process' factors. Vroom noted the factor of *expectancy*, arguing (reasonably enough) that a person's motivation is affected by the expectancy of fulfilment. He produced a calculus comprising: *valence* (i.e. a person's preference or need) x their *expectancy* of outcome = *motivation*. Lyman Porter and Edward Lawler added other process factors such as a person's *ability* to fulfill their expectancy and motivation and their *perception* of the equitableness of extrinsic rewards. The calculus then becomes: conditioning factors (*valence* x their *expectancy* of outcome) = *motivation*. As with many theories, such a calculus explains by objective, systematic analysis, but fails to help us act from a subjective, hermeneutic position. However, one managerial implication is that work objectives and job roles have to be spelt out and lines of communication have to be clear - openness and transparency, manifest equitableness and egalitarianism can be argued to be very important to any form of corporate success dependent upon employee satisfactions.

All of this theory is of interest to the design and project manager because it explores the issues involved in realising personal satisfaction and in offering it to others. In the latter instance the real motivation is economic: to make them happy in order to produce better work and success for the project, the team and the practice. But are the crucial factors internal motivations or external incentives? Or both? And if multiple factors are involved, which are the most important? When? To whom? Is the attempt to 'motivate' someone similar to the attempt to 'volunteer' them? There are no simple answers to such questions, but every manager knows they have to act as if there was, for without motivation (or morale as it can be interpreted), a team is set for a walk across a ploughed field. In any context this can become difficult, simply because of the number of considerations to be addressed. In a complex professional context such as the architectural project team, the simple determination to be 'professional' is a significant feature sustaining team ambitions.

Motivation

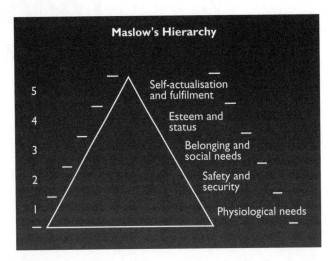

Maslow argued that a satisfied need no longer motivates. Once basic needs are satisfied, we want to move on. Of course, needs can return (e.g. hunger) or be only partially fulfilled.

If the top of maslow's pyramid is what is lost and to be found again, the bottom is what is inescapable and to be accepted.

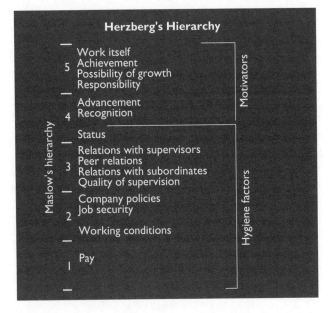

Frederick Herzberg differentiated between what he termed 'hygiene factors' (those which sustain life) and 'motivators' (what really concerns us). The former are 'satisfiers'; the latter are 'dissatisfiers' (causes of dissatisfaction). Managers must work to remove the causes of dissatisfaction and promote the factors of satisfaction. Herzberg called this 'job enrichment'. (But note: they aren't opposites - removing dissatisfaction is not the same as producing satisfaction.) As in much motivation theory, a key point concerns money. Herzberg would argue that it does not motivate, but lack of it will dis-motivate. The theory is not uncontentious (see Eunson, 1987), but it explains much about the motivations of professionals.

Leadership and team dynamics

You might be called upon to exercise it. Do you know what it is? Have you experienced it? Do you understand it? What is it? Leadership is about daring to undertake it and accepting its consequences. Some people don't have to really think about it and they sometimes come to be considered as 'born leaders'. Others adapt themselves to it and knowingly take on the responsibilities as an undertaking and, sometimes, a burden. On the other hand, some pretend to leadership and aren't suited.

Apart from such issues, leadership depends upon four factors:

1. Someone who dares to lead and accepts the responsibility.
2. A body of people willing to be led (power and authority are ceded).
3. Both the technical and interpersonal skills and abilities of the leader.
4. The authority of that leader.

The ideal Team

What is the ideal team? Ideal for what? Ideal in whose opinion? Ideal for what? Ideal in which circumstance? Is 'ideal' a fixed or relative quality? Must it be a dynamic quality?

Why is leadership necessary and what is it for? Edwards Deming argued that the aim of leadership is to remove the causes of failure so that people could then do a better job with less effort. His view is intrinsically positive about people's natural desire to do a good job and for teams to perform well - an attitude at odds with Taylorist presumptions. However, it would be unrealistic not to acknowledge that leadership is needed to focus the energies of the team, to effect decisions, to resolve conflicts, champion values, set an example and generally galvanise the team into effective performance across the project life-cycle and sometimes in spite of itself. Game theory suggests that someone has to lead simply in order that decisions can be made!

Leadership theory divides into three approaches:

Membership of the Team

Selection is important, but team membership is earned, every day. The conditions have to be fostered which enable this to happen and to be sustained.

1. *Trait theory*, concerned with the ostensibly inborn and inbred characteristics of those who become leaders. This is sometimes offered in the guise of vested self-interest or pretension: it's either in the genes or is the product of proper nurturing. Undoubtedly, some people are more 'naturally' leaders than others, but this is possibly largely attributable to their 'emotional intelligence' i.e. their ability and maturity in interpersonal relations.

2. Theory concerned with effective *leadership style* - as a *contingent behavioural* posturing and positioning that can be learned and adapted to circumstances. Such theory is really a response to the inadequacy of the trait approach with its fatalistic undertones. It takes the leadership issue apart, attempts to understand its contingent nature and identify what leadership behaviours appear to work and which do not..

Skills

There are three kinds of basic skill needed in any team:

- *technical skills*
- *interpersonal skills*
- *problem-solving and decision-making skills.*

3. The *functionalist* view: leadership is a matter of what leaders have to do. This is akin to the classical theory seeking to explain what a manager is. Leadership is explained in instrumental terms.

For example, the following four ways of considering leadership divide into trait and contingency perspectives:

- Leadership as a natural focus of *group processes* - e.g. the way leaders appear to naturally emerge out of particular social contexts.

- Leadership as forms of *social control and the exercise of power* - i.e. concepts of personal social control as the ability to influence, persuade and motivate others to pursue a mutual goal. Also concepts of power derived from legitimate authority within an organisation, or influence within social networks founded upon interdependency and mutual obligation.

• Leadership as a *pattern of behaviours and skills* functionally dependent upon situational appropriateness.

• Leadership as a form of *interactive relationship* between the leader and the led - i.e. the utilisation of the special or superior skills of the leader to benefit the group by the facilitation of appropriate and personally rewarding contributions. This is an emphasis upon the means and settings through which individuals can express themselves, develop and grow.

The trait theory approach might have merit, but can engender a 'so what?' question toward its analyses of class, sex, age, race, physical fitness, height, personality type, tolerance for stress and ambiguity, astrological birth sign, psychological type, parentage and the rest. These might be significant, but they are hardly theoretically sufficient and, arguably, an impractical basis for organising project teams. It is difficult how the trait theory helps us to realise project potential, to harness it in particular situations and to address the issue of shifting situational dynamics. In any case, research appears to have discovered no basis for a relationship between traits and organisational performance.

Contingency theory addresses the act of leadership as an adaptive behaviour that can benefit from learning. However, whilst it is easy to learn techniques it is something else to apply them - returning us to innate ability and potentiality. In other words, *both* character (an aspect of trait theory) and learned ability (an aspect of contingency theory) are relevant to any discussion of leadership.

The *functional* view of leadership seeks to deal with *what a leader does* e.g. team building, assigning roles and responsibilities, defining and clarifying goals, motivating the team, engendering loyalty, representing the group, serving as a role model, the nerve centre of the team, etc.

Another neo-functional view deals with *responsibilities*: to plan, investigate, organise, staff, direct, co-ordinate, report and budget. And *types* of leader have been characterised as authoritive (a dominator), persuasive (a crowd rouser), democratic (a group developer), intellectual (an eminent person), executive (an administrator), and representative (a spokesperson).

These viewpoints are not mutually exclusive and can be seen as interactive, as in the diagram on the overleaf.

The Status of Team Membership

1. Core team member: those who cover the entire project scope between them. They meet as a group chaired by the project manager. Each can state what the project is about and describe its status. As a group, they are responsible to the project sponsor or the sponsor's steering group.

2. Extended team member: responsible to the core group and sometimes meets with it as a larger group. These people have specific roles, tasks, duties, scope of authority and accountability.

3. Stakeholder: involved and interested, but without core or extended team status.

But is the core team really a team? Or is it a working group? Most architectural projects have the latter rather than the former. On such projects, real teams tend only exist within the individual agencies. This is an intrinsic difficulty with them. On the other hand, there is little reason to presume real teams exist within the agencies themselves (a typical argument in favour of 'design and build').

Power and Influence

It is helpful to see forms of power and its influence together, as a set of varying interactions, emphases, and nuances which are never exclusive, varies with circumstances, and can even vary between leadership (which is more than simply 'the leader') and individual team members.

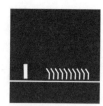

2 **Power.** A key aspect of the leadership issue concerns power and authority. Power is exercised strategically as direct or indirect influence over the behaviours of others. This might be in the form of persuasion, the imposition of rules and procedures, an ability to negotiate and bargain, the exercising of charisma, or the weight of expertise.

Four principal forms of power and two subsidiary ones can be readily identified:

1. *Legitimate or position power* derived from formal position, lending its holder invisible rights such as the rights to access and to organise, and power and influence over information.

2. *Expert power* derived from acknowledged expertise - a form of authority subject to dispute and competition from other experts, and subject to the skills of persuasion.

3. *Referent or personal power* deriving from personality or charisma. Its principal medium is persuasion.

4. *Reward or resource power*, and its obverse, *coercive power*, both deriving from an ability to bargain, negotiate, cajole, and from friendship and status. Reward power includes an ability to offer work challenge.

Subsidiary forms:

• *Connection power* deriving from political connections and influences and *information power* deriving from control over the flow and content of information.

In turn, effecting influence by those in power can be considered in three ways, none of which is exclusive:

1. *As compliance.* Force or the imposition of rules to modify behaviour or attitudes.

2. *As identification.* The individuals concerned adapt to the content of the influence because of admiration, persuasion, or identification. Behaviours are influenced in a more pleasant and motivated way.

3. *As internalisation.* Individuals now fully adopt the content of the influence, making it their own and thus a part of their motivational complex. This is the most difficult but most lasting form of influence. It is also the least common.

Subordinates tend to rank authority as the most important means of exercising influence, but higher levels of motivation can be expected by managers who can use expert power and work challenge as a way to elicit following.

3 **Team Life-cycles.** Apart from the issue of what leadership is and how sources of power exercise influence, there is another issue of particular interest to project managers: *team life-cycles*.

Teams evolve through distinct phases. These have been described as: *forming, storming, norming, working, uniting, being maintained,* and *winding down / breaking up*. These phases can be considered in terms of distinct 'waves', as described below, each dominated by a particular set of concerns. Whether one would add to or take away from these stages, amend the denotations or whatever, is less important than the point that team building is a dynamic issue.

First wave: *forming, storming and norming*. This is a wave concerned with goal setting, initiating work planning, and power distribution. It is a crucial period for forming a sense of team membership within the context of tackling the first stages of project work. It is a time for feelings of belonging, a knowledge that

Power and influence make up the fine texture of organisation, and indeed of all interactions.
Charles Handy.

individual contributions count, and a sense that the individual inhabits a project environment in which they can enjoy themselves and grow. Team members come together, start working, becoming familiar with one another, jockeying for position, status and influence as an authority structure is sorted out.

It is only when these initial phases of forming and storming have been sufficiently worked through that 'norming' can be established. This is manifest as a distinct pattern of behaviours and routines having a socio-psychological dimension beneath the surface. Clearly, the team leader needs to reach this stage as rapidly as possible, but it can only be done in the context of the work being undertaken. The process can be accelerated by meetings, bonding rituals, weekend workshops and the like. Once the front-end players are in place, new members of the team have to be inducted and taken through the same process whilst work progresses.

Practice Finders are quite likely to underestimate the significance of this internal team-building wave. Instead, they will focus upon the project content and inter-agency bonding, taking internal team-building for granted (as an aspect of an already established 'family') or leaving the problem to Minders with ambiguous status and authority.

Second wave: *performing*. This is the stage of teamwork, that parallels 'norming' and grows out of it. Some key questions arise: How do we keep up momentum and team morale? How do we maintain standards? How do we stay on track?

Initial achievements are likely to bring a uniting within the team - feelings of comradeship and effective team structure. But this has to be maintained. Further storming and norming might have to be dealt with as a consequence of team or work changes, and ongoing conflict resolution will become an everyday feature of team-life. Team leadership not only has to continue with kinds of planning, analysis and control, but also to keep a close eye on social issues and watch for dysfunctional symptoms (the leader as diagnostically skilled manager, relating technical and social behaviours). Team members should be involved, mutually trustful, feeling professionally challenged and satisfied - only then will there be the spontaneous participation that constitutes the necessary underpinning of a high performing team. However, this second wave is likely to be that stage subsequent to the scheme design i.e. when the team has to settle down to less glamourous, more routine work in translating a scheme into the realised potential of complete specifications. Strong schedule and budgetary problems can reduce the perceived job challenge and potential reward, producing low morale and even the 'bailing out' that is a common way of coping with tediousness and disenchantment.

Third wave: *winding down to project closure*. Winding down has to be managed. Those leaving the team must feel they are being forced to let go without experiencing completion and closure. Those staying must not feel they

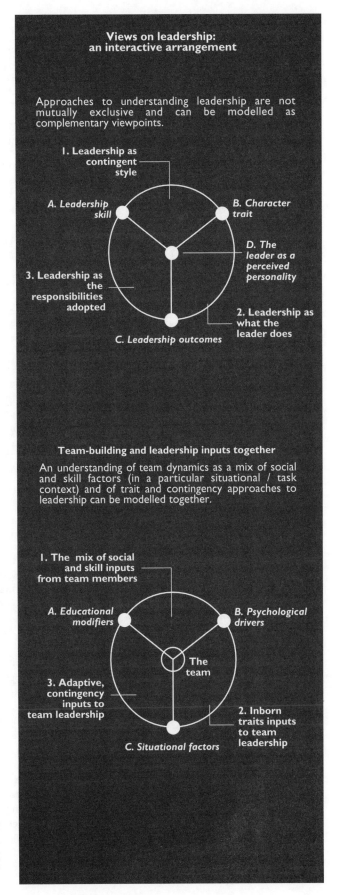

Views on leadership: an interactive arrangement

Approaches to understanding leadership are not mutually exclusive and can be modelled as complementary viewpoints.

1. Leadership as contingent style
A. Leadership skill
B. Character trait
D. The leader as a perceived personality
3. Leadership as the responsibilities adopted
2. Leadership as what the leader does
C. Leadership outcomes

Team-building and leadership inputs together

An understanding of team dynamics as a mix of social and skill factors (in a particular situational / task context) and of trait and contingency approaches to leadership can be modelled together.

1. The mix of social and skill inputs from team members
A. Educational modifiers
B. Psychological drivers
The team
3. Adaptive, contingency inputs to team leadership
2. Inborn traits inputs to team leadership
C. Situational factors

are hanging on whilst others move on to new projects and fresh challenges.

The notion of team waves - especially when linked with the more task-oriented concept of project stages - suggests that the leadership challenge shifts in 'structural' terms. The situation and the mix of issues faced by the members of a team and by its leaders have to be seen as something dynamic.

Dealing with Staff

When a project ends there is the problem of dealing with the staff. Does a firm get rid of them or keep them on? There key alternatives stand out:

- *Get rid of them.*
- *Put key staff on redeployment basis until a new project arises. make them redundant when it doesn't..*
- *Put them on a 'pay and rations' basis until another suitable project arises.*

Ground Rules for Meetings:

- *Use facts and data*
- *No secrets*
- *Whining is OK, occasionally*
- *Prepare a plan, find a way*
- *Listen to each other*
- *Help each other, include everyone*
- *Enjoy each other and the journey*
- *Emotional resilience*

Practised at Boeing's Programme and Review Meetings (Sabbagh, 1995)

4 Chemistries. One version of the trait theory that gets much publicity is the *chemical* approach. This theory argues that teams should be a suitable mix of psychological types whose interpersonal chemistry is suited to situation and undertaking. The presumption is that, if the appropriate types are in place, then appropriate team roles and tasks can be naturally dealt with - i.e that such a team is already a long way down the road to success.

Types identified by the chemical approach include such people / role characterisations as: the initiator (who suggests ideas and new means); the information seeker (who pursues factual adequacy); the information giver (who offers expert facts or generalisations); the opinion giver (who is looking for relevant opinions and values rather than facts); the evaluator (who assesses feasibility, imposes standards, etc.); the implementor (who executes group decisions); the procedural technician (who deals with logistics, detail, etc.); and the recorder (who acts as the group memory).

Other lists include encouragers, compromisers, confronters, withdrawers, blockers, recognition seekers, moaners, and the rest - attempts to link team character with psychological type. This can also include consideration of Jungian personality types. For example, the Myers-Briggs Indicator is a listing of types in terms of Jungian character and natural problem-solving strategies founded upon the ways individuals gather and use information (by sensing, intuition, thinking or feeling).

Kolb's model of decision-making uses a matrix of introvert / extrovert and people / things orientations to identify four types: the divergers, the assimilators, the convergers, and the accommodators / executors.

Kolb Type	Team character
1. *Diverger*	• Good at interpersonal relations and generating alternatives; comfortable with ambiguity; reliant on feelings rather than facts; tending toward introvertness, etc.
2. *Assimilator*	• Logical, reflective personalities with wide viewpoints; interested in means and look for whole patterns, although tending toward impracticality.
3. *Converger*	• Argue deductively; are goal-oriented, and experimental; seek single answers; tend toward extroversion; avoid ambiguity and do not like uncertainty.
4. *Accommodator / Executor*	• Action-oriented, interested in other *people*, like to deal with concrete experience and experimentation, mistrust theory and tend toward being good at crisis management.

Such 'chemical' approaches seek to identify the ideal team mix. But ideal for whom? How does one properly understand type? What about availability and shifting needs? What about available funds? Implicitly rooted in scientific management, the theory fails to deal with situational dynamics and does not account for the practicalities of team-building and team management. Only in Hollywood movies can the ideal team be easily assembled and made instrumentally effective by an accord with ostensibly natural social and psychological principles (as well as according to work content demands).

5 Conflict. The page opposite notes some important issues in something almost all projects inevitably suffer: kinds of conflict (not contention - which can be useful) between its participants. The point is not just that conflict must be anticipated, but that its sources appear to vary from stage to stage within the life-cycle.

Reducing conflict within the team can be promoted in a number of ways:

- By means of careful project planning, obviating bottlenecks, anticipating

Forging Teams

Teams might be described in terms of personal chemistries, patterns of conflict, issues of leadership and life-cycles, but how do they come about? How are they forged from the material at hand in the context of prevailing pressures?

Katzenbach and Smith (*The Wisdom of Teams*) offer many insights derived from research. One of their key points is that one has to differentiate between *high-performance teams, real teams, potential teams, pseudo-teams* and *working groups.*

• **Working groups** rely upon the sum of individual efforts. They thrive in large, hierarchical organisations. The focus is upon individual performances. Work is often delegated to others. There is no search for the magnified performance impact sought for within a real team. A managerial board or group of directors or associates in an architectural practice often work this way. A so-called project team made up of separate agencies also works this way.

• **Pseudo-teams** have the potential to magnify mutual performances, but they lack focus and shared purpose. Interactions are individualised and frequently detract from one another's performances. Politics is rife. Hierarchical rituals are adhered to. Leaders are always being criticised. These are probably the weakest of team types. The pseudo-team pretends to team-ness but does not *practically* deliver it on a day to day basis. It's a lie. It faces a dilemma of choice: between effectiveness as a working group, and the risks associated with moving toward genuine team commitments.

• **Potential teams** do better. They have a shared, identified purpose and are really trying to improve performances and realise some form of success. However, these teams often lack clarity, specific goals, and discipline. They need to move toward true interdependence, trust and the management of conflict.

• **Real Teams** are defined as '*a small number of people with complementary skills who are equally committed to a common purpose, goals, and working approach for which they hold themselves mutually accountable*'.

• **High-performance teams** meet all the criteria for 'real teams', but also offer a deep commitment to one another's personal growth and success. It is the comparative rarity, but lies there as a potentiality for most other team types.

Katzenbach and Smith offer five simple criteria which test a groups and define It:

• Is it small enough in number? About 10 people is a possible maximum that can form a tight group and easily communicate.

• Is there an adequate level of complementary skills (actually there or there in potential)? Teams should be skill based rather than personality based. Skills can be developed after a team has been formed (but this implies willingness, candour, trust, time and opportunity).

• Does the group have a truly meaningful (urgent and worthwhile) purpose? This will help form and galvanise the group, but more is needed. A general sense of purpose and vision has to serve the firm, but this isn't enough - specific goals have to focus the team. Many groups cannot make this leap: 'What will it take for us to achieve significant performance results?'

• Does it have specific goals (concrete accomplishments) it can identify? Do they know what is expected? Without such goals a team cannot be forged. It is the challenge itself which achieves this.

• Does the group have a clear working approach? The focus has to be on the issues not the people involved. Rules need to be set and enforced. Does the group spend a lot of time together (the group has to learn to be a team)? Is there candour? Are issues openly confronted? Does the group play together as well as work together?

There appears to be five consistent indicators of true team behaviour: enthusiasm and energy; event-driven histories which can be recalled; personal commitments; themes of identity (symbols, logos, etc.); and real performance achievement.

The challenge is summarised in the following diagram:

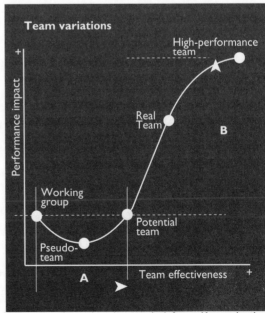

(Diagram adapted and amended from Katzenbach & Smith):

Conflict

One of the most important responsibilities of a leader is to address conflict within the team. Sometimes this means to resolve and obviate its destructive aspects; sometimes it means to turn conflict to the benefit of the project - it would be a tedious and perhaps unchallenging team without disagreements and debate. Conflict can also be looked upon as a surfacing of problems that need to be dealt with.

Thamain and Wilemon's oft quoted research into conflict (1974 and 1975) highlights two things: sources of conflict and their likelihood within the project life cycle. Those sources of conflict above the 'average' line indicate where attention should be directed.

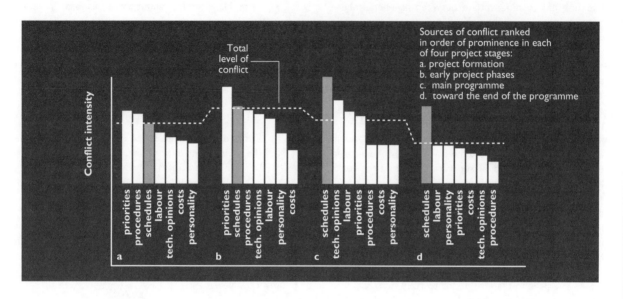

The diagram represents Thamain & Wilemon's findings which consensus seems to agree still apply today. However, another study by Posner (1986) suggests that some factors - particularly costs - have dramatically changed position in the ranking of mean conflict intensity over the project life cycle.

Rank in Thamain & Wilemon studies (1975):
1. *schedules*
2. priorities
3. staffing
4. technical issues
5. procedures
6. personality
7. **costs**

Rank in Posner's study (1986)
1. *schedules*
2. **costs**
3. priorities
4. staffing
5. technical issues
6. personality
7. procedures

How can conflict be handled? Five strategies stand out: *forcing* (power or dominance), *confrontation* (and collaboration), *compromising* (negotiation), *smoothing* (suppression), and *withdrawal* (denial and retreating).
Forcing and withdrawal have been found by Thamain & Wilemon to be associated with increased conflict. Confrontation, compromise and smoothing were associated with reduced degrees of conflict. The collaborative approach is favoured because it seeks to be a win / win situation rather than win / lose, but the strategy adopted will depend on factors such as the authority of the project manager / leader, the risks involved and a willingness to give something up.

Note: research quoted earlier argued that after a project is over the perception of success or failure tends to deny the place of schedule and budgetary factors (Baker et al., 1974). Technical or performative success in terms of fulfilling the project mission is what tends to stick in the minds of participants, especially if this has been achieved and there are memories of good interpersonal relations and coordination.

resource problems, personal chemistries, etc..
- By open communication within the team, implying honesty and trust.
- By using power and influence, status and charisma to support conflict management.
- By using work challenge, which appears to reduce conflict.
- By that old adage: listening.

When the inevitable happens, the manager has a variety of options:

- Confrontation rather than avoidance.
- Compromise through negotiation.
- Smoothing out areas of disagreement.
- Forcing a resolution.
- Withdrawing from potential or actual disagreement.

The leader's position-power and need to win will constrain circumstances and affect the options available. Without strong position power, for example, forcing is likely to be impossible. Low position power suggests the need to resort to smoothing, compromise and withdrawal. Similarly, the need to win implies a lot is at stake and this will also influence the possible courses of action (in fact, it might predetermine them). It is worth noting that sexual politics sometimes places the woman into a weak position but, when position power is strongly in her favour, the average woman appears more able to switch between, say, forcing or smoothing, than the average man. This is certainly the conventional wisdom currently in favour of women in team situations.

The key background requirement is that all situations should seek to solve the problems at issue, for example by identifying and agreeing the crucial issues, by agreeing the impact on the project, looking at available courses of action, etc.

As in negotiating, there should be a separation of the issues from the individuals involved. The focus should be on issues, not positions. There should be a search for objective criteria in the project's favour, and the search for options should seek to provide mutual gain.

6 **Reform the Environment, not the Man.** Team-building theory clearly raises a variety of fundamental questions to be decided upon, but a common (and erroneous) presumption is that the team is being formed on a *tabula rasa*. In fact, architectural project teams are usually formed within *particular* situational and cultural frameworks and even within the context of long-standing traditions characterising the profession and the building industry. Team building (and unbuilding) issues have to be seen against this background.

A key issue that arises in much current debate about teams is a concern with the

Facing Up to It

How should detrimental team behaviour be dealt with? It's difficult. One course of action is the following:

- *Tell the person what they are doing.*
- *Tell them how you (or others) feel about it.*
- *Tell them the consequences.*

Leadership Style and Confrontation

Contention can be useful in a team, but conflict is usually destructive. Conflict will always arise and four classic strategies exist for dealing with it, each of which can be expressed in terms of two factors: the position power of the leader and the need to win.

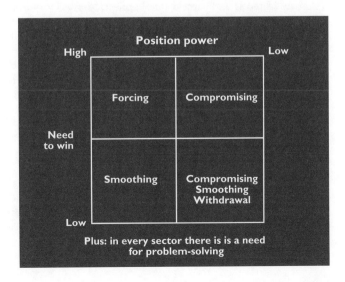

Dependence

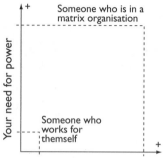

The personal power held by a leader is, clearly, important. The more a project manager is dependent upon others, the more he or she needs a source of power. The following diagram is one way of expressing this concept:

Sources of power vary. They include authority, reward and coercive powers, expert power, referent power (the degree to which team members identify with the leader), etc.

style of leadership. Should it be *democratic* (consultative, participatory and reliant upon the leader's expert and referent influences, upon personality, etc.), or *authoritarian* (reliant upon position, an ability to structure and direct, to reward and punish)?

Political correctness leans toward the former view and, undoubtedly, participation, open communications and task involvement are important. For example, in a study for NASA by Baker et al. (1974) it was found that lack of project team participation in decision-making and problem solving, lack of team spirit, a sense of mission, job security and sufficient influence from the project manager were all variables associated with perceived project failure. Participation in setting schedules and budgets was significantly related to perceived project success. However, I have already argued that the successful architectural firm does appear to be a power culture rather than a task culture. Perhaps the answer is never either / or, but always both / and - for example, the advice that planning should be democratically formulated but autocratically executed. The two elements are always present.

Feidler's work in this area is significant (39). He argued that both the directive, task-oriented leader and the nondirective, human relations-oriented leader could be successful. *Which* style is best depends upon the *situation* more than any other factor.

Feidler differentiated between two leadership styles. The first was that of *the task motivated leader* who preferred structured work and paralleled their liking for a person with how well that person accomplished tasks; poor performance equalled dislike. The task-motivated leader seeks esteem and satisfaction from tangible evidence of competence. When a situation is uncertain, they will concentrate on task completion; when they obtain confidence about this goal they will relax and devote more time to building sound inter-personal relationships. The poor co-worker is disliked.

The second leadership style was that of *the relationship motivated leader* who distinguished between the task performance and personal qualities attributable to a person. They seek to establish good relationships and to accomplish tasks through these relations. The poor co-worker can also be seen as pleasant and friendly. Once the support of co-workers and subordinates is assured, they shift attention toward support and esteem in the eyes of others who are important; if approbation is given for good task performance, then the leader's will devote themselves to this undertaking.

The two tendencies are found as a normal statistical distribution, but Feidler looked at the stereotypes in order to make his point: that a contextural change in what Feidler called situational control would alter the effectiveness of these two styles.

Situational control was made up of three variables:

1. *The quality of leader - team member relations* (weighted as 4 and therefore very important) i.e. the degree to which the leader is or feels accepted and supported by team members.

2. *The degree of task structuring* e.g. clear and structured or unclear and vague (weighted as 2). In architectural projects, this will vary from stage to stage, and even from project to project. The 'engineering' stage of most projects will necessarily have to be heavily structured (certainly in terms of outputs, even if the content is uncertain at the time of planning).

3. *The leader's position power* i.e. the authority to reward or punish in order to obtain compliance (weighted as1). In architectural practices, this authority is usually weak or ambiguous below a partner or director level. Minders will have limited authority except over relative juniors in the team.

An example of good situational control might be: a building site manager who is well liked and respected (strong leader-member relations), and who personally hires the workers (strong position power) to construct according to a full set of drawings (highly structured tasks). The leadership task is relatively favourable. An example of low situational control might be a tour leader who suffers a tough interpersonal relations (poor leader-member relationship), is serving a varied group of clients (has weak position power), and has conflicting opinions about where to go and what to do (low task structuring). The leadership task is relatively unfavourable.

Three other factors were important: *experience* (which could to shift control form low to moderate); *training* (which can either add to structuring by, for example, more training, or reduce the degree of structuring by fostering participative leadership); and *turbulence* (which could destabilize a situation and therefore lower control).

Feidler noticed that the task-motivated style worked best when the situational control was either high or low. Conversely, a relationship-motivated style worked best when situational control was only moderately favourable.

In *non-stressful* situations (good situational control), the task-motivated (directive) leader relaxes and builds relations. Conversely, the relations-motivated leader concentrates upon task-relevant behaviours. However, in *stressful* conditions (poor situational control), leadership style reverted to the predominant mode - the task leader emphasising task accomplishment, and the relations leader emphasising interpersonal relations which furthers performance and obviates conflict. A similar pattern occurs with respect to rewards and punishments. In *turbulent* conditions the task-motivated leader *reduces* rewards whilst the relations-motivated leader *increases* them. In the same conditions, the *inexperienced* relationship leaders (i.e. having less situational control) offer less punitive behaviour and the inexperienced task leader offers more. *Experienced* leaders of both types do the reverse.

Feidler's aim was to aim at *restructuring situational control* rather than attempting to change the natural behaviours of the leader (arguably impossible). In project management terms, situational control should be relatively high after scheme approval. In this situation the task-motivated leader will obtain better results. It is only when the situational can be said to enjoy moderate control that the relationship-motivated leadership style will work best. Feidler had argued that in organisational situations such as matrix and project work, "The requirements of the organisation call for immediate top performance and . . . the organisation must then be prepared to accept the possibility that a particular leader, who has been assigned to the job for an extended period of time, is likely to become less effective and must again be moved to a more challenging job."

A difficulty with Feidler's model is that it can be argued to call for another, background, overseeing person who can change the leadership style on a project or affect the conditions. This might be asking too much and draws us into a regressive argument.

7 Leaders and Followers. Hershey and Blanchard (1977) adapted earlier research and Feidler's leadership concepts into a model accounting for three principal factors:

1. The *behavioural support, massaging and feedback* the leader should provide.

2. The amount of *task structuring and directing* the leader provides.

3. The *maturity level of the leader's followers* - something that can be expected to evolve as the team becomes familiar with its undertaking.

The model is presented above in terms of a natural project progression. It is dynamic and generates four managerial modes (or the need to lead in a particular style):

1. Sector One: *Telling* - the early stages of team-building, during which there will be goal-setting and the leader's approach tends to be directive in accord with the need to set the team in position, establish a goal-orientation, etc.

2. Sector Two: *Selling* - equivalent to the 'working' stage of team formation, when tasks are better understood, procedures are in place and interpersonal relationships are developing. The leader now has a degree of trust and respect and will be involved with exploring, clarifying, persuading and selling. The aim is to get team members to 'buy-into' decisions. This style might also be appropriate to a customer.

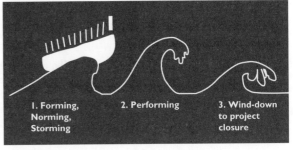

Riding Team Waves

Managing a project team is a dynamic affair. Leadership issues shift in relation to a number of factors: who is on the team; the stage of the project and therefore of the team's life-cycle; and the tasks being undertaken as the project progresses from stage to stage, deals with contingent issues, etc.

Valuing Action Two

Try to get people to do things differently. Once they do, attitude will follow. . . intellectual training pales in comparison with the urgency created by pushing someone out of the airplane and telling them, 'The ripcord is in front; you should probably pull it!'
Smith and Preston

3. Sector Three: *Participating* - the implementation stage, when there is more a unity among team members who are consulted about issues and their resolution, and are able to take the initiative and decisions for themselves. Encouragement, collaboration and commitment are given as key words for this situation. The leader is now a facilitator.

4. Sector Four: *Delegating* - the final project stage when the leader is reliant upon delegation and must play a background role, being non-directive and low-profile. Low supervision is in order, so that the leader might shift to simply monitoring.

The model presumes that the leader is able to adapt his or her style. In effect, there is only one dimension of adaptation: to lend more or less behavioural support.

Like Feidler's model, the Hershey and Blanchard version appears interesting and to offer information, but it drops Feidler's crucial point focused upon changing the context of leadership, even if it does add another new factor (the maturity of followers). It also ignores the premise that leaders are disposed to be task or relationally motivated. In effect, it is two-thirds of Feidler's model, taking a project from medium situational control through to low control. But do projects always begin here? Also, does one have to accept that the 'maturity of followers' is independent of other factors determining situational control? For example, is this latter maturity not also linked to the cultural nature of the organisation? Isn't there a large difference between the power culture run autocratically and the consensus-seeking, expert culture?

In other words, a translation of these models into project management might have to account for other factors (apart from natural leader style, the quality of leader-member relations, the degree of task structuring, the leader's position power, training, turbulence, etc.) such as:

1. The context of intrinsic project limitation, developing as a project evolves from inception through to completion (maturity in terms of project stage).

2. The context of organisational culture, how supportive it is, how directive or consensual, how motivating or alienating.

3. Maturity as the product of intrinsic follower intelligence, motivation, capability and experience.

Considerations such as these shake the original constructs. Whilst the models are not invalidated, managers will shrink back to intuition and judgement, with all its intrinsic prejudicial bias. People issues, it might be concluded, are just too complex, too variable, too difficult to determine and too intractable to resolve. And yet it cannot be denied that the theories and research do help us to understand, even if they fail to provide instant answers. Internalising that learning - difficult as it might be - is the maturing of the manager's natural behaviours.

Feidler's Concept of Contingency Management and Situational Control

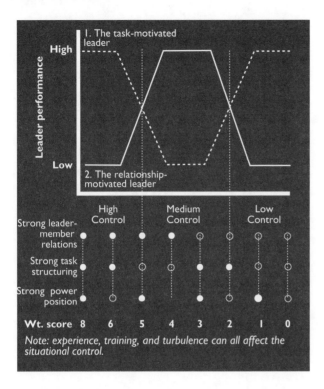

Note: experience, training, and turbulence can all affect the situational control.

Situational Leadership

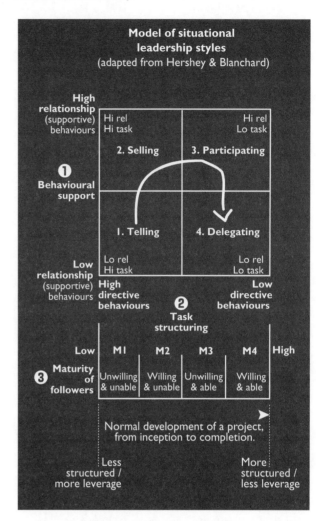

In brief, Feidler's model states that situational control affects leader behaviour which, in turn, affects team performances. Behaviour and performance change as the situational control of the leader alters.

In Feidler's model, experience (which correlates with understanding about how to get things done and can be affected by training) can effectively increase the structuring of a situation, promote the establishment of better relations, and enable the leader to use the power available. Control is increased. This implies that the inexperienced leader in a situation of weak control should be task-motivated, but that their performance will decrease as experience and the passage of time produces moderate situational control. Conversely, relationship-motivated leaders will perform less well at first, but improve as control is enhanced. If control is moderate at the beginning, the relationship-motivated leader will perform best, but effectiveness will decrease as control becomes high. The opposite of this is true for the task-motivated leader. How long it takes a leader to move from 'inexperienced' to 'experienced' appears to vary with occupation as well as the content of time on the job. 'Good fit' is not a static issue.

Training will produce similar results as experience, but much training is oriented toward participative styles which, generally speaking, might reduce situational control. Similarly, training in more technical forms of understanding can increase situational control and markedly affect performances e.g. in a situation of poor control, such training will probably decrease the effectiveness of the task-motivated leader, shifting them to moderate levels of control.

The great difficulty with all leadership theory lies with a kind of 'nature or nurture' predicament. Those people with natural and appropriate leadership qualities are hardly available on demand. The challenge is to bring out leadership qualities, or to teach them (or enhance them). However, this delves into an realm of intractable human traits. Can leadership be qualities be nurtured? Can they be effectively taught? Can instinctual behavioural norms be extended? The issue is complex.

Contingency leadership - which, in its fullest development, implies an acceptance that people have different leadership capabilities and that it is either the leadership context which should be amended, else the leader should be changed as a project develops - is only a partial answer to such issues. It still begs questions such as: how do we measure situational control? How do we actually exercise contingency management?

Situational leadership is a middle ground. It presumes that a leader is able to shift style with circumstances, as a project develops and team members mature in their roles. However, it also begs the question: how? Perhaps appreciation of the issues is half the battle.

● Part Five:

Concluding Section

Throughout this book there has been the deliberate toying with contradiction: that project process engenders product and is therefore all important, but that process is meaningless without prime importance being given to the project goal. These two - process and product, means and end - are, in other words, the two sides of the same coin. Many architects are rightly focused upon product but wrongly neglectful of process. Their joys and - more critically - the appraisal of peers and critics - are centred within outcomes, not processes. These outcomes have to stand alone, as it were, ready to be appraised as completed buildings, their process histories irrelevant to their adjudged value. And yet, all architects know that every completed building has a secret life rooted in the joys and difficulties, the motivations and enthusiasms of process, of getting there. This is what they gossip about. This is the inside story, rather than the abstracted, post-rationalisations offered by the press and academics (and to clients).

Design and project management have to root themselves in process - of that there is no doubt. And architects have to become positively enculturalised with respect to the art of management. But thank God they never forget end purposes and that they also frame this in terms other than the abstract media of money and power. However, if they are to sustain their art they must learn to cope with an instrumental context in order to realise the project potential. It's a difficult position to be in, filled with contradiction and ambiguity. But in essence, it's nothing new: only the terms of reference have changed.

Head in the clouds / feet on the ground

This book grows out of an interest in action systems - perhaps a pretentious term for the mundane things people do when they get out of bed in the morning, but nevertheless things which can be generalised, stereotyped and abstracted, only to return (once again) to a prosaic reality which characterises the human condition - even of architects. This paradox - that ordinary praxis can be of philosophical significance - is familiar to many architects, people who easily switch from mundane activity to chattering about ostensibly deeper meanings in the twinkle of an eye, who are always yearning to lend their practice overtones of significance - it would not be 'architecture' if this were not the case. But it is not always a comfortable position to be in.

The situation is summed up by a Clifford Odette play of 1949 in which a romantic idealist who is the hero of the drama (and might well be, but is not, an architect) is told by a ruthless pragmatist that he should "Stop philosophying about life and get used to it". The advice - ostensibly banal - is of profound significance. It attempts to return the hero to the unavoidable realm of ordinary actions, to the notion that who we are and what we represent are inescapably reducible to the ubiquitous truth that the sun relentlessly rises and sets all of its own accord, even over the heads of philosophers and dreamers. If you want, its a reminder that product goes with process and that getting there is all important to being there.

To 'stop philosophying and get used to life' is advice architects might always have been preferred, throughout the discipline's history. The predicament they find themselves in has always been one of potential conflict between their own ideals and agenda, and the purposes to which their expertise and talents are employed. It makes architects peculiarly prone to a sense of loss - the notion that there is something missing and needs to be regained, refound or reinstituted - and thus supports an alchemical ambition. In the guise of the ideology of Modernism this sense of loss leant toward the promise of the future, of change and its potential to improve the human condition by a poetic translation of instrumental thinking. But the movement was blind to its own true content. The values which engendered Modernism have developed to a point characterised by what Jurgen Habermas has convincingly articulated as an unprecedented penetration of our cultural lifeworld, producing all kinds of previously unexperienced predicaments and crises. The architectural profession's confrontation with project management is somewhere in there: a dramatic stage of contemporary architecture, upon which the architect acts so as to be either in business or to suffer being out of practice (a practise context in which a hegemony of managerial values and their implicitly instrumental criteria are something one might condemn or condone, but they aren't going away). Arising from the roots of modernism and the Industrial revolution like some primeval force, the mind-set resulting from these values increasingly appears to sustain itself independently of issues of social justice or political persuasion.

Whilst some react to this condition by calling upon us to remember that the modernist project (in terms of its 18th century liberal-humanist ambitions) is unfinished, others have floundered about to define a post-Modernism. Meanwhile, the sun rises and sets and architects must practise their creative, design artistry, aware that the social changes theorists seek to articulate are also mundane realities, particularly in the form of the decline of professional status, deregulation and a battle for professional jurisdiction between architects, other established professions, and relative newcomers to the scene such as project managers.

This book has sought to outline aspects of the situation with deliberate ambivalence, its aim being to mediate between designers and that purposive, instrumental climate of values which they have to address. In the background lies a challenge to redefine a purely architectural ideology to fit the *zeitgeist*, but this lies well outside the scope of the text. I would only suggest that the forms of architectural justification and validation that rest upon an exaggeration of the art paradigm, abstruse intellectualisations and anti-instrumental ambitions (e.g. notions of 'free space' or escapes to 'cyberspace') are better read as symptoms of the disease than realistic prescriptions of remedy. If an appropriate ideological direction is to manifest and develop it must positively confront the realities of contemporary professional practice in the manner of design disciplines born in the later decades of the modernist era (such as product design, graphics, corporate identities, media work, etc.). Inevitably, any new ideology must find ways of implicitly addressing the instrumental mind-set and negotiate a new contract which realises, rather than constrains, the potential of design. Re-empowerment of the profession and reinforcement of its jurisdiction is a project only architects can undertake. At the heart of that project should be the optimism that behind the instrumental mind-set characterising managerial values - especially corporate ones - lies the appetites of average human beings who probably drive home each day to a domestic environment redolent with compensating values. It is the architect's challenge to find ways of insinuating non-instrumental values, but this will only be achieved sympathetically rather than adversarially.

Project management has developed within a suitable climate of need, but to see it only as a professional enemy eroding the architect's area of professional jurisdiction and distorting the client's criteria is to miss the point. The erosion must be countered, but this can only be achieved by an understanding of where project management comes from and what it is all about - deep down, as well as on the surface. If there is a fundamental message to this book, it is that management is a fascinating subject, but that it is no panacea, nor does it possess any quick, simple answers in the form of the fads and, especially, the techniques it enthuses about.

Architects have always sought to resolve many conflicting factors, some of them contradictory. They can handle project management, too. They must, if the profession is not to become a shadow of its former self and the project potential it seeks to realise is not to be narrowed to cosmetic palliatives. Such an undertaking begins in the schools of architecture and in the professional associations who are there to govern the profession's educational content as a part of their contract with the state. However, current debate on the subject is expressed in the narrowest of terms and sometimes unable to see beneath the surface or beyond superficial issues of self-interest. Gating to the profession is still in terms of a professional examination which formally deals with administrative, legal and ethical issues and is anachronistic not for this, but for the over-riding topic it leaves out: the management of design and of projects. But that's institutions for you. Out there, on the street, there's still hope . . . Architects aren't exactly about to give up and move over! But they have to be quick: project management is the wave of a future already upon us.

A brief project management dictionary

Action Plan

A purposive orientation toward achieving ambitions, resulting in pre-planned and programmed activities.

The identification of principal activities should be anticipatory, but it can rarely be synoptic (see 'rolling wave'). Activities are usually principal groups of tasks allocated to a place within the planning network. They must be accounted for in terms of responsibility, beginning with the major design areas and the agencies who undertake them.

Activity Based Costing (ABC)

Sometimes called transactions accounting. A method of analysing organisational processes in order to identify where value is (and is not) being added. Related to process engineering, re-engineering, etc.

Added Value

Defined by Kay (1993) as the difference between the (comprehensively accounted) value of a firm's output and the (comprehensively accounted) cost of the firm's inputs. The underlying concern is to maximise benefit (of all kinds, particularly to the end user) and minimise waste in the provision of services and products. Related to the process concept of a 'value chain' (of events). Firms seek to 'add value' and thus enhance customer satisfaction, their market potential, etc.

Administration

To be differentiated from 'management'. Usually concerned with procedural matters and technical forms of expertise, as in 'to act as a minister or agent', applying rules, directives, etc. e.g. 'job administration'.

Approval

A ubiquitous feature of projects. Often formalised as a planning milestone, typically when the client agrees to what has been done and what is proposed to be done, when a departmental head authorises a scheme, or when an expert agrees to a specification. Often formalised as a 'sign-off'. See Gating.

Architecture

A set of holistically, configurationally and thematically considered strategic, and purposeful relationships, formulated 'by design'. The term can be applied to dealing with buildings, products, landscapes, ships, computers, software, political schemes, financial arrangements, organisations, plans, and much more (e.g. 'Chairman Deng was the architect of economic transformation in China'). Professionally registered architects are presumed to be the architects of buildings. The detailed, substantial forms in which an informing architecture manifests itself (sometimes described as features) can vary; however they should fulfil the architectural intent and not contradict it (the degree of acceptable tolerance is a subject in itself).

Art

Increasingly ambiguous expressionistic activity of high cultural status, offering a pretentious aesthetic agenda and barely concealed commercial concerns. Rooted in the notion of opposition to bourgeois culture and the ambition of shocking or 'awakening' it from narrow materialism and self-interest. A relative to design because of shared aesthetic concerns. Truly antipathetical to project management unless isolated as high risk or transformed into a goal-oriented, professionalised feature (paradoxically, usually something easy to achieve).

Audit

A periodic review and evaluation exercise, usually aimed at seeing if a plan or intent is being adhered to. It can apply to cost plans, quality control procedures, facilities programming, etc.

Barriers

Understood as an obstacle in the project path. See 'drivers'.

Bench-mark

A construction-derived term meaning a set standard against which efforts, achievements, products, systems, quality standards and the like can be measured. Often used to define best practice industry standards (competitive 'benchmarking') and important in process engineering and management.

Bias

A form of irrational and usually unperceived distortion of our judgement. Very difficult to counter, suggesting the leadership theory of contingency management and the notion of structurally changing conditions rather than people.

Brief

A concept derived from law practice, suggesting a succinct distillation of the situational-problematic to be addressed. Related to 'problem-framing' and 'problem-finding' as opposed to 'problem-solving'. Employed by designers as a statement of essentials.

Budget

The global financial expenditure anticipated and / or approved for a project or a part of it. A goal within which the project team is (not unreasonably) expected to contain its expenditures. Sometimes overrun, resulting in client uncertainty, anxiety and distress. See Cost Plan, Design to Cost.

Change

What projects are meant to address - as a goal, a managed transition, and a final realisation. Also a problem once plans are determined and set out as a form of agreed action guidance.

Change Control

The concept of procedurally managing arising change of whatever kind, especially contingent change arising after a scheme design agreement and approval. The aim is to constrain any negative impact and facilitate orderly and acceptable trade-offs in order to produce prediction / outcome alignment.

Collaboration

An inherent aspect of team behaviours and to be differentiated from co-ordination (e.g. teams collaborate; work groups co-ordinate).

Complexity

More than one can easily cope with, generating a law of diminishing returns. At once a desirable feature of the evolved, sophisticated organisation, and the problem of how to manage it. Usually best avoided, although often unavoidable.

Complexity Slope / Curve

The concept that the complexity content of a system (e.g. its managerial overhead) increases with growth in scale, scope and content. For example, the greater the component content, the greater the co-ordinative interfaces between them, producing an increasing managerial overhead. A complexity curve might increase by, say, 120% for every 100% increase in scope. \

Concurrent

A term used to describe activities carried out in parallel in order to save time and promote consultation and coordination. The opposite of a 'pass-the-baton' concept in which completed or almost completed packages of information are handed between agencies. Increasingly common in industry, where time-compression replaced quality as the concern of the 1990's.

Contracts

Modes of formalising interpersonal and/or inter-agency relations rooted in some form of exchange agreement, whether this be material or psychological. The three basic forms are: Spot, Classical and Relational. The Classical contract is increasingly common - to the point where it is in danger of stifling exchanges and forming them as the litigious battleground of the disappointed, disillusioned, abused or predatory (what has been broadly described by Jurgen Habermas as the process of societal juridification). The extent to which this is true draws a focus upon the ideal of the relational contract and its implicit forms of co-operation based upon an element of trust and (importantly) the expectancy of a repeat relationship.

Consummate Co-operation

A form of positive and willing co-operation, given without any form of coercion (by definition, usually an ideal).

Conflict

(As in contention.) An inevitability when people and agencies are brought together. It used to be considered a bad thing, but is now accepted as a healthy feature of competitive attitudes and organisational transformation (see Pascale, 1990). The key to dealing with project conflict is to confront it. However, skill is required to confront it in the right way in order to obtain a positive outcome.

Contingency

The anticipation that the unexpected will happen and has to be allowed for. Also an acceptance of the limitations of the planning intent. Usually a financial component of the budget, sometimes a specific plan of action held in reserve, just in case.

Co-ordination

(Related to synchronisation.) A fundamental feature of planning and day-to-day project relations. Interaction and adjacency do not necessarily produce coordination, but they can help. Depends upon openness of intent, anticipation, sharing of information, a creative quotient. Coordination is a fundamental problem among the professional agencies contributing to a building project - partly an issue of discipline, partly of disparate organisations, values, needs, priorities, etc.

Cost Drivers

The notion of particular and most significant drivers of cost allocation and expenditures. See ABC.

Cost Plan

A breakdown and allocation of the budget into discrete cost sectors. A principal means of cost control during design development, commonly used in managing trade-offs within an overall budget. Can be formulated from a 'bottom-up' or 'top-down' basis. Becomes a basis for monitoring and controlling project efforts.

Critical Path

The notionally irreducible, longest path through an activity network. Delay to activities on this path will consequently delay the whole project. The dynamics of project implementation can alter the crucial path, necessitating periodic plan reviews. The concept has probably influenced the related concept of 'critical success factors'. Developed at Du Pont in 1957-58 by Kelly and Walker.

Critical Ratio

A measure of productivity which accounts for both progress and costs, indicating whether deviations are serious or not.

Critical Success Factors

Those strategic considerations most pertinent to project success. A fundamental aspect of all design and design practice. Helpful concept when using heuristic. Implies 'editing' abilities.

Culture

The behavioural and value-loaded product of organisational groupings and a characteristic way of processing what the organisation deals with, and how it services its clients and customers. Culture comprises more than instrumental features. It is equivalent to an underlying organisational architecture (or 'deep structure') - rich, complex, never experienced directly, but clearly manifest in a symptomatic way as 'the way we do things around here'. It is easy to identify, difficult to change (particularly from the bottom-up), and almost impossible to copy.

Cybernetics

Term formulated by Norbert Weiner just after WW II. It derives from the greek for 'steermanship' and became an important aspect of systems theory and computerisation.

Deductive Reasoning / Inductive Reasoning

Deductive reasoning works from the facts to generalities. Inductive reasoning is the opposite and proceeds, for example, from *a priori* values or ideas to their implication as policies of implementation. Inductive reasoning was once the ideal of scientific method - until discredited. Deduction has served as the basis of policy and strategy determination in the public sector (as in PPBS), but has been flawed by synoptic ambitions with regard to noting all relevant criteria, weighting them, searching for options, etc.

Design

To deliberately place intent into events. Short-hand for 'product design', engineering design', architectural design', etc. Usually has a social and cultural, as well as an instrumental and economic, agenda.

Design Management

An outcome of business realising that design is important to added value. Now the meeting ground of design and instrumental value systems. The term now refers to any set of managerial techniques which aim to realise the potential of design as some form of socio-economic benefit.

Design To Cost

The notion of setting a 'cost target' (usually on the low side) for designers to work toward. Related to 'bench-marking'.

Division of Labour

An inherent principal of planning efforts, enabling the allocation of responsibilities and tasks. Conversely, it necessitates co-ordinative efforts to integrate what has been divided. The concept originates with early industrialists (John Taylor, Josiah

Wedgewood, Robert Owen, Richard Arkwright, etc.) and the massive gains in productivity they were able to obtain by employing the concept. The theory was publicised by Babbage in 1832 (although it had been around for some time). Since the early 18th.c. it became basic to the notion that the successful capitalist enterprise had to be structured and managed, thus slowly fostering a managerial class which replaced the familial basis of ownership and management. The concept reached its most iconic development with Henry Ford's Machine Age production line, but its organisational implications were more importantly developed by Alfred Sloane, at Chrysler, who developed the divisional conglomerate in the 1920's. The stereotypical bureaucracy of the Modernist era was founded on this principle of the division of labour, rooted in class divisions.

Downsizing

A late 80's/ early 90's fad that attempted to address efficiencies in organisations and process engineering by delayering in the search for the 'lean and mean' business firm. It reached the inevitable point where it had to spawn its sister, upsizing, as an attempt to cope with the fact that the only people left in the organisation hadn't been there long enough to know what was going on and were so worried about being made redundant that they didn't care (i.e. weak relational contracts and all they engender). Related to minimal effort / maximal effectiveness approach to process engineering. Whilst no longer a fad, its underlying principles are very much in force.

Drivers

As in 'drivers and barriers' to success. The concept of drivers helps to focus on critical success factors. The concept of barriers helps to remove them e.g. as when potential causes of dissatisfaction are removed.

Economy

A fundamental law applying to all three principal dimensions of a project (costs, performance, schedule). Why spend more, take longer, or do more than you have to? It applies to any activity that is purposeful, even when it is frivolous.

Ends

As in means / ends. The purpose of the project (outcome or deliverable), or the state of change realised by the project. See Goals.

Executive

Despite the implied meaning of someone who executes, the term has come to apply to suit-wearing policy-makers and planners with 'executive' influence, position power and authority. More usually associated with project sponsors rather than project managers or team participants.

Feasible

Concerning what it is possible to achieve (it can be done).

Fishbone (diagram)

A Japanese invention, sometimes called a cause and effect diagram which focuses upon main activity planning and maps a hierarchy of what is primary, secondary and tertiary.

Float

A network planning concept used to describe a period of time available to stretch out an activity, or deal with contingency or uncertainty.

Focus

A management fad of the 1990's, basically amounting to an attempt to simplify decision-making and management strategies by consistently focusing upon prime considerations (Critical Success Factors).

Focused Quality Control (FQC)

Child of TQM, but premised upon a targeting of quality initiatives at improving the particular processes that will have the greatest impact on what occurs (rather than a global approach to all aspects of process).

Fordism

Term describing Frederick Taylor's ideas (and the implicit concept of the division of labour) as applied on Henry Ford's car production lines. The kind of production attitude which brought the likes of Ford and General Motors to crisis in the 1970's and 1980's, when confronted by Japanese production techniques.

Framing

The concept that how we address problems is informed and determined by how we conceive and describe them. The 'framing' of a situational-problematic is the basis of how we tackle it and offer creative propositions. What is discussed as creativity in decision-making and problem-solving theory often amounts to framing variants (lateral thinking, brain-storming, etc.) All design involves appropriate framing. So does management.

Game Theory

A formal, mathematical set of techniques for dealing with understanding, explaining and predicting, the rational actions of systems, individuals or organisations in a described relationship with one another. Attributed to von Neumann and Morgenstern (1947).

Gantt Charts

Graphic planning technique invented by Henry Gantt around 1900, employed as an aid to military planning and adopted for civilian projects. Also referred to as bar charts. Requires the breakdown and conceptual coordination of efforts, represented by graphic bars set against a time-line.

Gate

Control concept related to planned staging, the handover of information, etc. Essential if a project is not to flow forward (or wherever).

Getting it Right First Time.

The concept of having only one bite at the cherry and the importance of timeliness. A concept poorly understood and appreciated by designers oriented toward the (expressionistic) art paradigm.

Getting it Right Up-Front.

As opposed to getting it right later on when options are normally reduced, constraints are tighter and more resources are required (leverage is reduced). Linked with project set-up and the maxim that, early on, problems are hard to see and easy to fix; later, they are easy to see and hard to fix.

Goals

Goals / Objectives 'state what is to be achieved and when results are to be accomplished' (Quinn, 1980). Fundamental to projects and teams. See Policies and Tactics.

Goal Orientation

The purposeful focusing of project efforts (the means) toward ends which justify the project enterprise. Also refers to local and subsidiary ambitions - see Milestone.

Gating

Project gates can be open or closed. Criteria, people, and planning, for example, all set up gates within the project - sometimes positively, sometimes unconstructively. A milestone can be a gate when it has to be navigated and criteria have to be satisfied to get through. Information control and approvals are gates. Gating is an important project management concept.

Gozinto chart

Tree-like, hierarchical diagram named after Professor Zepartzat Gozinto, an Italian mathematician invented by Professor Andrew Vazsonyi (Meredith & Mantel, 1995)

Guru

Term used to characterise an influential managerial figure who will often be responsible for publicising a fad ostensibly offering an answer to your problems (a 'quick fix'). Very '80's / '90's.

Heuristic

Guidance (or rules of thumb) based upon experience.

Implementation

What happens when a plan is put in to action. Related to 'procurement' in the sense of post-specification actions aimed at realising those specifications in a tangible or substantial form.

Inception

Term used by architects to describe when a project begins - which usually means long after it was brought to birth in the mind of the project sponsor (i.e. it's a relative concept).

Instrumentalism

The product of means/ends thinking and purposive rationality: means are instruments that serve stated ends; all capitalist business activity becomes *instrumental* to the service of the profit motive. Instrumental thinking is interested in results and what produces it. Its value system is usually qualitatively described, as is its goals and the means employed.

Iterative Enhancement

Repeatedly going over the same ground and incrementally addressing the same issue to advantage each time. A common idea of how design proceeds from general idea to detailed proposal.

Leadership

To lead is to both orient, direct and motivate those who are led. It takes place at a number of levels within a project, but is usually considered with reference to the senior project personnel, particularly to the project manager and the principals responsible for team performance. Leadership is very necessary at moments of difficulty and crisis, when democratic, participative organisations usually revert to a power culture.

Leverage

Refers to the strategic ability to effect a change of course. What is available at the beginning of a project but not later on.

Life -cycle

A concept deriving from the marketing of consumer products, describing the history of investment and return, attempting to maximise the latter and anticipate demise and replacement. The concept has been applied to buildings and to projects as a way of conceptualising a life-to-death or inception to closure history of investment.

Linear Responsibility Charts

A simple matrix translating project planning networks and task schedules into a way of graphically relating tasks to individuals who are responsible for their execution.

Management

To be differentiated from 'administration'. If the latter is more concerned with systems and procedures, the former is concerned with inventive, purposive, goal-oriented decision-making.

Mapping Techniques

In project management, various ways of 'picturing' the (projected) ground ahead or the way forward. Usually in one of two general formats:

• Gantt (bar) charts which graphically make visible 'chunks' of effort as tasks or pieces of work undertaken.
• Networks (Programme Evaluation and Review Technique and Critical Path Method) which identify dependencies and a critical path.

Means

(Implicitly to an end.) What gets the team to its desired end; the project *process* that produces the deliverable or realises the required change. Also refers to the project *deliverable* considered in terms of its place within a *larger* business or organisational plan.

Measurement

Quantification. As in the oft-quoted notion that 'if it can't be measured, it can't be managed'. Fundamental to all forms of technocratic rationality. Necessary for monitoring action plans.

Meetings

Project rituals, a means of coordinating and synchronising actions, and confronting issues on a face to face basis between those responsible. Occasions when leadership can be demonstrated and authority effected. Should have a purpose, an agenda (plan), and a useful outcome.

Milestone

A significant project route-marker. Used in planning as a way of breaking the overall path to the project goal into a series of sub-goals. Often key administrative and managerial points when approval is needed before the team can proceed to the next milestone (or set of milestones).

Modularisation

Management concept of breaking a whole (e.g. the production effort)into significant and managerially meaningful parts.

Motivation

Crucial factor in project success, manifesting at the personal and team level. Key names include Maslow (hierarchy of motivating factors) and McGregor (Theory X and Y; later added to with 'X' - a way of being 'both/and' rather than 'either/or'). Features in the work of the human-relations movement (e.g. Hawthorn experiments).

Muddling Through

A facetious term invented by Charles Lindblom in the 1960's to refer to decision-making processes in administration which proceeds incrementally, moving away from problems rather than toward visions i.e. the basis of most managerial actions and always a significant feature of decision-making within a project. The concept is influenced both by experience and Karl Popper's theory.

Murphy's Life-cycle

A cynical, five-stage (sometimes seven-stage) concept of the project life-cycle: euphoria; disillusion; a search for the guilty; the punishment of the innocent; the reward of the uninvolved.

Network

Planning technique depending upon having a reasonably full understanding of what is being undertaken; common in construction, where the specification of works is known. Rarely used by architects, who are often dealing with uncertainty and formulating what has to be done, although crucial to proper planning for more complex projects and the scheduling of inter-related activities with maximum economy of time. Networks allow the identification of a critical temporal path and therefore of critical activities on that path. They are usually divided into two types: activity on arrow and activity on node. See Critical Path and the Network primer on page 191. Also see networking Primer after this section.

One Bite at the Cherry
Related to Getting it Right First Time. The idea that the same opportunity and circumstances rarely repeat themselves. Especially pertinent to projects where the end-date means just that and failures cannot be revisited.

Optimism
As in over-optimism. Often associated with bias and common at the beginning of projects. To be avoided (although optimism in itself should not be avoided!).

Percentage Complete
Monitoring term referring to reported progress as a percentage of completion. Intrinsically difficult to estimate when the work includes decision-making. Often dealt with over-optimistically and best translated into percentage or effort remaining.

Perceptions of Project Failure and Success
A variable depending upon whether you are a project sponsor or a project agent. Suggested by research to be more dependent upon technical and human relations problems than cost and schedule.

Performance
A project term derived from military weapons systems, but more generally referring to the instrumental characteristics of any project deliverable. The term is used in to describe what that deliverable does, not what it feels like (although it could). Like 'budget', 'programme', and 'schedule', the term is rather awkward and inadequate.

Perfunctory Cooperation
The cooperation given reluctantly or in a limited way, not wholeheartedly. Often accompanied by classical contracts.

PERT
Project Evaluation and Review Technique. Developed in conjunction with the US Polaris weapons systems programme during the later 1950's by D.G. Malcolm and others. Its major concern was to deal with uncertainty. See network.

Planning
The anticipatory, speculative mapping of future activities. Project planning is inherently anticipatory and, to some degree, speculative.

Policies
'Policies are the rules or guidelines that express the limits within which action should occur' (Quinn, 1980).

Preliminary Design Concept
Term sometimes used to denote the final scheme proposal agreed by all parties concerned and the basis of subsequent planning effort. Plausibility has been accepted. Feasibility has been tested. Viability has been agreed. Final goals for Performance, Schedule and Cost are determined at this stage.

Priorities
An acknowledgement of difference and hierarchy. What all decision-makers need to be aware of given that available resources (time, money, personnel, skills, interest, patience, etc.) will always be in limited supply. Related to the brief (as client needs) and to the concept of 'critical success factors' within the framework of project actions.

Procurement
A word referring to the process of acquisition, usually used with reference to the project goal. Sometimes referred to what is done after a specification is complete and the end-goal is entirely known (as when a building contractor engages in procurement on the basis of a set of specifications).

Productivity
An input / output ratio, as in planned progress (as an allocation related to available fee income and temporal constraint) / actual progress. See Critical ratio.

Professionalism
A Victorian embodiment of technical rationality and expertise posing as a gentlemanly and disinterested vocation, ideally founded upon self-regulating, governmentally-sanctioned association formed for the purposes of market and jurisdictional control. Currently a somewhat devalued concept and the resort of anyone with a mix of vocational expertise and ethical pretensions, but still very important to both society and architectural practice. Originating in the notion of 'professing' to a faith.

Programme
The outcome of activity planning; also an alternative to action plan 'schedule'. Used in the American sense, it can refer to a configured medium in the sense that software is 'a programme' which processes inputs - in this usage, similar to 'the briefing statement' i.e. it is as inadequate a word as 'budget' and 'performance'. Quinn (1980) defines programme as that which specifies *'step by step sequences of actions necessary to achieve major objectives'*. He sees strategy-making as building a posture.

Programming
The intentional, strategic way a (building's) design can be configured to deliver the intended service(s). Sometimes a specialist consultant service to a project which formulates the brief and then works with the team and audits its work in order to ensure conformance.

Progress
A measure of achievement along a path from inception to the goal of project completion. Dependent upon travel in the right direction, usually in synchronised co-ordination with others. Crudely measured by time-sheets as something on-going. Inherently difficult to properly measure except in terms of milestones and stages reached and/or completed.

Project Management
Increasingly the prevalent behaviour of organisations who are constantly managing change on a number of fronts. Projects are to be differentiated from the strategies, policies and programmes which they seek to implement i.e to transform into action or realisation.

PPBS
Planning Programming Budgeting System. Advocated after WW II and introduced in order to manage the Cold War effort (significant during the Johnson era). It attempted to ensure a success-oriented, purposive way of allocating available monies and effectively relating expenditures to stated goals which are shared across many agencies. The period was enamoured with 'systems theory' and the rational-deductive ideal. Systematic comparative analysis was undertaken in the famous Rand Corp.,

who compared weapons systems for the US Air Force and became known as a 'think-tank' daring to anticipate the future. At the time, systems inspired approaches to administration and management were hailed as the greatest advance in government since the introduction of a civil service based on competence (see M.Ways, The Way to 1977, Fortune, Jan. 1967). The US Defense department, under Robert McNamara, (one of the so-called 'whizz kids' who went from the Air Force to Ford Motor Co., to the government under Kennedy), was restructured along these lines.

Purposive Rationality

A strategic way of thinking justifying actions in terms of a purpose they serve and the extent to which they lead to success. Used in relation to an instrumental attitude.

Quality assurance

(As in Quality Management.) Overused concept (as in Total Quality Management, TQM), often employed by people who have never read their Juran or Deming (the fathers of quality management) and usually related to a bureaucratic, procedural postures reliant upon a purposive, technical rationality. Focused Quality Management (FQM) is an attempt to deal just with those aspects of process that are critical to success. Theory developed in the USA and exported to Japan where, after WWII, it was a huge success and re-exported to the West. In project management, quality is entirely related to the perception of the users of the deliverable.

Rational Deductive ideal

Deductive thinking elevated to an ideal. Generally proceeds from a problem statement, through criteria description, their weighting, the generation of alternative forms of action, their evaluation in terms of the criteria, and the selection of a most beneficial (effective, success generating) option.

Reengineering

An early 90's fad related to process engineering, activity planning, downsizing, etc. and made famous by the management consultants, Hammer and Champney (1993). By the mid-90's Champny was writing more cautiously about the subject and admitting its failures as well as its successes. Criticised for its destructive affects upon corporate culture and distinctive capabilities. See 'Downsizing'.

Responsibilities

What individuals and organisations willingly take on or are allocated in return for vocational reward, cudos and remuneration. Associated with liability. Often a scheduled aspect of work planning, sometimes discussed as a 'responsibility matrix'.

Resource levelling

An attempt to prevent excessive team peaking and to reallocate activities in order to prevent this happening.

Result path

A goal-oriented route between a less and more desired condition; a path to change between one milestone and another and a concept for considering the related activities on this path. Often one of many concurrent activities, as in network planning.

Risk

The possibility that something will go wrong and threaten a plan. In the sense that risk can be assigned a probability, it is different to uncertainty (which can't be assigned a probability).

Satisficing

The term for the process of looking for a needle sharp enough to sew with, rather than the sharpest in the haystack. Originally employed by Herbert Simon and James March during the 1950's as a way of dealing with 'bounded rationality' (i.e kinds of constraint).

Schedule

A term describing the listed products of planning e.g. who does what, when. Basically any list or table as well as a time-table. Also frequently used to refer specifically to the temporal sequencing (timetabling) of activities.

Scheme

The plan of a way forward which will satisfy project criteria and realise its goals. Implicitly well-considered and tested for validity ostensible feasibility, and potential viability. Often not considered thoroughly enough as a basis for further project action.

Scientific Management

Modernity's instrumental attempt to mix management theory with an ostensibly scientific method. Rooted in late Victorian engineering enterprise and the need to control and optimise the productive utilisation of manpower and material resources by the application of purposive-rationality; later informed by post-war systems theory.

Sign-offs

The formal agreement to a proposal, enabling work to progress. Used as a gating mechanism, as a means of encouraging decision-making, and sometimes as an insurance. ("I can't sign-off because it's an inadequate proposal." "Failure to achieve a sign-off will delay the project." "If you disagreed with it, you should not have signed it off.")

Smith, Adam

Eighteenth century Scots, social and economic theorist who is credited with articulating the concept of the division of labour.

Sponsor

The client and initiator of the project. The one with the cheque book and most at stake, either financially, politically or in terms of health and well-being. Usually pigeon-holed as 'good', or 'bad' by architects, depending on the extent to which the latter's agenda is endorsed.

Stages

A concept of dividing the project whole into manageable parts, each with its own defining characteristics. Each stage completion will be marked by a major milestone and normally gated before further development is allowed. See Life-cycle.

Start-up Meeting

An important project ritual that seeks to introduce and orient participants (especially when they belong to different agencies) and begin the process of bonding them together.

Strategy

The great hope of post-war management thinking and still an important feature of business practice. To act strategically is to seek to influence events or the behaviours of others (usually to one's own benefit). See Mintzberg. Quinn(1980) defines strategy as, 'the pattern or plan that integrates an organisation's major goals, policies, and action sequences into a cohesive whole. . . [It] helps to marshal and allocate an organisation's resources into a unique and viable posture based upon its relative internal competences and shortcomings, anticipated changes in the environment, and contingent moves by intelligent opponents'.

Status

In project management, a relational concept concerning a measure of what is or is not in accordance with an intention or plan. Fundamental to progress reports.

Stretch-out
Term used to denote delays and extensions to the project. Acute stretch-out is one-off outcome; chronic stretch-out indicates fundamental project problems that keep asserting themselves in various forms of poor performance.

Systems Theory
Body of theory, principally developed after WWII, which seeks to identify and explain the way sets of related things can be differentiated from their environment and explain their interaction with that environment. Originates in biology and the work of von Bertalanffy (General Systems Theory). Associated with names such as Stafford Beer, Ashby, Turing, Pask, Norbert Weiner, etc.

Tactics
Tactics *are the short-duration, adaptive, action-interaction realignments that opposing forces use to accomplish limited goals after their initial contact* (Quinn, 1980). See Goals and Policies. This neo-militaristic language has a long history inn management theory.

Target Cost Management (TCM)
The concept of identifying a cost target and engineering toward it (as a goal). Originates in the US defence system.

Task
The most basic unit of effort identified in work planning. The local undertaking of a team member which can become an end in itself if not related to some larger goal. See Work Breakdown Structure.

Taylorism
Term used to characterise a form of technical rationality developed as a work planning method by Frederick Taylor (1856-1917), as outlined in his book *Principles of Scientific Management* (1911). It extends Smith's principle of the division of labour to the study of work, the separation of policy from execution, etc. and especially referred to the idea of what is 'scientific' as that which is systematically observed and measured. Originally to benefit workers as well as owners. Taylor's work was gathered together and re-published in 1947 as *Scientific Management*. Since Taylorism is essentially an 'Input-Process-Output' (IPO) method founded on time and motion studies it ignores many 'soft' aspects of a business such as marketing, personnel, research, etc. For this reason it has often being superseded by the 'Workflow' concept (WF) which is concerned with value chains, activity based costing and the use of computers to track what is actually happening within a process. The concept of customers, performers, and transactions between them is also employed.

Team
A comparatively small, collaborative and purposeful work group, exhibiting individual and mutal accountability as well as goal orientation and knowledge of success criteria. To be differentiated from 'work group'.

Team Cycle
When a group of people are brought together to form a team, they commonly experience a series of project stages; forming; storming, norming; performing.

Team Motivation
Vital to team progress and project success. Often taken for granted until absent - when it is probably too late and the pro-

ject becomes a proverbial walk across a ploughed field. Leadership has a prime responsibility for motivation and building its foundations.

Technique
Tool, lever or procedural aid to effectiveness used to quickly and effectively produce results. Sometimes grasped as a life-belt by those who poorly (or don't) understand that the word is inherently a euphemism for a concept and the methods derived from it.

Theory
'All that theory can do is give the artist or soldier points of reference and standards of evaluation . . . with the ultimate purpose of not telling him how to act but of developing his judgement'. (C.Von Clausewitz, *Vom Kreige*, quoted by Quinn, 1980. Von Clausewitz was a Prussian famous for the dictum that *' War is but a continuation of politics by other means.'*) Theory embodied in books (like this) is useful as orienting preparation for future experience, or for making sense of past experience.

Time
An unavoidable project expenditure to be dealt with economically. Less time often means less effort, less cost, less hassle. Claimed by some industries to produce quality and productivity yields. Rarely adequate and usually claimed to be either in short supply or wastefully expended.

Time Sheets
The way practices measure (and thus monitor) the expenditure of available temporal resources. Fundamental to practice management, underscoring the reality that today's professional sells the effective utilisation of time, as well as expertise.

Timely information
The need not only to produce *adequate* information, but to produce it in a timely fashion appropriate to the needs of the team. Failure to produce timely information is often linked with poor co-ordination and collaboration, an inability to finish and a failure to appreciate the needs of other project agencies. Because procurement contracts with builders are usually of the 'classical' form, the timeliness of information often becomes an issue of conflict and litigation.

Trapezoidal Method
A heuristic and graphic method of picturing project efforts against a time-line and estimating durations, peak team sizes, etc. Based on the concept of three phases: build-up; peaking; and run-down.

Utilisation
A term referring to time usage within a time allocation or availability, usually broken down into kinds of activity such as fee earning, non-fee earning, administration, sickness, vacation, etc. In effect, an indicator of efficiency and productivity. When over 100%, this means the contracted time available has been exceeded (which is common).

Validity
Concerning the right thing to propose or do.

Value Engineering
A cost management technique of 'engineering' value for money by assigning costs to functions. Engineering implies quantification, both of what has been referred to as 'use' values and 'esteem' values (the latter sometimes becoming a means of pricing the percentage for the 'architecture'). Better value is a means that achieves the same ends with less expenditure,

increased profits or greater benefit. Related to the concept of 'functional analysis'.

Verification

The check that something is being done or is performing properly (as intended).

Viability

Concerning what 'sustains life'.

Work Breakdown Structure

A planning concept that employs the Gozinto tree to break down a whole complex undertaking into a hierarchical series of tasks. Each level gathers together the tasks at the subsidiary level, leading to higher levels of generality. Its difficulty is the crossing of categories and reintegration.

Workflow

See Taylorism.

Work Group

Common and useful organisational feature, but no more than the sum of its parts and typified by boards and committees. Intrinsically incapable of realising the synergistic success of teams. Usually individualised, politicised, hierarchical and subject to ritual. See Teams.

A network primer

This book leaves little room for any extended discussion of network mapping techniques such as Critical Path Analysis. In principle, the concept is very simple and most architects will find the more complex and abstruse aspects of little or no relevance to their practice. However, some brief notes and hints are necessary. These are garnished from a number of sources, but Lockyer & Gordon's book (Pitman, 1996) is recommended. Much of what is said below is adapted from that work.

Networks deal with the relationships between *events* and *activities*. It is impossible to draw them without some notion of what these relationships are and which activities precede others. The next stage is to add temporal information: how long does an activity take? what time lag exists between the start and / or finish of a preceding activity? etc.

There are two ways of drawing simple networks: Activity-on-arrow (AOA), and activity-on-node (AON). The milestone examples given in previous sections were Activity-on-arrow, leaving the nodes to be assigned as events.

The difficulty most designers face with networks is their plodding, mechanical aspect. Life isn't like that. Designing isn't like that - it's more fluid. This reasonable criticism should not deny the usefulness of networks, particularly after post-scheme design and especially as the work becomes more specific e.g. when a contractor accepts a set of 'specification to build' documents. In other words, networks will be less useful in the indeterminacy of early design and most useful in the determinacy of construction. Inbetween is a gray area where the logic of schedules and working out relationships is valuable in itself.

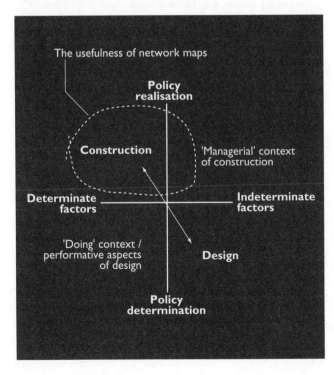

Activity

What is undertaken e.g. a task. What lies between events. Can be drawn on the arrow between event nodes, or on the nodes themselves (but only one technique can be employed within a network - consistency is all important.) It is useful to ask about the most significant or crucial activities and to apply the test of 'needfulness' to the project being undertaken and mapped by the network.

Note: Network activities to focus upon for simple time reduction:
- those under your control
- the early, easy, and long ones
- the ones which don't cost much to accelerate
- the ones for which resources are readily available
- the least risky / crucial ones.

Activity-on-arrow (AOA)

As in Critical Path, which is activity oriented and often used in construction.

Activity-on-node (AON)

As in PERT, which is more event oriented and can take account of probabilities of durations. Rarely employed in construction.

Arrow

The line drawn between nodes. Given a consistent direction, usually left to right. Sometimes assigned an activity (Activity on Arrow, AOA). The length of an arrow has no significance.

Critical Path

A temporarily defined path through the network., from start to finish The longest path whose extension will result in an extended project programme: the path which is therefore 'critical'.

Dangling activity

Logic fault, producing an activity which 'dangles', without further connection within the network.

Discontinuous Activities

It is rarely practical to employ the 'pass the baton' concept in network planning. Some degree of concurrent activity is almost unavoidable. The simplest conceptual breakdown is three deliberately vague stages of an activity: start, continuation, finish.

Dependency Rule

The basis of network logic. The relationship stated between activities. The direction of an arrow indicates the dependent relationship - the head being dependent on the tail.

Duration

The time given to an activity. Also the times between combinations of starts and finishes of activities. As the longest cumulative path through a network, duration is the Critical Path. Durations are usually written underneath the line with AOA diagrams. AOA and AON have a variety of accepted notations in or around the node.

For Activity-on-node EST is the earliest start time, LST is the latest starting time, LET is the earliest finishing time, and LFT is the latest finishing time. EST and LST are usually the most significant.

For AOA, the times are described as event times e.g. EET (earliest event time) and LET (latest event time).

The total project time is a forward pass, adding the earliest start times. The critical path results from a backward pass adding up the latest finishing times of activities. The concepts ' 'float' and 'slack' simply refer to available time on non-critical paths.

Dummy activities

Often necessary in order to make a network functional. They are

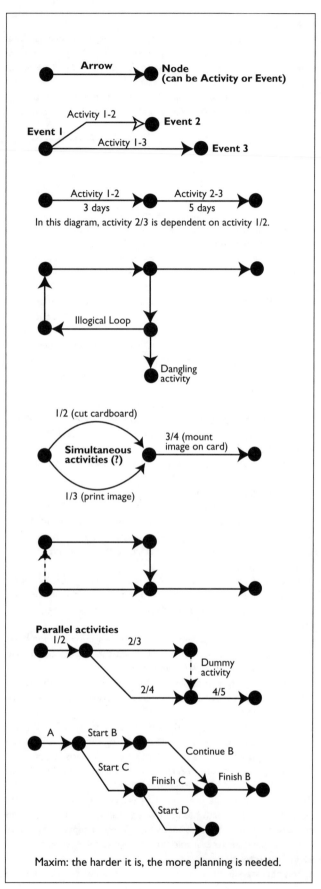

In this diagram, activity 2/3 is dependent on activity 1/2.

Maxim: the harder it is, the more planning is needed.

a logical link between nodes, but are 'activities' without resources. They can be used to indicate lapsed time between two nodes.

Event

An event is a realised state. It begins and ends an activity. A milestone is a kind of event. An event does not occur until all activities leading into it are complete.

Lag

The time between one activity and another - for example as start to start, finish to start, etc. This is an important concept because it enables networks to describe a variety of temporal relationships rather than the most simple one which requires the completion of a preceding activity before a subsequent one can begin. A start to start, for example, could allow activity B to start even though activity A is not finished. It is sometimes useful to consider activities in three phases: start; continuation, and finish.

Logic

The logic of a network 'map' or diagram should be apparent and consistent. It helps if basic rules are followed and not varied.

Loop

A logic fault caused when a series of arrows and nodes lead back on themselves.

Milestones

More important or significant events. Often considered as the goal toward which efforts are directed and thus a possible starting point for drawing a 'goal-oriented' network.

Node

Nodes complement the arrows which link them, together forming the basis of a network diagram. Nodes can either signify activities (AON) or events such as the start or completion of an activity (or set of them).

Parallel Activities

Typically generate the need for dummy activities drawn on the network. Initially best dealt with as start, continuation, and finish phases of the activity. Can be further sub-divided as necessary.

Preceding / Succeeding

Reference to the relationship between activities and nodes. The preceding is sometimes denoted as 'i'; the succeeding is 'j'.

Result Path

It is usually possible to identify sets of activities which link together and form 'paths' through a part or the whole of a network. It is also possible to draw a network with this concept in mind. Substructure and superstructure is the most general breakdown. The latter might then be broken down into structural frame, envelope, services, and finishes. (See page 56.)

Time

Flows in one direction, usually left to right.

Fees 1

A new fee scale calculus. The diagram to the left sets out the principles of a revision and reformatting of the former RIBA fee scale. The overall shape of the fee window has been retained, but the content has been abstracted so that it can be used by different practice cultures to suit themselves. Practices need to establish their own bench-marks with reference to their own experience and the jobs for which they have a history. With enough data, an entirely practice-specific fee window can be constructed.

This diagram is derived from the former RIBA fee scale (Blue Book). The overall shape of the fee window has not been changed.

Percentages refer to those given in the original RIBA fee scale. These can be adjusted as necessary relative to any selected reference point.

C1 - C5 refer to the RIBA Classes (see page 113).

The shaded, upper section of the diagram refers to Work to Existing Buildings. The lower section refers to New Work.

Fee Factors (FF) refer back to the simplest job i.e. lowest overall construction value and Class One new build project.

Input / Output figures refer back to the same point and, across the scale, illustrate presumed productivity gains from larger scale jobs.

The Design Complexity Factor on the left presumes that the fees directly reflect the work effort required. Reference is again made to the simplest Class, cheapest job.

The Volume Response Curves (VRC) have been calculated within the three bands as rates applying to doublings of job volume'. Unit production costs decrease at the lesser rate, as indicated.

Note:
Input / output ratios are indicatedbeneath the Fee Factor. These reference a Class One, newwork job as 100. The percentages should be adjusted as necessaryrelative to a base eg max. complexity / min. cost. Any reference point can be chosen.

Shaded area is current RIBA Work to Existing complexity range.

Design complexity factor 200 FF200

% 16 15 14 13 12 11 10 9 8 7 6 5

FF151 264   FF131 305   FF127 (314)   FF121 321

FF112 197   FF96 236   FF93 (236)   FF85 242

FF103 181   FF89 211   FF85 (221)   FF84 229

FF74 135   FF63 159   FF62 (161)   FF60 165

FF150   FF136   FF100

S1   S2   S3   S4   S5   S6

Design complexity rating 10 9 8 7 6 5 4 3 2 1

Design complexity factor 1.0 set at Fee Factor 100

Job Class (original) C5 C4 C3 C2 C1 C5 C4 C3 C2 C1

Percentage Fee (original) % 16 15 14 13 12 11 10 9 8 7 6 5

Band One	Band Two	Band Three
VRC = 182%	VRC = 190%	VRC = 198%

VRC = 197%	VRC = 199%

One unit of construction value   8 units   64 units   (256 units)   512 units

Note: between 64 - 256 units of construction value, the averaged Volume Response Curve for this band is 197%. Between 256 - 512 it is 199%.

Fees 2

Fee comparisons: RIBA scale (1982-94) to survey (1985-90)

Inflation has shifted the surveyed fee window to the right. There is also a marked difference between the shapes for Works to Existing buildings and New Work. A significant gap has opened up between about 8.5 and 12.5% at the low construction value end. There is also a distinct belly around middle values.

Actual fees realised over the period 1985-90, are more complicated than the Blue Book recommended scales, although the same general principles apply, confirming the general pattern of the fee window. For example, although the Class curves for New Works overlap, the average volume response slope remains similar

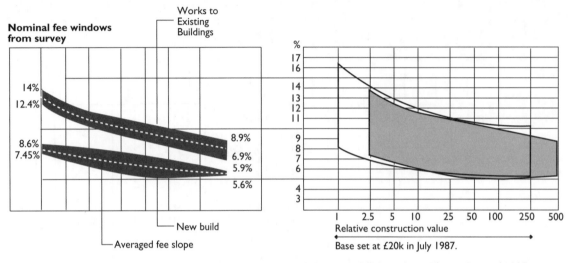

Nominal fee windows from survey

Works to Existing Buildings

14%
12.4%
8.6%
7.45%
8.9%
6.9%
5.9%
5.6%

New build

Averaged fee slope

Relative construction value

Base set at £20k in July 1987.

Solid line is RIBA preferred fee scale as of 1987.
Shaded area is 1985-90 survey (% in brackets).
The movement to the right is accounted for by inflation and survey limitations.

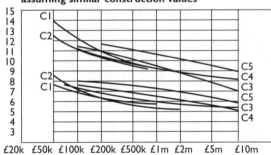

Survey results (1985-90) for Types and Classes assuming similar construction values

C1
C2
C2
C1
C5
C4
C3
C5
C3
C4

£20k £50k £100k £200k £500k £1m £2m £5m £10m

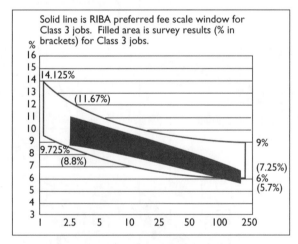

Solid line is RIBA preferred fee scale window for Class 3 jobs. Filled area is survey results (% in brackets) for Class 3 jobs.

14.125%
(11.67%)
9.725%
(8.8%)
9%
(7.25%)
6%
(5.7%)

Note: UK building costs index gives 1985 as 100. On that basis the index for 1991 was at 140, for 1995 it was at 160, and it should be at about 180 in 1997. This will vary from region to region.
Also note that a 'unit of effort' in the above table is relative and will vary from practice to practice.

References

Good books are of two kinds: those which orient your perceptions and are thus prepatory to learning; and those which help to make sense of your experience - the ones which really 'talk' to you. I have found the following references useful. Each will lead you to many other sources not quoted. The list is not comprehensive, but I'm a big believer in edited information and it should offer interesting starting points that will open up other avenues of exploration. Works that cross categories are not mentioned twice.

Architectural and construction viewpoints
Of the architectural books, a few landmark books stand out. On the construction scene the key book that comes to mind is that from Reading University (but see comment).

• K. Allinson, *The Wild Card of Design*, Butterworth Architecture (1993).
The first part is the best, covering fundamental issues in the nature and history of professionalism in relation to management and project management.
• Coxe et al., *Success Strategies for Design Professionals*, McGraw Hill (1987).
I can't accept the basic practice practice / business premise of this book, but recommend it as essential reading for anyone interested in the cultures of practice. Read it for its wealth of commentary on relative design cultures. Maister was on the team of writers.
• D. Cuff, *Architecture: The Story of Practice*, MIT Press (1991).
Dana in Wonderland - an intelligent, informed and informative ramble through the complexities and contradictions of contemporary architectural practice (in America).
• C. Gray et al., *The Successful Management of Design*, University of Reading (1994).
I'm ambivalent about this book: glad its there, grateful for its construction-manager viewpoint, appaled by a lack of understanding of design that mocks its title. In a nutshell, its key to success is to shift as quickly (and politely) as possible from those risky designers toward an engineering posture. Read it with this major health warning, but milk it for what you can.
• R. Gutman, *Architectural Practice - A Critical View*, Princeton Architectural Press (1988).
Gutman is a sociologist cum-architectural groupie; he's always worth reading for his sensitive, informed and intelligent considerations. This is a book about the state of the architectural profession in the USA in the late-'80's; what he says is still relevant.
• G. Golzen, *How Architects Get Work*, Architecture and Building Practice Design Guides, (1984).
A post-deregulation look at how architects got work when they were (as then, after changes between 1979-83) allowed to procure, advertise and practice as limited liability companies - in effect, the end of a profession ostensibly dedicated to service rather than profit. 34 practices are discussed. Useful reading, if only to see where some famous practices were and what they then had to say about themselves.
• R. Green, *The Architect's Guide to Running a Job*, Butterworth Architecture first published 1962; last ed. 1995).
This is job *administration* rather than design and project *management*. Its underpinning is a traditional concept of professional practice and the notion of proper procedures. It's all good stuff and required support, but it invites the danger of being unable to see the wood for the trees.
• B. Hubbard, *A Theory for Practice*, MIT Press (1995).
An excellent book in the currently fashionable, narrative style of offering architectural theory. Hubbard differentiates between three equally valid perspectives: that of the market (a concern with results); that of designers (a concern with order); and that of the community (a concern with the values we share between us). Excellent book with a feeling of great humanity about it.
• *Strategic Studies*, RIBA (1993).
Promoted by Doctor Frank Duffy, President 1993-5, these studies are a rich series that begin with reports on how clients look at architects. The reports follow in the tradition of the an earlier report, The Architect in his Office, 1962 (the principal authors of which wrote a book called *Management Applied to Architectural Practice*, The Builder Ltd., 1964 - worth a look to see how matters have and have not changed).
• Edward Robbins, *Why Architects Draw*, MIT Press (1994)
This is a book to read 'between the lines'. It will tell you much about how offices are run, especially the implicit power structures which relate the controlling partners / directors to lower level professionals.
• Andrew Saint, *The Image of the Architect*, Yale (1983).
Excellent book on the nature of the profession.
• M. Symes et al, *Architects and Their Practices - A Changing Profession*, Butterworth Architecture (1995).
A look at the British profession and changes over two decades - examined through the nature and work of seven UK

practices. Good stuff, but difficult to know what the authors' point is.

Costs

Not the most stimulating subject to read at bedtime, but its worth knowing what the trends are. The following book should be a good starting point:

- M. Tanaka, T. Yoshikawa, J. Innes and F. Mitchell, *Contemporary Cost Management*, Chapman & Hall, (1993).

Decision-making and Heuristic

Books on decision-making are heavily biased toward the rational-deductive ideal and usually distil down to some variation upon it. Designers might find long-term best sellers like De Bono ('lateral thinking') only superficially entertaining and not very useful. Two of the most important books are by Donald Schon - they'll give you pride in your designer-thinking to set against the weight of rational-deductive thinking. Other books worth looking at have titles like 'team decision-making' and will address brainstorming, ranking and weighting techniques, etc. (all very rational and strongly resisted by most designers). However, the most illuminating books are those by Karl Popper (although they do not deal with design or art directly).

- M.Bazerman, *Managerial Decision Making*, John Wiley(1990)
Good coverage of all kinds of heuristic bias, but biased itself toward perceptual and general judgemental issues.
- P. Medawar, The Limits of Science (1984). Useful, accessible and short.
- D. Schon, *The Reflective Practitioner*, Josey-Bass Inc. (1987).
The beginnings of an understanding of the design mind. Also, *Educating the Reflective Practitioner* (1983).
- R. Townsend, *Up the Organisation* (1970) and *Further Up The Organisation* (1984). Irreverent books by a great believer in 'Theory Y', who succeeded in turning a loss-making company around. Townsend was one of the first of the laddish, 'how-to, quick-answer' writers whose profound understanding is mismatched with the popularised, short shelf-life of their examples.
- G. Polya, *How To Solve It*, Doubleday (1957).
A simple, original book on heuristic by a mathematics professor who knows his stuff and is a delight to read.
- Karl Popper stands out as a 20th century philosopher who has given an explanation of scientific method which has had a profound influence in many fields, notably with E.H. Gombrich's *Art and Illusion*. Popper's works include: *The Logic of Scientific Discovery* (originally published 1934); *The Open Society and its Enemies* (5th. ed.1966); *The Poverty of Historicism*(1957); *Conjectures and Refutations: The Growth of Scientific Knowledge* (originally published1963); etc.

Gurus

If you're interested in management, you should know about the following (there are more, but this is a good starting point). Significantly, most are American. However, be warned: since Tom Peters and ISoE, an industry has developed around inventing faddish ideas and selling them through consultancies. A book on the subject usually leads the way. And beware of the same generic idea being repackaged as something original (reengineering also became business transformation and business process redesign). Consultants are now convinced there is a revolution going on in their business, shifting them away from doing reports to ensuring results. At the time of writing (1997) books are starting to come through aimed at debunking management gurus and fads; Scott Adams' The Dilbert Principle is a best-selling example.

- Peter Drucker - the grand-daddy of gurus, with great faith in the power of management for the benefit of society. Virtually invented the serious study of management all on his own. Famous for MBO, advocated in the 1960's and still influencing people. See *The Practice of Management* (1954), *Managing for Results* (1964), etc.
- Michael Hammer and James Champny - early 1990's gurus and fathers of process reengineering (see *Reengineering the Corporation*, 1993). Failures became blamed on a questionable concurrency of the concept with the down-sizing phenomenon, but process reengineering looks as if its here to stay, even with a more sensible and humane face coloured by latterday enthusiasms for loyalty, corporate memory, etc. See *Reengineering the Corporation - A Manifesto for Business Revolution*, 1993 (which sold 17m copies). Champny has since written books tempering his early enthusiasms for universal reengineering. Both authors have become very successful consultants.
- Charles Handy - Irish guru at the London Business School. Started off writing a source book called Understanding Organisations (Penguin) and moved into guru phase with *The Age of Unreason* (Business Books Ltd., 1989). Increasing sociological and Christian bent to his work.
- Moss Kanter - has a background in sociology and is very people oriented.
- John Kay - English; LBS. See *Foundations of Corporate Success* (1993). An excellent book on the nature of competitive advantage.
- Henry Mintzberg - Canadian teacher and commentator on strategy. Has worked on design management with Angela Dumas at the London Business School. Try, *Mintzberg on Management*, The Free Press (1989); this includes his Harvard Business Review article, *The Manager's Job: Folklore and Fact* (1975).
- J. Nickelthwaite, *The Witch Doctors*, William Heinemann (1996).
Managerial ones, that is, their ideas described and criticised. Good, sceptical guide to that entire scene.
- Tom Peters - *the* Tom Peters, ex-McKinsey consultants. Big breakthrough was *In Search of Excellence* (1982, with Robert

Waterman), a review of best practice at the time (and bad practice a few years later!). The book has sold over 5m copies. See also *A Passion for Excellence* (1985), and *Thriving on Chaos: Handbook for Management Revolution,* (1989).

• Michael Porter - mixes economics with management. Strategic thinking, possibly over-arching for most designers. See *Competitive Strategy* (1980), *Competitive Advantage* (1985), *The Competitive Advantage of Nations* (1990).

• Other names: Kenichi Ohmae, C.K. Prahalad, Gary Hamel. Major consultancies in the ideas generation game include McKinsey & Co., Anderen Consulting, Ernst & Young, Coopers & Lybrand Consulting, KMPG Peat Marwick, Arthur Andersen, Deloite & Touche, Mercer Consulting, Price Waterhouse, and many more.

The Internet
Anything I mention might be out of date by the time you read this. Nevertheless, the net is worth exploring, even though the process reminds me of the fairy tale prince fighting his way through the brambles in order to get to the sleeping princess.

Simply searching on 'design management' is likely to bring up thousands of references. Among these, the pages of the Design Management Institute, in Boston, are a useful starting point. Other interesting sources unlikely to quickly disappear include: The Consummate Design Center (TCDC - a good place for other links and a broad spectrum of information); the Netherlands Design Institute; the Project Management Institute (an American organisation); the International PMI; and the Association of Project Managers (UK, founded in 1972). The PMI offer information services such as the PMI Body of Knowledge and the PMI Project Manager's Desk Reference. Whilst on computers, it is worth noting that, at the time of writing, Chronos (by Broad Bay Software) was an administration programme suited to architecture and design out as a demo on the Web. This is a project *administration* package rather than a project planning aid.

Lessons and Commentary from Other Fields

• D. Berstein, *Company Image and Reality*, Holt, Rinegart and Winston (1984)
A book on communication management by an old hand at the game (founder of the Creative Business in 1972). Also see *The Corporate Personality*, by Wally Olins, (1978). The gane hasn't really changed since these books were written.

• P. Burger, *Theory of the Avant-Garde*, University of Minnesota Press (1984).
Another German writer, discussing fundamental points about the institution of art and art's status in society - it should be required reading for all architects who doubtful that art is just another production sector of the economy.

• Rachel Cooper & Mike Press, *The Design Agenda*, (1995) John Wiley.
Design Management. Good, but more like a case for it rather than a 'how to' book.

• M. Cusumano and R. Selby, *Microsoft Secrets,* Harper Collins (1996).
Managers looking in on Microsoft. An excellent study in high-powered, creative product development strategies and to be compared with Moody's perspective. If you're interested in Microsoft as such, try James Wallace's *Hardrive* (1994) and *Overdrive* (1997).

• Stuart Crainer, *All Corvettes are Red,* (1996) Simon & Schuster.
A journalist spending eight years with Chevrolet, following the development of the C5 car.

• Roger Evans & Peter Russell, *The Creative Manager* (1989).
Parallels some of the concerns of Schon, but adopts a more 'feely' approach with lots of emphasis on mind-sets, imagination, intuition, etc.

• J. Habermas, *The Theory of Communicative Action (Reason and the Rationalisation of Society)*, Polity Press (1987).
Being an architect, my approach to philosophy is founded upon whether or not a theoretician helps to make sense of the facts of one's experience. Habermas does that. See also Habermas's *The Structural Transformation of the Public Sphere* (1982), and other works.

• R.F. Hartley, *Bullseyes and Blunders*, Wiley (1987).
Lots of case studies (Harley Davidson, Honda, McDonalds, Chrysler, Coors, Adidas, Nike, Apple, etc.) and the managerial importance of learning from experience.

• T. Kidder, *The Soul of a New Machine,* Avon Books (1981).
A work on the development of a computer, for which Kidder won a Pulitzer prize.

• T. Kidder, *House,* Picador (1985).
A simple project and the motivation of its three principal protagonists: architect, client, builders. It's all very familiar and Kidder's attempt to validate each perspective is valuable.

• Peter Linebaugh, *The London Hanged*, Penguin (1991).
Actually about 18th. century socio-economic change, with interesting sections on the docks and similar issues relating to the formation of capitalist enterprise and the changes it entailed. I think it's highly relevant, but there's nothing about design as such in here (apart from begging questions about the nascent professionalism then being form by architects such as Sir John Soane and William Chambers).

• Christopher Lorenz, *The Design Dimension,* Blackwell (1986).
Excellent book on product design, with case studies and a background on industrial design.

• F. Moody, *I Sing the Body Electronic*, Hodder & Sloughton (1995).

A journalist sitting in on Microsoft for a year and watching how they really do it. He couldn't quite believe what he experienced! Worth comparing with Microsoft Secrets for less managerial analysis and more feeling for the angst of the creative process.

• Akito Morita, *Made in Japan,* (1994) Harper Collins.

Sony - from the mouth of its most senior executive.

• David Ogilvy, *Ogilvy on Advertising*, Pan Books (1983).

One of the most famous figures in advertising offering the inside view on imagery that worked. Architects should read more of this stuff rather than being disdainful of its commercial content.

• Stuart Pugh, *Total Design: Integrated Methods for Successful Product Engineering*, Addison-Wesley (1991).

Good book with many examples and explanation of product design and engineering techniques. Will be illuminating for most architects.

• Karl Sabbagh, *21st Century Jet,* Pan (1995)

Managing the Boeing 777project through its 2000 day history, with an emphasis on people and how they achieve such amazing things. Like the books on IBM, general Motors, Microsoft, etc., these examinations of the project process are worth reading. The original, in the architectural realm, was probably *The Honeywood File, by H.B. Cresswell (1930).*

Management

Management books generally divide into the academic, the technical and the faddish / how to variety, although some cross-over between these categories. Academic works are often compilations; those offering the original, classic sources are very informative and should not be overlooked simply because they ostensibly lack fashionable topicality (go to the original source whenever possible). Technical books are unlikely to appeal to designers because of their emphasis upon quantitative decision-making and purely instrumental criteria, although those seeking to review product innovation can be fascinating. Anything under the label 'strategy' begins to introduce managerial thinking in terms of an overview of organisations, their structuring and ways of operating relative to their markets. The faddish section is huge and loaded toward the charismatic gurus and best-sellers who touch a topical key-note and ostensibly offer a magic key. Many books are by consultants seeking to drum up clients. It is surprising how many brilliant 'answers' look jaded a few years on, but do not underestimate the power and influence of these waves of fashion among otherwise instrumentally-minded managers. Surprisingly, anything of a more historical and philosophical bent is hard to find - the exact opposite of the architectural bookshop. The emphasis is upon action rather than reflection. Anyone wishing to get beyond this moves toward organisational theory or human-relations theory. The former tracks quickly back to Max Weber (1864-1920), the sociological content of his work linking across to a vast area human relations and motivation theory. Jurgen Habermas continues some aspects of Weber's work.

• A.D. Chandler, *The Visible Hand,* Harvard University Press (1977).

By which Chandler means the visible hand of management replacing the 'invisible hand' of market forces (Adam Smith) - the key to the development of management. One of those classics which can now be seen to characterise a certain era and attitude to management.

• Stuart Crainer, *Key Management Ideas*, Pitman Publishing (1996).

Useful primer on management concepts and all those fads.

• Baden Eunson, *Behaving,: Managing Yourself and Others*, McGraw Hill (1987).

Good, thorough summary (as many Australian books are) of the many concepts and commentaries in the field. Lots of references for further reading.

• C. Hickman & M. Silva, *The Future 500*, Unwin (1988).

Useful for its attempt to place current trends in a historical context rather than for what Hickman and Silva say about those trends.

• L. Iacocca, *Iacocca - An Autobiography*, Bantam (1984).

Necessarily ego-centric, but revealing, especially for the history of the famous Mustang. A part of the 'you-too-can-do-it-like-me' era of management books so prevalent from the late '60's on (e.g. Robert Townsend's *Up The Organisation*, 1970).

• J. Kay, *Foundations of Corporate Success*, Oxford University Press (1993).

Excellent book concerned with identifying competitive advantage.

• Mark McCormack, *What They Didn't Teach You at Harvard Business School*, 1984. Another example of the 'charismatic manager tells all' approach common in the '80's.

• R. Pascale & A. Athos, *The Art of Japanese Management*, Simon & Schuster (1981).

In which the authors introduce the 7-S Framework, - the result of applied research in McKinsey and later used by Peters and Waterman in In Search of Excellence (see below).

• R. Pascale, *Managing on the Edge,* Simon & Schuster (1990).

A good, post-excellence book (Peters & Waterman, 1982) that notes in its introduction that, "we keep applying the tools of transformation without a corresponding shift in our managerial mindset". The book is about creative contention as a vehicle of corporate transformation. It is also about the importance of people and how large organisations address (or do not) all-important cultural factors. Above all, it is about coping with paradigm shifts.

• S. Pollard, *The Genesis of Modern Management,* Edward Arnold (1959)

Lttle is written about managerial history, although a new journal is now about (and can be visited on the Internet). Books on 18th c. engineering (especially in the coal-fields and related construction work) are another area to look. This book is recommended to those seeking to parallel managerial beginnings with nascent architectural professionalism.

• D.S. Pugh & D.J. Hickson, *Writers on Organisations*, Penguin (1989).

Good summary of what key figures had to say (Weber, Drucker, Simon, Lindblom, Herzberg, Feidler, Peters, Mintzberg, March, Chandler and others, with lists of references. Recommended.

• D.S. Pugh (ed.), *Organisation Theory: Selected Readings,* Penguin (1988).

Another selection of originals, this time from Weber, Fayol, Taylor, Mayo, Sloan, Simon, McGregor, and others. Recommended.

• J. Rojot, *Negotiation: From Theory to Practice*, Macmillan (1991).

A good book on a subject which has become so important to architects and designers.

• A. Sampson, *Company Man,* Harper Collins (1995).

Informative book about management history. Loaded with literary references that give a 'feel' for conditions.

• A. Sloan, *My Years with General Motors*, Penguin (1963).

Still selling - a classic how to / case study book. An inside view on how big corporations work from someone who ran general Motors for almost 40 years. Not so self-obsessed as Iacocca's similar book.

• V. Vroom & E. Deci (eds.), *Management and Motivation* (1989).

Good reprint of sources: Maslow, Herzberg, Simon, Taylor, Leavitt and others, with lists of references.

Magazines

Stick with the Economist for a mix of politics, social issues, management and all kind of topics of interest to your average intelligent managerial reader. Forbes, Business Week, Fortune and others might attract you, but they have an off-putting wizzy, breathless kind of journalism. From a design (rather than a managerial) perspective, most weekly and monthly magazines are introspective, gossipy, promotional; and rarely discuss managerial issues in an interesting way. Try the journal from the Design Management Institute for something more learned.

Miscellaneous

• *Strategic Study of The Profession: Phase Two - Clients and Architects*, RIBA (Oct. 1993).

• *Code of Practice for Project Management for Construction and Development,* The Chartered Institute of Building (1992).

The administrative side of project management. Useful in terms of checklists, the inclusion of the RICS form of Agreement for the appointment of a project manager, and other such matters.

• BS 4000 Part 4:1996, Design Management Systems. 'Relational contract' stuff applicable to architectural practice. Dry, but important to have on the shelf.

• Publications from the RIBA are useful for the procedural and administrative aspects of project work. These include its ageing *Plan of Work*, the *Job Book*, and the *Practice management Handbook*.

Professionalism

It is important to grasp what is happening to all professionals in a late-capitalist era. Sociological perspectives dominate the scene, although there are some historical ones, too. Studies of what the architectural profession actually is tend to be ignored by architects themselves, but these studies are of interest (meanwhile, the profession goes its own merry way).

• A. Abbott, *The System of Professions*, University of Chicago Press (1988).

An important perspective that emphasises the notion of competition for professional jurisdictions and takes us through a series of historical paradigms that dominate the story of the professions.

• J. Blau, *Architects and Firms - A Sociological Perspective on Architectural Practice*, MIT Press (1984).

Blau's study of architects is ageing, but it's full of insights that are worth picking out from the generality of the research text.

• M. Brawne, *From Idea to Building*, Butterworth Architecture (1992).

An erudite book on the nature of architectural design, deeply rooted in Popper's work.

• M.S. Briggs, *The Architect in History*, 1927

• D. Cuff, *Architecture: The Story of Practice*, MIT Press (1991)..

A fine, wide ranging book on contemporary (American) practice,although not readily inaccessible.

• Dingwall & Lewis (eds), *The Sociology of the professions*, Macmillan (1983).

Good source book.

• R. Gutman, *Architectural Practice - A Critical View*, Princeton Architectural Press (1988).

• B. Hubbard Jr, *A Theory for Practice - Architecture in Three Discourses*, MIT Press (1995).

An excellent book about resolving three conflicting perspectives and the contemporary architectural design predicament: Order (what the architect is interested in), Results (instrumental, purposeful thinking; design as an effectuator of results), and Values(whether personal or shared). Every architect should read this book. Every student should be made to.

• F. Jenkins, *Architect and Patron* (1961)

- Barrington Kaye, *The Development of the Architectural Profession* (1960)
- B. Kimball, *The True Professional Ideal in America*, Basil Blackwell (1992).

Excellent because it takes us back to the roots of professionalism in the act of 'professing'.
- S.K. Kostoff, ed., *The Architect: Chapters in the History of a Profession,* 1977.
- M. Larsen, *The Rise of Professionalism*, University of California Press (1977).

A key work by a famous sociologist.
- K. Macdonald, *The Sociology of the Professions*, Sage (1995).

You could do worse than beginning here. The early sections give a review of sociological viewpoints on the profession, with an especial nod toward Margali Larsen, the dominating figure of all research and commentary on the professions.
- D.H. Maister, *Managing The Professional Service Firm*, Free Press (1993).

Maister was a part of the Coxe team (see below). This is an excellent practice management book aimed at professionals.
- H. Perkin, *The Rise of Professional Society*, Routledge (1989).

An historian's perspective on the British professions that leads up to the current general decline in status.
- J.Raelin, *The Clash of Cultures*, Harvard Business School (1985).

This book attempts to address managers who have to employ that strange breed called professionals. Since there are not many books that look at the difference between professionals and managers, this one is still worth a look. Based on research, it has many references.

Project Management

Most project management books underscore the purposive thinking of the practical, instrumentally-minded man. Only in recent years has there been a significant shift toward an interest in the project as a general managerial tool, resulting in a more lively and interesting discussion. Many of the books give huge emphasis to network planning techniques that will rarely if ever affect the average designer - pick a simple and direct text. Do not expect too much at all that adopts the designer's viewpoint (or is even mildly empathetic with it); however, expect more of these to come forward as managers realise how dependent they are on design and have lots to learn from it.

- E. Andersen et al., (1984), *Goal Directed Project Management*, Kogan Page. Now in a 2and (revised edition).

I like this book. It's a managerial viewpoint from Norwegian consultants and gets straight to the point: being goal oriented. They slip in heuristic guidance, which is good.
- N. Augustin (preface; book from The Harvard Review), *Managing Projects and Programs* (1989).

Articles in this book range from 1959-89 and its reassuring to see that nothing much changes in project management.
- Robert Buttrick, *The Project Workout*, (1997), Pitman Publishing.

You'll probably like this book. It's lively, knowledgeable and has a good presentation (apart from Buttrick's attempt at cartoon). It's entirely business oriented, demonstrating project management as a tool for constant change and will give an excellent insight into the notion of project orientation as a business norm. On the other hand, there's a disappointing understanding of design and creativity, so you'll have to translate the ideas (which, as usual, reduce creativity to no more than 'brainstorming').
- D.Cleland & W. King, (eds.), *Project Management Handbook*, Von Nostrand Reinhold, (1988).

Thick and expensive. 997 pages. Good source book. More academic (in the best sense of the term) than Kerzner et al.
- D. Cleland, *Project Management*, (1994), McGraw Hill.

More succinct version of Cleland's approach.
- Kevin Forsberg et al., *Visualising Project Management.* (1996), John Wiley & Son.

An approach from people with backgrounds in aerospace and computers. Good, but I wouldn't go out of my way . . . Truly instrumental and deductive approach to problem solving. Good on risk and control.
- H. Kerzner, *Project Management - A Systems Approach to Planning, Scheduling, and Controlling*, Von Nostrand Reinhold, (1984).

The title says it all. Orthodox, but very thorough.
- D. Kezbom, D. Schilling and K. Edward, (1989), *Dynamic Project Management*.

Why 'dynamic' is rather unclear. Two of the authors are, unusually on this scene, women. Good, general book.
- K. Lockyer and J. Gordon, *Project Management and Project Network Techniques* (6th edition), (1996).

The PM stuff is the usual, although fine, but read this for the network techniques. You have the feeling they know what they're talking about and it's all being informed by heuristic.
- J. Meredith & S. Mantel, *Project Management - A Managerial Approach,* John Wiley (3rd ed.), (1995).

All the usual stuff plus some case studies and material from elsewhere, packed into 766 pages; lots of references. If in doubt about selecting a general book, try this. Recommended.

Time

Both the following books are good introductions to the subject of time awareness in contemporary business enterprise. The former has an engineering bias,; Stalk & Hout are more general.

- P. Smith & D. Reinertsen, *Developing Products in Half the Time*, Van Nostrand Reinhold (1991).
- G. Stalk & T. Hout, *Competing Against Time*, Free Press (1990).

Quality

What a band-wagon that was! Now we're into disillusionment with the self–contradictory bureaucracy foisted onto the design professions, it's possibly time to make a more balanced reappraisal that goes back to roots. The bookshelves will be lined with works on quality, the later ones discussing the failures as well as the success stories. Start with the two fathers, Deming and Juran who, in the 1920's, worked together under Walter Shewhart at Bell Labs, pioneering statistical quality control. Nelson's book is good, especially if you edit out one or two faddish enthusiasms.

- Philip Crosby, *Quality is Free: The Art of Making Quality Certain*, 1978. Also *Quality Without Tears* (1984), *Let's Talk Quality* (1989), *Quality is Still Free* (1996).

Devisor of the slogan 'zero defects', which Deming dismisses as nonsense . . . but Crosby is a big name in this field.

- Edwards Deming, (1982), *Out of The Crisis*, Cambridge University Press.

Think of him as the Bucky Fuller of quality assurance - an engineer's practical mind and little tolerance for fools or bureaucracy. The other key figure in quality assurance is Juran.

- J.M. Juran, *Juran on Quality by Design: The New Steps for Planning Quality into Goods and Services*, Free Press (1991). Also *Quality Planning & Analysis* (1988), *Juran on Leadership for Quality*, Free Press (1989), *Managerial Breakthrough* (1994), etc.
- Charles Nelson, *TQM & ISO 9000 for Architects and Designers* 1996.

Thorough and lively coverage of the subject by an Australian consultant, but one gets the feeling he hasn't really read Deming.

Teams

Although techniques are attractive, the truth of the matter is that books on teams, human relations, psychology and the like will bring you nearer to the real issues at stake. However, by their nature, such issues are more intractable and less likely to provide the ostensible quick fix that a technique proffers. I confess to having found little of inspiration in this field, although Katzenbach and Smith(1994) stands out..]Anything with a case study in it will usually tell you (indirectly) something about how teams work.

- D. Cleland & H. Kerzner, *Engineering Team Management,* Van Nostrand Reinhold (1986).

Lots in there, but do they mean *engineering* team management or engineering *team* management? Rather technocratic in approach.

- Paul Dinsmore, *Human Factors in Project Management*, American Management Association(1990).

Cross-over between a discussion of project management and team issues.

- W. Fletcher, *Creative People*, Hutchinson Business Books (1988). Fletcher is in advertising.

This is one of the rare books written by someone in his position (perhaps the only one). Somewhat condescending about those pesky creative types, but interesting. The book offers some references to other works that are relevant.

- D. Goleman, *Emotional Intelligence*, Bloomsbury (1996).

This US best-seller is a must for anyone interested in how emotional maturity and skill in interpersonal relations affects success and happiness. It therefore becomes crucially important to managers concerned with teamwork. The basic message is simple: measures of IQ are not indicators of socio-economic success (then Goleman tells us why).

- Jon Katzenbach & Douglas Smith, *The Wisdom of Teams*, (McGraw Hill / Harvard Business School Press).

Research based, this books strikes a key-note of correspondence with experience, helping to make sense of it and thus promoting learning (especially their points about working groups, pseudo-teams and real teams). It's a good, straight-forward, book. If you read no other on teams, try this one.

- O. Kharbanda & E. Stallworthy, *Project Teams: the Human factors*, Blackwell (1990).

Lots of knowledge in there, but the book does leave you wondering what the message is.

- T. Peters & N. Austin, *A Passion for Excellence - The Leadership Difference*, Collins (1985).

A big follow-up to an even bigger fore-runner, *In Search of Excellence*, Harper & Row (1982). Their problem is that lots of the 'excellent' companies later nose-dived (e.g. IBM), but they weren't to know that at the time. Still worth reading.

- Michael Schrage, *No More Teams!*, (1995), Currency Doubleday)

An emphasis upon collaboration and media; lots of references to books which have described it in action.

Notes

1. J.B. Quinn, *Strategies for Change - Logical Incrementalism,* 1980. Quinn seeks to differ from Lindblom in lending 'incrementalism' the coherence and control with which post-war management reassures itself.

2. See Henry Mintzberg, *The Manager's Job: Folklore and Fact,* Harvard, 1975. This text is still quoted and is the basis of much that Mintzberg had to say in his later research. Also, see Donald Schon's arguments(Schon,1983 and 1987) in favour of learning from the way designers think, teach and practise.

3. 'Satisficing' was a term used by Herbert Simon. See H.A. Simon, *Models of Man,* 1957; and J.G. March & H.A. Simon, *Organisations,* Wiley, 1958.

4. See: Braybrooke and Lindblom, *A Strategy of Decision,* Free Press, 1963. Also, C.E. Lindblom, *The Policy-Making Process,* Yale University, 1968. These are both old books, but still worth reading if you have any interest in Lindblom's perspective (Pascale, for example, quotes Lindblom, although his interest is in those circumstances shifting policy-makers outside of 'disjoint ed incrementalism' i.e. when a paradigm shift is called for). 'Muddling through' is sometimes quoted without apparent benefit of having read Lindblom's convincing rationale. In the earlier work, Lindblom quotes Karl Popper in a way that sheds light on the former's concepts of administrative and strategic policy-making: "Popper rightly holds that the problem of evaluation is simpli fied by a concentration on social evils rather than on utopias; that limits on man's competence are acknowledged in reforms that alter only relatively small parts of the social structure at any one time; that continuity in readjustment diminishes the need to be right in any single decision; that aims change with experience with policies; and that experiments in social reform teach some things that cannot be learned in any other way." (Braybooke and Lindblom, p82) Lindblom fails to tell us how choices are generated (the essential creative conundrum), but he says a lot about the frame of reference, the scope of consideration and the way solutions are reached by a process of incremental consideration of marginal differences between limited choices. Lindblom's theory does not preclude radical change, but his notion that ' a rational problem solver wants what he can get and does not try to get what he wants except after identifying what he wants by examining what he can get', was an attempt to examine and explain prevailing normative processes rather than expound myths concerning problem solving.

5. See Donald Schon, *Educating The Reflective Practitioner,* 1987. This is a follow-up to *The Reflective Practitioner,* 1983. Schon is/was Ford Professor of Urban Studies at MIT and an honourary fellow of the RIBA. His ideas partly derive from sitting in on MIT architecture classes for a year and watching how architects design and are taught.

6. Quoted in V. Scully, *The Shingle Style and the Stick Style,* Yale, 1971, pp 51-52.

7. D.H. Maister, *Managing the Professional Service Firm,* Free Press, 1993. This book is recommended to anyone dealing with practice management and practice marketing.

8. There is a darker side to all this: the way in which the ideas of inspiration and alchemy are connected to the role of art in contemporary society. The architectural profession's retreat to a justificatory posture rooted in the art paradigm is an attempt to counter the strongly purposive, instrumental climate they now practise in - a context that was once celebrated and became the inspiration of Modernism. However, this restatement of an alliance with artists returns architects to a period one hundred years ago when the process of professionalisation engendered vociferous arguments concerning formal registration (and mar ket control). Many architects (among them, men like Norman Shaw and others belonging to the Arts and Crafts Movement) deemed such trade unionism as an affront to their elevated artistic status. Their battle was lost and the fully professionalised body of British architects after WWII enjoyed the fruits of their contract with the state in the form of extensive patronage and programme control, especially in the housing field. The current situation has returned us to some of the debates of 100 years ago. The art paradigm and an alliance with painters and sculptors has often been resurrected as a defence against what is seen as excessive instrumentality. The difficulty is that, for a long time, art has been a fully institutionalised feature of consumerist society and the game of 'shock the bourgeoisie' has become a rather hackneyed posture to adopt (shock - as Duchamp discov ered - quickly translates into a price tag). Many artists nowadays have agents and enjoy a socio-economic role as performers, much like actors, performing on demand. The alchemy of design is not quite the same as the enlightenment sought by art, just as the alchemy of *architectural* design is different to that of interior or decorative design. To cite aesthetics as common ground hardly illuminates the issues at stake. It would take another volume to explore this topic properly, but it appears to me to be self-evident that architectural design as inspiration and alchemy are rooted in the sense in which a design finds the 'right answer' in its own, unique, particular circumstances i.e. it is 'on target' and is therefore *authentic.* Terms such as 'problem-find ing', 'problem-framing' and 'unlocking potential' are actually impoverished and technocratic descriptions for locating and identi fying this authenticity and its possible ramifications.

9. The concept was strongly promoted in Charles Handy's book, *The Age of Unreason,* Business Books, 1989, and characterised by him as a 'shamrock' organisation.

10. See C. Gray et al., (1994), *The Successful Management of Design,* University of Reading. The authors' concept of how to successfully manage design is to transform it - as quickly as possible - into an engineering function.

11. Adapted from *Microsoft Secrets,* M.A. Cusumano & R.W. Selby, Harper Collins (1995). This is a thorough look at how Microsoft actually works and is a must for anyone interested in case studies from other fields. Also see Moody (1995).

12. This might strike some architects as an offensively pragmatic statement. Those adopting the art paradigm would reject it and argue for architectural acts imbued with social and even political comment (a critical posture). They might argue for a clear differentiation between 'architecture' and 'building', the former manifesting qualities of self-consciousness, transcendence and originality elevating it above the latter; they would require a definition of architecture before they could make an architectural act; they would reject the implied commerciality and gross instrumentality of pragmatism; they would find no inspiration in the notion that architecture is a design profession. Such attitudes are widely prevalent in an over-populated profession in which frustrations of the exiled becomes the peculiar ideology of academics (dangerous because they teach another generation). In turn, I reject this art paradigm as irrelevant to design practice; it profoundly misses the point. I would argue for all ideological postures to return themselves to a world of action and the realities of what architecture always has been and, probably, will be. There is a place in this philosophy for the profound and sublime, for political awareness and social justice, but these are necessarily rooted in the mundaneity from which architecture arises and the limitations of influence it has to accept. This contradiction is the point, the challenge and joy of architecture. Making architecture does not require *a priori* definitions. Good design does not have to be original (although it should seek to be authentic). It does not have to adopt a critical posture. The fact that any excellent work of architecture is realised is sufficient in itself - an amazing achievement that has wrested from mundaneity something that people inhabit, enjoy and value. Art can only be jealous of this rootedness in praxis that makes architecture as exciting as it can often be. In the words of the late Esther Harding, "*We rarely reflect how essential it is that all things should wear out and decay. We forget that it is not in our creations, the things we make, the order we establish, but in our func tioning that life is fulfilled in us*". (Esther Harding, *Woman's Mysteries*, 1982.)

13. See note 4.

14. See note 3.

15. See note 1.

16. See J.G. March & JP Olsen, *Ambiguity and Choice in Organisation,* Universitetsforlaget (1976).

17. See C. Lindblom, *The Policy-Making Process,* Yale (1968). Also, note (4).

18. G. Polya, *How to Solve it,* Doubleday (1945). An excellent, relatively short book by this former Professor at Stanford University.

19. This advocacy of an incremental approach is counter-intuitive, contradicting media-generated cults of personality and the 'Eureka!' myth. When examples are analysed they commonly reveal that the ostensibly radical innovation has been worked upon consistently, vigorously and incrementally. Many case studies make this point e.g. Cusumano & Selby's look at Microsoft. Similarly, marketing success stories such as Sony's Walkman, introduced in 1970, was an unattractive buy rapidly turned into a huge success by constant, quickly established but incremental changes.

20. See P. Drucker, *Innovation and Entrepreneurship*, Harper & Row(1985).

20. L.A. Bennington, *TREND: A Project Management Tool,* Proceedings of the Project Management Conference, Philadelphia, Oct. (1972). Meredith and Mantel (1995) discuss Bennington's technique, but I have not come across it in other project management works.

21. The reader is referred to Meredith & Mantel (1995) for a succinct summation of networking, particularly of probabilistic techniques and their statistical basis. It's slightly short-hand and therefore cryptic, so those of you averse to maths might refer to D. Rowntree, *Statistics Without tears - A Primer for Non-mathematicians,* Penguin, 1981. Another recommended book to use as an introduction to networking is Lockyer and Gordon (1996). Most of the older and more conventional books on project management discuss network techniques; the newer, more managerially oriented ones ignore it.

22. The classic work by W.Edwards Deming is *Out of the Crisis* (1982). This is the Bucky Fuller of quality assurance, a man who emphasised the importance of a statistical and systems approach to quality control - which, oddly, ended up deeply humanistic and considerate of workers (he died in 1993 at the age of 93). The other large figure in quality is J.M. Juran, a former colleague of Demings at Bell Laboratories. Both had immense influence in Japan after WWII.

23. H.J. Thamain & D.L. Wilemon, (1986), *Criteria for Controlling Projects According to Plan,* Project Management Institute Journal, 6.1986. Similar research was carried out at about the same time by Pinto & Slevin, using 50 managers in order to identify what the researchers termed 'Critical Success factors in Project Implementation'; it's intelligent and useful, but the results were common sense, despite the heavy scientific justifications. Lots of project management research uses the same tedious, overly pedantic application of technical rationality. This is where research carried out by Thamain and Wilmon stands out as not only rational and scientific, but sane and without hype.

24. Anderson et al (1984, since revised) is a good source. Another is any work by Thamain & Wilemon.

25. B. Baker, D. Murphy, D. Fisher, *Factors Affecting Project Success* (1974), reproduced in Cleland & King (1988). The research was among 650 projects.

26. ibid.

27. See Tanaka, Yoshikawa, Innes & Mitchell (1993). This section is indebted to the review of Tanaka et al's book and its discussion of costing techniques.

28. See PG Smith & DG Reinersten, *Developing Products in Half the Time,* von Nostrand Reinhold, 1991. The authors also quote material from Ford, General Motors, and Westinghouse that confirms this finding.

29. See Stalk & Hout (1990). Smith & Reinersten (1991) cover the same ground.

30. ibid.

31. A range of 20 medium to large size London practices were interviewed by the author in 1994. All undertook

similar kinds of work. They included North American as well as British practices. The interviews were with the Managing Director or Senior Partner, often accompanied by the Finance Director, Senior Associate involved, or similar. Although informally supported by the President of the RIBA, the research failed to obtain the base data sufficient to generate a revised fee calculus.

32. The idea of the trapezoid originates from an article in Cleland & KIng (1988) by James Bent, a former engineer with companies such as Mobil and Kellogg.

33. See John Kay, *Foundations of Corporate Success*, Oxford University Press (1993)

34. One of the best reviews of the history of professionalism, with summaries of contending viewpoints and references is MacDonald (1995).

35. *Emotional Intelligence*, Daniel Goleman, (1995).

36. See C. Handy, *Understanding Organisations*, Penguin (1976)

37. A report called *Constructing Quality* (DOE 1996) reviewed quality certification schemes in the UK and severely criticised them. Clients were often more dissatisfied after certification. Small firms were daunted by the costs. Firms criticised the bureaucracy involved and a restrictive culture which prevented them innovating. A similar paper called *Quality Management for the Constructional Professional: What a Mess* was published as an RICS research paper in 1995.

38. H. Herzberg, *Work and The Nature of Man*, (1966), Excerpt reprinted in *Motivation & Management*, eds. V.Vroom and E. Deci, Penguin (1970). Another good book on motivation, covering many aspects of the subject, is *Behaving*, B.Eunson, (1987).

39. Feidler, Address to NATO,1976. Reprinted in Pugh (1988)

Readers interested in Feidler's research are advised to look up the original - lack of space in this work prevents a discusion of the nuances in Feidler's findings. His comments on the impact and value of training are instructive.

Index